THE LORD OF THE RINGS
POPULAR CULTURE IN GLOBAL CONTEXT

THE LORD OF THE RINGS
POPULAR CULTURE IN GLOBAL CONTEXT

edited by Ernest Mathijs

WALLFLOWER PRESS
LONDON & NEW YORK

First published in Great Britain in 2006 by
Wallflower Press
6a Middleton Place, Langham Street, London W1W 7TE
www.wallflowerpress.co.uk

A catalogue record for this book is available from the British Library

ISBN 1-904764-82-7 (pbk)
ISBN 1-904764-83-5 (hbk)

Printed by Replika Press Pvt Ltd, India

Contents

SECTION 3: ANCILLARY CONTEXTS

Acknowledgements

Edited books are not just a collection of people rallying under a joint banner, to use a *Lord of the Rings* metaphor. More than a cause and concern, they share interests, commitments and differences. The fellowship of this book was designed to be carefully delineated, less impromptu perhaps than other collections. It has a very clear brief to discuss only the public presence of the *Lord of the Rings* film phenomenon. I want to thank all the contributors for keeping to this brief and for not letting the limits imposed on them impair the vitality and quality of their arguments. A special thank you to Brian Sibley for his thoughts and comments, and for writing the foreword to the volume. All remaining errors are, of course, mine.

One essay in this collection also appears elsewhere: Erik Hedling's 'Framing Tolkien: Trailers, High Concept, and the Ring' is also published, in a different version, in W. Wolf & W. Bernhart (eds) (2006) *Framing Borders in Literature and Other Media, Studies in Intermediality 1*, Amsterdam: Rodopi. I thank Rodopi for their permission to publish it in this volume as well.

The images in this collection remain the property of the copyright owners and are reproduced here in the spirit of fair use, and the promotion of the films concerned. Figure 1 is reprinted courtesy of myirony.com, Figure 2 appears courtesy of the *Radio Times*, Figure 3 appears courtesy of theonering.net, Figure 4 appears courtesy of *The Times*, Figure 7 is courtesy of compleatseanbean.com, Figure 8 is the property of New Line Cinema and Figure 10 appears courtesy of Seduction Cinema.

I thank the following fellow travellers for their continuous support and encouragement: Yoram Allon, Martin Barker, Daniel Biltereyst, Kate Egan, Janet Jones, Philippe Meers, Dirk Reynders, Kristin Thompson, and all the collaborators of the 'International Lord of the Rings Research Project'. Special thanks to Hedwig Mathijs for the internet services provided.

This book is for Emily, for our life to be.

Ernest Mathijs
Vancouver, BC
September 2006

List of Illustrations

List of figures

List of tables

Notes on Contributors

MARTIN BARKER is Professor of Film and Television Studies at the University of Wales, Aberystwyth. He has worked in the field of audience and cultural research for more than twenty years. He is author of *The Video Nasties: Freedom and Censorship in the Arts* (1984), co-author of *The Crash Controversy: Censorship Campaigns and Film Reception* (2001), and co-editor of *Ill Effects: The Media/Violence Debate* (1997) and *Knowing Audiences: Judge Dredd, its Friends, Fans and Foes* (1997). He was director of the 'International Lord of the Rings Research Project'. He is editor of *Particip@tions*, the only journal devoted to the field of audience research.

BRONWYN BEATTY is a PhD candidate at Massey University, Auckland, New Zealand. She is currently writing her doctoral thesis on the popularity of heroic fantasy, with particular reference to the books and film adaptations of *Lord of the Rings* and *Harry Potter*. Her research interests include children's literature, the New Zealand film industry and cultural theory.

DANIEL BILTEREYST is Professor in Film, Television and Cultural Media Studies at Ghent University, Belgium. He has published in the *European Journal of Communication, Media, Culture and Society* and the *European Journal of Cultural Studies*, and in the anthologies *Understanding Reality TV* (2004), *Media Cultures in a Changing Europe* (2004), *Big Brother International: Formats, Critics and Publics* (2004), *Communication Theory and Research in Europe* (2005), *Rebel Without a Cause: Approaches to a Maverick Masterwork* (2005) and *Adolescents in International Cinema* (2006). His recent work is on controversial film and censorship, and the role of the media in public debate.

WARREN BUCKLAND is Associate Professor of Film Studies at Chapman University, Southern California. He is author of *The Cognitive Semiotics of Film* (2000), *Film Studies* (2003) and *Directed by Steven Spielberg* (2006), co-author, with Thomas Elsaesser, of *Contemporary American Film: A Guide to Movie Analysis* (2002) and editor of *The Film Spectator: From Sign to Mind* (1995). He is also editor of *New Review of Film and Television Studies*, and is currently editing a volume entitled *Complex Storytelling in Contemporary World Cinema*.

K. J. DONNELLY is Lecturer in Film Studies at the University of Wales, Aberystwyth. He is the author of *Pop Music in British Cinema* (2001) and *The Spectre of Sound*

(2005), and the editor of *Film Music* (2001). He is currently writing a book about British film music and film musicals.

JONATHAN DOVEY is Reader in Screen Media at the University of Bristol, UK. He is a media producer and writer, and has previously written on Reality TV in *Freak-shows – First Person Media and Factual TV* (2000). He has recently co-authored, with Helen W. Kennedy, a book entitled *Game Cultures*.

SUSANNE EICHNER is Lecturer in the Media Studies Department at the Konrad Wolf Academy of Film and Television in Potsdam-Babelsberg, Germany. Her main research interest is the structure and reception of interactive media formats with a focus on video games. She has published in *Archiv der Jugendkulturen*, and has chapters in collections such as *Handbuch Qualitativer Medienforschung*. She is chairwoman of the Association of the International Student Film Festival SehSüchte and member of the (Digital Games Research Association). Currently, she is working on her PhD thesis on the reception of interactive formats.

BRIAN SIBLEY has had an on-going association with the works of J.R.R. Tolkien for over twenty years. He was co-dramatist of the BBC's acclaimed radio adaptation of *The Lord of the Rings* and subsequently dramatised several of Tolkien's shorter works of fiction including *Farmer Giles of Ham*. In collaboration with artist John Howe, he has written a series of publications about the maps in Tolkien's books and, most recently, various volumes chronicling the making of the *Lord of the Rings* film trilogy.

JONATHAN GRAY is Assistant Professor of Communication and Media Studies at Fordham University. He is author of *Watching With The Simpsons: Television, Parody, and Intertextuality* (2006). With Bertha Chin, he wrote on *Lord of the Rings* and pre-fans before release of the first film in the trilogy in *Intensities: The Journal of Cult Media*, has also published on fandom, antifandom and textuality in the *International Journal of Cultural Studies*, and has contributed to *The Blade Runner Experience: The Legacy of a Science Fiction Classic* (2005).

ERIK HEDLING is Professor of Comparative Literature at Lund University, Sweden. He is the author of *Lindsay Anderson, Maverick Film-Maker* (1998) and *British Fictions: Intermedial Studies in Film, TV, Drama, Prose, and Poetry* (2001). He is also the co-editor of *Interart Poetics: Essays on the Interrelations of the Arts and Media* (1997) and *Cultural Functions of Intermedial Exploration* (2002).

MATT HILLS is Senior Lecturer in Media and Cultural Studies at the Cardiff School of Journalism, Media and Cultural Studies, Cardiff University. He is the author of

Fan Cultures (2002), *The Pleasures of Horror* (2005) and *How to Do Things With Cultural Theory* (2005). He has also written on the issue of the 'mainstream cult' in edited collections such as *Movie Blockbusters* (2003) and *Teen TV* (2004).

I. Q. HUNTER is Principal Lecturer and Subject Leader, Film Studies at De Montfort University, UK. He is co-editor of Routledge's British Popular Cinema series, for which he edited *British Science Fiction Cinema* (1999). Among his other publications are the co-edited books *Pulping Fictions* (1996), *Trash Aesthetics* (1997) and *Retrovisions* (2001). His recent work has focused on Paul Verhoeven, British exploitation cinema, and Hammer's science fiction and fantasy films.

ANNE JERSLEV is Associate Professor of Film and Media Studies in the Department of Media, Cognition and Communication of the University of Copenhagen. She is the author of various books about David Lynch, cult movies, horror films and video film reception. She is the editor of *Realism and 'Reality' in Film and Media* (2002) and co-editor of *Performative Realism: Interdisciplinary Studies in Art and Media* (2005).

STAN JONES is a Senior Lecturer in Screen and Media at the University of Waikato, Hamilton, New Zealand. He has published on modern German literature and German and New Zealand cinema in collections as *European Identity in Cinema* and *New Zealand Filmmakers*, and journals such as *Metro* and *Illusions*. His current research interest is in cross-cultural influences and identity questions in contemporary cinema.

HELEN W. KENNEDY is Senior Lecturer and MA Award Leader in the School of Cultural Studies at the University of the West of England. Her general research interest is gender and technology with a recent focus on computer games. She is Chair of the Play Research Group within the School which has organised a number of international conferences and symposia on the subject of computer games. She has published on the subject of feminist readings of Lara Croft, female *Quake* players and game studies more generally. She has recently co-authored, with Jon Dovey, a book entitled *Game Cultures*.

JENNIFER LAWN is Senior Lecturer in the School of Social and Cultural Studies, Massey University, Auckland, New Zealand. Her research and teaching interests include the Gothic, New Zealand cultural studies, Canadian literature and the representation of trauma in literature and film. She is a co-editor of *Gothic NZ* (2006) and has published recently on Kiwi Gothic in *New Literatures Review* (2002) and the *Journal of New Zealand Literature* (2004), on Margaret Atwood and Janet

Frame in *New Windows on a Woman's World* (2005) and on national branding and the New Zealand film industry in *PostScript* (2005).

CHRISTOPHER LONG, a former day trader, has an MA in Film Studies from Chapman University, Southern California. He is a freelance writer who has had articles published in the *New Review of Film and Television Studies* and in *Cineaste*. He is also a film critic at dvdtown.com.

MARIANO LONGO is Associate Professor of Sociology at the University of Lecce, Italy. His research interest is in the theoretical aspects of communication, with regard to system theory and phenomenology. His works include chapters in *Net sociology: Interazione tra Internet e scienze sociali* (2002) and *Immaginario e società globale* (2005).

ERNEST MATHIJS is Assistant Professor in Film and Drama at the University of British Columbia, Vancouver. He is the editor of *Cinema of the Low Countries* (2004) and co-editor of *Big Brother International: Formats, Critics and Publics*, with Janet Jones (2004) and *Alternative Europe: Eurotrash and Exploitation Cinema Since 1945*, with Xavier Mendik (2004). He has published widely on the reception of alternative cinema including articles in *Screen* and *Cinema Journal*, and is part of the research team investigating the worldwide launch and reception of *Lord of the Rings: The Return of the King*. He is also series co-editor, with Jamie Sexton, of a major new series of studies of individual cult films, *Cultographies*, beginning in 2007.

PHILIPPE MEERS is Assistant Professor in Communication Studies at the University of Antwerp, Belgium. His research focuses on popular media culture, film audiences, European film and international fiction flows. He has published in *Media, Culture and Society*, the *Journal of Popular Film and Television* and the collections *Hollywood Abroad: Audiences and Cultural Relations* (2004) and *Het on(be)grijpbare publiek/The Ungraspable Audience* (2004). He is editing a reader on genre and co-editing a book series on *Film & TV Studies*, both with Daniel Biltereyst.

LOTHAR MIKOS is Professor of Television Studies in the Media Studies Department at the Konrad Wolf Academy of Film and Television in Potsdam-Babelsberg, Germany. His main research interests are in audience studies, popular culture and genres and formats. He is the author of *Im Auge der Kamera. Das Fernsehereignis Big Brother* (2000) and *Film- und Fernsehanalyse* (2003), and co-editor of *Qualitative Medienforschung* (2005). He has also contributed to *Intertextuality and the Media: From Genre to Everyday Life* (2000) and *Big Brother International: Formats, Critics and Publics* (2004).

KIRSTEN PULLEN is an Assistant Professor of English and Performance Studies at the University of Calgary. She is the author of *Actresses and Whores: On Stage and In*

Society (2006). Her previous research on Internet fan activity includes articles in *Web.Studies: Rewiring Media Studies for the Digital Age* (2000) and *Web.Studies* (second edition) (2004), and her current research focuses on how Zsa Zsa Gabor challenged Cold War domestic ideology.

JUDITH E. ROSENBAUM is a doctoral candidate at the Department of Communication, Radboud University Nijmegen, the Netherlands. Her research interests include media literacy, media education and reception research. She co-edited *Action Theory and Communication Research: Recent Developments in Europe* (2004), and has published on the reconceptualisation of media literacy in *Communications: The European Journal of Communication research*. Her 2003 ICA paper entitled 'How media literacy is defined: A review' received a Top-Student Paper Award.

GOVIND SHANADI is a doctoral student in the School of Journalism and Communication at the University of Oregon. He collaborated on the 'International Lord of the Rings Research Project', and presented results of his research on the *Lord of the Rings* games and merchandising at the 2005 ICA conference in New York.

DAVINIA THORNLEY is Lecturer in New Zealand cinema in the Film and Media Studies Programme at the University of Otago. She has published journal articles in *National Identities*, the *Quarterly Review of Film and Video* and *Film Criticism*, and has contributed to *Film Studies: Women in Contemporary World Cinema* (2002) on New Zealand film and nationality. Her current project is an ethnographic study of how cinema literally crosses the borders of nation-states and creates a sense of community among dispersed New Zealand citizens.

JANET WASKO is the Knight Chair for Communication Research at the University of Oregon. She is the author of *Hollywood in the Information Age* (1994), *Understanding Disney: The Manufacture of Fantasy* (2001) and *How Hollywood Works* (2003), and editor of *Dazzled by Disney?: The Global Disney Audience Project* (2001) and *A Companion to Television* (2005), as well as other volumes on the political economy of communication and democratic media.

MICHAEL WEDEL is Assistant Professor at the Media Studies Department of the University of Amsterdam. He is the author of *Der deutsche Musikfilm: Archäologie eines Genres* (2006), and is co-editor of *A Second Life: German Cinema's First Decades* (1996), *The BFI Companion to German Cinema* (1999), *Kino der Kaiserzeit: Zwischen Tradition und Moderne* (2002) and *Die Spur durch den Spiegel: Der Film in der Kultur der Moderne* (2004). His articles on early cinema, German film history and contemporary Hollywood have appeared in a number of edited collections and in journals such *Film History, Iris* and *New German Critique*.

Foreword

Every once in a while a book escapes. Somehow, a story – the unique creation of an inventive mind – breaks out and goes running off, footloose and fancy free, with never so much as a by-your-leave or a backward glance at 'the onlie begetter' who gave it life. *Frankenstein* is a good example – especially since it is the tale of a creator who loses control of his creation – but there are many others: *Dracula, Don Quixote, Moby Dick, Alice's Adventures in Wonderland* and *The Hunchback of Notre Dame* along with several plays by Shakespeare, a good few novels by Dickens and more or less any story featuring Sherlock Holmes or James Bond. And to these, and sundry other titles and characters, must now be added *The Lord of the Rings* and its cast of hobbits, wizards, dwarves and elves.

Whenever a book escapes, it firstly severs the umbilical cord by which it was hitherto attached to an author, and then wisely (or foolishly) adopts any number of surrogate guardians – illustrators, dramatists, filmmakers, actors, composers, singers, choreographers and dancers – willing to devote their individual and combined talents to ensure its continued existence and ever-widening fame. This phenomenon – for it is rare enough to be so categorised – occurs with works that, through some lightning-strike of originality or quirk of vision, have laid siege to the public imagination and, as a result, inspired a diversity of creative artists to interpret or translate its narrative into other, non-literary, media. It is, however, a process that cannot be accomplished without change: the requirements of a film, opera, musical, ballet or radio play will always require some measure of extrapolation or a degree of compression; there will, invariably, be additions (possibly inspired, occasionally silly) and, in all likelihood, there will be many deletions: nips and tucks, even violent carvings and cuttings, in order to speed up the storytelling, simplify the plot or just pander to the adaptor's egocentric need to leave an identifying thumb-print on the original. Once this process is embarked upon, there is no turning back – the escape is underway…

Rarely has any book escaped in so spectacular a fashion as J.R.R. Tolkien's *The Lord of the Rings*. Never has a work of fiction been so single-handedly redefined in the global consciousness as is the case with Peter Jackson's filmic retelling of Tolkien's chronicle of the War of the Ring. Even the achievements of its nearest runners-up – *The Wizard of Oz* and *Gone With the Wind* – pale into insignificance, mainly because they were produced in the year 1939 when the concepts of marketing and merchandising were only vague foreshadowings of what we mean by those terms today. What has ensured that the *Lord of the Rings* trilogy stands alone in the realm of Hollywood sequels is that – revitalised every twelve months for three years and augmented by intermediary releases of videos and DVDs – the movie saga attained a staggering, annually increasing, domination of worldwide cinema box-office returns.

The success of *The Lord of the Rings* – both in terms of financial performance and critical perception – was not achieved simply as a result of the staggering 9 hours 18 minutes combined running-times of the three theatrical releases or even the 11 hours 22 minutes of the 'extended DVD editions', but the fact that millions of people (perhaps the majority of whom had never read a word of Tolkien's book) embraced this cinematic epic with a passion, loyalty and devotion unrivalled in over a century of movie-going. Underpinning the experience of seeing the films (a process, in the case of the devout, involving multiple viewings) was a promotional campaign of behemoth proportions – beginning prior to the opening of *The Fellowship of the Ring* and running through to the extended version of *The Return of the King* – carried through with unflagging commercial zeal. The films were further endorsed by an almost four-year-long marketing bonanza which resulted in a tidal wave of books, magazines and comics, limited-edition artworks, two-a-penny toys, fast-food tie-ins and a seemingly limitless supply of gewgaws, gimcracks and miscellaneous knick-knackery of which my personal favourite remains the 'One Ring key-ring'! What better way to safeguard against mislaying one's keys to Orthanc, Barad-dûr or Bag End!

The value of this thought-provoking collection of essays is that it rightly gives equal consideration to the artistry and the commerce that constructed and then sold the *Lord of the Rings* phenomenon to the world. Not everyone, of course, will agree with all of the arguments put forward or all of the conclusions reached. Few, however, are likely to quibble with the thoroughness of the research involved and only the purblind will refuse to allow their own judgements and evaluations to be challenged. Without question, Peter Jackson's *The Lord of the Rings* trilogy will stand for all time as a landmark achievement in motion-picture making. Similarly, for many years – or decades – to come, the films and the spin-offs that spun-off them will continue to be reassessed, aesthetically and sociologically, so that the present editor and his authors will be well aware that their contributions are unlikely to be the last word on the subject. That fact, however, is singular proof of the validity of the studies they have undertaken into the whys and wherefores of how a famous book came to effect so amazing an escape from the shackled restraints of an author's words and the close confinement of the bookbinder's prison, to live at large as if it were now in total control of its own destiny...

This story is, without doubt, a true Promethean myth for our age.

Brian Sibley
London, UK
September 2006

Popular Culture in Global Context: The *Lord of the Rings* Phenomenon

Ernest Mathijs

The public presence and commercial contexts of *The Lord of the Rings*

> So Jackson has done it. After seven years of work, the young New Zealander has pulled off one of the most ambitious and phenomenally successful dream projects of all time, a complete visual rendering of a 1,000-page literary classic beloved by countless readers internationally, a set of films that both satisfies Tolkien purists and will generate well upwards of $3 billion in all markets ... Ancillary benefits from various versions and packaging will continue to issue forth close to forever. (McCarthy 2003)

> The only problem ... is who counts the money. (Johnson 2003)

It is difficult to overstate the worldwide public presence of *The Lord of the Rings*. In the half-century since its inception it has become a globally recognised range of products, ranging from the original 1950s books by J.R.R. Tolkien, through film adaptations, to all sorts of accompanying and associated materials. At the same time, less tangibly but perhaps even more pervasively, it has also become a global brand and cultural point of reference, both a fiercely protected copyrighted trademark influencing dozens of franchises and management deals and a popular shorthand for addressing all sorts of topical and culturally pressing topics, from astronomy (the Rings around Saturn), through politics ('Frodo Has Failed', see Figure 1, overleaf), to sports (the comparisons between Elf Legolas and footballer David Beckham).

The textual properties and idiosyncrasies of *The Lord of the Rings* have provided a wellspring of parallels between fictional characters/events and real-life (and historical) figures and events, regardless of how Tolkien's own discomfort with

Figure 1: 'Frodo Has Failed' (courtesy of www.myirony.com)

such allegorical interpretations. Although he famously said of the story that 'it is neither allegorical nor topical' (1966: xvii), it has been used to support opinions on practically every cultural discourse from racism to vintage cuisine. Above all, the decades-long popularity of *The Lord of the Rings* – as underground counter-cultural symbol, as source of inspiration for spin-offs and rip-offs, tributes and spoofs, and as global commercial entertainment – has spawned legions of audiences of different plumage: militant fans, literati, indifferent accidental viewers, hostile opponents and shrugging consumers unfazed at yet another marketing offensive. As such, it has been present in the lives of billions of people for more than fifty years.

This edited collection of essays is both testimony to that popularity, and a serious academic attempt to investigate its multiple facets and appearances. Since the mere scale of the *Lord of the Rings* phenomenon warrants modesty, this collection only addresses the public presence and commercial contexts of the three *Lord of the Rings* films directed by Peter Jackson, produced by New Line Cinema, and released between December 2001 and December 2003. It does not address the public presence and commercial contexts of the books (in whatever editions). Importantly, it also refrains from analyzing the text, i.e. the properties of the films contained within the narrative and *mise-en-scène*, and their inherent or derivative meanings (for an exploration from such a perspective, see Mathijs & Pomerance 2006). Rather, this volume deals exclusively with its public presence, the multiple formats through which that text is presented to a worldwide audience, and its subsequent place in the public sphere.

That place is undeniably significant. The trilogy's production and success have been widely publicised, but the details are worth repeating (see Table 1).[1]

Title	Production Budget	Marketing Budget	Release Date	Length
The Fellowship of the Ring	$93m	$50m	19.12.01	2h58m
The Two Towers	$94m	$45m	18.12.02	2h59m
The Return of the King	$94m	$50m	19.12.03	3h20m
TOTAL	$281m	$145m		9h17m

Table 1: *The Lord of the Rings* production and marketing budgets
Source: http://www.boxofficemojo.com/movies

The three parts were shot together ('back-to-back' in Hollywood jargon), with an original budget of $281 million. This amount apparently mushroomed to $310 million (Johnson 2003), although others claim it was closer to $330 million. Another $210 million (much more than the listed $145 million) was said to be spent on marketing the three films, which included a $2.5 million party at Cannes in 2003. Only a small percentage of these funds were contributed by New Line Cinema. Depending on the source, it is reported that New Line paid between $25 to $80 million for the films, with another $200 million having been advanced from international distributors. Interestingly, the Weinstein Brothers (of Miramax) were said to be involved with a 2.5% stake, while the Disney company held another 2.5%. Of special interest is the claim that 10% of the budget was raised by selling rights to 'video games, toys and merchandise companies' (Holson 2003). In addition, about $11 million came from deals with Burger King, JVC Electronics, Barnes & Noble, and other companies (Ward 2003).

Upon their domestic openings, the three *Lord of the Rings* films grossed more than $181million (47,211,490; 62,007,528; and 72,629,713 respectively). Nine months after the release of *The Return of the King* the three films had attracted around $3 billion worldwide (see Table 2). And, more recently, New Line has claimed that the films have attracted well over $3 billion worldwide. Meanwhile, the films are ranked 7th, 11th and 16th on *Variety*'s all time US box office list (see Table 3). And on *Box Office Mojo*'s list of worldwide gross receipts they even rank 2nd, 4th and 9th (see Table 4).

Title	US	Overseas	Worldwide	Theatres
The Fellowship of the Ring	$314,776,170 (36.1%)	$556,592,194 (63.9%)	$871,368,364	3,703
The Two Towers	$341,786,758 (36.9%)	$584,500,642 (63.1%)	$926,287,400	3,622
The Return of the King	$377,027,325 (33.7%)	$741,861,654 (66.3%)	$1,118,888,979	3,359
TOTAL	$1,033,590,253 (35.3%)	$1,882,954,490 (64.7%)	$2,916,544,743	3,359

Table 2: Box office figures for *The Lord of the Rings*
Source: http://www.boxofficemojo.com/movies

#	Title (studio, year)	Gross (US)
1	*Titanic* (Paramount, 1997)	$600.9m
2	*Star Wars* (20th Century Fox, 1977)	$461m
3	*Shrek 2* (Dreamworks, 2004)	$436.7m
4	*E.T. – Extraterrestrial* (Universal, 1982)	$435m
5	*Star Wars: Episode 1–The Phantom Menace* (20th Century Fox, 1999)	$431.1m
6	*Spider Man* (Sony, 2002)	$403.7m
7	*The Lord of the Rings: The Return of the King* (New Line, 2003)	$377m
8	*The Passion of the Christ* (Newmarket, 2004)	$370.2m
9	*Spider Man 2* (Sony, 2004)	$368.4m
10	*Jurassic Park* (Universal, 1993)	$357.1m
11	*The Lord of the Rings: The Two Towers* (New Line, 2002)	$341.8m
12	*Finding Nemo* (Buena Vista, 2003)	$339.7m
13	*Forrest Gump* (Paramount, 1994)	$329.7m
14	*The Lion King* (Buena Vista/Disney, 1994)	$328.5m
15	*Harry Potter and the Philosopher's Stone* (Warner, 2001)	$317.6m
16	*The Lord of the Rings: The Fellowship of the Ring* (New Line, 2001)	$314.8m
17	*Star Wars: Episode 3 – Attack of the Clones* (20th Century Fox, 2002)	$310.7m
18	*Star Wars: Return of the Jedi* (20th Century Fox, 1983)	$309.2m
19	*Independence Day* (20th Century Fox, 1996)	$306.2m
20	*Pirates of the Carribean: Curse of the Black Pearl* (Buena Vista, 2003)	$305.4m
21	*The Sixth Sense* (Buena Vista, 2001)	$293.5m
22	*Star Wars: The Empire Strikes Back* (20th Century Fox, 1981)	$290.3m
23	*Home Alone* (20th Century Fox, 1990)	$285.8m
24	*The Matrix Reloaded* (Warner, 2003)	$281.5m
25	*Shrek* (Dreamworks, 2001)	$267.7m

Table 3: *Variety*'s Top 25 Films of All Time
Source: http://www.variety.com/index.asp?layout=chart_top_250&dept=Film

#	Title (studio, year)	Gross (world)
1	*Titanic* (Paramount, 1997)	$1,244m
2	*The Lord of the Rings: The Return of the King* (New Line, 2003)	$1,118.9m
3	*Harry Potter and the Philosopher's Stone* (Warner, 2001)	$976.5m
4	*The Lord of the Rings: The Two Towers* (New Line, 2002)	$926.3m
5	*Star Wars: Episode 1 – The Phantom Menace* (20th Century Fox, 1999)	$924.3m
6	*Shrek 2* (Dreamworks, 2004)	$920.7m
7	*Jurassic Park* (Universal, 1993)	$914.7m
8	*Harry Potter and the Chamber of Secrets* (Warner, 2002)	$876.7m
9	*The Lord of the Rings: The Fellowship of the Ring* (New Line, 2001)	$871.4m
10	*Finding Nemo* (Buena Vista, 2003)	$864.6m

Table 4: *Box Office Mojo*'s Top 10 Films, worldwide
Source: http://www.boxofficemojo.com/movies

The Lord of the Rings also represents the third most successful film franchise (see Table 5). However, when Ralph Bakshi's animated 1978 film is excluded, the average box office for the New Line trilogy is higher than any other franchise. Note also that *Box Office Mojo*'s list reports only revenues from domestic theatrical box office.

Franchise	Total Gross	Number of films	Average per film
Star Wars	$1,861.1m	6	$431.1m
James Bond	$1,272.7m	21	$60.6m
The Lord of the Rings	$1,033.6m	4	$265.6m
Batman	$832.7m	6	$251.2m
Harry Potter	$827.3m	3	$275.8m
Jurassic Park	$767.3m	3	$255.8m
Star Trek	$755.6m	10	$75.6m

Table 5: *Box Office Mojo*'s top franchises
Source: http://www.boxofficemojo.com/franchises

The various DVD/video versions of the first two *Lord of the Rings* films generated an estimated $634 million in sales and about $70 million in rental revenue. *The Fellowship of the Ring* has sold just less than 19 million copies and *The Two Towers* 17.3 million. *The Return of the King* has sold about 12 million copies, and its extended DVD, released in December 2004, added to that total significantly.

Finally, *The Lord of the Rings* also broke records in terms of critical acclaim and appraisal. The trilogy won 17 Academy Awards in total (see Table 6), capturing the Award for best Visual Effects three years running. It also won 4 Golden Globe Awards, the MTV Movie Award for Best Movie (three years in a row), a wide selection of professional awards (Director's Guild, Society of Cinematographers, Screen Actors Guild), from the British, Australian and Japanese Academies, and from practically every Film Critics' Circle in the US. It also won 16 Saturn Awards of the Academy of Science-Fiction, Fantasy and Horror Films.

Category	The Fellowship of the Ring	The Two Towers	The Return of the King
Motion Picture	Nominated	Nominated	Won
Director	Nominated		Won
Screenplay (adaptation)	Nominated		Won
Supporting Actor	Nominated		
Music, original score	Won		Won
Music, original song	Nominated		Won
Cinematography	Won		
Sound	Nominated	Nominated	Won
Editing	Nominated	Nominated	Won
Sound Editing		Won	
Visual Effects	Won	Won	Won
Make Up	Won		Won
Art Direction	Nominated	Nominated	Won
Costume Design	Nominated		Won

Table 6: Academy Awards for *The Lord of the Rings*
Source: www.imdb.com

Studying the public presence and commercial contexts of global popular culture

These impressive figures and lists demonstrate the pressing importance of studying the public presence of cinema, not just for blockbusters, but for cinema in general. This collection takes as its starting point the assumption that a film text's public presence is its primary condition for existing, and the lens beneath which its meanings are consummated. It holds that private, discrete interpretations of cinema have no real function if they refuse to take the public presence of cinema into account. In other words, and mirroring in very crude philosophical terms a well-known metaphor ('if a tree falls in the woods and no one is around, does it make a sound?'), this volume maintains that a film without public presence has no relevance. It is only through its interaction with mechanisms of production, distribution, reception and consumption that a film acquires any meaning for society.

In itself this is not such a novel position to take. Janet Staiger has famously argued the same issue in *Interpreting Films* (1992). But Staiger limited her public presence to the classic public sphere. This term, conceptualised most prominently by Jürgen Habermas (1962), is a zone between the private environment of the family (often delineated by a household and informal routines and habits), and the official state environment of governance and judiciary (often delineated by bureaucracy and formal laws) that form the two most recognisable poles of cultures and societies. In its most classical sense, the public sphere is a forum where these two meet, a place (sometimes literally so) where private citizens meet to discuss official affairs. Habermas links the public sphere to eighteenth- and nineteenth-century bourgeoisie and its success to carve out a space, independent of state, church and individual, where cultural affairs and politics could be discussed outside any immediate interest (see also Eagleton 1984). In this classic concept of the public sphere, the central figure is the disinterested yet well-educated, financially quasi-independent connoisseur of taste and the human condition who is willing and capable to share his opinion, and make judgement, on a variety of topics. A bit like the wet dream of a middle-class intellectual, or a film critic (Bordwell 1989). Since the twentieth century, however, Habermas and others note a decline of that forum: no one individual seems to be able to detach themselves from interests (we all speak for our own sakes), and the mass-production of cultural goods has made the informed discussion of their value subordinate to profit and immediate gratification. While in some recent discussions of the public sphere the role of the media is put forward as a saviour (see, for example, Kellner 1995), the inability to ignore commercial elements is usually seen as the main reason for the decline of the public sphere.

I want to use the term 'public presence' as an extension to 'public sphere', inclusive of its commercial contexts. This is especially relevant for cinema studies. Walter Benjamin and Siegfried Kracauer pointed out as early as in the 1930s, that the public sphere of cinema (in other words, the forum where cinema gets discussed and its cultural meaning forged) is not confined to the largely non-commercial, disinterestedness and amateur-entrepreneurship that characterised the original bourgeois public sphere and which lives on in the institution of film criticism. In fact, its place outside that traditional frame of reference is noted as one of its main typicalities (see Benjamin 1969 and Kracauer 1995; also see Bourdieu 1984). Benjamin may mourn the loss of the aura of uniqueness so typical for cultural product appreciation, but he sees the study of the reproductive character of film, and its wide distribution and impact, as an opportunity for emancipating audiences. Kracauer writes eloquently that because films and other cultural products are produced for (and indeed contain) the masses, they are 'ornaments' more than artefacts, yet he insists that 'the ornament, detached from its bearers, must be understood rationally' (1995: 77). That includes an analysis of its production and reception circumstances, for 'the production process runs its secret course in public' (1995: 78). It therefore warrants scrutiny. The term 'public presence', then, including its commercial contexts as used in this volume, refers to the conditions of production, distribution, reception and consumption, as well as to the larger cultural frameworks by which they are governed and in which they operate.

On the production level, or the ways in which films are conceived and created, the public presence includes the conditions of the particular decision-making processes of producers, directors and crew, not just as aesthetic choices, but as choices informed by an awareness of existing opinions (of fans or of executives), routines (of production but also of legal implications) and of possibilities (of budget or of shooting conditions). In the case of *The Lord of the Rings* it means taking into account copyright issues as well as physical and political concerns when discussing the adaptation of the source material.

On the distribution level, or the ways in which films are presented to the public, the public presence includes circuits of circulation of genre and art-house films, the dangers and limits of festival submissions, award ceremonies, and the fetishist breakdowns of box office figures to show upward or downward trends. In the case of *The Lord of the Rings* it means, and this may be anecdotal but it is telling, taking into consideration the fact that in the US films premiere on Fridays and that the *Lord of the Rings* episodes were released on Wednesdays.

On the reception level, or the ways in which film is received by audiences, the public presence includes awareness of how local and international receptions feed off each other (why every critic feels compelled to address, if only implicitly, the *Variety* or *Cahiers du cinéma* reviews), of how topical, regional references appear in local media, and of the shape and intensities (in tone as well as over time) online discussions take. In the case of *The Lord of the Rings* it means being sensitive to the fact that a story with a British origin, American financing and a New Zealand political and cultural appropriation will register differently on the radars of those cultures. It also means being capable of using discourses of audiences to understand the real impact of a film on its real viewers. In the case of *The Lord of the Rings*, the attempts of fans to intervene in production played such an important role that any study of the films that does not make them part of its subject risks rendering itself irrelevant.

On the level of consumption, or the ways in which film is used to satisfy needs or to manufacture other goods, the public presence encompasses the ancillary materials circulating around the main text. It means knowing what types of spin-offs, tie-ins, merchandising and associated materials (like computer games, trailers, DVD extras) are available and how these are being presented. In the case of *The Lord of the Rings* it means being prepared to study video and role-playing games, or, very specifically, being in the know about how widespread *Lord of the Rings*-inspired music is as a subcultural (and commercial) phenomenon. While the production level is arguably closest to the text itself, the consumption level may well have nothing to do with the film texts. Yet its role in the synthesis of textual meanings is equally significant.

It has taken cinema studies several decades to acknowledge this, but the public presence and commercial contexts of films is now firmly becoming a focus of academic interest, as part of three strands: the study of film consumption, or reception studies (see Staiger 1992 and 2000; Klinger 1997); the study of the film industry, or the political economy of film (Wasko 1994), including research into hyping and branding (Austin 2002; Grainge 2004); and the study of the public and commercial implications of a text, as part of the textual interpretation of film (most notable here are Rick Altman's discussion of genre (1999) and Thomas Elsaesser's discussion of blockbusters (2001)).

Usually, film studies curricula have had difficulties linking these three strands together, although everyone agrees they are intrinsically linked. But it seems hard to find examples which really show this connection. *The Lord of the Rings* is such an example. Its presence on the screen had been announced for years, partly through a well-considered system of publicity, merchandising, franchising and branding, and partly through spontaneous fan activities, public interest in its allegorical meaning and even rivals (the *Harry Potter* and *The Matrix* series). Never before have the attempts to manage the public presence of films been so elaborate. Producer New Line Cinema's existence, director Peter Jackson's reputation and writer J.R.R. Tolkien's standing depended on how the adaptation of the trilogy was announced, how its production was publiciced and how its reception was anticipated and managed. At the same time other interested parties, such as fan communities, local economics, aping producers and all Hollywood seemed to be willing to jump on the train and benefit from it. As the first significant tent-pole production of the twenty-first century, *The Lord of the Rings* has been setting a standard for (dealing with) the public presence of films, a standard which extends beyond blockbusters to include generic produce and art-house fare alike.

Outline and methodology

No one researcher or project can cover all the angles of the public presence and commercial contexts of contemporary cinema. Like micro-historiography, it is doomed to remain single-minded, and bound by the limits of the individual (or team). That is why edited collections, like this one, have a crucial function in presenting the diversity of the public presence of cinema today.

This volume aims at offering an introduction to the study of the public presence and commercial contexts of contemporary cinema through *The Lord of the Rings*. The focus on one film text allows for comparisons between different approaches, stances and opinions. Through such a focus, this volume introduces the three approaches mentioned above: the study of the political economy of film; the study of film reception; and the study of textual meaning in a public context. As a 'dispersible and ancillary text' (a text whose meaning is derived from its public presence; see Austin 2002), *The Lord of the Rings* brings together elements of popular culture, and informs our view of the film, as entertainment, as an event and as a 'sign of the times'.

There are numerous ways to investigate the public presence and commercial contexts of a phenomenon the size of *The Lord of the Rings*. While this volume has not imposed a single top-down methodological approach on its contributions, it insists on a descriptive analysis of the presence and contexts of the phenomenon. This is essential given its scale. Preventing the individual elements of contexts from collapsing into one grand narrative requires an effort; it is all too easy to jump from considerations of the films' production contexts to interpretations of spin-offs without offering readers the necessary information and detailed analysis of each of the parts. The public presence and commercial contexts of *The Lord of the Rings* need to be descriptively analysed precisely because they are so variously complex, and because getting the facts straight matters.

There are other strong methodological connections in this volume. One is the affiliation with The 'International Lord of the Rings Research Project' (see www.lordoftheringsresearch.net), a worldwide study of the launch and reception of *The Return of the King* in twenty countries (Australia, Austria, Belgium, Canada, China, Colombia, Denmark, France, Germany, Greece, Italy, the Netherlands, New Zealand, Norway, Russia, Slovenia, Spain, Turkey, the United Kingdom and the United States), directed from the University of Wales, Aberystwyth.[2] The project had three stages: a study of the prefigurative materials in each country (marketing and publicity, press, magazine, radio and television coverage); a databased questionnaire combining multiple-choice with free-text responses, available online but also completed on paper in a number of countries; and follow-up interviews with individuals chosen to typify response-positions from the questionnaire responses. The volume and density of materials produced by the project is enormous – 24,739 questionnaires across the world. Because of this, it permits systematic investigation of many questions which have, to date, been mainly the subject of speculative claims (see Barker & Mathijs, forthcoming). Several of the contributors in this volume were part of the research teams (Barker; Biltereyst & Meers; Eichner, Mikos & Wedel; Jerslev; Jones; Longo; Mathijs; Wasko & Shanadi), while others were closely associated with its activities (Donnelly; Hedling; Hunter; Rosenbaum). While this collection is in no way a reflection of this project, it does give it an international scope. Many film textbooks stipulate how crucial it is to understand contemporary cinema as a global phenomenon, yet most refuse to take an international (or internationalist) perspective to its study. This volume offers snapshots from different cultures and invites comparisons between them in order to obtain a more informed view of global cinema in the twenty-first century.

Structure of the book

This volume consists of three sections, and it has three threads running through it. The first thread is, of course, the focus on *The Lord of the Rings*. Though no chapter actually discusses the films as such, but instead approaches them across different presences, they all use them as an ultimate point of reference; it is the text that binds the contexts.

The second is what I propose to call the timeline of the public presence of *The Lord of the Rings*, namely its trajectory through time from inception to consumption. The first chapter stands closest to its inception, in explaining the corporate backgrounds within which it was created, and in analysing the materials that accompanied or announced its release. The last is one that studies how *The Lord of the Rings'* reputation was a starting point for erotic spin-offs, months after its release. In between, discussions of funding, politics, online fandom, DVD extras and tourist spin-offs designate stages of its cultural evolution. As such the timeline is indicative of the trajectory a film text follows during its time in the public eye.

Parallel to this timeline runs a thread that indicates degrees of remoteness from the core text. The first chapters address issues that are pivotal to the creation of *The Lord of the Rings*, like financing and preparing the product for release. The last chapters concentrate on far less official (and hence more remote) issues such as spoofs, music inspired by the narratives or unofficial guidebooks to the locations. The trajectory here is one from greatest control by the corporate machine, through issues of reception still somewhat under control (by virtue of their shared interests in the text – like fans, or in cinema in general – like reviewers), to ancillary materials riding on the back of the success and popularity of the original text.

Section 1: Political Economy and Commercial Contexts

The first section investigates the ways in which strategies to ensure success guide the trilogy's construction and release. It analyses processes of policy, marketing, hyping, branding, distribution and box office performance (and the presentation of these as evidence of 'success') to provide an overall view of how the production and release of films of such magnitude is managed. The chapter 'More than Just Rings: Merchandise for Them All' by Janet Wasko and Govind Shanadi presents an overview of the merchandising associated with *The Lord of the Rings*. The discussion traces the background of copyright and ownership rights for *The Lord of the Rings* and the success of the recent films. The chapter describes the wide range of merchandising that accompanied the films and includes some discussion of the corporate synergy within Time Warner that promoted the films. Wasko and Shanadi argue that the *Lord of the Rings* trilogy represents an ideal franchise for a diversified entertainment conglomerate because of its already established popularity, the appeal across demographic groups and the merchandising potential.

Moving slightly away from the corporation and materials directly affiliated with the production, the next three chapters analyse efforts to facilitate its inception and release. Taking a materialist approach, Jenny Lawn and Bronwyn Beatty's chapter '"On the Brink of a New Threshold of Opportunity": *The Lord of the Rings* and New Zealand Cultural Policy' considers the impact of Peter Jackson's achievement on the New Zealand national economy, on the government's export-driven creative industries policy and on the longer-term shape and sustainability of local film production in New Zealand. The chapter traces the significant role that the New Zealand government has played in accommodating the *Lord of the Rings* production through its cultural policy, funding initiatives and tax incentives, and discusses the economic and cultural implications of the government's policy to make feature films a 'value-added' export industry.

Also departing from a cultural politics perspective, but exchanging the New Zealand context for that of Thatcherite Britain of the early 1980s, Martin Barker's chapter 'Making Middle Earth Sound Real: *The Lord of the Rings* and the Cultural Politics of the BBC Radio Edition' argues that the edition of the story that was dramatised by BBC Radio 4 needs to be seen as a part of radio drama's attempt to appropriate *The Lord of the Rings*' reputation as a middle-brow national treasure. The technology and acting used to make the edition as 'realistic' as possible fitted the BBC's political programme in the period of Margaret Thatcher's reign. The chapter discusses how this led to alterations to the story's original narrative, which have, in a different rhetorical framework, been appropriated by Peter Jackson and New Line cinema, giving the national context of the BBC editions an international resonance, but also stripping them of their significance.

Inspired by discourse analyses and theories on (media) events, Daniel Bil-tereyst and Philippe Meers' chapter 'Blockbusters and/as Events: Distributing and Launching *The Lord of the Rings*' investigates the growth and evolution of *The Lord of the Rings* as a carefully constructed worldwide event. Framing the films as blockbusters, they look at the strategies in launching them, at New Line Cinema's extremely strict guidelines for distributors, at the creation of events around *The Lord of the Rings*, film criticism and media coverage, as well as the advertising discourse around the movie(s), taking Belgium as a case study. The chapter builds on Walter Benjamin's concept of 'aura' to understand how a carefully constructed discourse successfully influences advertising, media coverage, reviewing, horizons of expectations and – possibly – actual viewing practices.

The final chapter of this section makes the first move towards reception, albeit still from a decidedly political economy point of view. Warren Buckland and Chris Long's chapter 'Following the Money: *The Lord of the Rings* and the Culture of Box Office Figures' approaches the first film in the trilogy, *The Fellowship of the Ring*, as a blockbuster from one particular perspective, that of box office figures. Avoiding the superficial use of box office figures common in film studies, they analyse them in depth, using several variables such as weekend figures, percentage change in box office from week to week, number of engagements, weekly average earnings per engagement, the film's release pattern, and so on. Buckland and Long analyse the economic performance of the film in the marketplace by examining and interpreting its international box office performance week by week for several months after its initial theatrical release.

Section 2: Public Receptions

The second section of this volume analyses the trilogy's actual reception in different local circumstances and cultural environments, including its appeal with critics, fansites and with fans and avid viewers. The chapter by Davinia Thornley, '"Wellywood" and Peter Jackson: The Local Reception of *The Lord of the Rings* in Wellington, New Zealand' sketches the reception of the films in Wellington, one of New Zealand's major cities, closely associated with the shooting of the films. Using Wellington respondents' answers to an email questionnaire, she portrays how media reports were largely occupied with three main topics. The first charted the unprecedented impact the production had (and has) on Wellington. The second highlighted New Zealand's role as a filmmaking nation. Third, there is the role of Peter Jackson as a 'great man' in the New Zealand film industry. In discussing these topics Thornley exposes the colonialist ramifications of the transfer of international capital from geographical centre (United States) to periphery (New Zealand).

The next two chapters investigate local receptions less directly involved in the making of the films. Ernest Mathijs' chapter 'The Critical Reception of *The Lord of the Rings* in the United Kingdom' analyses previews and reviews from all national British newspapers in order to paint a picture of how the UK press received *The Return of the King*. Emphasising the differences between discussions and opinions published in the run-up to the release, and following the release (and noting the increasing tendency to anticipate the release by publishing previews), Mathijs singles out the editorial politics of *The Times* and *The Independent* as symptomatic examples of two ways to frame *The Lord of the Rings* culturally. While occupying opposite camps of appreciation, both newspapers deploy similar rhetorics and terminology, reflecting their politics (and that of their readers).

'"*Apocalypse Now* in Middle Earth": "Genre" in the Critical Reception of *The Lord of the Rings* in Germany', by Susanne Eichner, Lothar Mikos and Michael Wedel, focuses on the critical reception of *The Return of the King* in Germany. Setting the films up as examples of both the blockbuster and the fantasy genre, they trace how the German press both applied and resisted these genre-labels, and it developed strategies to link the set-ups to other generic references, such as splatter-horror (through Peter Jackson's pedigree) and to the war film (through a complex set of arguments linking *The Lord of the Rings* both to contemporary conflicts such as the Iraq War or historical ones such as World War Two). The chapter also investigates which conceptions of the fan viewer are used in the German press, and how this equips the fantasy genre label with a certain reputation.

The next two chapters maintain interest in blockbusters and reputations, but move the emphasis from reviewers and professionals to fans and regular viewers. Matt Hills' chapter 'Realising the Cult Blockbuster: *The Lord of the Rings* Fandom and Residual/Emergent Cult Status in "the Mainstream"' considers how the 'cult' and 'blockbuster' statuses of *The Lord of the Rings* intersect. 'Cult' is usually seen as 'anti-mainstream' and as indicating a subcultural, minority or specialist taste, whereas 'blockbuster' denotes commonness (in numbers attendance if nothing else). Hills argues that *The Lord of the Rings*' 'residual' or carry-over cult status, where a new text is read through preceding iterations, can be contrasted to its 'emergent' cult blockbuster, where a new film text itself becomes the originating source and focus of cult fan activities. This binary opposition, Hills argues, is complicated by the fact that *The Lord of the Rings*' cult status is multiple: it may relate as much to Peter Jackson's preceding career and J.R.R. Tolkien's status as author, as to the films. As such, then, it remains important to analyse cult status as overdetermined rather than as a singular and somehow inherently 'anti-mainstream' bid for audience distinction.

Kirsten Pullen's chapter '*The Lord of the Rings* Online Blockbuster Fandom: Pleasure and Commerce' discusses how internet fans were crucial to the *Lord of the Rings* global marketing campaign, and how the lines between 'authentic' fan communities and commercially motivated and sponsored fan activity became increasingly blurred. She argues that the large number of sites as well as the meanings and activities attached to different online articulations of *Lord of the Rings* online fandom expand understandings of what fan activity might look like. Examining dedicated websites (especially www.theonering.net, but also looking at fan fiction), she pays particular attention to notions of community, of branding and hype, and to the excess of sites and fan activity associated with these texts, and how, as a blockbuster text, *The Lord of the Rings* illuminates the increasingly tangled relationship between 'commercial' and 'private' use of media texts.

Also questioning fandom, Judith Rosenbaum's chapter '"This is What it Must Look Like': *The Lord of the Rings* Fandom and Media Literacy' uses techniques from the study of media literacy to empirically investigate both self-declared fans and non-fans in order to investigate claims that fans show any kind of inclination or desire to perceive the world created in their favourite films as real, and to test their understanding of the construction of fan objects, on both narrative and technical levels. Rosenbaum builds on findings from an exploratory study conducted among the local *Lord of the Rings* fan communities in the Netherlands to compare the level of media literacy of these fans with that of non-fans, concluding that, as far as perceptions of reality are concerned, fans appear to be as critical (and hence as media literate) as non-fans.

Anne Jerslev's chapter 'Sacred Viewing: Emotional Responses to *The Lord of the Rings*' closes this section. Her contribution focuses on the way viewers are absorbed into the *Lord of the Rings* films, the impact of absorption on their direct viewing experiences and on their abilities to retell or cognitively appreciate the films. Using empirical data from an online questionnaire on *The Return of the King*, and relying on cognitive theories of film perception, she investigates the use of emotional languages viewers employ to describe their wonder, amazement and awe. Distinguishing between two main sorts of emotional attachments to *The Lord of the Rings*, namely those relating to the fictional universe of the films, and those in relation to the making of that universe, she identifies five kinds of emotional reactions (immediate, contextual, thematic, formal and situational), while also reserving space for a 'sacred viewing' category akin to the sublime, nearly intangible but very real in its effects.

Section 3: Ancillary Contexts

The third and final section of this volume relates the trilogy's public presence to the textual structure and form of products associated with it. It is not the intention of this section to provide isolated analyses of the textual features of the film. Rather its aim is to offer discussions that demonstrate how the trilogy's textual features also inform cultural products in their own sense – as if specific elements of the films live on 'outside' in other products.

The first four chapters in this section take as their subject ancillary materials created, promoted and/or endorsed by the copyright holders of the *Lord of the Rings* franchise. Erik Hedling's chapter 'Framing Tolkien: Trailers, High Concept, and the Ring' deals with the film trailers advertising *The Lord of the Rings*. Framing the trailers as an attempt to evoke the modern aesthetic of High Concept, a strategy employed by Hollywood for integrating product and marketing in the most commercially effective way, Hedling analyses them with reference to 'the book' (the source material), 'the look' (the style) and 'the hook' (the main point of attraction). Building on aesthetic theories of paratextuality, he discusses how issues of fidelity, stardom and spectacle (battle scenes as well as special effects) are used to attract millions to the cinemas and also to promote sales of various merchandise – tourism, DVDs, computer games – connected to the films, concluding with the observation that the trailers generated so much interest that they were advertised in themselves as cinema attractions.

Pushing theories of textuality and aesthetics Jonathan Gray's chapter 'Bonus Material: The DVD Layering of *The Lord of the Rings*' uses Walter Benjamin's 'aura'

concept to argue how the extras on the DVDs of *The Lord of the Rings* (and especially the luxuriously edited extended versions) have become an integral part of the
core text, essential to any meaning-making of the story and its background. Gray
questions the proliferation and continuation of *The Lord of the Rings*' textuality
through the DVDs, and it asks what they do to 'the text'. Performing a close reading of *The Two Towers*' DVD bonus material, the chapter examines hierarchies and
interrelations of texts within the supposedly solitary text; the industry literacy that
commentary tracks teach; and how DVDs are initiating multiple new modes of
audience interaction. In conclusion, the chapter seeks to understand the increasing
complexity and development of the public presence of different versions of a text.

The next two chapters concentrate on the *Lord of the Rings* games, and its
place in and implications for game culture. Jonathan Dovey and Helen Kennedy's
chapter 'Playing the Ring: Intermediality and Ludic Narratives in the *Lord of the
Rings* Games' presents an observational pilot study of eight young people playing
the board game, the computer game and watching the second part of the trilogy.
Dovey and Kennedy's objectives are twofold. First they investigate the proposition
that the circulation of popular media texts across a number of platforms function
to invite the user into a storyworld, and explore how the platform determines the
users' experience of that storyworld. Second, they question the positions of ludologists and narratologists by investigating how users choose to play the game (on
the basis of filmic character or on the basis of the characters' functionality in the
gameworld), thus examining the relative importance of narrative and gameplay
pleasures in each of the platforms examined.

Mariano Longo's 'Cooperation versus Violence: An Ethnographical Analysis of
the *Return of the King* Video Game' also concentrates upon the games associated
with the films. Like Dovey and Kennedy he addresses the distinction between
narratological and ludic attitudes to the game to isolate its main theme and aim:
cooperation. Using an ethnographic approach, and describing in detail the social
rules and routines that playing relies upon, Longo adopts a sociological perspective
that enables him to treat what happens on the screen as actual social situations,
albeit simulated ones. Longo also studies the ideological dimensions of the *Lord of
the Rings* game through a focus on five aspects (action, interaction, violence, the
representation of the enemies, time and space) which he analyses through a qualitative approach to content analysis.

The last three chapters in this section move away from officially endorsed ancillary materials, into the grey zone of materials inspired by *The Lord of the Rings*
and condoned (at best) by the copyright holders. The areas of subcultural and local contexts within which these materials operate show how widespread the public
presence of *The Lord of the Rings* is. The fact that all of them (at least the ones discussed here) have either been created to gain profit, or have not refused such profits
when they became available, shows, once more, how intrinsic the commercial con-

text is to that presence. The chapter by Stan Jones 'Fixing a Heritage: Inscribing Middle Earth onto New Zealand' addresses the adjunct initiatives spawned across New Zealand attempting to profit from the popularity of the films. Jones concentrates on four such initiatives, namely the Location Guidebook by Ian Brodie, the national television documentary by New Zealand public television, the Te Papa Exhibition, and Hobbiton, the preservation of the only remaining film set of the shoot. Jones argues that these activities need not be seen as opportunistic endeavours towards profit, but rather function as builders of a local heritage, thus helping to link local history and the authenticity of New Zealand culture (which had after all been appropriated by the production) to its contemporary exploitation.

Kevin Donnelly's chapter 'Musical Middle Earth' elaborates on the numerous musical imaginings of *The Lord of the Rings*, such as those by Leonard Rosenman, Bo Hansson and Howard Shore (the official soundtrack). His chapter looks at how these musical versions have articulated aspects of the original text, noting what has been foregrounded and what has been marginalised, looking for a musical 'centre' to *The Lord of the Rings* as both a cinematic and musical object. In so doing he forms an argument which relates contemporary popular music culture (of different strands) to how music is being used (applied, abused, added, distorted) in film culture, including its employment as a publicity tool.

The final chapter of the volume, 'Tolkien Dirty', by I. Q. Hunter, discusses *The Lord of the G-Strings*, an erotic spin-off of the films, a lesbian-themed rip-off of *The Fellowship of the Ring*, which recounts the erotic adventures of Dildo Saggins, a Throbbit of Diddle-Earth. Hunter interrogates contemporary cinema's ability to attract and facilitate spin-off spoofs. His chapter places the *Lord of the Rings* phenomenon within the context of exploitation popular culture, and argues that *The Lord of the G-String* is an attempt to 'correct' the original's sexual politics by exploiting its covert homo-eroticism and repression of female sexuality. Thus, he argues, it impacts upon strategies of ironic readings and textual poaching, akin to fan fiction, which challenge the purity of the original solely by presenting it with an outrageous alternative in its public presence.

Conclusion

Whether focusing on descriptive analysis, or employing empirical research of the particular presence or context they investigate, or textually researching a particular ancillary media, all chapters in this volume converge in their treatment of *The Lord of the Rings* as a milestone in contemporary cinema – not so much because of its intrinsic qualities, but because multifarious popular culture is so saturate with its manifestations. The contributions in the first section touch upon theories and concepts of merchandising, franchising, synergy, distribution, cultural policy, blockbusters and techniques of cinema release; in the second section they address theories of auteurism, genre, political rhetorics, reception studies, internet studies, fandom, media literacy and cognitive perception; in the third they discuss modern aesthetics, textual analysis, game culture, ideology, authenticity, musical theory and exploitation cinema.

This diversity demonstrates the vast terrain that the public presence of cinema in fact traverses. *The Lord of the Rings* is the ideal case study for charting this emerging territory, because of its sheer enormity, significance and popularity. But not to miss the forest for the Ents: *The Lord of the Rings* may be an unprecedented marvel, but the scope of its *présence* inevitably reshapes the nature of film in general, as revealed by a multitude of public and commercial dimensions. In order to fully comprehend the true impact of cinema in the twenty-first century, it is nothing less than essential to take such multiple dimensions into account.

Notes

1   I want to thank Janet Wasko and Govind Shanadi for providing the information for this part of the analysis.
2   This project was made possible by a grant from the UK Economic and Social Research Council (ESRC Grant No. 000-22-0323) to whom we record our gratitude.

Works cited

Altman, R. (1999) *Film/Genre*. London: British Film Institute.
Austin, T. (2002) *Hollywood, Hype and Audiences*. Manchester: Manchester University Press.
Barker, M. and E. Mathijs (eds) (forthcoming) *Watching The Lord of the Rings: World Audiences for the Film Adaptation*. New York: Peter Lang.
Benjamin, W. (1969) *Illuminations*. New York: Schocken Books.
Bordwell, D. (1989) *Making Meaning: Inference and Rhetoric in the Interpretation of Cinema*. Cambridge, MA: Harvard University Press.
Bourdieu, P. (1984) *Distinction: A Social Critique of the Judgement of Taste*. London: Routledge.
Elsaesser, T. (2001) 'The Blockbuster: Everything Connects, but Not Everything Goes', in J. Lewis (ed.) *The End of Cinema as We Know It: American Film in the Nineties*. New York: New York University Press, 11–22.
Eagleton, T. (1984) *The Function of Criticism*. London: Verso.
Grainge, P. (2004) 'Branding Hollywood: Studio Logos and the Aesthetics of Memory and Hype', *Screen*, 45, 4, 344–62.
Habermas, J. (1962) *Strukturwandel der Offentlichkeit*. Frankfurt am-Main: Suhrkamp.
Holson, L. M. (2003) 'A franchise fantasy', *New York Times*, 9 November.
Johnson, T. (2003) 'Is "King" the golden ring?', *Variety*, 12 October, 1.

Kellner, D. (1995) *Media Culture: Cultural Studies, Identity and Politics Between the Modern and the Postmodern*. London: Routledge.

Klinger, B. (1997) 'Film History Terminable and Interminable: Recovering the Past in Reception Studies', *Screen*, 38, 2, 107–28.

Kracauer, S. (1995) *The Mass Ornament: Weimar Essays*. Cambridge, MA: Harvard University Press.

Mathijs, E. and M. Pomerance (eds) (2006) *From Hobbits to Hollywood: Essays on Peter Jackson's The Lord of the Rings*. New York: Editions Rodopi.

MacCarthy, T. (2003) 'Review: *The Lord of the Rings: The Return of the King*', *Variety*, 5 December, 9.

Staiger, J. (1992) *Interpreting Films: The Historical Reception of American Cinema*. New York. Princeton University Press.

_____ *Perverse Specators: Practices of Film Reception*. New York: New York University Press.

Tolkien, J. R. R. (1966) *The Lord of the Rings: The Fellowship of the Ring*, second edition. London: HarperCollins.

Ward, B. (2003) '37 things about Lord of the Rings', *Ottawa Citizen*, 18, 13 December.

Wasko, J. (1994) *Hollywood in the Information Age: Beyond the Silver Screen*. Austin: University of Texas Press.

SECTION 1
POLITICAL ECONOMY AND COMMERCIAL CONTEXTS

More than Just Rings: Merchandise for Them All

Janet Wasko and Govind Shanadi[1]

Introduction

> For sheer commerciality, *Rings* has arguably become the most profitable fictional
> work of all time. (Gilsdorf 2003: 10)

New Line Cinema claims that it is a 'pioneer in franchise filmmaking and its *Lord
of the Rings* trilogy ... is one of the most successful and most honored film franchises in history' (New Line Entertainment 2004). Thus, it may be of interest to
understand more about the commercial context of these films, and more specifically, to identify the commodities that accompanied their release and continues to
attract revenues. This chapter presents an overview of the merchandising associated with *The Lord of the Rings*. The discussion traces the background of copyright
and ownership rights for *The Lord of the Rings*. As well as discussing the corporate
synergy within Time Warner that promoted the films we will analyse the wide
range of merchandising that accompanied the films. We argue that the *Lord of the
Rings* trilogy represents an ideal franchise for a diversified entertainment conglomerate because of its already established popularity, the appeal across demographic
groups and the evident merchandising potential.

It may be helpful to first define some of the terms used in discussing film
merchandise generally, especially because some of these concepts are sometimes
used rather loosely. 'Merchandise' includes commodities that derive from a film,
while 'tie-ins' represent already existing products featuring (tied to) a film. 'Product
placements' are products that are featured in a film. The concept of a 'franchise',
as it relates to film or entertainment, has been defined by some to mean simply
sequels. However, a better description is a property or concept that is repeatable
in multiple media platforms or outlets with merchandising and tie-in potential.
It works particularly well if the franchise includes reoccurring and copyrightable

characters and story elements. Our basic point is that *The Lord of the Rings* represents a nearly ideal franchise because of three reasons:

1. Its already established popularity – The three *Lord of the Rings* films draw on an already successful set of books and thus tap into a huge potential audience already familiar with the story and characters. The books are sometimes considered children's literature (or what *Variety* calls 'kiddie lit'), which has become a common standby for Hollywood blockbusters or franchises (an obvious example is the *Harry Potter* franchise). As *Variety* explains:

> The run on kiddie lit owes something to demographics and market trends; chiefly, films skewing towards a younger mass audience and studio execs jumping on the 'Potter' bandwagon. But at the root of this trend is a deeper tectonic change in Hollywood. For the vertically integrated congloms that own the studios, kiddie properties aren't just a popular fad: they're *the perfect fuel for the synergy machine*. (Bing & Dunkley 2002: 1; emphasis added)

2. Its appeal across demographic groups – Even though *Variety* may characterise *The Lord of the Rings* as 'kiddie lit', it is obvious that the books have had a much wider appeal. Indeed, *The Lord of the Rings* is one of the recent film franchises that hoped to appeal to a wide range of age groups – and succeeded. According to a New Line executive, the only audience group that has not been particularly attracted is the '50+ woman' who are called the 'Achilles heel' of the franchise (Rooney 2004).

3. Its merchandise potential – The movies offer countless merchandising possibilities due to this wide appeal, as well as the huge numbers of characters with costumes, jewelry, swords and other weapons.

All of these points are captured rather well in a statement by the CEO of Toy Biz (one of *The Lord of the Rings*' key merchandisers):

> With its intricately detailed fantasy world, incredible range of highly unique fantasy characters, and a story that has captivated kids and adults alike for more than 40 years, *The Lord of the Rings* has enormous potential in the marketplace. (Anon. 2000).

To further illustrate these three points, we focus in this study on the range of merchandising and the context in which it has been produced and distributed.

The property/copyright

It is important to trace the ownership of the rights to *The Lord of the Rings* to understand who controls and benefits from the extensive merchandising associated with the books and the films. Initially, J.R.R. Tolkien signed a contract to publish *The Lord of the Rings* with the publishing house of George Allen and Unwin, which included a 50/50 profit sharing deal. Because of its length, the book was published in three parts. In August 1954, 3,500 copies of the first installment, *The Fellowship of the Rings*, were released. It was republished six weeks later because of its initial success. The second installment, *The Two Towers*, was published in November 1954. The third and final installment, *The Return of the King*, was published in October 1955 (see White 2002). The American publisher for the books was Houghton Mifflin. Both the critical and commercial success in the United States was initially only moderate. However, in June 1965, a pirated Ace Publishers paperback edition made its appearance in the United States, which was a huge success. By Christmas 1965, an official Ballantine paperback edition was issued and Ace reached an out-of-court settlement to pay royalties for its illegal sales. The Ballantine edition had sold 3 million copies by 1968.

In 1967, Tolkien sold the film and other merchandising rights for *The Lord of the Rings* to United Artists. In 1976, United Artists sold the movie and merchandising rights to a Hollywood producer, Saul Zaentz.[2] In 1977, Rankin/Bass Productions created an animated television movie titled *The Hobbit* which aired on ABC-TV and was subsequently distributed on video. The next year, Ralph Bakshi produced a $10million, truncated, animated version of *The Lord of the Rings*, which was distributed by United Artists. The film received cool critical reviews and attracted relatively paltry box office receipts (Lowson *et al.* 2002). Hollywood's reintroduction to *The Lord of the Rings* began in 1998, when the Saul Zaentz Company, doing business as Tolkien Enterprises, granted a license to film the trilogy to New Line Cinema, a subsidiary of Time Warner (which we will discuss further below). Under the terms of the contract, New Line Cinema also received the license for renderings based on the movie depictions of the characters. However, Tolkien Enterprises still held the rights to the *Lord of the Rings* characters in a more general sense. Merchandisers who want to use a likeness of a character in the film must go through New Line. However, a more generic depiction of the character must be licensed through Tolkien Enterprises (National Arbitration Forum 2002). While the exact terms of New Line's contract are unavailable, it is reported that the arrangement involves a profit-sharing scheme. In fact, Zaentz filed a suit against New Line for £11million, claiming that his share of the profits from the first movie, *The Fellowship of the Rings*, was based on net profits rather than gross receipts (Davies 2004).

In addition, HarperCollins Publishing in London holds the rights to some 'printed published matter based on non-film artwork' (Tolkien Enterprises 2004). On the other hand, the Tolkien family receives no money from any of the merchandising. Recall that Tolkien sold the rights to United Artists in 1967. The family does receive 50% of the profits from book sales, which will be discussed below

(White 2002). Meanwhille, Zaentz is reported to be working on a West End theatre production of *The Lord of the Rings* (Davies 2004).

The conglomerate: Time Warner

> ...the Mordor-like conglomerate that owns New Line. (Anon. 2003a)

We need to look closer at the organisation that has produced and distributed *The Lord of the Rings* to understand the commercial context of the films. Time Warner Inc. is generally considered to be the world's largest media company (Anon. 2004). Revenues in 2003 were $39.6 billion (Time Warner Inc. 2004). Time Warner is listed on the New York Stock Exchange with a ticker symbol of 'TWX'. With 4.4 billion shares outstanding, they have a market capitalisation of $73.31 billion (MSN Money Central 2004b). Time Warner was 29th on *Fortune*'s annual 'Fortune 500' list in 2003. By comparison, *Fortune* ranked Microsoft at 47th and Disney at 61st. The company is the result of the merger of Time Warner and America Online on 11 January 2001, after which it was known as AOL Time Warner. The name was changed back to Time Warner in October 2003 (Munk 2004). The company is currently divided into five 'segments': 'America Online', 'Cable', 'Filmed Entertainment', 'Networks', and 'Publishing'. But these five categories do not fully capture the size of the company. AOL is still the leading provider of Internet access in the United States, and operates in many other countries around the world. AOL also operates Mapquest.com and Moviefone. Time Warner Cable serves 10.9 million customers in the US. The filmed entertainment division includes Warner Bros. Studios, as well as Castle Rock Entertainment and New Line Cinema. The Networks division includes the Turner Broadcasting System, which itself includes CNN, TBS Superstation, TNT, Turner Classic Movies and The Cartoon Network. The Networks division also includes the WB Network, as well as HBO and Cinemax. Finally, the Publications division includes many of the largest circulating magazines, including *Time, Sports Illustrated, People, InStyle, Fortune, Entertainment Weekly, Real Simple, Money, Southern Living, Sunset, Golf, Field and Stream, Ideal Home* and *Country Life*, as well as many more niche publications.

The company is a classic vertically and horizontally integrated company, which the it describes in the following way: the Filmed Entertainment segment generates content revenue by licensing television and theatrical programming to the Networks segment; the Networks segment generates subscription revenues by selling cable network programming to the Cable segment; the AOL, Cable, Networks and Publishing segments generate advertising revenue by cross-promoting the products and services of all Time Warner segments; the AOL segment generates Other Revenue by providing the Cable segment's customers access to the AOL Transit Data

Network (ATDN) for high-speed access to the Internet (Time Warner Inc. 2004). The company had been under investigation by the Securities and Exchange Commission and the Department of Justice because of possible accounting irregularities by America Online. Nina Munk (2004) reports that between the time the dot.com bubble burst and the merger with Time Warner went through, AOL engaged in 'creative accounting' to keep their advertising revenue high, even though many of their Internet advertisers were going bankrupt and were not going to be able to meet their contracts with AOL. However, a settlement of a fine of $510 million and independent monitoring of the AOL division is close to being reached (Fabrikant 2004). Other lawsuits have been filed by shareholders who were upset by the merger. The Chairman and CEO of Time Warner is Richard Parsons, while the largest single investor is Capital Research & Management Company, which owns 7.7%, and the largest individual owner is R. E. 'Ted' Turner, who owns 3.23% (MSN Money Central 2004a).

Revenues	2002	2003	% change
AOL	$9.094bn	$8.600bn	-5
Cable	$7.035bn	$7.699bn	+9
Filmed Entertainment	$10.040bn	$10.967bn	+9
Networks	$7.655bn	$8.434bn	+10
Publishing	$5.422bn	$5.533bn	+2
Intersegment Eliminations	$(1.932bn)	$(1.668bn)	-13
TOTAL	$37.314bn	$39.565bn	+6

Table 7: Time Warner in 2002–03
Source: Time Warner Inc. 28 January 2004 press release

Founded in 1967, New Line claims to be an 'independent' film company, even though it is fully owned by Time Warner. In 2003, New Line generated the highest revenue in its existence. In 2003, it accounted for a 10% share of the US film market with $924million in box-office grosses, making it the fifth-ranked studio in the US for the second year in a row, in terms of revenue. The success of the *Lord of the Rings* trilogy obviously contributed a good deal to New Line's recent success. Other contributions for 2003 were *Elf* (Jon Favreau 2003) which grossed more than $175 million (domestically), and two other modestly budgeted releases, *The Texas Chainsaw Massacre* (Marcus Nispel, 2003) and *Freddy vs. Jason* (Ronny Yu, 2003), which each grossed more than $80 million. The various segments of New Line include New Line Cinema, Fine Line Features, New Line Home Entertainment, New Line International Releasing, New Line New Media, New Line Television, New Line Distribution, New Line Merchandising/Licensing and New Line Music.

The merchandise

> Great for *Lord of the Rings* fans ages 300 years old and younger. (lordoftherings-catalog.com 2004)

Before New Line/Peter Jackson, there was already a significant amount of merchandise. However, with the New Line trilogy, the flood gates opened even wider. Merchandising was even involved in the budgeting of the films. It is claimed that 10% of the budget was raised by selling rights to 'video games, toys and merchandise companies' (Holson 2003). Another source says that '$11 million came from Burger King, JVC Electronics, Barnes & Noble, and other toy and merchandising companies' (Ward 2003).

Movie merchandise is not unusual and represents a huge global market, with $2.5 billion in royalties from entertainment properties reported in 2001 (Goldsmith 2002: 1). However, many, if not most, movies do not translate well into merchandise. In addition, studios and licensees have been cautious after some significant losses in the past. One problem is that Hollywood-related merchandise has a relatively short time to prove itself on retail shelves before the next big property arrives. As Andrea Hein, Viacom's president of consumer products, explains: 'Licensing is all about wanting a piece of something. You've got to have the time and place for that property to be nurtured' (quoted in ibid.). And the success of the merchandise is tied directly to the success of the film. A representative of the International Licensing Industry Merchandisers' Association (LIMA) states that, 'marketing and merchandising is [*sic*] never the major driving force behind a film. If a film's no good, no one will buy the product' (quoted in Monahan 2003).

By most accounts, the films as well as the merchandise have been successful. One assertion is that 'the range of merchandise launched to tie-in with the new *Lord of the Rings* film is almost unprecedented in the movie world' (Anon. 2003c). Allegedly, the merchandise was released rather slowly. One reporter states that New Line 'held back a merchandise blitz at the start of the trilogy in 2000 to build the property slowly', while David Imhoff, New Line's senior executive vice president of worldwide licensing, explained: 'It was about letting the marketplace build on its own, and it's worked out wonderfully' (quoted in Howard 2003). For instance, Hasbro added *Lord of the Rings* Monopoly and Trivial Pursuit in 2003 to its first game tie-in, Risk. A Hasbro spokesperson explained: 'We had a nice success with Risk, and that inspired us to do more' (ibid.). While there was apparently less *Return of the King*-tied merchandise, new products were released around *Return of the King* and another new range of products was offered for 2004, with the release of *Return of the King* in video/DVD formats, including fifty new action figures, new games and collectibles, and so on (Anon. 2004b). One reference has noted that the merchandising of *The Lord of the Rings* is an example of 'dual merchandising' – the classic products as well as the movie-tied products. There seems to be some kind of agreement not to overlap in some areas, but there still is quite a bit of duplication. While the movie-tied products stress connections to the films, the movies have increased the revenues for classic products (Mathews 2001). One store owner explained: '*Lord of the Rings* is popular with both young and old', and observed that parents were introducing their kids to the trilogy through the films. Furthermore, 'customers have included people not normally associated with the purchase of science-fiction and fantasy paraphernalia' (Anon. 2003c: 6).

It is nearly impossible to obtain accurate accounts of the amount of revenues or profits that are associated with film merchandise, as companies rarely report such revenues. Various reports in the *Hollywood Reporter* have noted that between $1billion to $1.2billion has been generated from the worldwide sale of *The Lord of the Rings* merchandising (Schiller 2004). More recently, New Line noted on its website that the *The Lord of the Rings* DVDs and videos, plus 'related merchandise' had attracted $2.5billion. Another indication of *The Lord of the Rings*'s merchandise clout is the award that one of the films received for best entertainment brand license of the year at the 2003 Licensing Show sponsored by LIMA (ibid.). It is also difficult to accurately assess the number of licensees or the amount of merchandise. Mark Rahner (2003) states that there were more than 300 licensees worldwide, while other reports are much lower. Typically, a producer or distributor receives an advance payment for such products, as well as royalty payments, often 5–10% of gross revenues from sales to retailers (that is, the wholesale price). However, royalties for *The Lord of the Rings* properties were reported to be 10–15% of the wholesale price (Monahan 2003). Whatever the revenues or profits have been, New Line has expressed satisfaction with the results. As David Imhoff explains:

> We are tremendously pleased with the dedication and commitment Toy Biz, Burger King, and the other licensees have brought to this process and thrilled to see their work being embraced across the globe. They never lost sight of the history and intricacies of the books, as well as the characters of Tolkien and Peter Jackson's Middle Earth. (Quoted in Anon. 2002b)

The Lord of the Rings involves quite a lot of typical merchandise associated with film franchises, but also introduces some unique categories of merchandise. We will only present a brief overview of these categories and some examples, with special attention to books and games.

Books, books and more books...

It is not unusual for films to be accompanied by a wide range of books. Of course, the Tolkien texts are the source of the film, and not necessarily products initiated by the film. However, they still might be considered merchandise in this context, in addition to the wide range of books that have been inspired by the films. *The Hobbit* and *The Lord of the Rings* have been translated into over forty languages, with an estimated 100 million copies sold (White 2002). *Boston Globe* reporter Ethan Gilsdorf concludes that 'Tolkien has spawned a whole international sub-culture of escapism and fueled a boom in science fiction and fantasy that's now 10% of the total trade-book business' (2003: 10). The success of the films has undoubtedly influenced the sale of the 'classic' books. Ballantine had sold 32 million copies of the mass market paperback edition between 1965 and 2001. It sold 14 million from the release of the first film through the end of December 2003 (Seiler 2003). Meanwhile, Houghton Mifflin, owned by Vivendi Universal, had received $43.5million from the novels by the end of 2001, up more than $5.2million from previous years (Mathews 2001). One report claims that from 2000 to 2004, 25 million copies of various versions of the trilogy and *The Hobbit* were sold. Houghton Mifflin's Tolkien-related books generated $48million in sales in 2001 and $54million in 2002. Unlike most classic novels, it remains available in hardback editions. 'For a book that's fifty years old, it's unprecedented', said Houghton Mifflin projects director Clay Harper (quoted in Schorow 2004: 24). But there are also countless books and other publications that are directly linked with the film. With the release of *The Return of the King*, Houghton Mifflin's various tie-in editions and books about the films filled four pages in its 2004 catalogue.

The typical merchandise: toys, t-shirts and tankards

The list of products associated with *The Lord of the Rings* seems endless. However, many of the products are similar to those associated with other Hollywood blockbuster films. A wide variety of toys have been available, with Marvel's Toy Biz alone, as the 'master licensee', producing from 450–500 items (Rahner 2003). A huge number of different action figures have been produced, which apparently have been more successful than anticipated. A Marvel representative explained early in 2002:

> The action figures are selling phenomenally ... we expected that it would be a collector line that would appeal to an older demographic. Apparently kids are buying the products as well. (Quoted in Anon. 2002b)

Not one set, but many sets of action figures, continue to be produced. Other toys include skateboards, toy swords, bow and arrow sets, 'standees' (life-size standups), puzzles, 'head Nodderz' (bobble-head dolls), plush dolls, as well as a *Lord of the Rings* version of Barbie (as Galadriel) and Ken (as Legolas). Paper supplies include calendars, maps, bookmarks, journals, paperweights, posters, post cards, stickers sheets and prints. Of course, trading cards are available, sometimes associated with games that will be discussed below. Household items consist of everything from mugs, cups and glasses to bed sheets and pillows. Party items include invitations, wrapping paper, balloons, hats, favour packs, loot bags, blow-outs, paper plates, cups and napkins, table covers, cake decorations, thank you notes, and so on. Halloween costumes feature a wide variety of masks, helmets and capes, plus Hobbit feet, wigs and Elven ears. Other holiday fare includes Christmas tree ornaments and Valentine cards. There is a wide range of boxes, waterglobes, snowglobes, tins, plastic cubes, photo frames and other curios. Typical clothing items include t-shirts, caps and jackets, plus watches, key chains, umbrellas, ties ('the one tie') and scarves. Of course, backpacks and lunch boxes are also available.

It is worth noting that in many of these categories, there is not only one product available, but multiple products corresponding to the different films or characters. For instance, there are around twenty posters available on the New Line *The Lord of the Rings* site, including a five-foot cast poster for *The Return of the King*. Of course, there is a wide range of musical products connected to the films. In addition to the soundtracks and sheet music from the films, other music is promoted as 'inspired by the film'. (In fact, one album is entitled 'Music Inspired by *The Lord of the Rings*', featuring the Middle Earth Orchestra). At least 41 other musical products relating to *The Lord of the Rings* are listed on Amazon.com.[3] Also, computer programs (not including games, which will be discussed below) have included *Lord of the Rings* Activity Studio (produced by IMSI) and *Lord of the Rings* CD Cards (produced by Serious USA).

The not-so-typical and high-end merchandise: stamps, swords, jewelry and furniture

Again, *The Lord of the Rings* films are not unique in inspiring more expensive merchandise, as other films that attract avid fans also offer high-end products. For instance, one could site the life-size replicas of *Star Wars* characters, ranging from $4,500 for the helmeted bounty hunter Boba Fett to $13,000 for the robot C-3P0 (Christenson 1999). But it seems that pricey *Lord of the Rings* products abound. To begin with, high-priced goblets, shot glasses, mugs, flasks and pipes are available, again, corresponding to the many characters in the film. A variety of products are drawn directly from settings or props from the films; for instance, the Phial of Galadriel ($75). High-priced clothing includes everything from exclusive, limited edition Elven cloaks (made from the fabric produced only in New Zealand from rare Stansborough Gotland sheep at $600 each), to elegant flowing gowns, ties (or, as advertised, 'the one tie' for $70), aviator jackets ($249), and so on. Other high-priced items include many types of headdresses, helmets/helms, staffs, swords and other weapons. One can purchase the Gauntlet of the Dark Lord Sauron for $399.95, as well as Gimli's helmet for around $300. Indeed, there is quite a wide range of weaponry, including regular size and miniature swords, axes, knives and scimitars that correspond to most of the main characters in the films. Obviously, there is a wide variety of jewelry as well: necklaces, earrings and brooches, plus lots of Elven pins. And, of course, there are the rings. While the trilogy features One Ring to rule them all, there were actually twenty rings in the story. But there are far more than that available for sale. As the *Rough Guide to The Lord of the Rings* observes:

> Let's be clear about this. There is no One Ring. There are millions of them. You can get one anywhere, for just about any price, of almost any material that can be made ring-shaped and will take an impression of Elvish script. Unfortunately, none of them have the power to make you invisible, it's doubtful they'll remain cool to the touch after being in fire and they certainly won't prolong your life (Simpson 2003: 251).

Again, as with many blockbuster or film franchises, there are many products called 'collectibles' – which could include anything from original art work to decorative plates. Weta Digital, the company that helped create the visual effects for *The Lord of the Rings*, sells many 'collectible' products that draw on the settings of the films. Thus, one can buy limited edition 'poly stone environments' such as Minas Morgul, Minas Tirith and the Mines of Moria. Weta works with a company called Sideshow Collectibles to produce these items, plus a wide range of statues, figures, plaques, busts, weapon sets and medallions. One of the highest priced items is a bronze statue of Gandalf, which sold for $6,495, when it was available. (At the time of writing, it was supposedly sold out.) In an example of cross-promotional deals between the merchandising companies, Sideshow/Weta worked with Houghton Mifflin to sell a special set of bookends together with a single-volume hard cover edition of *The Lord of the Rings*. Among the most expensive merchandise are extremely limited versions of furniture produced in England by Middle Earth Furniture: the One Ring table and Darkness & Light chairs sell for £19,750 and original pinball art from a *Lord of the Rings* pinball machine, as for sale on eBay for $40,000. And, finally, in a somewhat unique situation, *The Lord of the Rings* has been 'honoured' with the release of stamps and coins, both in New Zealand and in the UK. Of course, these also represent merchandise, available online at the New Line and other *The Lord of the Rings* websites.

The games

The wide range of games that are tied to the *Lord of the Rings* trilogy is representative of the 'richness' of the *Lord of the Rings* franchise. Several different categories will be discussed in more detail below, including traditional board games, video games and role-playing type games.

1. Traditional games – The traditional board games might have been mentioned above under typical merchandise; however, the number of different games that have been converted to *The Lord of the Rings* may be somewhat unusual. First, there is a *Lord of the Rings* board game based on each of the New Line films, as well as other board games not tied to the film. But also, there are versions of Monopoly, Trivial Pursuit, Risk and Stratego (all produced by Hasbro), plus dominoes, backgammon, checkers and chess (including some very high-end chess sets). Hasbro also produces a Lord of the Rings Battle for Middle Earth Mission TV Game, plus Top Trumps Lord of the Rings Card Game.

2. Video Games – Video game versions of each film were produced for various formats (PlayStation2, GameCube, Xbox, GameBoy) by the fast-growing game company, EA. Another EA game is The Lord of the Rings: The Third Age, and others are planned for the future. Meanwhile, Vivendi Universal (VU Games) produces video games from the classic *The Lord of the Rings* licensed by Tolkien Enterprises. The Nintendo version produced by Interplay is also drawn from the classic Tolkien and not film-related.

3. Computer games – EA has produced several games and are planning more. Meanwhile, Vivendi Universal Games offers 'The Lord of the Rings: War of the Ring', a PC strategy game, plus others, again using the classic Tolkien. Several years ago, Black Label Games, a studio of Vivendi Universal Games, announced it had entered into a production agreement with Liquid Entertainment to develop 'The Lord of the Rings: The War of the Ring,' a real-time strategy (RTS) game for the PC platform. The game was to be developed through VU Games' long-term agreement with Tolkien Enterprises and was to be released in early 2004. VU Games announced in May 2003 that it had entered into a production agreement with Turbine Entertainment Software Corp. to develop 'Middle Earth Online,' a massive multiplayer (MMP) game which was launched in 2005.

4. Role-playing games – Various kinds of role-playing games have grown in popularity over the last few decades. One of the first of this type was the Dungeons and Dragons role-playing game introduced in 1970 which claimed to be directly inspired by Tolkien's books (Ward 2003). There are least three types of these games that draw on *The Lord of the Rings*: strategy or tabletop battle games, tradeable miniatures games, and trading-card games. Online activities are sometimes associated with some of these games. The Lord of the Rings Tabletop Battle Games are produced by Games Workshop and based on the motion pictures. Games Workshop's website explains:

The Lord of the Rings Strategy Battle Game gives you and your friends every opportunity to relive the excitement of the motion picture. Do you want to refight the tense and action-packed scenes from the Battle for Minas Tirith? You can! Will Frodo, Sam, and their companions make it to Mordor and destroy The Ring in the fires of Mount Doom? Play the game to find out! All you need is an opponent, a handful of dice, a flat surface to play on and, of course, some *The Lord of the Rings* miniatures, and you're ready to take the first steps down the path of Miniature Gaming. (Games Workshop 2004)

Games Workshop claims to be the world's largest hobby wargames company and is based in Nottingham, UK. Games Workshop also owns Sabertooth Games, which produces The Lord of the Rings Tradable Miniatures Game, featuring pre-painted miniature figures. The game was released around Christmas 2003, and featured over 120 expertly painted miniatures, based on all of the key characters from the *Lord of the Rings* movie trilogy. New products continue to be released, including booster or expansion packs, individual character figures, maps, special dice, and so on. There are leagues, tournaments and events associated with the game around the United States and in other countries. The website features products for sale, plus listings for tournaments and events, a Hall of Champions and 'battle lore' – army lists, battle reports, strategy briefings and the like, to assist players.

Finally, Decipher, Inc. produces a widely distributed collectible trading-card game based on *The Lord of the Rings*. These products 'combine the appeal of collecting and strategic game play' (Free Dictionary 2004) and follow the tradition established by the widely-known collectible card games, Wizards of the Coast and Magic: The Gathering, which were first introduced in the early 1990s. Decipher is based in Norfolk, Virginia, and also produces the *Star Trek* Customisable Card Game, first introduced in 1994. However, their most successful game is The Lord of the Rings Trading Card Game, a collectible card game that includes images taken from the films, as well as artwork depicting characters from the novel absent from the films produced by Weta Workshop for use on cards. The game cards are sold in starter sets, as well as other 'booster packs'. A total of ten sets have been produced (plus other 'boutique products', such as The Return of the King Anthology), with another ten planned through July 2007.

Obviously, it is impossible to list all of the products associated with *The Lord of the Rings*. However, even without including all of the products, it is still possible to observe that the *Lord of the Rings* merchandise which continues to be manufactured and marketed is wide-ranging and has been aimed successfully at a multiplicity of consumers.

The merchandise sites

Similar to other blockbuster films, *The Lord of the Rings* merchandise is promoted in various ways and sold in multiple outlets. One of the more interesting strategies, however, is Internet marketing. Again, similar to other media conglomerates, the

Lord of the Rings trilogy has been promoted on a wide array of websites. New Line featured the films on their website and continues to sell a long list of merchandise at the New Line Cinema Studio Store (http://shop.newline.com). The New Line site offers an interesting Affiliate Program to merchandisers. If they place banners and links to NewLineShop.com on their websites, they then receive 10% commissions on items sold as a result of someone clicking on those banners/links. The program also features access to graphics, special offers, promotions and a monthly newsletter with recommended links, hot selling products and NewLineShop. com insider information. And, of course 'It's FREE to join the NewLineShop. com affiliate program'. On the Lord of the Rings Fanatics Link Directory, 19 merchandise sites are listed (and rated).[4] For instance, The Lord of the Rings Fanatics Shop (http://www.lotrfanshop.com) 'currently sells 600+ Tolkien-related products through multiple affiliate programs and also has Product Specials and Reviews to aid your shopping and keep you up-to-date on upcoming Movie Merchandising' (Table 8 includes the product categories included on this site). In addition, many of the fan sites include shops that sell merchandise or lists/links to merchandise. Another set of sites sells the cards and game pieces, as noted above. (Interestingly, Tolkien Enterprises has a website with licensing information, but no products for sale. See http://www.tolkien-ent.com.)

Action Figures	Electronics	Pewters
Audiobooks	Games	Pewter Figures
Battlegames	Headdresses	Pipes
Boardgames	Helmets	Posters
Bobble Heads	Jewelry	Puzzles
Books	Keychains	Rings
Brows	Life Standups	Secret Boxes
Brooches	Lighters	Site Products
Calendars	Maps	Statues/Busts
Caps & Hats	Masks	Stamps
Card Games	Medallions	Swords
CD Cardz	Movies	Tin Boxes
Chess Sets	Mousepads	Toys
Coins	Mugs & Cups	T-Shirts
Costumes	Music	The One Ring
DVD/VHS	Necklaces	Videogames
Earrings	Ornaments	WaterGlobes
Figures	Pendants	Weapons

Table 8: Merchandise categories for the Lord of the Rings Fanatics Shop
Source: http://www.lotrfanshop.com

There is constant promotion of these sites via email for customers who order products or sign-up for further information. For example, a promotional message received from lordoftheringscatalog.com around Halloween: 'Have a Mysteriously Spooky Halloween with the Evil Spirits of Mordor.' The ad features a Grima Worm-tongue Bust, Saruman Standee, Sauron, Ringwraith and Ugluck action figures, The Eye of Sauron Fossil Watch, Saruman and the Dark Forces Poster, and a Witchking Candle Holder. Another extremely interesting development is a site that features fans with merchandise. While other sites may include this feature, TheOneRing. Net has extensive archives with photos sent of fans displaying their *Lord of the Rings* merchandise (see www.theonering.net/scrapbook). While they encourage this activity with periodic campaigns ('Show Us Your Speagol', 'Show Us Your DVD', and so on), it is amazing to view the large number of consumers who are anxious to display such images in a public space.

The tie-ins and the promotion

There are no Whoppers in Middle Earth. (Rose 2002)

Because product placements were not possible for the *Lord of the Rings* films, tie-ins became especially important. While these activities represent further commercialisation and commodification of the films (and sometimes involved additional merchandise), they also are connected with the promotion of the films and the merchandise. Only a few of the numerous tie-ins and promotional activities will be mentioned here. The first film involved tie-ins with Burger King; however, the arrangement did not continue for the second or third films. Several reasons were given, including the quote above, as well as the tie-ins taking away from the 'high-class image' of the film (ibid.). Meanwhile, Verizon arranged a two-year promotion deal and helped promote the films and the Verizon products associated with the film (for instance, a Verizon ad is included on *The Two Towers* video). New Line shared in the sales of ring tones and game. A Verizon representative explained: 'We see *Lord of the Rings* as a phenomenon – a community of raving fans that also has mass-market appeal' (ibid.). Other tie-in products and services have included Pringles, Cheerios, A&W, Cadbury, Bassett's Candy, HP Baked Beans, Air New Zealand, JVC and France Telecom. In addition, *National Geographic* produced several programmes and featured the film on a National Geographic Special. The programmes also are sold on video/DVD.

One of the biggest promotions involving tie-ins consisted of an 'Adventure Card' in conjunction with the second and third films. The promotional partners included Dr. Pepper/Seven Up, Air New Zealand, Chrysler, Duracell, Verizon Wireless, America Online and EA Games, as well as the retail partners Target, Best Buy and Circuit City. Adventure Cards were packed in more than 10 million

DVDs and single VHS copies of the movies, and consumers were directed to the website (www.lotradventurecard.com), which required a pin number included on the card. At the site, there were coupons including everything from $5 for Duracell batteries to a $500 'cash allowance good towards the purchase' of a new minivan. Dr. Pepper and Seven Up featured *Lord of the Rings* imagery on their products and 'Liquidloot' points which customers could use to bid on *Lord of the Rings* merchandise on the adventure card website, presented by eBay. Air New Zealand featured a vacation package that included round-trip airfare, accommodation, car rental and Rings Location Guidebook for purchase at the website. Verizon gave all new subscribers a free video and a chance to win a trip to New Zealand. Verizon also made *The Lord of the Rings*-ring tones available for their phones (New Line Entertainment 2003).

One of the many other promotional strategies was the arrangement that New Line made with the entertainment promotions agency Planet Report to distribute bookmarks and posters to millions of junior high and high school students (Rose 2002). Planet Report distributed 26 million *Lord of the Rings: The Return of the King* bookmarks, which the company claimed 'provided enormous buzz among nation's youth in the 2 weeks prior to the film's release' (Anon. 2003b).

The synergy

> *Harry Potter* and *The Lord of the Rings* are so successful, they are threatening to re-place Bugs Bunny as the symbol of AOL Time Warner. (Bing & Dunkley 2002: 1).

The *Lord of the Rings* merchandise does not necessarily sell itself and is accompanied by extensive advertising and promotion. Some of this promotion is associated with publicity that accompanied the films themselves. While an extensive discussion of the marketing and publicity cannot be presented here, a few notes will be offered about some of the strategies used.

Time Warner is similar to other diversified entertainment conglomerates in attempting to cross-promote its products throughout its organisation in synergistic fashion. Synergy has been defined as 'the cooperative action of different parts for a greater effect' (Wasko 2003: 170) and companies such as Time Warner are not shy about explaining this line of attack. In fact, Time Warner's 2003 Factbook states that

> AOL Time Warner is more than a random collection of great brands and businesses. Each and every franchise plays an important role in helping people be informed, entertained and connected. Our focus is on developing, strengthening and taking advantage of the natural overlaps to make each part stronger than it would be alone, and the whole greater than the sum of its parts. (2003: 4)

A few examples of how this worked for *The Lord of the Rings* would include a TV special on the Time Warner-owned WB network on the making of the film; a nine-page cover story in *Time* (9 December 2002), featuring Aragorn, Frodo and Gandalf on the cover; a cover story in *Entertainment Weekly* (26 December/ 2 January 2004), with the cover featuring Aragorn and Frodo; and CNN's Larry King interview of Ian McKellen (Gandalf) in February 2004. While there are numerous other examples, often described extensively in company press releases, an interesting description of these various activities, especially as they related to AOL, is offered by *The Economist*:

> Together, AOL and New Line created a 'community' of fans who were offered a tantalising advance snippet of the film on the Internet in April 2000; this was downloaded over 1.7 million times. To keep them coming back, the official website is continuously updated, and will feed visitors a steady supply of exclusive morsels throughout the life of the trilogy. AOL subscribers, however, were treated to more: a chance to enter a competition to be flown to the movie's world première in New Zealand (where it was filmed) – if, that is, they upgraded to AOL 7.0. In two weeks, 800,000 community members signed up. Few corners of the AOL Time Warner empire have not been turned into marketing outlets for the film, from the WB network, which first aired the movie trailer, to *Entertainment Weekly*, part of the Time Inc stable, which ran a special competition to win 'figurines', little toys based on the film's characters. Given that yet another of the group's films, Warner Bros.' *Harry Potter and the Philosopher's Stone*, broke box office records last year, and that both films have brought in lucrative merchandising and licensing deals, this might look like vindication of the AOL Time Warner synergy model. (Anon. 2002a)

Thus, for a company such as Time Warner, *The Lord of the Rings* not only offered huge merchandise potential, but also *'the perfect fuel for the synergy machine'* – a franchise that the company continues to promote across its various businesses.

Conclusion

This discussion of merchandise and some of the promotional strategies associated with New Line's trilogy demonstrates the ideal nature of the *Lord of the Rings* property/franchise for a diversified entertainment conglomerate such as Time Warner. But what can be said about the consequences of such activities? In an interesting and thoughtful piece about the implications of the commercialisation of Tolkien's work, Ethan Gilsdorf offered the following comments:

> Make no mistake. Rings is serious, and the money-grubbing and hype do not jibe with Tolkien's medieval aesthetic or his sober themes. Commercialisation degrades

his creation to a lowest-common-denominator enterprise. Market forces pare down a nuanced story to its superficial aspects, confusing the experience of literature with buying mass-produced plastic junk. But die-hards can take solace in remembering that Middle Earth's sudden surge of middle-of-the-road appeal was not driven solely by marketers. Tolkien's creation is popular because it still responds to the zeitgeist. That his visceral fiction works on so many levels – as escapism, scholarship, community, lucrative revenue stream – remains a testament to a unique genius. Even the worst aspects of the commercial machine are a backhanded tribute to what Tolkien created. (2003: 12).

Beyond the hand-wringing over the insults to creativity and the trivialisation of 'classic literature', the wide range of merchandise associated with *The Lord of the Rings* suggests the extent to which literature/films have become commercialised, turning vehicles of fantasy and escape into an endless array of commodities. In other words, the proliferation and marketing of merchandise related to films such as *The Lord of the Rings* must be seen as contributing to the commodification of culture as well as reinforcing a consumer society, with all its contingent problems that have been persistently discussed by numerous scholars and other observers (see, for instance, Ewen 1977; Berger 2000). In other words, it is not enough to merely (pay to) see the movie(s), but one is encouraged to buy more products and, in the case of some of the games, to continue buying additional items that renew the original products. Thus, literature/entertainment/fantasy/escape becomes tied to consumption. And what about the profits from such activities? Peter Jackson is certainly making a fortune (see Schorow 2004), but it is the copyright holder, Time Warner and other companies that stand to benefit from any merchandise success.

In addition, this study points to the ability of integrated entertainment conglomerates (such as Time Warner) to promote their products across their various businesses in synergistic fashion, including the promotion of entertainment products in 'news' outlets. Even one of Time Warner's owners has commented on this issue recently. In a critique of media consolidation offered by Ted Turner at a recent industry gathering, he noted that such concentration has an impact on news operations, making companies less critical. Turner further pointed out that 'We need to be very well informed. We need less Hollywood news and a little more hard news' (quoted in Guider 2005: 1). Furthermore, it might be argued that these companies wielding so much weight in our media-saturated world make decisions about the kind of films (and other cultural products) that are produced and distributed based on the potential for commodification, not for artistic, creative or communicative goals. In other words, 'merchandise for them all' is not intended as a process of sharing culture, but of accumulating wealth.

Notes

1 This chapter was developed as part of the 'International Lord of the Rings Research Project'. It was made possible by a grant from the UK Economic and Social Research Council (ESRC Grant No. 000-22-0323) to whom we record our gratitude.

2 There is a discrepancy in the reporting of ownerships rights at this point in time. Lowson *et al.* (2002) say that United Artists maintained some rights, but the National Arbitration Forum (2002) states that Zaentz has held the rights since 1976.

3 Our favorite example: The Brobdingnagian Bards, billed as an 'Original Celtic Renaissance music duo from Austin, Texas'. They have produced 'Memories of Middle Earth: Musical Tribute to JRR Tolkien's *The Hobbit* and *The Lord of the Rings* Music CD', which includes 'Psychopathic, Chronic, Schizophrenic Gollum Blues' and 'Like a Hobbit in a Mushroom Field'.

4 Interestingly, the list does not include the New Line Cinema site, which is listed under 'Official Sites,' along with the 'Official Fan Club' site (http://lotr.fanhq.com), which features tons of merchandise and is owned by Decipher, Inc.

Works cited

Anon. (2000) 'Toy Biz granted master toy license for one of the most highly-anticipated film franchises of all-time', *Business Wire*. Online. Available at http://www.licensingmedia.com/news/html/ddhistory2000.html (accessed 30 April 2004).

_____ (2002a) 'Who's afraid of AOL Time Warner?', *The Economist*, 24 January. Online. Available at http://www.economist.com/agenda/displayStory.cfm?Story_ID=952225 (accessed 1 December 2004).

_____ (2002b) 'New Line Cinema's "Lord of the Rings: The Fellowship of the Rings" ignites marketplace', *PR Newswire*, 15 January.

_____ (2003a) 'The gamble that was the "Ring"', *Hollywood Reporter*, 7 January, 1.

_____ (2003b) '26 million Lord of the Rings bookmarks help deliver youth audience', *PR Web*. Online. Available at http://www.prweb.com/rclcascs/2003/12/prweb95721.htm (accessed 1 December 2004).

_____ (2003c) 'Movie's merchandise proving a big hit', *The Sentinel*, 19 December.

_____ (2004c) 'Fortune 500', *Fortune.com*. Online. Available at http://www.fortune.com/fortune/fortune500/company/top500 (accessed 12 March 2004).

_____ (2004a) 'Who owns what', *Columbia Journalism Review*. Online. Available at http://www.cjr.org/tools/owners/timewarner.asp (accessed 12 March 2004).

_____ (2004b) 'Rings merchandise hits $1.2 billion', *Dominion Post*, 30 April.

Berger, A. (2000) *Ads, Fads and Consumer Culture*. Lanham, MD: Rowman & Littlefield.

Bing, J. and C. Dunkley (2002) 'Kiddy litter rules H'wood', *Variety*, 8 January, 1.

Christenson, D. (1999) 'Star Wars: Return of the collector', *The Old Times*. Online. Available at http://www.theoldtimes.com/past/699_1.html (accessed 1 September 2004).

Davies, H. (2004) 'Lord of the Rings royalties owner issues £11m writ', *Daily Telegraph*, 20 August.

Ewen, S. (1977) *Captains of Consciousness: Advertising and the Social Roots of the Consumer Culture*. New York: McGraw Hill.

Fabrikant, G. (2004) 'Time Warner Settles 2 Cases Over AOL Unit', *New York Times*, C1, 16 December.

Free Dictionary (2004) 'Collectible card game'. Online. Available at http://encyclopedia.thefreedictionary.com/collectible%20card%20game (accessed 1 December 2004).

Games Workshop (2004) '*The Lord of the Rings* Strategy Battle Game'. Online. Available at http://us.games-workshop.com/games/lotr/sbg/default.htm (accessed 1 February 2005).

Gilsdorf, E. (2003) 'Lord of the gold ring', *Boston Globe*, 15 November, 10.

Goldsmith, J. (2000) 'Licensing show has little to buzz about from H'wood: It's not child's play', *Variety*, 12 June, 1.

_____ (2002) 'With billions at stake, toy biz is no longer child's play', *Variety*, 9 June, 1.

Guider, E. (2005) 'Frustrated maven: Turner chews out congloms at NATPE sesh', *Variety*, 2 February, 1.

Howard, T. (2003) 'Now playing at a toy store near you', *USA Today*, 10B, 8 December.

Holson, L. M. (2003) 'A franchise fantasy', *New York Times*, 9 November.

Lordoftheringscatalog.com (2004) Online. Available at http://lordoftheringsguide.com/ (accessed 20 April 2004).

Lowson, I., K. Marshall and D. O'Brien (2002) *World of the Rings: The Unauthorized Guide to the World of J.R.R. Tolkien*. London: Reynolds and Hearn.

Mathews, A. W. (2001) 'Companies in licensing face-off over "rings"', *San Diego Union-Tribune*, E-7, 21 December.

Monahan, D. (2003) 'Lining merchandisers' pockets', *Daily Telegraph*. Online. Available at http://www.TheOneRing.net (accessed 23 January 2005).

MSN Money Central (2004a) 'Time Warner quote'. Online. Available at http://money-central.msn.com/scripts/webquote.dll?iPage=qd&Symbol=twx (accessed 12 March 2004).

MSN Money Central (2004b) 'Time Warner ownership'. Online. Available at http://money-central.msn.com/investor/invsub/ownership/ownership.asp (accessed 19 March 2004).

Munk, N. (2004) *Fools Rush In*. New York: HarperCollins.

National Arbitration Forum (2002) 'Start-up trademark opposition policy decision: The Saul Zaentz Company v. Gandalf R.r.l.', Claim Number: FA0112000103063, 19 February.

New Line Entertainment (2003) 'New Line Home Entertainment breaks new ground with the Lord of the Rings: The Two Towers Adventure Card', press release, 13 August.

_____ (2004) 'About Us'. Online. Available at http://www.newline.com/about/index.shtml (accessed 28 January 2004).

Rahner, M. (2003) 'Lords of merchandising churn out tchotchkes', *Seattle Times*, K4, 14

December.

Rose, M. M. (2002) 'NL "Rings" in new strategy', *Hollywood Reporter*, 5 December.

Rooney, D. (2004) 'Not of this earth', *Variety*, 4 January, 1.

Schiller, G. (2004) 'NEWS: MARKETING', *Hollywood Reporter*, 10 June.

Schorow, S. (2004) 'Beloved Tolkien trilogy sets cash registers ringing', *Boston Herald*, 23 October.

Seiler, A. (2003) '"Rings" comes full circle', *USA Today*, 26 December.

Simpson, P. (ed.) (2003) *Rough Guide to The Lord of the Rings*. London: Penguin Books.

Time Warner Inc. (2004) 'Time Warner Reports Results for 2003 Full Year and Fourth Quarter', press release, 29 January.

Time Warner Factbook (2003) New York: Time Warner Inc.

Tolkien Enterprises (2005) Online. Available at http://www.tolkien-ent.com (accessed 10 January 2005).

Ward, B. (2003) '37 things about Lord of the Rings', *Ottawa Citizen*, I8, 13 December.

Wasko, J. (2003) *How Hollywood Works*. London: Sage.

White, M. (2002) *The Life and Work of J.R.R. Tolkien*. Indianapolis: Alpha Publishers.

'On the Brink of a New Threshold of Opportunity': The Lord of the Rings and New Zealand Cultural Policy

Jennifer Lawn and Bronwyn Beatty[1]

Introduction

In 1999 right-wing economist Gareth Morgan dismissed a call by Jane Wright, head of the Screen Producers and Directors Association, for state funding in New Zealand to aid big-budget film production:

> Since when has quality been synonymous with budget? Hollywood manages to make bad movies with big budgets. It's sad Jane but we can't afford to enter the race to Mars either. Get real. (Morgan 1999)

These four sentences suggest numerous assumptions about the nature and purpose of filmmaking: that quality is the objective of state funding of film; that quality can be achieved by low-budget films; that film industry workers need not be paid very much, even if they do produce quality; that 'reality' is the privileged epistemological register; that the New Zealand film industry, like its engineering counterpart, should face reality and curb any ambition to 'shoot for the stars'; and that uppity cultural advocates need to be chastened by the voice of disinterested economic reason. The tenor of Morgan's comment expresses some truths of the fragmented and depleted cultural sector that the incoming Labour coalition government, led by Helen Clark, inherited in 1999 (see Volkerling 1994). Although not antipathetic to state support for culture, the National government of 1990–99 had given the cultural sector a taste of the extensive economic and social restructuring that had occurred from 1984 onwards (Waller 1996: 255). The New Zealand Film Commission, which is charged with the funding and promotion of films with significant New Zealand content, saw its budget decline in real terms from 1990 to 1998.[2] Reeling, the arts community had still not, in any co-ordinated strategy, appropriated and turned to its advantage the discourse of neoliberalism: commer-cialisation, competition, branding, fiscal accountability and quantifiable outputs (Easton 1999: 183).

The state-subsidised arts were thus an easy target for free-market enthusiasts such as Gareth Morgan, but he could not have anticipated that New Zealand was about to embark on its own star quest: an ambitious, integrated initiative to expand its tiny market share of the global entertainment industry, estimated at half a tril-lion US dollars (Vogel 2001: xvii). For in the same year, the Labour government reluctantly allowed *The Lord of the Rings* production to qualify for a tax shelter constituting a risk to the public purse of approximately $219million.[3] On finan-cial, technological, artistic and logistical counts, the project fantastically exceeded the orbit of any previous New Zealand film production. The subject itself was audacious. The $600million production involved some 23,000 New Zealanders,[4] prompted the appointment of a dedicated Cabinet Minister (Pete Hodgson, the Minister of the Rings), furnished the material for Te Papa's most successful museum exhibition, secured (with the 2002 America's Cup defence) a share of a $9million government package to promote spin-offs, and attracted a $4million government subsidy to stage *The Return of the King* premiere in December 2003. In just four years, almost all of the assumptions underlying Morgan's comment had been over-turned in New Zealand cultural policy discourse. Films are no longer judged by aesthetic and expressive criteria of 'quality' but rather by 'quantity' – their capacity to generate foreign exchange. Fantasy has become permissible in the Kiwi imagi-nary, not only as a cinematic genre but also as the capacity to imagine ambitious futures, and the New Zealand government now woos foreign, big-budget film production with all the trappings of expensive star talent. Furthermore, where arts agencies were encouraged to behave more like businesses during the 1990s, busi-nesses are now urged to act more like arts agencies, for 'creativity is at the heart of innovation' (*Growing an Innovative New Zealand* 2002: 56).

In this chapter we suggest that the *Lord of the Rings* phenomenon – encompass-ing the production's political, governmental, technological, economic, social and national impacts – functioned as a gravitational force around which a relatively incoherent set of ideas about the nature and purpose of national culture could coalesce into a highly integrated, cross-sectoral cultural development policy based on a vision of government-industry partnership, a close alignment of cultural and economic interests, and the promotion of an export-oriented creative imaginary. Given Jackson's publicly announced distaste for state-funded mandarins, this gov-ernmental analysis may seem to neutralise the anti-bureaucratic energies associated with Jackson's persona. However, we take as a grounding assumption Theodor Adorno's dictum that 'whoever speaks of culture speaks of administration as well, whether that is his intention or not' (1991: 107). Furthermore, in its anthropo-logical dimension policy is 'an increasingly central concept and instrument in the organisation of contemporary societies' (Shore & Wright 1997: 4). The first part of our discussion thus traces the development of a New Zealand 'creative industries' platform from 2000 to 2003, with particular attention on the opportunities for cross-sectoral leveraging. We then discuss how film funding initiatives have been intended to stimulate and channel economic activity. Despite being heavily talked-up or 'hyped', the 'Frodo economy' has not received an objective cost-benefit analysis, and we outline the critical factors in this discussion. Finally, we contemplate that in the postmodern and post-nationalist policy environment ushered into New Zealand by *The Lord of the Rings*, 'talking up' may in itself prove productive, even if economic revenues have been overstated. The enduring policy legacy of the production may be the government's insight that the screen industry can become a policy instrument, a *'means of acting* on the social' (Bennett 1998: 11), to promote an ethos of creative entrepreneurship. It is through 'Brand Jackson' and its associated values – chutzpah, determination, technological innovation, fierce independence, 'instinct and nerve' (Downie 2002: 2) – that economic policy penetrates, or attaches itself, to members of the population. Our analysis thus focuses on the aspirational or 'prognostic' dimension of cultural policy, the way in which it gestures 'always towards "something beyond itself" – new sets of relations, identifications, forms of value, or of cultural citizenship that it struggles to bring into being' (Werry 2004: 2). We conclude that the government is employing culture in general, and the *Lord of the Rings* phenomenon in particular, to achieve national consensus by upholding the sign of the nation while evacuating its substance. At a structural level, the present cultural policy framework thus exemplifies an insight made in the mid-twentieth century by journalist Gordon Mirams: 'If there is any such thing as a "New Zealand culture", it is to a large extent the creation of Hollywood' (1945: 5).

The policy vision: the globalised creative imaginary

Cultural policy has been a highly active and visible field of public policy in New Zealand under Helen Clark's Prime Ministership. The policy directions may be characterised as a potent convergence of expressive nationalism, aesthetic protectionism, populism and market-driven economic pragmatism. A highly flexible discursive repertoire has developed through which government speakers have wooed the diverse constituencies of business, creative industry workers, middle-class consumers of high culture and advocates of popular culture by, in effect, implying that they have the same interests in common. The *Lord of the Rings* phenomenon has furthered this 'becoming cultural of the economic, and the becoming economic of the cultural' (Jameson 1998: 60). In a series of initiatives the New Zealand government has attempted to resolve – or more accurately, *dissolve* – numerous policy tensions: the differing demands of 'art', 'cultural development' and 'creative industry'; production for domestic versus international audiences; aesthetic versus commercial criteria for quality; state funding of production versus foreign direct investment; the degree of state interventionism in funding mechanisms and signals; and the effort to capture the distribution of culture as well as its production. The film industry occupies a central place in such discussions because, as Nick Reid paraphrases Orson Welles, 'only an idiot would talk about films for more than five minutes without mentioning money' (1986: 13). However, where the 1985 New Zealand Film Commission annual report could figure the film industry as 'a constant tug of war between finance, investment and economic returns on the one hand and art, culture and national identity on the other', by 2001 a glossy circularity is asserted by the Commission's CEO:

> There is no place in the new economy for the type of thinking which sees a disjunction between the business world and the art world. Cultural industries are based on national identity. National identity is key to creating a unique positioning for our goods and services. (Harley 2001)

'National identity' becomes a vacant category as it equates, literally and figuratively, to 'selling ourselves'.

A lengthier and more sophisticated articulation of this absorption of the aesthetic within the economic can be found in *The Heart of the Nation* (2000), a strategic plan for the cultural sector commissioned by the government. Unlike its Australian counterpart *Creative Nation* (1994), the report cannot be regarded as a formal policy statement. Indeed it was quickly rejected on the grounds that it recommended structural changes to government when a 'self-help' plan had been envisaged (Matthews 2000). Yet in many respects the authors theorise the cultural sector in terms entirely consonant with the government policy that has subsequently evolved. In a sweeping vision, both cultural development and creative industry models are endorsed.[5] A 'strong and confident cultural identity' can emerge through 'a strong creative industry sector which provides sustainable employment and is able to contribute to economic growth and prosperity' (*The Heart of the Nation* 2000: 20). No tension is presumed to arise between these twin imperatives, culture and commerce. The report envisages an 'ideal of a global cultural commons as the foundation for post-national civil society' (Werry 2004: 11). The central economic development strategy lies in the orientation of cultural production toward *export* substitution, through which New Zealand diversifies its foreign exchange earning capacities. This strategy considerably extends and in some ways distorts the dispensation of *import* substitution under which the New Zealand Film Commission was established in 1978, through which representations of the local were to supplant, or at least supplement, the images imported through foreign film. However, when New Zealand film allies with promotional industries such as tourism, a structural impasse emerges through the effort to inject 'nation' into a merchant-dominated entertainment world which 'is not concerned about the "nationality" of the cultural product, just as it is not necessarily concerned with the film itself' (Hozic 2001: 75) – a conundrum that we return to below.

In theory, film presents itself as an ideal value-added substitute for bulk commodity exports for a nation located 2,200 kilometres from its nearest trading partner. 'In essence', as the strategy document *Growing an Innovative New Zealand* puts it, 'our exports need to reduce in weight and become heavier in knowledge and value' (2002: 32). Although the upfront costs of film production and marketing are high, the costs of distribution are minimal. A film can be quickly distributed through multiple cinema release; the *Lord of the Rings* release required 10,000 prints worldwide (*Scoping the Lasting Effects* 2002: 49). A film can be re-released in 'director's cut' and 'extended' versions, and it can be reformatted for video, DVD and gaming. Ancillary markets such as network and syndicated television, pay cable and home video, have 'collectively far overshadowed revenues derived from theatrical release' since the mid-1980s (Vogel 2001: 58). Copyright and royalties (including merchandising) generate income for decades after production, although it should be noted that relatively few films will generate the high utilisation of 'classics': the proportion of feature-film titles held by Hollywood majors that will be deployed in any one year in the American and international markets has been estimated at just 5% (Vogel 2001: 65). As the *Lord of the Rings* experience shows, cross-marketing, sponsorship and leveraged initiatives also offer good returns for responsive entrepreneurs, ranging from Resene Paint's launching of a new colour called 'Wellywood' and Ian Brodie's bestseller *The Lord of the Rings Location Book* (2002) to Air New Zealand's fleet of *The Lord of the Rings*-themed planes and Telecom's provision of simultaneous voice, video and data links, which enabled Jackson to monitor and direct up to three scenes remotely – a commercial coup which the telecommunications company touted in a wall-sized advertising display at Wellington's domestic airport.

The *Lord of the Rings* project also exemplified how the screen production industry can both exploit and originate technological innovations that enhance the competitiveness of seemingly unrelated industries. Peter Jackson's special effects company Weta Workshop adapted 3D imaging techniques developed by Christchurch firm Applied Research Associates for the meat packaging industry to make digital body doubles of principal characters. In turn, production innovations can themselves be saleable, such as Weta's development of Massive software for staging large-scale fight scenes.[6] Weta itself became only the second visual effects facility outside of California to win an Academy Award for visual effects (see Calder 2003: 10). The story of the making of the trilogy provided the central narrative of the Te Papa Tongarewa-Museum of New Zealand exhibition *The Lord of the Rings:*

The Motion Picture Trilogy, a further leveraged commodity, which attracted over 200,000 visitors to the museum in Wellington and toured venues in Singapore, the United Kingdom, the United States and Australia. Documentaries and books on 'the making of' the trilogy, such as Brian Sibley's *The Lord of the Rings: Official Movie Guide* (2001), likewise emphasise technological innovation, though whether viewers of such texts attribute the craft and attention to detail to New Zealand's information technology and design sectors, or simply to Peter Jackson, is unclear. As Rod Oram cautions, the prevailing cinematic representation of New Zealand as 'mythically medieval' is not likely to convince investors to 'bankroll a sophisticated software or biotech business here' (2001/02: 42).

By far the greatest cross-sectoral energy generated by the *Lord of the Rings* production, however, has been in the tourism sector. *The Lord of the Rings*-based Fantasy tourism ventures such as Red Carpet Tours, Extreme Green Rafting and Hobbiton Tours have emerged, and Tourism New Zealand implemented a marketing campaign projecting New Zealand as Middle Earth. New Zealand tourism was rewarded with *Lonely Planet's* designation of 'Hot Spot for 2003' (Anon. 2003: 8), the *Daily Telegraph* Travel Award for 2004 (displacing four-time winner Italy), and the *Guardian & Observer's* People's Choice award for best long-haul travel destination. Astonishingly, foreign exchange earnings from tourism outperformed the dairy industry in 2004, and government documents routinely juxtapose film industry achievements with comments about New Zealand's tourist appeal: Brad McGann's *In My Father's Den* is 'a powerful piece of social commentary with stunning New Zealand backdrops', boasts Minister of Economic Development Jim Anderton (2004), while a recent press release implicitly credits runaway Bollywood productions for Indian tourism and the export education market: 'Over 100 Bollywood productions have been filmed in New Zealand since 1995. An estimated 18,000 Indian tourists visit New Zealand each year with 2,500 Indian students studying in the country' (ibid.). However, the extent to which the tourism increase can be attributed to New Zealand's profile in the global entertainment market is debatable. It has been noted that visitor numbers increased even more dramatically in Australia during a similar period (Calder 2003: 10), and that increased visitor numbers do not necessarily translate to higher net earnings in this very low-margin, highly seasonal service industry (Rotherham 2003).

It is equally difficult to quantify the equivalent advertising value of the *Lord of the Rings* phenomenon to the self-promotional interests of central and regional politicians. For with the Large Budget Grants Scheme effective from 1 July 2003, the Labour government is specifically wooing star vehicles that provide photo opportunities of politicians in close embrace – sometimes literally – with the likes of Elijah Wood, Gwyneth Paltrow (*Sylvia* (Christine Jeffs, 2003)) and Tom Cruise (*The Last Samurai* (Edward Zwick, 2003)). When the Television New Zealand news featured Helen Clark visiting the set of *King Kong* (26 January 2005), anchor Judy Bailey quipped 'Maybe they'll give her [Clark] a bit part'. No doubt intended to be ironic, the comment acknowledges that most politicians crave the exposure of the silver screen. Peter Jackson's media pull and capacity to attract capital investment led to his being ranked second, behind Clark, in a *New Zealand Listener* listing of the most powerful people in New Zealand (Watkin 2004). Clark may carry more political power than Jackson, in the institutional sense of the term 'political'; however, in terms of global exposure Clark truly does play a tiny 'bit part' relative to Jackson. The creative industries policy effectively acknowledges that 'Brand Jackson' – and 'Brand Tom Cruise' for that matter – is far more widely recognised than 'Brand Helen Clark' or even 'Brand New Zealand'. One brand thus piggy-backs on another that carries more international reach while conveying compatible values. As Stan Sutter notes, paraphrasing Coca-Cola Company CEO Steve Heyer: 'A brand icon like Coke, with its global distribution clout, media buys and near ubiquitous consumer presence, is actually a more powerful media network than the ones offered by most, if not all, media companies' (2003: 18). Such vicarious star exposure can be maximised without taking on any of the financial risk of production, for stars always attract media attention, even when their movies flop. In an essentially American turn, New Zealand national politics and showbusiness have never been more difficult to distinguish – though the government is yet to be led by a movie star, as has occurred in California and the United States. In the next section, however, we enter into the rather greyer matter of policy pronouncements, and ask whether the government's economic projections for film development are 'realistic' – as Gareth Morgan might urge – or rather 'hyperrealistic'.

Policy implementation and evaluation

Since 1999, Labour Coalition governments have pushed policy initiatives towards a three-tiered New Zealand film industry. At the first tier is state-supported domestic production administered by the New Zealand Film Commission, limited to films with significant New Zealand content or creative input. The arduous application process, the purported lack of consultation with industry representatives and the risibly small grants allowed have provoked strong criticism from outspoken directors and producers; as Geoff Murphy complains, 'Man, you'd have to love making films to put up with this sort of shit!' (*Onfilm* 2004/05b: 18). These constraints were partially eased by the one-off Film Production Fund of $22million, established in the Labour administration's May 2000 'cultural recovery' package. The fund supports commercially viable films with significant New Zealand content, where external funding sources provide about 40% of investment. The fund was designed to serve as a bridge for early-career directors and producers between their first, state-supported feature films, to the wholly commercial competition of securing private investment.[7] However, the fund has not been renewed despite successful outcomes. The New Zealand Film Commission instead received additional funding of $10million in 2004, part of which allowed it to take over the Film Fund mandate, though critics say this move 'simply inflation-proofs the funding agency's low-budget commitments' (Wakefield 2004: 3).

At the second tier of the government's creative industries policy lie runaway productions, where the film is shot in New Zealand though the production company, financing and creative talent are sourced from overseas. Local companies provide services such as location scouting facilities and 'below the line' production staff who work on non-union contracts without benefits and who are subject to lay-offs when budgets are tightened (Elmer 2002).[8] The transnational 'unbundling' of film production tends to drive place competition, a feature of economic globalisation in which capital can move rapidly to whichever location offers the cheapest production opportunities, the most advantageous exchange rates and the optimal local incentives at any one time.[9] The continuity of a local industry is compromised, for while a nation may be perceived as a 'cool and groovy' place to shoot films for a period of time, runaway production may dry up when another nation offers a more competitive incentive (Gaylene Preston in Knight 2004: A4). Local workers fear becoming 'hewers of wood and carriers of water' (John Barnett in Campbell 2001: 27) if the New Zealand film industry contracts to a mere 'export processing zone' serving foreign producers (Werry 2004: 4). However, runaway productions are just as likely to put *upward* rather than *downward* pressure on local wages. Foreign producers often pay more than local companies, particularly when the exchange rate differential between the nations is high, forcing up wages and studio fees and making it more attractive to work as a freelancer on an international production than to generate local material. Ironically, precisely by being 'pretty careful not to pay too much' the *Lord of the Rings* producers managed not to alienate local production companies (Dave Gibson in Campbell 2003: 24).

The principal value of runaway productions lies less in generating export receipts so much as raising the general level of experience and global enterprise nous across the local industry. Big-budget runaway productions also tend to carry comprehensive media publicity packages, including promotional machinery around the filmmaking process itself: dedicated websites, media interviews with creative talent, and documentaries showing 'the making of the film' which are regarded, by New Zealand tourism agencies, as invaluable international exposure. These aspirations underlie the government's Large Budget Grant Scheme. Any screen production company spending $15–$50million on production within New Zealand (where that amount equates to at least 70% of the total production expenditure) receives a 12.5% rebate upon completion of the project, from a maximum grant pool of $40million in the first year.[10] Although not excluded from the grants scheme, budget constraints mean that few solely New Zealand productions are likely to qualify unless screen production bundling, including television, is allowed (Anon. 2004; *Onfilm* 2004/05a). The scheme compensates somewhat for the 1999 rescinding of the tax loophole that supported *The Lord of the Rings*. However, Peter Jackson has attacked the instability of film-funding policy, accusing the government of sending confusing policy signals and drawing producers into 'some kind of bait and switch routine' (quoted in Wakefield 2003: 1).[11]

A larger, more intransigent difficulty underlying both tax incentives and the Large Budget Grant Scheme is precisely that they are designed to encourage production rather than distribution, a move dictated by the structure of the film industry. A studio incurs large fixed annual operating costs to establish a large-scale distribution network, but once established, the marginal cost of distributing and marketing a product is relatively small. Because economies of scale apply only at a relatively large scale, distribution is characterised by oligopolistic production/distribution/financing organisations. The service and production sector, by contrast, is characterised by fragmented, small and specialised firms (Vogel 2001: 41). The New Zealand Trade and Enterprise Creative Industries section established in 2003 encourages cluster development to mobilise regional, national and international networks to manage this 'assembling and disassembling' of creative teams 'from one deal and one picture and one technology to the next' (ibid.). However, the pressures of transnational capitalism marginalise the sphere of production, as a convergence between entertainment and media communications technologies enables the film industry to accumulate its profits by 'recycling the same product through a number of distribution venues' (Hozic 2001: 59). Companies that exercise control at the point of consumption, rather than production, benefit most from the economies of scale that can be achieved. Recognising this industry development, the Screen Production Taskforce has given priority to improving the industry's 'market intelligence' to encourage greater vertical integration and to drive demand by developing more widespread consumer taste for local production (*Taking on the World* 2002: 21). One modest proposal suggests boosting New Zealand Film Commission funding available for marketing New Zealand film, currently averaging around $35,000 per feature-film.[12]

We now arrive at the third tier of the government's film industry policy, the one which pertains to the *Lord of the Rings*: the development of productions that receive foreign investment while being creatively driven from New Zealand. The economic rationale for favouring such productions is that New Zealand interests are able to retain and exploit intellectual property rights. The government has taken no specific policy steps (other than the Large Budget Grant Scheme) to implement this vision, in contrast to Australian tax incentives, introduced in the 1980s, which allow investors a 100% write-off in the year the film is made provided that it meets 'Australian content' criteria including creative control and copyright ownership. Yet the benefit of the *Lord of the Rings* production to the New Zealand economy has not yet been reliably ascertained. Opponents of tax-funded incentives for foreign film investment are often rebutted by the claim that without such incentives such films would not be made in New Zealand, but the latter view assumes, in a circular way, that making foreign films in New Zealand is good for the country. On this faith John Anderton is willing to 'subsidise the devil incarnate if there is a net economic benefit to New Zealand' (quoted in Calder 2004: B3), no idle threat from a practising Catholic. But on what economic basis do we make such a judgement? Without attempting to decide the case – a task for specialised cultural economists – we point out some of the policy implications of the scoping report on the *Lord of the Rings* production, published in 2002.

Scoping the Lasting Effects of The Lord of the Rings was commissioned by the New Zealand Film Commission and conducted by the privately-funded New Zealand Institute of Economic Research for a cost reported at $90,000 (Drinnan 2002). The term 'effects' encompasses both short-run economic impact – the net injections of new spending in New Zealand as a direct result of the production, particularly employment – and the expansion of capacity in the local film industry's skills, technology, international relationships, brands, intellectual capital and scale. The Institute estimates that from mid-1998 to early 2002, spanning from pre- to post-production for *The Fellowship of the Rings*, the production contributed $352.7 million of expenditure to the New Zealand economy. The report acknowledges that any attempt to accurately interpret short-term data on the film industry is fraught with difficulty, given that the industry is subject to 'economic peaks and troughs because of the time between development, raising finance and going into production' (Screen Production and Development Association of New Zealand 2003). Furthermore, in a small economy, single productions can make dramatic percentage increases in financing figures.

Even considering these caveats, the methodology of the *Scoping the Lasting Effects* study was poor. The report does not present or justify its own methodology in any detailed way, nor does it refer to similar reports or protocols for cultural revenue projections developed in comparable economies. Neither New Line nor Peter Jackson's own production companies released production budget information to the Institute, which based its data on a speculative sum published in a newspaper report. No quotations are sourced, except for an endorsement of Telecom that appears to be reprinted from a Telecom advertisement. The Institute also overestimated the percentage spent in New Zealand, almost exclusively interviewed people with a vested interest in a positive outcome, and failed to take into account the tax break which facilitated the production (Barnett 2002). A more recent economic impact assessment for the filming of *The Last Samurai* in Taranaki considerably improves upon these methodological errors (*Economic Impact Assessment* 2004).

However, as is typical of economic impact studies in the cultural sector, both reports fail to consider the costs as well as benefits of a cultural activity, including the ramifications of intra-regional competition for film production within New Zealand. It is also rare for advocates of the state-supported creative industries to demonstrate that taxpayer funding was better spent on the creative sector than on some other activity that makes a competing claim for the public purse (Seaman 2003: 226; Towse 2003: 9).

These methodological weaknesses do not necessarily mean that the *Scoping the Lasting Effects* report's findings are inaccurate, as economic projections may prove inadvertently accurate if they overestimate short-term impacts but underestimate longer-term multiplier effects (Seaman 2003: 228). Data from 2001–02 gives some qualified evidence of increased capacity and investment. Although 'production expenditure in Wellington has dropped by 45% to $133million with the wrap of *The Lord of the Rings* ... Wellington expenditure is still well ahead of 1999 levels, indicating lasting effects on the Wellington industry despite a lean local production year'; however, industry employment also 'returned to pre-*Lord of the Rings* levels', noted as 'largely a loss of independent contractor positions' (*Onfilm* 2003: 9). In 2002–03, the increased value of feature-film production masked declines in television production, while levels of employment across the screen production industry remained relatively stable (*Onfilm* 2003: 2–3). The more interesting question, in terms of government policy strategy, is why an economic impact report should be commissioned so soon after the production wrap-up, before the medium- to long-term effects could be ascertained with any degree of certainty. Given that state support had already been committed to the project in the form of the tax shelter, the report seems to present an *ex post facto* justification, suggesting that the neoliberal machinery of policy evaluation, objective 'quality control' and 'accountability' for public spending has been invoked in a rather hollow manner.

What the *Scoping the Lasting Effects* report does contribute to, however, is the 'feel-good effect' of the appearance of success blazoned through the constant self-congratulatory repetition of 'How we created world-class performance', to borrow a title from Ruth Harley (2002). The nation is perpetually poised 'on the brink of a new threshold of opportunity', as one Labour Member of Parliament expresses the new confidence (Cunliffe 2004). The very uncertainty of Hollywood, where it is said that 'nobody knows anything', generates such a countervailing language of confidence. In a postmodern policy environment, this 'appeal to appeal' (Werry 2004: 9) carries its own momentum and implied value: the impression of success is perceived as necessary to breed success for 'us' all, without probing further into the constitution of this 'us'. 'How could [*The Lord of the Rings*] not be a success', observes John Downie, 'when the very terms of its cranking up, its momentum, and its manufacture were always posited on a final idea of the "success" it must of necessity be?' (2004: 3).

Conclusion

One can admire Peter Jackson's auretic populism and management genius while also paying attention to the complexities of the way in which the *Lord of the Rings* phenomenon has been pressed into the service of the commodified nation. Through a mimicry of organic social inclusion Jackson's team achieved what governing politicians long for, a 'subtly compelling public consent' (Werry 2004: 7). Jackson engaged the New Zealand army as extras for Orcs; stayed onside with the Ngai Tahu tribe and the Department of Conservation with his ecologically-friendly filming practices (Phillipson 2002/03); roused a crowd at Wellington's Westpac Trust stadium to record the foot-stamps of the oliphants in *The Return of the King*; paraded down the streets of Wellington; and altogether 'firmly inserted the kiwi into the Tolkien bestiary' (Downie 2004: 5). The sentimental Middle Earth analogy for this heroic national effort proved irresistible, invariably with the scenic tag attached: 'Just as the little hobbits helped restore Middle Earth the little guys of New Zealand, ordinary kiwis, helped produce the success of the Rings trilogy from within the scenic magnificence of their own back yard' (*The Real Middle Earth* 2004). However, this seductive 'cyclone of the hyperreal' (Downie 2004: 4) instantiates 'production fetishism', in which a nation proudly appropriates as 'ours' an entity that is largely owned and controlled overseas, creating an illusion of 'local control, national productivity and territorial sovereignty' that obscures the transnationalism of a product (Appadurai 1993: 306).

> And so it came to pass that most of New Zealand's sparse and ever-willing proletariat, it seemed, became defined as goblins and elves and hobbits ... a population transformed before our eyes, courtesy of covert American investment. (Downie, 2002: 2)

Yet the rhetoric of 'creative entrepreneurship' and 'cultural capital' tends to elide the analytical distinction between the 'proletariat' and those who control capital. The concept of 'capital' has progressively softened to include not only physical and financial capital, but also human, cultural and creative capital. Just as everybody 'has' culture in the anthropological sense, so everybody can contribute to cultural capital, defined as 'cultural networks and relationships that support human activity' (Throsby 2003: 168).[13] Likewise, while very few of us are professional artists, almost all of us could be flattered into believing that we have some creative capability. After all, creativity is a flexible and appealing term, powerful precisely because of its unassailability: who could possibly be against it (Corballis 2003: 59)? This democratisation of both culture and creativity produces new heroes: where the New Zealand media profiled wealthy financiers such as Bob Jones, Michael Fay and Ron Trotter during the 1980s, it is now ruffle-headed Peter Jackson who has become the 'poster-boy for fast capitalism' (Jutel 2003).

New Zealand's creative industries policy not only makes a bid for improved economic outcomes, but it also helps to bring into being new perceptions and social relationships. While *The Lord of the Rings* story tells of the destruction of Sauron's *industrial* hell,[14] the government's utilisation of Peter Jackson's project as a policy vehicle orients the population toward the entrepreneurial creativity deemed necessary to survive the global competition in the trading of images that characterises the *post-industrial* world. Somewhat ironically, this policy-driven enticement to creative adventurism has been underwritten by the injection of millions of dollars of public funding. In a further irony, the discursive positioning of creative vision at the centre of cultural and economic development policy tends to increase, not lessen, the politicisation of both the film production and the film product. Whether this export-oriented creative excitement will be sustained is difficult to tell, though the history of policy cycles and Kiwi export mythologies suggests that its use-by date is limited. As Michael Volkerling phlegmatically observes, the 'strategy of spectacularisation positions the state as an indulgent host of a celebration which it never fully understands nor fully controls', and which it 'seems to tolerate only until the party turns sour' (Volkerling 1995).

Notes

1 The research for this chapter was completed during a residency at the Stout Research Centre at Victoria University of Wellington, and the support of the Centre is gratefully acknowledged.

2 The Film Commission's budget fell from approximately $12.965million in 1989–90 to $11.247million in 1998–99. The government proportion of funding relative to Lottery sources also fell over that time period, amounting to 7.2% in 1998–99 (Post Election Briefing 1999: Appendix B). The government grant for 2005–06 stands at $10.873million, representing approximately 53% of the Film Commission's total income, with Lotto sources providing approximately 39% of income. All budget figures in this chapter are in New Zealand dollars unless otherwise specified.

3 The tax shelter enabled the Australian-owned Bank of New Zealand to finance the production through a New Zealand-based subsidiary company, which wrote off the expenditure as a tax loss. Through a pre-arranged option the subsidiary was then sold back to the overseas producer, meaning that New Zealand taxpayers effectively shouldered one third of the financial risk of production amounting to approximately $219million in foregone tax revenue (Campbell 2000: 21). By comparison, reported tax revenues from around 600 New Zealand film, video and sound companies amounted to a mere $7.6million, or 0.17% of total net revenue in the 2002–03 financial year (Clifton 2003: 15).

4   This figure was stated by Pete Hodgson, the 'Minister of the Rings', at the Parliamentary reception for Peter Jackson and the *Lord of the Rings* talent at the Wellington premiere of *The Return of the King*.

5   Lisanne Gibson and Tom O'Regan elaborate upon these policy frameworks. Briefly, the 'cultural development' model aims to 'establish viable and sustainable *cultural ecologies*' through a 'dual focus upon cultural diversity and economic sustainability'. The 'creative industries' model stresses business competitiveness and economic growth by 'stimulat[ing] connection and synergies among the arts-related industries' (2002: 5). A major initiative in the Labour government's cultural development is the requirement that local government planning enhance 'cultural well-being' (Local Government Act 2002).

6   This software spawned the urban myth that the virtual warriors exhibited sufficient intelligence to run away from battle through fear. In fact when the virtual warriors on the margins of a battle scene could not find an enemy warrior to engage, as they had been programmed to do, they displayed random behaviour.

7   Films funded under this scheme include Nicky Caro's *Whale Rider* (2002) and Gaylene Preston's *Perfect Strangers* (2003). Co-production negotiation can require compromises in content such as the insertion of a German love interest in *Whale Rider* to meet the terms of German co-financer ApolloMedia. Compromises in intellectual property ownership may also be called for to meet the subsidy criteria set by other foreign film-funding bodies. At one stage of financing negotiations for *Her Majesty* (2001) director Mark Gordon 'was given the option (by the Australians) of giving up or sharing my screenwriting credit with an Australian producer in order for the "package" to have enough co-production points to qualify for funds. Obviously that did not go over too well' (*Onfilm* 2004/05c: 20).

8   The Employment Relations Act (2000) claws back some of the deregulation in the labour market that occurred during the neoliberal period. A Supreme Court decision interpreting this Act designated one of the set technicians on *The Lord of the Rings* production as an employee, rather than an independent contractor (James Bryson v Three Foot Six Limited). The case has generated debate in Parliament about whether the government's labour and creative industries policies counteract each other.

9   *Variety* (2003) magazine conveniently compares such incentive schemes as at November 2003. Toby Miller notes that place competition led to the establishment of 31 film commissions across the globe, many of them (such as Film New Zealand, established in 1994) solely concerned with attracting foreign capital (2003: 135). Australia has felt the pinch of an appreciating dollar relative to the greenback, as '[runaway] production dropped by 23% between 2001–02 and 2002–03 and local feature production followed suit, dropping a whopping 63%' (Calder 2004: B3).

10 The Goods and Services Tax is 12.5% in New Zealand, making the scheme comparable to the Australian scheme introduced in September 2001, although the New Zealand version also applies to television production. The Australian protections have been

allowed as a reservation to the Australia-US Free Trade Agreement.

11 Jackson's criticism of 'constant revisionism' in film-funding policy and processes dates back to 1997 when he published a comprehensive attack on the New Zealand Film Commission (cited in Heal 1997: 64). Jackson has more recently castigated the New Zealand Film Commission for encouraging a producer-led industry, rather than fostering writers and directors, and for 'supporting anybody who can fill out the forms correctly and jump through the hoops' (cited in 'Jackson Berates Bureaucrats' 2004: 4). On policy uncertainty in other economies, see Inverne (2004) for a discussion on the consequences for the United Kingdom film industry when the government closed a tax loophole without warning on 10 February 2004, now referred to as 'black Tuesday' within the local industry.

12 Personal communication with Jasmine McSweeney of the New Zealand Film Commission, 1 February 2005. For comparison, a 30-second prime-time advertisement on Television New Zealand costs up to $10,000, while the *average* marketing budget for the top seven Hollywood studios in 2003 was US$39million (Germaine 2004). On the challenges that European cinema faces in developing distribution networks, see Farouky 2004.

13 The theorisation of cultural capital is associated with the work of David Throsby (2001; 2003) and, in the New Zealand context, with George Barker (2000), whose monograph *Cultural Capital and Policy* was commissioned by the New Zealand Film Commission.

14 Te Papa's *Lord of the Rings* exhibition shows how Jackson's costume design team incorporated a pre-industrial ethos to their team by, for example, individualising each character's armour.

Works cited

Adorno, T. (1991) *The Culture Industry: Selected Essays on Mass Culture*, ed. J. M. Bernstein. London: Routledge.

Anderton, J. (2004) 'Address to Screen Production (SPADA) Conference', 19 November. On-line. Available at http://www.beehive.govt.nz/ViewDocument.cfm?DocumentID =21550 (accessed 30 January 2005).

Anon. (2003) 'IMP Success Story', *Tourism News*, May, 8–9.

_____ (2004) 'Hollywood Wins as Locals Lose', *The New Zealand Herald*, 12 January, A10.

Appadurai, A. (1993) 'Disjuncture and Difference in the Global Cultural Economy', in M. Featherstone (ed.) *Global Culture: Nationalism, Globalization, and Modernity.* London: Sage, 295–310.

Barker, G. (2000) *Cultural Capital and Policy.* Wellington: Australian National University Centre for Law and Economics.

Barnett, J. (2002) 'Shaky Statistics Don't Help Film', *National Business Review*, 10 May, 17.

Bennett, T. (1998) *Culture: A Reformer's Science*. St. Leonard's, NSW: Allen & Unwin.

Brodie, I. (2002) *The Lord of the Rings Location Book*. Auckland: HarperCollins.

Calder, P. (2003) 'The Hoard of the Rings', *The New Zealand Herald Canvas Magazine*, 29–30 November, 10–13.

_____ (2004) 'Banking on Hollywood', *New Zealand Herald*, 10–11 January 2004, B3.

Campbell, G. (2000) 'Lord of the Tax Deals', *NZ Listener*, 21 October, 18–24.

_____ (2001) 'Shoot and Scoot', *NZ Listener*, 22 September 2001, 26–7.

_____ (2003) 'The Lion, the Witch and the Wardrobe Department', *New Zealand Listener*, 23 August, 22–4.

Clifton, J. (2003) 'Ring Wrath', *NZ Listener*, 13 December, 14–15.

Corballis, T. (2003) 'Against Creativity', *Landfall*, 205, 53–65.

Creative Nation: Commonwealth Cultural Policy (1994). Canberra: Department of Communication and the Arts.

Cunliffe, D. (2004) 'Building a Capable New Zealand Economy: Towards a "New Zealand-Inc."', 24 November. Online. Available at http://www.cunliffe.org.nz/6.news/articles/detail.asp?id=90 (accessed 24 January 2005).

Downie, J. (2002) 'A Milestone of Fabulous Digitalisation: *The Lord of the Rings: The Fellowship of the Ring*', *Illusions*, 34, 2–5.

_____ (2004) 'Cyclones, Seduction and the Middle Mind', *Illusions*, 36, 2–11.

Drinnan, J. (2002) 'Screen Taskforce Sets Economic Goals', *Onfilm*, June, 3.

Easton, B. (1999) *The Whimpering of the State: Policy after MMP*. Auckland: Auckland University Press.

Economic Impact Assessment for the Filming of The Last Samurai in Taranaki (2004). New Plymouth: Venture Taranaki.

Elmer, G. (2002) 'The Trouble with the Canadian "Body Double"': Runaway Productions and Foreign Location Shooting', *Screen*, 43, 4, 423–31.

Farouky, J. (2004) 'Playing Against the Big Boys', *Time Europe Magazine*, 163, 10, 8 March, 60–3. Online. Available at http://www.time.com/time/europe/magazine/printout/0,13155,901040308-596082,00.html (accessed 16 June 2005).

Germaine, D. (2004) 'Movies [*sic*] Costs Are Through the Roof', *CBS News*, 25 March. Online. Available at http://www.cbsnews.com/stories/2004/03/25/entertainment/main 608657.shtml (Accessed 30 January 2005).

Gibson, L. and T. O'Regan (2002) 'Culture: Development, Industry, Distribution', *Media International Australia*, 102, 5–8.

Growing an Innovative New Zealand. Online. Available at http://www.beehive.govt.nz/innovate/innovative.pdf (accessed 16 June 2005).

Harley, R. (2001) 'Cultural Capital and New Zealand's Knowledge Economy', Smart Wellington Interactive Breakfast Series, 26 June. Online. Available at http://www.r2.co.nz/20010626 (accessed 31 January 2005).

_____ (2002) 'How We Created World Class Performance', Innovate Conference, Christchurch, NZ, 6 March. On-line. Available at http://www.innovate.org.nz/speakers-notes/harley.html (accessed 31 January 2005).

Heal, A. (1997) 'Horror Story', *Metro*, December, 62–70.

The Heart of the Nation: A Cultural Strategy for Aotearoa New Zealand (2000). Wellington: McDermott Miller.

Hozic, A. A. (2001) 'The Political Economy of Global Culture', in R. Lukic and M. Brint (eds) *Culture, Politics, and Nationalism in the Age of Globalization*. Aldershot: Ashgate, 55–78.

Jameson, F. (1998) 'Notes on Globalization as a Philosophical Issue', in F. Jameson and M. Miyoshi (eds) *The Cultures of Globalization*. Durham, NC: Duke University Press, 54–77.

Jutel, T. (2003) '*The Lord of the Rings*: Landscape, Transformation and the Geography of the Virtual'. Paper presented at the New Zealand Studies Associaton Annual Conference, London, UK, 29 June.

Knight, K. (2004) 'New Zealand Films – Scene but not Heard, Says Top Director', *Sunday Star Times*, 11 January, A4.

Matthews, M. (2000) 'Report to the Minister on the Heart of the Nation Document'. Wellington: Ministry for Culture and Heritage. On-line. Available at http://www.mch. govt.nz/publications/hotn/hotn.htm (accessed 17 August 2003).

Miller, T. (2003) 'The Film Industry and the Government: "Endless Mr Beans and Mr Bonds"?' in J. Lewis and T. Miller (eds) *Critical Cultural Policy Studies: A Reader*. Malden, MA: Blackwell, 134–51.

Mirams, G. (1945) *Speaking Candidly: Films and People in New Zealand*. Hamilton, NZ: Paul's.

Morgan, G. (1999) 'Towards Rationalism in the Arts'. Online. Available http://nbr.info-metrics.co.nz/towards-rationalism-in-the-arts_81.html (accessed 25 January 2005).

Onfilm (2003) 'Screen Production Survey Highlights', December, 1, 9. Online. Available at http://www.onfilm.co.nz/editable/lotr/Onfilm_1202b.html (accessed 31 January 2005).

_____ (2004) 'Jackson Berates Bureaucrats and Bumblers', March, 4.

_____ (2004/05a) 'Thinking Bigger about LBGs', December/January, 4.

_____ (2004/05b) 'Murphy's Lore', December/January, 18–19.

_____ (2004/05c) 'Return of the Queen', December/January, 20–1.

Oram, R. (2001/02) 'Brand New Zealand', *Unlimited*, December/January, 40–6.

Phillipson, A. (2002/03) 'Dollarman vs *The Lord of the Rings*: The Battle of Nature and Progress', *World Literature Written in English*, 39, 2, 18–37.

The Real Middle Earth (2004). Television New Zealand, 22 February.

Reid, N. (1986) *A Decade of New Zealand Film: Sleeping Dogs to Came a Hot Friday*. Dunedin, NZ: McIndoe.

Rotherham, F. (2003) 'Why Less is More for Tourism', *Unlimited*, August, 31–9.

Scoping the Lasting Effects of The Lord of the Rings (2002). Wellington: New Zealand Institute of Economic Research.

Screen Production and Development Association of New Zealand (2003) 'Survey of Screen Production in New Zealand 2003'. Wellington: SPADA. On-line. Available at http://www.spada.co.nz/documents/Survey2003.pdf (accessed 28 January 2005).

Seaman, B. A. (2003) 'Economic Impact of the Arts', in R. Towse (ed.) *A Handbook of Cultural Economics*. Cheltenham, UK: Edward Elgar, 224–31.

Shore, C. and S. Wright (1997) 'Policy: A New Field of Anthropology', in C. Shore and S. Wright (eds) *Anthropology of Policy: Critical Perspectives on Governance and Power*. London: Routledge, 3–39.

Sibley, B. (2001) *The Lord of the Rings: Official Movie Guide*. London: Harper.

Simpson, P. (ed.) (2003) *The Rough Guide to The Lord of the Rings*. London: Haymarket.

Sutter, S. (2003) 'The Medium is the Brand', *Marketing Magazine*, 108, 6, 18.

Taking on the World (2002) Wellington: Screen Production Industry Taskforce.

Throsby, D. (2001) *Economics and Culture*. Cambridge: Cambridge University Press.

_____ (2003) 'Cultural Capital', in R. Towse (ed.) *A Handbook of Cultural Economics*. Cheltenham, UK: Edward Elgar, 166–9.

Towse, R. (2003) 'Introduction', In R. Towse (ed.) *A Handbook of Cultural Economics*. Chelthenham, UK: Edward Elgar, 1–14.

Variety (2003) 'Tax Incentives around the Globe', 3 November, 22–6.

Vogel, H. L. (2001) *Entertainment Industry Economics: A Guide for Financial Analysis*. Cambridge: Cambridge University Press.

Volkerling, M. (1994) 'Death or Transfiguration: The Future for Cultural Policy in New Zealand', *Culture and Policy*, 6, 1, 7–28.

_____ (1995) 'The State, the Arts, and Culture', Winter Lecture, University of Auckland, 18 July.

Wakefield, P. (2003) 'Jackson Attacks Tax Lax', *Onfilm*, May, 1, 5.

_____ (2004) 'Film Fund Finished?', *Onfilm*, March, 3, 5.

Waller, G. A. (1996) 'The New Zealand Film Commission: Promoting an Industry, Forging a National Identity', *Historical Journal of Film, Radio and Television*, 16, 2, 243–62.

Watkin, T. (2004) 'The Listener 2004 Power List', *New Zealand Listener*, 11 December, 14–30.

Werry, M. (2004) 'National Cinema, Global Markets, and the Politics of Post-Ethnicity: Notes from Middle Earth', *Occasional Papers on Globalization*, 1, 5. Tampa: University of South Florida. On-line. Available at http://www.globalgrn.org/publications/werry.pdf (accessed 25 January 2005).

Making Middle Earth Sound Real: *The Lord of the Rings* and the Cultural Politics of the BBC Radio Edition

Martin Barker

Sunday lunchtimes in the UK for half of 1981 were dominated for many thousands of people by compulsive radio-listening. Introduced by the sonorous music of Stephen Oliver, the half-hour slots of the first-ever broadcast of the BBC's dramatisation of *The Lord of the Rings* filled people's homes throughout the months of March to August. Houses would go quiet for half an hour as whole families listened. People made arrangements for friends to record episodes while they were away on holiday. Groups would meet to talk about the latest happenings in Middle Earth. When the programme replayed on the following Wednesday evening, many listened again. This glorious aural treat generated a huge mailbag of enthusiastic responses, and because of the demand the series was repeated as 13 hour-long episodes a year later, then re-broadcast at intervals thereafter. It played in Australia, and also in the United States where it eclipsed and made entirely forgettable a local version of Tolkien's books produced for The Mind's Eye. Although it never won a single award, the BBC's *Lord of the Rings* is arguably the single most remembered, and most re-listened, radio drama of all time – despite, or perhaps because of, its great length. The BBC's version of *The Lord of the Rings* has become for very many fans a touchstone for all adaptations, and a measure for evaluating Peter Jackson's film version. The series was issued on audiocassette in 1987, and then revised and reissued on CD in 2001.

The Lord of the Rings and prestige radio drama

The BBC had ventured into *Rings* territory before. In 1956, a reading of Tolkien's books went down badly – including with Tolkien himself, who called it a 'sillification' of his work. In 1971, two years before his death, the BBC managed to obtain a rare, long interview with Tolkien himself, in which he talked, among other things, about the status *The Lord of the Rings* had achieved. 1978 saw Ralph Bakshi's animated version of the first half of the trilogy – loved by some, panned by more. Its lacklustre box office performance ensured that the second half never got made. But it was one of the prompts for the BBC to consider a dramatisation. When it came to casting, the Bakshi version was sufficiently influential that two actors (Peter Woodthorpe (Gollum) and Michael Graham Cox (Boromir)) were invited to reprise their roles.

This was a prestigious production, strongly committed to fidelity to the books.[1] And expensive. Not just in its spread over 26 episodes – unprecedented for an adaptation – but in a range of other attributes. The BBC expected, even budgeted, to pay heavily for the rights to produce the story.[2] The cast they assembled included a number of major theatrical players: Ian Holm (Frodo), Robert Stephens (Aragorn) and Michael Hordern (Gandalf); major television figures like John Le Mesurier (Bilbo); and a number of radio luminaries, such as Marion Diamond (Galadriel). There was one crossover from the nation's most notable radio soap *The Archers*, Jack May as Theoden. Specially composed and recorded music, a company of trained singers, rehearsal times of a duration that would soon become inconceivable and a complicated post-production – all these added costs, and raised the quality stakes. Developed in some secrecy,[3] the series was released with great publicity, including a prestigious cover story in the *Radio Times*.[4]

Everything was done with a consistent *seriousness* at odds with Peter Jackson's inclusion of jokey by-plays among the hobbits, or around the character of Gimli.[5] Not that the characters did not laugh. The deep chuckle in response to Frodo's discomfort when he begins to describe how Aragorn would surely 'appear fairer, but feel fouler' if he really were a servant of the Enemy, and realises what he is thus implying; or Frodo's uncontrolled mirth at Sam's storytelling on the Stairs of Cirith Ungol: these are real, but they do not lighten the story. Rather, they redouble the humanity of the characters, but also the sense of the dangerous paths they walk. No, the BBC version made no concessions to 'children' – the narrative was played straight, with the added tension that it built each episode to a cliff-hanger. Each half-hour episode closed with a moment of decision or desperation – sufficiently, that when re-broadcast in hour-long episodes in 1982, additional narration by Gerard Murphy had to be recorded to form bridges. The most powerful have surely to be Gandalf's dying cry of 'Fly, you fools!' as he plummeted to his doom with the Balrog, from which the episode crashed into the closing music, or Sam's despair as Frodo claimed the Ring for himself on the brink of the Cracks of Doom. But whatever one's favourites, it is unarguable that elements of these kinds contributed to a sense, for first-time listeners, of *going on the journey* with the Companions.

All this and much more in the service of a very ambitious quality: a 'real' Middle Earth. The 2002 re-release of the BBC radio edition includes an extra CD,

'Microphones in Middle Earth', for which Brian Sibley, aided by narration from the now stellar Bill Nighy (Sam), talked to producers, actors and enthusiasts about the making of the series. Largely taken up with the production processes and anecdotes of some of the principal players, it nonetheless gives some vital information about its production, and includes one telling exchange between Sibley and Jane Morgan, its producer:

> Sibley: One of the things I remember very vividly, Jane, is your saying that you were determined that the series should sound 'real'. Now to many people that would be a sort of strange thing to say about a book which features dwarves and elves and wizards.
>
> Morgan: Yes, well it's a contradiction in terms, really. I didn't want us to have electronic sounds all the way through. I didn't want to treat the voices so that they sounded distorted. I wanted to find the attributes in every character … I tried to think of actors whose voices were going to sound real. I mean it's all very well having a wizard but unless you think he's an interesting wizard, and he has qualities in common with you and with humankind, then you're not really interested.

This exchange points to a set of operative assumptions which can only be properly grasped by examining the context at the BBC in this period.

The BBC in 1980

For the BBC as a whole, this was a nervous time. The new 1979 Conservative Government of Margaret Thatcher was playing politics with its licence fee, forcing annual bids, and encouraging both staff cuts and more commercial borrowing, as part of a general undermining of a Public Service commitment (Tracey 1998: 105–7). But while bearing its share of financial misery, radio was somewhat insulated from the worst political criticisms, which were aimed primarily at the more prestigious television. Radio as a whole had its own problems, originating in the impact of the 1960s pirate radio stations which had revealed its lack of contact with youth music tastes. The response had been drastic. The old Home Service and Light Programmes were replaced by Radio 1 (roughly equalling pop music), Radio 2 (easy listening with some comedy), Radio 3 (classical music with highbrow talks and dramas) and Radio 4 (news, current affairs, middle-brow talk and drama – including, of course, the longest-running staple *The Archers*). But radio drama to an extent had its own trajectory, regardless of station locations.

The late 1970s were giving rise to a phase of reflection on radio, its politics and potentials, in the UK. A Cinderella in academic terms – especially in the face of the wave of inflated spectator-centred theorisations of 'film texts' that swept into universities – it was also now marginal in professional and critical arenas, because of television. And it would be television, not radio, which in a few years' time would bear the brunt of the Thatcher Government's assault on the BBC's political role (arising from the Falklands War, in particular). But compared with Radio 1 and Radio 2 fighting to be the voice of popular music, this was almost an interregnum period at Radio 3 and Radio 4 (Street 2002: 91). This very marginality generated a will to explore radio drama's potentials. In 1981, the year of *The Lord of the Rings*, there came both John Drakakis's and Peter Lewis's edited volumes on the topic of radio studies. And in 1982, following a conference of academics and professionals which they organised, came Ian Rodger's (1982) thoughtful historical enquiry of the medium.

Rodger began from a rebuke to people like Cyril Connolly who once charged Louis MacNiece with 'wasting his time' on radio plays. A former critic from *The Listener* Rodger paints a narrative of the history of radio drama, from beginnings in the 1920 and 1930s in which experimental playwrights excited by the medium's possibilities were repeatedly constrained by bureaucratic nervous censorship, to a sea-change begun during World War Two. The then Head of Scripts, Val Gielgud, among others, persuaded the BBC's Board that radio could become the voice of the nation under attack; and that radio drama in particular could demonstrate Britain's support for eternal 'civilised values', by adapting classic novels and plays. The space thus generated attracted a generation of post-war writers to make the most of the medium. MacNiece, Dylan Thomas, Harold Pinter, Samuel Beckett, Alun Owen among others all wrote for the BBC, creating 'an explosion of dramatic talent which utilised radio, and created the second golden age in the history of British drama' (Rodger 1982: 5). Among their achievements was bringing into radio the many voices of 'the Nation'. From being the singular voice of middle-class England, now classes, regions and dialects were finding their place through these radical new dramas. This also gave rise to a new concept of a 'radio shape', self-consciously postulating the distinctive characteristics of a medium operating through intimate sound alone. But this ideal, Rodger believed, was now in danger from, among other things, new technologies (stereophony, radiophonic special effects and in-studio editing) which risked overwhelming the newly arrived 'real voices'.

Inflated or not, this vision was clearly circulating within BBC radio itself in this period. The functions of radio drama were not to be 'plays to hoover to' (Wade 1981: 221–2). BBC radio was a 'national theatre of the air', providing democratic access to Great Works. And it is not coincidental that the team producing *The Lord of the Rings* included Michael Bakewell, one of the early advocates of experimental work, when he pressed for the BBC to accept work from Beckett and Pinter. But I believe the influence of this self-conscious awareness goes deeper, into the formulation of that very notion of a 'real' Middle Earth, into the recognition of the specific challenges posed by dramatising Tolkien's work, and the solutions found.

Further indications of the enabling context can be gleaned from Peter Lewis's book. With a mix (unusual for its period) of academic and professional contributors, the book seeks to carve a space for the serious consideration of radio drama, covering its history and sociology, but also its production processes and aesthetics of this 'theatre of the imagination'. Through the book it is possible to build a picture of some of the further contextual factors (pressures, possibilities) driving radio drama in this period. Perhaps most relevantly, in a brief translated survey of the history of the BBC's radio drama, Horst Priessnitz identifies the tendency for Radio 4 to become an unembarrassed 'middle-brow' station, but that in the course of the 1970s the gap between that and the more high-brow Radio 3 narrowed, as Radio 4 shifted upwards. I want to suggest that *The Lord of the Rings* was one case, but a special one, of a will in this period for the BBC drama unit to speak to everyone in 'the Nation' in a high moral tone, and with nationally-popular materials.

'Shaping' *The Lord of the Rings*

To do *The Lord of the Rings* on the radio in this context was to do something special. This was a 'national treasure'. Largely now past its associations with 1960s counterculture, Tolkien's work was widely popular. Bakshi's film, even in failure, had boosted public awareness. But its 'middle-brow' associations had not yet sedimented into the sneering distaste that would so infect the BBC's *The Big Read* poll of most popular books ever in 2003. Rather, at the moment of the BBC radio version, an opportunity and a demand coincided. Self-confident radio drama producers had at their fingertips an array of technological possibilities, but also a sense of a project, that led them to want to make a monumental, national project. But the idea of 'national' was now being debated. From radio history had come a sense of inclusiveness, of multiple voices, speaking from regions and classes. With the arrival of Thatcherism, 'Englishness' was charged with new provocative meanings and debates. Radio drama would not address such things directly, not least because its makers knew that drama that preached would die. But a popular magical drama, which had pitched itself as a mythology for England, might *enact* the 'national'.[6]

What components of the series contribute to this? First, I would argue, the sheer attention to variety of voices. *The Lord of the Rings* posed a potential problem for radio – how to keep absolutely distinct even the nine voices for the Company, without repeatedly reminding us of their names. With two – significant – exceptions, they did this brilliantly. Second, the close intercutting of storylines, strongly disapproved of by Tolkien himself, emphasised the tension and unresolved nature of the story.[7] This was accentuated by a decision – copied by Jackson – to insert a back-story as a prologue. Where the book leaves us in uncertainty for a long time about the nature and origins of Frodo's Ring, both radio and film versions 'solve' that before the travellers ever set out.

What is so striking about the BBC version, however, is the simplicity of the devices to evoke settings and make it 'real'. Aside from some theme musics for characters and peoples, sound effects are used very sparingly. The Dead Marshes are evoked by small occasional scratchy violin strings – nothing more. The entire episode of Aragorn's mind-wrestling with Sauron is done by a slight echo to his side of an entirely one-sided conversation. Jane Morgan had learnt well the lessons of 'radio shape'.

In one respect, the 'Englishness' of the series does shine through, ahead of and beyond Peter Jackson, in the portrayal of the Shire. I pointed out earlier that the series is entirely serious. That is not *quite* true. When we meet the hobbits on their home territory, they are enacted as pleasant, narrow-minded country bump-kins with strong West Country accents. All, that is, apart from Frodo, Merry and Pippin. The latter two are the only ones whose voices – light, boyish, *very* middle-class and never portrayed as funny – are not immediately distinct: very different from their leprechaun-like characterisation in the films. And as well as keeping, generally, the Scouring of the Shire (entirely missing from the film adaptation), it highlights Frodo's pained recognition that having saved the Shire for others, he cannot enjoy it himself.

The sense of *journey*, the marvellous excitement of the first broadcast, dimin-ished a little – to some extent inevitably (re-listening is never quite the same as the first hearing) – but to some extent as a result of the changes introduced by the BBC. Going to hour-long episodes, the cliff-hangers were reduced and extra nar-ration bridged the spaces. Released on CD in 2002, they disappeared completely, and an additional layer of narration – voiced by a recalled Ian Holm – moved the story into a 'past', as he seemed to look back from after the events, recalling (some-times in pain) the events. It is as if BBC radio can *recall* doing this kind of work, but these possibilities are now past. The meanings of 'England', 'nation', 'middle-brow' and 'quality' are fraught in new ways and, like Frodo recalling his journey, can only be recollected in a kind of tranquillity.

From radio to film: real and rhetorical connections

So how in sum should we think about the relations between the radio and film adaptations of *The Lord of the Rings*? First and foremost, we must recognise that Peter Jackson and New Line Cinema were very aware of the need to 'manage' the fans. This meant dialoguing with them (Shefrin 2004). It meant researching what the fans cared about; and while Bakshi's film had at best mixed responses, clearly the BBC version was for very many (and in quite a few countries) a *legitimate* version. For this reason, it made sense to explore the BBC's narrative solutions.

The BBC's version was among the research materials used by company and crew for Jackson's film adaptation, and Ian Holm, Frodo for the BBC, was moved up a generation to play his uncle Bilbo in the film. And one of the two radio script-writers, Brian Sibley, who had shoe-horned himself into this role partly by being a pushy fan, was subsequently employed to write the Official Movie Guide for the trilogy. But as importantly as these personal connections, there are some important thematic continuities between radio and film versions. Jackson adopted the BBC's tactics of a prologue to provide the back-story of the Ring; lost many of the same scenes (for instance, everything involving Tom Bombadil[8]), and intercut the two journeys after the Company splits. Perhaps most notably, Elijah Wood very much followed Ian Holm in how he showed Frodo becoming possessed by the One Ring. It helped too to have on board Ian Holm, perhaps especially in the more fatherly role of Bilbo. Even Andy Serkis's voicing of Gollum recalls the distorted inflections so brilliantly deployed by Peter Woodthorpe.

But we should also recognise the *rhetorical work* put in to emphasise how safe the story was in Jackson's hands. If you believed them, Jackson had full editorial control. New Line Cinema simply handed over $300million and trusted him thereafter to make a 'quality' film; and all was sweetness and light.[9] In fact, from the bits of evidence we have, the story is much more complicated. From the beginning New Line worked hard to feed information and gather opinions via favoured websites. Unpopular decisions, such as the loss of the Scouring of the Shire, were 'handled' in advance through Jackson's apologias.

But while engaged in this public relations game with the fans, New Line had other concerns. Working from a very crude – but effective – quadripartite model of the audience, they realised that their major battle was elsewhere. Thence they construed the need to win over a tricky audience: the under-25 female audience, whom the first part of the trilogy had lost to the *Harry Potter* franchise. To this end, Jackson was urged to upgrade the part of sexy Orlando Bloom – and late extra filming and editing achieved exactly this. Albeit probably not in response to such an exact estimate of market conditions, making Gimli a figure of fun looks like a decision to play a game for a (young male) audience segment who would approach the films through the tenets of the chirpy action genre.

Jackson and New Line Cinema thus took what they could, and sought to inherit the prestige of the BBC's production, but used the image of 'hobbit Jackson' to disguise decisions made in response to a very different marketing environment – decisions which took them most away from the kind of 'fidelity' that the BBC had achieved.

Notes

1   This public commitment to faithful adaptation did not prevent the BBC from not only cutting sections, and borrowing convenient back-story from Tolkien's *Silmarillion*, but even 'cleaning' some famous lines. Bilbo's famous 'compliment' at his farewell party that 'I don't know half of you half as well as I should like, and I like less than half of you half as well as you deserve' was tidied by the removal of two 'halfs'.

2   Originally the BBC paid Saul Zaentz whose ownership of the rights had enabled Bakshi's production. Then it was discovered that he did not own radio rights, and they had to turn to the Tolkien estate, for permission – which led to Tolkien's son Christopher attaching a codicil of a right to review the script.

3   Brian Sibley has several times told the story of his encounter with Richard Imison, Head of the BBC's Script Unit. Sibley was engaged in a writing campaign to get work inside the BBC, and had mentioned that he would really most like to do Tolkien's books. On their next encounter, Imison ushered him into a side office, demanding to know how he had known of the BBC's plans to do *The Lord of the Rings*. It was clearly seen at this point as highly confidential information. See for instance Anon. 2003: 31.

4   The importance of the *Radio Times* recognition should not be underestimated. Recently Tim Crooks, one of the current generation of radio scholars, had this to say about the way in which the *Radio Times* relates to the BBC's self-obsessions: 'For the edition of 11th to 17th July 1998 the *Radio Times*, the largest selling magazine in Britain and with the BBC as the major shareholder, decided to invite its readers to "vote for your all-time greats". It explained: "As there are so many memorable programmes and people to choose from, we asked a panel of experts to help you decide by nominating what they have enjoyed most." The magazine explained that anyone was open to "disagree with their suggestions, just add your own". People sending in their votes were automatically entered for a competition to win a widescreen television. Here was an example of the BBC through its powerful *Radio Times* gathering together the "great and good" of broadcasting to identify the "best radio drama" in Britain produced and broadcast over the previous 75 years. Not surprisingly all the nominated productions had been made by the BBC. One of the panel, Paul Donovan, was to later declare in his *Sunday Times* newspaper column that the BBC had had virtually no competition in radio drama. Eight of the nominated productions were titles in the BBC's Radio Collection of audio cassettes which had a majority share of the spoken word market. The promotion therefore had a hidden commercial purpose and resonance masquerading as a cultural creative celebration and appreciation.' (Available at http://www.irdp.co.uk/britrad5.htm, accessed 18 December 2005.) Inevitably, *The Lord of the Rings* featured among that Top Ten.

5   Gimli was not only given dialogue emphasising his humorous role, he was also filmed in ways that emphasised this (the shot of him unable to see over the walls at Helm's Deep, for example). And he was taken as such – see the evidence garnered from audience research in Barker 2005.

6 Recently, the Tolkien Society published a very interesting pamphlet on this topic, drawing together its own intellectuals to discuss what Tolkien might have meant by thinking the *The Lord of the Rings* as a 'mythology for England' (Crawshaw 1999). Perhaps concerned with putting and keeping Tolkien on a high plain, this casts 'myth' by analogy with the Greek, Roman and Norse myths, and searches for sources there, and motifs and parallels with Tolkien's characters. I am not using 'myth' in this sense. Rather I am interested in the sense of a *marvellous ethical journey*, a theme that has emerged powerfully from researches into audiences for Jackson's films (see Barker & Mathijs, forthcoming).

7 Sibley, under Bakewell's sensible guidance, overcame his fannish hesitations about transgressing Tolkien's will on this. In fact it does leave some small chronological inexactitudes. My favourite is the scene in Ithilien where Frodo wakes many hours before Sam, after their rescue from Mount Doom. We have to suppose that while Frodo waited, he saw neither Merry nor Pippin, nor Aragorn – it was important to the emotional rush of the 'Praising' scene that he and Sam should be equally astonished at seeing their friends again!

8 If this seems too obvious to be worth mentioning, consider that no one even notices some other narrative omissions from both the BBC and the film version. What has happened to the Woses, the Wild Men of the Wood who enable the Riders of Rohan to reach Gondor in time, unseen? Their importance is more than this narrative advance – they represent an old, aboriginal culture whose rights will henceforth be respected.

9 This heavenly picture began to unravel when it emerged that Jackson's Wingnut Productions was suing New Line over its accounting practices.

Works cited

Anon. (2003) 'Voices off', *Expose*, 81, November, 28–33.

BBC, *The Lord of the Rings*, Audio CD series 2001 (based on the radio broadcasts, BBC Radio 4 1981). Bonus CD: 'Microphones in Middle Earth'.

Barker, M. (2005) '*The Lord of the Rings* and "identification": a critical encounter', *European Journal of Communication*, 20, 3, 353–78.

Barker, M. and E. Mathijs (eds) (forthcoming) *Watching The Lord of the Rings: World Audiences for the Film Adaptation*. New York: Peter Lang.

Crawshaw, R. (ed.) (1999) *Tolkien: A Mythology For England*. Telford: The Tolkien Society.

Drakakis, J. (ed.) (1981) *British Radio Drama*. Cambridge: Cambridge University Press.

Lewis, P. (ed.) (1981) *Radio Drama*. London: Longman.

Rodger, I (1982) *Radio Drama*. Basingstoke: Macmillan.

Shefrin, E. (2004) '*Lord of the Rings*, *Star Wars*, and participatory fandom: mapping new congruencies between the internet and media entertainment culture', *Critical Studies in Media Communication*, 21, 3, 261–81.

Street, S. (2002) *A Concise History of British Radio 1922–2002*. Tiverton: Kelly Books.

Tracey, M. (1998) *The Decline and Fall of Public Service Broadcasting*. Oxford: Oxford University Press.

Wade, D. (1981) 'British radio drama since 1960', in J. Drakakis (ed.) *British Radio Drama*. Cambridge: Cambridge University Press, 218-44.

Blockbusters and/as Events: Distributing and Launching *The Lord of the Rings*

Daniel Biltereyst and Philippe Meers

No picture has ever been made that is good enough to sell itself. (Samuel Arkoff, quoted in Wasko 2003: 188)

Introduction

The Hollywood blockbuster is intrinsically linked with a fascination for excess, hypes and events. One way of defining the blockbuster phenomenon is that it deals with *big event* pictures, which do not only perform extravaganza in terms of budgets, production values, special effects or high-priced stars. Blockbusters also refer to motion pictures with blockbuster *ambitions*, or the will to become something bigger than just a movie and eventually grow into an event or even a wider societal phenomenon. Especially in times of infrequent movie-going and an immense competition from other forms of public/private entertainment, people have to be attracted in ways which exceed ordinary publicity and marketing strategies.

From this perspective, *The Lord of the Rings* seems a new step in acquiring media attention, the next step after James Cameron's *Titanic* (1997), a movie often seen as the ultimate milestone in contemporary blockbuster history (Lubin 1999; Sandler & Studlar 1999; Krämer 2001). Supported by heavy marketing, the producers behind *Titanic* were able to attract critics' and audiences' fascination for the movie as a special event for a very long time. Several years before the movie received its premiere, *Titanic* was already discursively supported and constructed as a movie which would break all records. Even before its release the public was inundated with fascinating stories about its excessive production history in terms of a never heard-off gigantic budget, unique production conditions and revolutionary visual effects. In so doing, the producing studios Paramount and Twentieth Century Fox (and their local distributors) managed to install a certain discourse around their product. This included values and ideas about the exceptional character and uniqueness of the *Titanic* project on various levels of production, distribution and reception – many being covered by traditional cultural and film-related media (Blanchet 2003: 185). Appealing to a middle-brow cultural taste (Roberts 2003), *Titanic* also received serious attention from quality papers and other unexpected media outlets such as children's programming and even popular scientific media. As such, it succeeded to grow into a wider cultural and societal phenomenon or an *event*. By the latter we mean that it succeeded in leaving its intrinsic field of action and attention (that is, the domain of film criticism, distribution and exhibition, the field of popular star discourses in gossip and other popular magazines), and received an increasingly wider public attention, in effect becoming part of public discourses in general. It was used as a topic to discuss public matters, as a metaphor or as a point of reference in debates on contemporary cultural taste, the historical accuracy of popular entertainment, the educational value of historical movies, the actuality of history, the power of virtual technology, and so on. This process of becoming a wider media and societal event might be the ultimate (perverse) dream for producers in terms of marketing or in launching and attracting public attention to blockbusters – thus helping to break records in terms of media coverage, box office and merchandising revenues.

This chapter will study *The Lord of the Rings* as a constructed event. It starts by looking at blockbusters in relation to the 'event concept'; building on discourse analysis and sociological literature on media events, we investigate an event as a multidimensional concept, a connecting issue between marketing and public discourse management strategies, the (discursive) creation of a certain horizon of expectation, the promise of pleasure, spectacle and imagination, the attempt to mediate audiences' movie experiences, public reception and discourse. As an empirical case study this chapter will analyse the Belgian launch and distribution of *The Return of the King*. In arguing that the *Lord of the Rings* phenomenon has surpassed *Titanic* in many respects as a mega-blockbuster, we look at issues such as New Line Cinema's extremely strict guidelines for distributors, the creation of additional events, as well as advertising and media discourses surrounding the trilogy. The underlying premise of the chapter here is that the producers successfully developed a discourse around the trilogy, recruiting its unicity, historicity and magnitude of the overarching *Lord of the Rings* phenomenon to build a momentum they kept going for a considerable period. In conclusion we will speculate on how its revolutionary production and marketing budgets, record box office performance and excessiveness have made the *Lord of the Rings* phenomenon a new milestone in Hollywood's blockbuster history.

Events connect: *The Lord of the Rings* as a blockbuster milestone

The growing academic interest in movies such as *Titanic, The Matrix* (Andy and Larry Wachowski, 1999) or *The Lord of the Rings* is in line with the scholarly attention for the *productive* sides of the blockbuster phenomenon (Sandler & Studlar 1999; King 2000; Krämer 2001; Lewis 2001; Blanchet 2003; Stringer 2003; Gillis 2005). Blockbusters used to be considered as exemplifying brainless, spectacular and anti-*auteur*-oriented entertainment produced by major Hollywood studios. The blockbuster stood for the profit-driven mentality within global entertainment conglomerates, with its myopic drive to produce superficial, formulaic high-concept pictures. Recent blockbusters studies, however, tend to underline how these 'multipurpose entertainment machines', as Thomas Schatz (1993: 9) has called them, have superseded their purely industrial or economic contexts. They have become a more multidimensional research object. They are not only discussed in political-economic terms illustrating revolutionary changes in producing, distributing and marketing movies (Gomery 1998; Maltby 1998). Within blockbuster studies, intriguing questions are raised about the new textual dynamics within post-classical Hollywood cinema (spectacular narratives, stylistic fragmentation, the frontier experience; Krämer 1998; Neale & Smith 1998; Thompson 1999; Bordwell 2002); about blockbuster and authorship (Buckland 2003); about issues of critical and audience reception (on the local-global nexus in consuming Hollywood products; Meers 2004); and about discursive activities surrounding them. Acknowledging that 'the blockbuster is so important, both for the contemporary media scene (it is responsible for "saving" Hollywood and thus "saving" the cinema as a popular entertainment medium), and for understanding the history of the cinema in the last fifty years' (Elsaesser 2000: 42–3, our translation), Thomas Elsaesser argued that the power of blockbusters lies in how they connect different dimensions. He claims that we should think of blockbusters not only in terms of a macro-level of profit-oriented Hollywood with its different markets of exploitation and its marketing strategies. Blockbusters also work on a micro-level, as a pleasure-oriented device, as a text (with particular narratives, style, and so on) as well as an event (addressing and inviting social meaning).

While *Titanic* has been groundbreaking in all these dimensions *The Lord of the Rings* seems to be pushing the boundaries even further. This is quite clear for some obvious micro-level dimensions, such as the overall running time (a magnum opus of nearly ten hours in its theatrical version), the use of new technologies and the advances made in special effects. On a medium level, seeing *The Lord of the Rings* as an overarching *project* consisting of three movies, we come to a cumulated, record production budget of $290million ($200million for *Titanic*), a promotion and marketing budget of $145million ($40million for *Titanic*), and a cumulative box office of nearly $2000million (against $1845million).[1] Even on a macro-level *The*

Lord of the Rings also outclasses *Titanic*. Although the trilogy production company is New Line Cinema, a firm with strong connotations of an independent production company (Wyatt 1998), making sophisticated art-house-like movies such as *Magnolia* (Paul Thomas Anderson, 1999) and the *Nightmare on Elm Street* series (1984–94), it is also part of Time Warner (Wasko 2003: 61), a global multimedia corporation with links to network television (Turner network, HBO), film production (Warner Bros., New Line Cinema), the music industry (Warner), the world of publishing (*Time, People Illustrated*) and cable and internet services. This constructs a much stronger environment for synergy, marketing strategies and market control than the one in which *Titanic* was bred. It is no surprise, then, that *The Lord of the Rings* has also been an extraordinary and heavily (pre-)advertised and promoted multimedia phenomenon, with an astonishing array of advertising, publicity, marketing and merchandising activity (see the chapter by Janet Wasko and Govind Shanadi in this volume).

The Lord of the Rings as an 'event'

These political-economic dimensions should be firmly kept in mind when discussing how *The Lord of the Rings* became a major mediated social 'event'. In the literature, this 'event' label has been described in terms which detach it from the public sphere or the discursive environment in which they operate. For John Belton, for instance, blockbusters are simply 'big event pictures', where movies have to become 'a special event in order to drive the sometime spectator away from other leisure-time activities back into the movie theatre' (Belton 1994: 272–3). Many authors, talking about the event-character of blockbusters, do so from a marketing perspective. In an article on the marketing of American blockbusters in France, Martine Danan underlines how American film companies try to create 'media events on an international scale' through 'fast, high visibility', the technique 'to saturate foreign markets with prints' and the orchestration of 'media coverage' (Danan 1995: 132–3).

Besides this marketing perspective, there are also different meanings and levels to the event concept. In fact, 'event' is often used in various, overlapping senses. First, it can refer to a producer/distributor's concrete initiatives to attract wider attention, both from potential spectators and the media. These concrete initiatives or '*marketing events*' might be the organisation of a marathon screening event, a special party, fan meetings, and so on, all in the context of the release of a blockbuster movie. Second, as indicated by Danan, event movies are often linked to '*media events*'. This refers to the blockbuster's wider coverage and exposure through the media. In marketing and advertising literature,[2] as well as in blockbuster studies, the concept of the 'media event' is often under-theorised (Dayan & Katz 1992; Fiske 1996).[3] In sociological literature on media events, they are often associated with the metaphor of flows, waves or a river of discourses. John Fiske, for instance, in his critical analysis of race and gender representation in US media and politics, uses the concept of media events as referring to a dynamic river of discourses which heavily influence perception and reality in its own way. In a postmodern environment, media not only represent what happens, they also create their 'own reality, which gathers up into itself the reality of the event that may or may not have preceded it' (1996: 2). Referring to Jean Baudrillard's ideas on hyper-reality and the simulacrum, Fiske argues that a media event is basically a *discourse event*, thus a terrain of struggle or a 'continuous process of making sense and of circulating it socially' (1996: 6). From this perspective, a media event must be thought of as a relatively uncontrolled wave of public discourses triggered by a *key event* (for example as in the Rodney King case: the beating of a black man by police officers). This key event triggers a higher level of discourse than a media discourse itself, linking it to wider public discourses beyond the movies and the media. As such, talk about, say, *Big Brother* or *The Lord of the Rings* becomes metaphorical; the movies and media being used as a metaphor in the fields of the arts, politics, education, academia… We would like to call this level of event as a wider phenomenon a 'societal event'.

It is difficult to distinguish levels of *marketing events* (concrete initiatives by a producer/distributor to attract attention), *media events* (discourses produced by the media around a blockbuster) and *societal events* (wider discourses in society with references to the movie) because they tend to overlap with several other concepts in the tense relationship between 'reality', the media, public discourses and the public sphere.[4]

Dimensions and connections of events

There is also another way of looking at the event concept if we want to understand its importance for blockbusters. Thomas Elsaesser also talks about event movies, media events and film-as-an-event. Although he does not focus upon the event concept itself, it is interesting how Elsaesser indirectly links it to issues such as marketing strategies as well as to public discourse and audience experiences. As spectators, he claims, 'we want to see the movie that promises to be an event' (2001: 16), a promise made by advance advertising, word of mouth or a media blitz. These 'media events' are strategically put together as 'military campaigns, and that's one of the reasons why they cost so much to make' (2001: 17). The blockbuster can be related to 'certain production processes and marketing campaigns, which try to make a movie into an event' (2000: 43, our translation). Elsaesser also relates it to the promise of spectacle and the role blockbusters play in audience's time-management or in society's 'life calender' (2001: 21). The latter refers to the blockbuster's ability to play a role in our culture's time-management, similar to what seasons do.

Indirectly, Elsaesser also links the event character to the ability of blockbusters to build a community of spectators around the promise of the event movie. Claiming that it is precisely through this ability to be part of the 'contemporary economy of experience and to create an event that our experiences are intensified, our senses sharpened, and that we are provided with topics to discuss, what allows us to share and to exchange the feeling of "being there" and "having been there"' (2000: 43; our translation).

We would like to integrate Elsaesser's conceptualisation within the broader framework of our event types. Looking back at the *Titanic* phenomenon, it is precisely the event aspect or the success in becoming a media and a societal event, which enables us to connect different dimensions both on a micro- and a macro-level – from texts, publicity and marketing strategies, audiences' horizon of expectations and imagination, to media attention or public debate in society. Events remain, to a major degree, highly orchestrated (marketing events), at least at the start. They rely on traditional marketing and publicity techniques, of course, but also include the skills of something like public discourse management and the creation of a certain horizon of expectation (the promise of pleasure or imagination) and the use of a particular discursive arsenal (with specific words, ideas, metaphors such as *Titanic* as 'exceptional', 'unique', 'historical', 'a masterpiece'). When these initiatives work (and often they do not, as people in the industry know all too well) they go on to live a life of their own, and become an avalanche of media and public discourses with a growing media attention (media event), with people talking to each other about the movie, with increased fan activity on the internet, or even with public figures talking about it or referring to it in speeches (growing into a societal event). In this optimal scenario an event includes the idea of a growing, uncontrolled public attention and a spiralling public discourse around (in this case) a movie, involving various societal actors (audiences, critics, journalists, politicians, public figures).

When a movie such as *The Lord of the Rings* grows into such an event, it stimulates the audience's attention, imagination, as well as its willingness to pay for a ticket. This is where, on a micro-level, events meet spectators' imagination, experience and financial considerations. When the movie and the process of watching it fulfil the audiences' horizon of expectations, audiences will talk about it with friends and relatives, thus helping the movie-as-an-event to grow even further. The event perspective to the blockbuster phenomenon also deals, of course, with the ability to absorb media attention (at a relatively low cost). Traditionally, this works through media-supported publicity campaigns, promotional partnerships with media partners, and press services (such as interviews, press junkets, and so on). But in case a blockbuster grows into a wider event, other media and journalists than film or cultural critics come into play. One of the amazing observations about American blockbusters is that they often succeed to attract the mainstream media's attention. Even in Europe, where many quality news media still show an elitist anti-American rejection of blockbusters, it is remarkable that big-budget US movies such as *Star Wars* (George Lucas, 1977), *Independence Day* (Roland Emmerich, 1996) or *Saving Private Ryan* (Steven Spielberg, 1998) are seen as events newsworthy enough to be covered in mainstream news. Finally, as indicated in the introduction, an event movie such as *Titanic* might also be part of a much wider discourse where other groups or actors in society recognise, talk about or use it.

Looking at the event concept from this perspective, we might think of it as a Russian *matryoshka* (a nested doll) with various overlapping levels of spiralling public discourses with different layers. In the best case, the blockbuster (or another cultural phenomenon) as an event is widely picked up by film related media (criticism), mainstream media (reports on major awards, spectacular stories on production, distribution, box office and audience success), but also in fans' and audiences' discursive activities (talk, gossip, email, web), as well as in other fields and by other actors in society (politicians, scientists).

We see an event as consisting of different levels of intensity (from low- to high-level event, from marketing to societal events), while it also ultimately is a multi-dimensional concept, connecting both material (economy, concrete marketing strategies) and immaterial dimensions of the blockbuster phenomenon (audience's imagination and expectations, talk among movie fans, gossip). An event connects those levels and dimensions. Although events should be thought of as, to a major degree, highly orchestrated or professionally constructed (marketing and media events), we will use the case of *The Return of the King* to indicate how a blockbuster can enter a wider discursive play in society.

Distributing *The Return of the King*

The launch of a blockbuster trilogy such as *The Lord of the Rings* is a complex operation, involving global strategies with local adjustments. It is complex because, first, it needs planning over a longer time period with different movies released between 2001 and 2003. Different from most other blockbusters, *The Lord of the Rings* started off with an integrated project of 'sequelisation' around three movies (Lewis 2003). Second, as a global cultural project it involves both a central, cockpit-controlled planning of the worldwide distribution, marketing, publicity and other commercial strategies, as well as (partly) decentralised strategies to work upon local markets (Miller *et al.*, 2001). As such, *The Lord of the Rings* is an extremely fine example of how global strategies cannot be deployed without taking into account local market structures and cultural differences, or without displaying a variety of global and local marketing events. Third, of course, *The Lord of the Rings* is more than just a series of movies. The process of launching the trilogy involves a myriad of global/local activities such as different strategies of merchandising, publicity and advertising, of releasing the movies on video and DVD (in different editions), of publishing books and music, of coordinating and creating global and local (marketing and media) events, and so on.

We decided to look at one local market, Belgium, as a case study on how those mechanisms work and on how events emerge.[5] With its three official languages and its small population size (10.4 million), the Belgian film market might seem small. In terms of the gross receipts for *The Lord of the Rings*, however, the Belgian market is comparable to Austria, Brazil and even China. The gross box office for the first *Lord of the Rings* movie in Belgium was $6,094,454, $7,301,126 for the second and $9,902,589 for the third (boxofficemojo.com 2005). The Belgian case also perfectly illustrates the impact of an American blockbuster's impressive release strategies. This includes the strategic placement of the movies, high visibility or the attempt to saturate foreign markets with prints (Danan 1995; Lewis 2003). On the Belgian market only, with its 420 screens, *The Return of the King* was released on 113 prints, most of them subtitled (French and Dutch), while dubbed versions were also used. The movie circulated in sixty different locations, often with various copies and theatres playing the movie within one multiplex.[6]

American big-budget blockbusters are usually released through one of the many local branches of US major studios. This is also the case in Belgium, where the local distribution market is traditionally dominated by major US companies such as United International Pictures. The various small local distribution firms mostly do not possess the necessary budgets, know-how and personnel to release such big event movies. In the case of *The Lord of the Rings*, however, it was surprising that New Line Cinema chose not to work with one of these US branches. Similar to what happened in the Netherlands, for instance, where A Film released the movies, they contracted a smaller, local distributor. Cinéart can be characterised as a small firm specialised in alternative, art-house movies, mostly non-American pictures. Cinéart's history as a left-wing, alternative distribution firm lies in distributing world cinema, art-house movies and directors such as Theo Angelopoulos, Pedro Almodóvar or Ken Loach. One of the reasons for choosing Cinéart was New Line Cinema's positive experience with Cinéart's successful release of somewhat more alternative US pictures such as *Magnolia* (Paul Thomas Anderson, 1999). For the release of *The Lord of the Rings*, Cinéart had to change its normal distribution strategies in terms of the number of copies, marketing and promotion budgets, or personnel, and they had to live through a tight scenario of detailed guidelines on how, where and when to promote and release the trilogy. This included a system of regular reports from the Brussels-based distributor to New Line Cinema's headquarters in the USA.

For Cinéart this meant a sea change in scheduling marketing, publicity or release strategies of the movies. Taking *The Return of the King* as a case study,

activity	2003						2004	
	July	August	September	October	November	December	January	February
previous films			launch DVD Two Towers					
publicity in theaters	teaser posters			final trailers		final posters		
advertising						standees, banners, postcards, lobby cards	billboards / tv spots ads in daily newspapers	relaunch (Academy Awards)
free media campaigns (preferential media partnerships)						publicity campaign tv & radio internet	world premiere European premiere LOTR trilogy party	pedagogical project schools (Ministery of Education)
promotional partnerships (brands)						Quick (international France): in-store campaign, Pepsi (internat onal): retail, in-store, ad campaign, sponsoring party, Microsoft: special screening event, Belgacom /Skynet: local LOTR website , ads		
promotional partnerships (tie-ins & special)					Electronic arts: games posters, add campaign, Fortis Bank contest agendas & calendars	print & TV media: free holidays to NZ, book editors, Warner music: soundtrack, posters		
marathon screenings						trilogy event party 13-12 Marathon 16-12		
merchandising						New Line, local benelux licensees		
press contacts						long lead junket NY, interview London International press junket & coverage, European premiere, Berlin newsletters		

Table 9: Marketing *The Return of the King* in Belgium

various stages can be identified (see Table 9).[7] While the movie received its world premiere on 17 December 2003, the poster campaign started as far back as July 2003, soon followed by the release of *The Two Towers* DVD. This first stage of (public) identification of the movie (July–September 2003) was followed by the wider proliferation (October–November 2003). In this period, Cinéart started to trailer the movies in theatres, while the first advertisements appeared, followed by the final posters, standees, banners and the release of the official Belgian *Return of the King* Internet site. In this period, we also witness the starting-point of the news flow, where news about the arrival of the movie was spread through the different media as a major media event, resulting in the first regular articles, radio spots and television reports in the mainstream media.

A third, decisive stage in building up the event around *The Return of the King* (December 2003) included a further interaction and intensification with the start of publicity campaigns using billboards in Belgian cities, television spots, an advertising campaign in the print media, as well as special public actions with preferential partners such as Quick Belgium (a local fast food chain) and Pepsi. A major public relations stunt in this period, attracting major news media coverage, consisted of a series of well-publicised marketing events such as an exclusive *Lord of the Rings* party, and several successful marathon screenings. In December, film reviewers and journalists were invited to press junkets and special screenings. This process of intensification only went into crescendo during the worldwide release week (mid-December 2003).

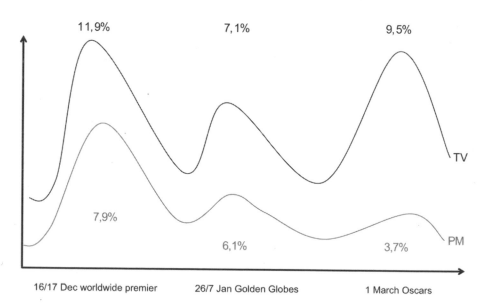

Table 10: Media coverage of *The Return of the King* in Belgium: three peaks in the news flows (television and print media)

Cinéart's marketing and publicity campaigns soon resulted into growing public attention and increasing media coverage (see Tables 9 and 10), including press which usually did not address film or popular culture. A first peak in this media coverage of *The Return of the King*'s release resulted into both a full-page advertising and news coverage, including in quality newspapers such as *De Morgen* (left-liberal) and *De Standaard* (leading conservative). The European (in Berlin) and local premieres also featured well on television, both in traditional news and gossip magazines, and even more on the public service broadcaster than on commercial channels. This first peak in the media attention was followed by a gradual extinction. What is interesting in this media attention for *The Return of the King* is that not one but three peaks can be observed. Besides the premiere in December, an additional peak appeared at the end of January 2004, with the Golden Globe Awards, followed by one in the beginning of March with the Academy Awards. This extended career was widely supported by Cinéart's additional efforts in terms of a re-launch of advertising and marketing, leading to a boost at the box office (8 million Euro) and the total attendance (1.25 million tickets).[8]

Overall, the patterns of the launch of *The Return of the King* indicate how Cinéart's and New Line Cinema's publicity and wider marketing strategies were successful in gradually building up media and public attention, leading to three peaks in terms of the amount of time and space spent on it by local news media. Closely following New Line Cinema's script, the local distributor used a wide arsenal of typical blockbuster means to obtain this attention and participation from partners – from specific distribution strategies and market saturation release, through multiple-level advertising, merchandising, tie-ins and press strategies, to the creation of marathons and other events.

A discursive aura of art, unicity, magnitude

Launching a movie involves more than just the use of traditional marketing and publicity techniques, of course. As we have already argued, it also includes a strong discursive play around the movie, as well as the producer/distributor's attempt to guide and set boundaries to these discourses (Austin 2002). This public discourse management reveals itself in many ways. The launch of the movies went hand in hand with the use of particular words and ideas in terms of genre, references to art and literature, or the creation of a certain horizon of expectation through particular actions. Through this, we argue, the producer and the distributor successfully created an aura-like discourse of unicity, historicity, art and magnitude around the *Lord of the Rings* movies.

From the very start, New Line Cinema tried to underline the trilogy was not just another blockbuster sequel. It was actively marketed as appealing to *middle-class blockbuster taste* as well as to the cultural repertoires mostly associated with *art-*

house film audiences. The Belgian and Dutch use of art-house-oriented distributors helped to underline this double strategy. Looking at Cinéart's marketing report for *The Return of the King,* it is clear that this orientation is part of the wider strategy. Advertising was not restricted to popular wide-audience media, but prominently included quality papers and magazines. The latter were also among the few preferential media partners, while the exclusive marathon was held in the '*most prestigious cinema*' (Cinéma Eldorado in Brussels; Cinéart 2004). This process of distinction (close to how Pierre Bourdieu used the term) was activated again in the re-launch of advertising at the occasion of the announcements and final ceremony around the Golden Globes and the Academy Awards.

An analysis of the Belgian media coverage indicates how *The Return of the King* received more attention in some of the quality newspapers than in the popular ones, while negative coverage was nearly absent (only three percent of all articles in the mainstream newspapers and magazines). One might speculate about the impact of advertising and preferential partnership on the editorial pages, but now that Cinéart distributed the movies, serious film critics and their media seemed to have followed the double repertoire of the movie as a blockbuster and a work of art. In other words, they inscribed themselves, willingly or not, in the discursive framework constructed by the industry and its marketing strategies. Most articles also focused upon the awards, which seemed to act as a legitimacy of *The Return of the King* as an art masterpiece. In advertising, press and other material *The Return of the King* was referred to not as a piece of fantasy, but rather in other generic terms such as an 'epos' ('epic') or a 'mythic legend'. There were also explicit references to other fields of the arts, literature and classical myths (for example, Tolkien as a serious writer with an immense impact on various generations; Peter Jackson as an 'auteur' with an 'oeuvre'; *The Lord of the Rings* as a 'magnum opus'). In this sense, the trilogy was discursively constructed as incomparable, a unique *project* with – we dare say – Wagnerian aspirations (indicated, for instance, by the re-creation of a closed, manicheistic world of fantasy with references to a mixture of mythical stories and biblical themes; technical and artistic grandeur; cyclical narrative). It is symptomatic that one marketing event, well featured in the press and underlining the unicity of *The Return of the King,* involved coverage of the extreme – and rather over the top – security measures when the first copy of *The Return of the King* came to Belgium.

Another feature illustrating the will to position the movie as something unique and different referred to how the distributor (and the producer in the USA) tried to construct the movie as a pedagogical tool. In Belgium, but also in other countries such as the United States, different initiatives were taken to attract the attention of schools, the Ministry of Education and their media outlets. This pedagogical project included the large-scale publicity support of national pedagogical outlets (edited by the Ministry of Education) exclusively reserved to teachers, parents and children. Cinéart succeeded in securing a contract with the official popular magazine for educators, *Klasse* (with a circulation of 1.2 million copies), to ensure coverage of the film in an educational context. Another marketing event was the organisation of a special 'Fantasy & Film' pedagogic day focusing on the *Lord of the Rings* trilogy, with private screenings for teachers in three main cities. In a special issue of *Klasse* for teachers, the educational potentials of the movie were explained, including the fascinating world of fairy tales, the fantasy genre and the world of Tolkien. The issue introduced ways of analysing these literary genres 'seriously', including references to approaches such as those of Vladimir Propp. It approached the *Lord of the Rings* trilogy as more than just a couple of movies, but rather as a fascinating adaptation of a twentieth-century classic literary milestone, written by a master of fantasy and fairy tales.

These examples indicate how distribution and marketing strategies were accompanied by a discursive play around the unique, historical character of the movie and the books. *The Return of the King* was presented as part of a unique, prestigious project referencing history, mythology and the wider world of the arts and (high) culture. These references should be seen as constituting a vague discursive play of words, creating a nebula or aura of connotations and expectations around the movie. This aura is less concrete than hard marketing figures and budgets, but important in allowing a cultural product such as a blockbuster to grow into a media event and, potentially, a societal event. The high coverage and the positive evaluation of the movie underline how the movie grew into a media event. Even elite or quality papers were only marginally critical to the blockbuster they would usually be more hostile to, and they even took over many of the ideas and words circulating around *The Return of the King*.

Metaphorical and wider use

To grow into societal events, blockbusters need to be discussed or referred to in wider forums, beyond their immediate relevance. This can take very different forms, such as direct references to the movie in public speeches or the metaphorical use of characters, themes or situations in the movie to discuss completely different public matters. This is only possible when the blockbuster has become a public good or part of public knowledge. It is also the domain where the movie discursively leaves its intrinsic field of action.

Looking at the Belgian case, it is clear that *The Return of the King* grew into such a societal event. In the quality newspaper *De Standaard*, for instance, more than 220 articles (published between the beginning of December 2003 and the start of 2004) mentioned the movies, most of them directly referring to the field of the movie itself (production, distribution, reviews, gossip, awards). But references to *The Lord of the Rings* were also abundant in unexpected circumstances. The movie was discussed in relation to concerts by Howard Shore, the boost of tourism in New Zealand, articles on science and technology, on changes in the local censorship system as well as on politics (for example John Rhys-Davies' support for the British National Party).

Another illustration of how global cultural products such as *The Lord of the Rings* can be part of a wider field of common knowledge and reference lies in a metaphorical use. The President of the International Olympic Committee, Belgian Jacques Rogge, was nicknamed the 'Lord of the Rings', not only for his executive post in the field of sports, but also because he developed a hard policy for clean sports. There was a strong enough assumption of a wide knowledge of the world of *The Lord of the Rings* to invite a connotation with Rogge's explicit profile as the hard fighter against the use of doping in sports. Another example deals with a public speech delivered by one of the most controversial politicians in the country, Filip Dewinter, the main spokesman of the extreme right-wing, nationalist party Vlaams Blok (which since its conviction for racism changed its name into Vlaams Belang). In a climactic moment of a public speech for party members, in the midst of an electoral campaign he shouted the quote: 'Stand, men of the west, and fight!' News reporters will choose such a quote, of course, given its topicality, and it thus becomes part of an ongoing societal event. This is yet another, extreme, example, illustrating how the movie, with its ideas, sentences, characters, themes, inspired a wide public domain and started to live a life on its own.

Conclusion

One way of defining blockbusters is that they are *event movies*. What this really means is not very clear. Referring to the changing motion-picture experience from the 1950s onwards, it often referred to high-budgeted, spectacular movies that try to create a special (marketing) event in order to draw the spectator back into the movie theatre. In this chapter we have indicated how movies such as *The Lord of the Rings* can become something more, and rise to a higher level of event, from a media to a societal event. We have also underlined that events deal with different dimensions of globalised popular media culture: the movie business, meaning and experiences. Events allow cultural industrial products such as blockbusters to grow into something more than the art of making a marketing event out of a movie.

Concentrating on the launch of the third *Lord of the Rings* movie, *The Return of the King*, we have also argued that even in the case of a media and societal event we should take into account the constructed character of it, or the producer's skills in terms of orchestrating an event around the movie(s). This includes the attempts to set in motion a snowball effect of attention, carefully trying to keep control over the discourses surrounding it. This is not to say, of course, that the tremendous financial, box office and audience success of blockbusters such as *The Lord of the Rings* is completely reducible to marketing, publicity or the industry's professional skills in creating events. Many authors have been looking at textual, aesthetic or technical features of this extraordinary picture, or at the audience and wider societal reception of it. These various analyses of the blockbuster phenomenon, however crucial they remain, should not overlook a critical political economy approach towards the discursive power of the Hollywood marketing machine. This includes the power to *create* events (what we see as a connecting issue), and through these events eventually *guide* expectations, reception and imagination.

Notes

1   See: www.boxofficemojo.com/alltime/world.
2   See for instance the advertising and marketing literature on how to organise successfully a media event, http://advertising.about.com/od/publicrelationsresources/a/handlemedia.htm.
3   In their standard work *Media Events* (1992), Daniel Dayan and Elihu Katz mainly concentrate upon the role of television in creating events. They define different types and dimensions, one of them being major televised ceremonial events (such as royal weddings). Dayan and Katz look at media events mainly as non-routine breaking news, disrupting social life.
4   We cannot go into details here, but the issue of *events* and *media events* poach on other territories such as the one of *media scandals* (Lull & Hinerman 1997; McLean & Cook 2001), *moral panics* (Cohen 1980; Thompson 1998; Biltereyst 2004), *media controversy* (de Young 2002) or *media hype* (Vasterman 2000).
5   This analysis is based on the research project 'The Export of Fantasy: The Lord of the Rings, global film culture and blockbusters' (2004–5, BOF, Ghent University Research fund). This research project combines a political-economic analysis of the distribution, marketing and exhibition of *The Return of the King*, with a discourse analysis of the press and media coverage in Belgium and a wide-ranging audience and reception analysis of the movie. In this chapter we rely upon the political-economy part of the project as well as on media coverage analysis. The research was also developed as part of the 'International Lord of the Rings Research Project', supported by a grant from the UK Economic and Social Research Council (ESRC Grant No. 000-22-0323) to whom we record our gratitude.
6   Information based on an interview with Mrs Chantal Moens (Cinéart), December 2003, upon Cinéart's marketing report (Cinéart 2004), and upon an email from Moens 24 January 2005.
7   The following analysis of different stages in the launch and public reception of *The Return of the King* is inspired by Peter Vasterman's (2004) work on media hypes.
8   Email correspondence by Chantal Moens (Cinéart), 24 January 2005.

Works cited

Austin, T. (2002) *Hollywood, Hype and Audiences*. Manchester: Manchester University Press.

Belton, J. (1994) *American Cinema/American Culture*. New York: McGraw-Hill.

Biltereyst, D. (2004) 'Reality TV, troublesome pictures and panics', in S. Holmes and D. Jermyn (eds) *Understanding Reality TV*. London: Routledge, 91–110.

Blanchet, R. (2003) *Blockbuster. Ästhetik, Ökonomie und Geschichte des Postklassischen Hollywoodkinos*. Marburg: Schüren.

Bordwell, D. (2002) 'Intensified Continuity: Visual Style in Contemporary American Film', *Film Quarterly* 55, 3, 16–28.

Buckland, W. (2003) 'The Role of the Auteur in the Age of the Blockbuster: Steven Spielberg and DreamWorks', in J. Stringer (ed.) *Movie Blockbusters*. London: Routledge, 84–98.

Cinéart (2004) *Return of the King: Marketing Report Belgium*.

Cohen, S. (1980) *Folk Devils and Moral Panics: The Creation of the Mods and Rockers*. Oxford: Martin Robertson.

Danan, M. (1995) 'Marketing the Hollywood blockbuster in France', *Journal of Popular Film and Television*, 23, 3, 131–41.

Dayan, D. and E. Katz (1992) *Media Events: The Live Broadcasting of History*. Harvard: Harvard University Press.

de Young, M. (2002) *The Ritual Abuse Controversy*. Jefferson: McFarland.

Elsaesser, T. (2000) 'De blockbuster als motor van de hedendaagse mediacultuur', in T. Elsaesser and P. Hesselberth (eds) *Hollywood op straat*. Amsterdam: Amsterdam University Press, 27–44.

_____ (2001) 'The Blockbuster: Everything Connects, but not Anything Goes', in J. Lewis (ed.) *The End of Cinema as We Know It: American Film in the Nineties*. New York: New York University Press, 11–22.

Fiske, J. (1996) *Media Matters: Race and Gender in U.S. Politics*. Minneapolis: University of Minnesota Press.

Gillis, S. (2005) *The Matrix Trilogy: Cyberpunk Reloaded*. London: Wallflower Press.

Gomery, D. (1998) 'Hollywood Corporate Business Practice and Periodizing Contemporary Film History', in S. Neale and M. Smith (eds) *Contemporary Hollywood Cinema*. London: Routledge, 47–57.

King, G. (2000) *Spectacular Narratives: Hollywood in the Age of the Blockbuster*. London: I.B. Tauris/New York: St Martin's Press.

Krämer, P. (1998) 'Would You Take Your Child to See This Film? The Cultural and Social Work of the Family-oriented Movie', in S. Neale and M. Smith (eds) *Contemporary Hollywood Cinema*. London: Routledge, 294–311.

_____ (2001) *The Big Picture: Hollywood Cinema from Star Wars to Titanic*. London: British Film Institute.

Lewis, J. (ed.) (2001) *The End of Cinema as We Know It: American Film in the Nineties*. New York: New York University Press.

_____ (2003) 'Following the Money in America's Sunniest Company Town', in J. Stringer (ed.) *Movie Blockbusters*. London: Routledge, 61–71.

Lubin, D. M. (1999) *Titanic*. London: British Film Institute.

Lull, J. and S. Hinerman (eds) (1997) *Media Scandals*. New York: Columbia University Press.

Maltby, R. (1998) 'Nobody knows everything: Post-classical historiographies and consolidated entertainment', in S. Neale and M. Smith (eds) *Contemporary Hollywood Cinema*. London: Routledge, 21–44.

McLean, A. L. and D. A. Cook (eds) (2001) *Headline Hollywood: A Century of Film Scandal*. New Brunswick: Rutgers University Press.

Meers, P. (2004) 'It's the language of film!': Young Film Audiences on Hollywood', in M. Stokes and R. Maltby (eds) *Hollywood Abroad: Audiences and Cultural Exchange*, London: British Film Institute, 158–75.

Miller, T., N. Govil, J. McMurria and R. Maxwell (2001) *Global Hollywood*. London: British Film Institute.

Neale, S. and M. Smith (eds) (1998) *Contemporary Hollywood Cinema*. London: Routledge.

Roberts, G. (2003) 'Circulations of Taste: *Titanic*, the Oscars and the middle-brow', in J. Stringer (ed.) *Movie Blockbusters*. London: Routledge, 155–65.

Sandler, K. S. and G. Studlar (1999) *Titanic: Anatomy of a Blockbuster*. New Brunswick: Rutgers University Press.

Schatz, T. (1993) 'The New Hollywood', in J. Collins, H. Radner and A. P. Collins (eds) *Film Theory Goes to the Movies*. London: Routledge.

Thompson, K. (1998) *Moral Panics*. London: Routledge.

Thompson, Kr. (1999) *Storytelling in the New Hollywood*. Cambridge, MA: Harvard University Press.

Stringer, J. (ed.) (2003) *Movie Blockbuster*. London: Routledge.

Vasterman, P. (2000) 'Dynamiek van de mediahypes', *Tijdschrift voor Communicatiewetenschap*, 28, 1, 2–25.

Wasko, J. (2003) *How Hollywood Works*. London: Sage.

Wyatt, J. (1994) *High Concept: Movies and Marketing in Hollywood*. Austin: University of Texas Press.

Following the Money: *The Lord of the Rings* and the Culture of Box Office Figures

Warren Buckland and Christopher Long[1]

Nobody can truly participate in the motion picture business without looking at numbers of all kinds, and especially those numbers which represent the collective and comparative decisions of paying customers. Box office grosses must be looked at constantly – on almost EVERY film, on almost EVERY day. Far from being mere numbers, box office grosses represent the responses of PEOPLE to films. To ignore those numbers – and those people – is to risk business failure and – worse – to inhabit the catatonic world of the compulsive aesthete. (A. D. Murphy, quoted in Hayes & Bing 2004: 291)

Introduction

Movies offer highly variable income to their financial backers. Bank-rolling movies is a high-risk strategy – especially now, after the demise of the classical Hollywood studio system whose vertical integration stabilised risk by ensuring an outlet for its films. The divorcement of theatres from the major studios, plus the outlawing of blind-selling and block-booking, means that each individual film takes on more importance for it has to be sold to exhibitors on its own merits. Production values of each film have increased, and the differentiation (primarily through stars, directors and special effects) of films from each other has intensified.

These industrial and economic changes functioned as incentives to the rise of blockbusters in the film industry. Economists comment that 'the growing emphasis on blockbusters reflects a rational adaptation by risk adverse firms to changing market conditions' (Garvin 1981: 2). Blockbusters are formulaic because they adopt the same types of risk adverse self-insurance: they rely on pre-sold elements (such as a successful novel or comic); they look back to and continually borrow from classical Hollywood and its genres (creating a neo-classical form of filmmaking); they employ well-known performers who play characters embodying simple, clear-cut moral values; and there is a predominance of elements of spectacle and special effects.

Box office figures were a specialised short-term economic indicator of a film's performance in the marketplace for studio executives seeking confirmation of their risk adverse strategies. In the twenty-first century, however, box office figures have become a national obsession (see Hayes & Bing 2004). Yet these figures enter the mainstream in the form of a sound bite, usually a new release's final weekend gross – a single variable taken out of context. We demonstrate below that multiple variables are involved in the data mining of box office figures. We offer a straightforward outline of ten of the most significant variables, before applying them to *The Lord of the Rings: The Fellowship of the Ring* (2001).

How to read a film's box office figures: a ten-step process

1. Opening weekend – One of the most visible aspects of box office figures is of course a film's performance on its opening weekend. Most mainstream films now have a saturated (or wide) release, as opposed to a platform (or tailored) release. As Arthur De Vany writes: 'A wide release on many screens draws a large, simultaneous sample in many theaters and cities. A tailored release strategy samples sequentially, starting at a few theaters and using the information from that sample to adjust bookings if the film builds an audience' (2004: 13). At the end of the year, some Academy Award contenders are given a platform release and a saturation release later in the New Year. (Simply by being released on a few screens in December, the film can then qualify for Academy Award nomination; it is then 'properly' released in January.) In terms of the split in the takings between studio and exhibitor, the rule of thumb is that it is evenly split 50/50. However, the studio takes the biggest percentage of the box office in the opening weeks (around 90%), before the percentages even out in the following weeks. This is beneficial to the studio because the exhibitor only earns a bigger percentage of the taking if it keeps the film on screens for a long time, which keeps the studio's product in the marketplace. Exhibitors are also contractually obliged to show a film for a minimum of four weeks. According to De Vany 'the contract to exhibit a film usually requires the theater to show it for a minimum number of weeks; 4 weeks is a common minimum, although 6 and 8 week minimums are sometimes used. In addition, the contract contains a hold-over clause that requires the theater to continue exhibiting the film another week if the previous week's box office revenue exceeds a stipulated amount' (2004: 14). The law of diminishing returns also plays a role in determining when a film will be pulled from the screens, since the exhibitor will calculate when it can earn more money from a new release (even though its percentage of the takings is much lower) than from keeping an old release on its screens.

2. Full week – The industry trade journals *Variety* and *Hollywood Reporter* (as well as numerous websites) list the weekend box office figures and the full week figures (which they obtain from Nielsen EDI, the film industry's ultimate source

for box office figures). Even a quick glance at these figures reveals that about 80% of a film's weekly revenue derives from the three-day weekend (Friday to Sunday night).

3. Number of engagements/screens – This number simply indicates how many theatres the film is being shown in. A film can be released in just one theatre or 3,000 (the normal number for the release of a blockbuster in the United States). Number of engagements is distinct from the actual number of screens a film is shown on, because the same theatre may show the film on more than one screen. For example, *Spider-Man* (Sam Raimi, 2002) opened in 3,672 engagements but on 7,500 screens – an average of two screens per theatre in its opening week. Raw box office figures by themselves are not a good indication of a film's success; success also depends on how many theatres show it and on how many screens. A film may have accumulated what seems to be a large box office for the week, but this may simply be because it appears in thousands of theatres, and each one may be half empty. One of the best indications of a film's success is therefore to consider the following category.

4. Week's average $ per engagement – By dividing the full week's box office by the number of engagements, one ends up with the week's average takings per engagement (per theatre). This is the best indication of a film's success because the figures are ratios, not raw numbers; ratios create averages that can be compared fairly: the average amount of money a film takes per theatre per week is a criterion that applies to any film, whether showing on one screen or 3,000. Of course, a popular film released in a few theatres will restrict supply and therefore increase demand, thereby artificially inflating the week's average per engagement. *The Royal Tenenbaums* (Wes Anderson, 2001) opened at just five engagements on its first weekend, generating $276,981 or a per engagement average of $55,400.

5. Percentage change in box office – Opening weekend box office figures are only one indication of a new film's success. Another indication is the percentage change in box office from the opening weekend to the second weekend (and, less importantly, the second weekend to the third, and so on). Most films fall steadily from week to week. If the number of engagements remains the same, a 40% fall from week 1 to week 2 is normal. A smaller drop is unusual. A drop of over 60% spells failure and is caused by bad word-of-mouth. (The box office of *The Hulk* (Ang Lee, 2003) dropped 70%, while *Gigli* (Martin Brest, 2003) holds the record with a drop of 82% from week 1 to 2.) An increase in box office is exceptional (unless the film is released in a substantially larger number of theatres in the second week). The success of *Titanic* (James Cameron, 1997) was evident primarily in its second week, since it achieved the almost impossible of actually increasing its box office from week 1 to 2 without an appreciable increase in the number of theatres. In its opening weekend, the film did well, making $28.64million from 2,674 engagements, generating an explosive average of $10,710 per engagement.

(However, this was not good news to Twentieth Century Fox and Paramount, the two studios that financed the film for almost $200million, for these figures suggested that the film would never go into profit.) In its second week, *Titanic's* box office *increased* 24% to $35.45 million, an average of $13,078 per engagement. It finished with a domestic box office of $601million.[2] Increasingly, the relation between the opening Friday night and Saturday night box office is scrutinised to determine if a film will be successful or not. An increase of around 20% is not exceptional (since Saturday night is the busiest night for cinema going). If the figure actually drops from the opening Friday to Saturday, the film is considered to be box office poison.

6. Number of weeks in release, at number one, and in the top ten – Saturation releases reap most of their box office in the opening few weeks (some say in the opening weekend). A platform release will take months to make the same amount of money. A saturation release will also have expensive saturation advertising, which cannot be maintained over many months. The trend is towards intensification: extracting all the box office takings in a shorter number of weeks (preferably at number one for at least a week), achieved through the super-saturation release of blockbusters (over 4,000 theatres), accompanied by heavy advertising. The distributors of blockbusters attempt to achieve a huge opening weekend, preferably at number one in the box office charts, and hope that word of mouth keeps the film in the top ten. However, few films stay in the marketplace for more than six weeks. De Vany argues that 'a film has less than a 25% chance of lasting 7 weeks and less than 15% chance of lasting more than 10 weeks' (2004: 7).

7. Domestic, foreign and worldwide box office cumulative – A film's worldwide accumulative box office is simply the total amount of money it makes in the United States (domestic) and overseas (foreign) markets. Some blockbusters that only gain an average or mediocre domestic box office make huge sums overseas. For example, Steven Spielberg's *A.I.: Artificial Intelligence* (2001) made only $78million in the United States but collected $158million overseas. Also, Tom Cruise's films receive far more overseas than domestic box office. For example, *The Last Samurai* (Edward Zwick, 2003) accumulated $110.1million at the United States box office but over $310.5million in foreign box office.

8. Ratio between opening weekend box office and final box office – How much of the final box office is collected in the first weekend? This measures a film's durability, or its staying power in the marketplace. A low ratio indicates that a film collected most of its box office in its first few weeks and then disappeared, whereas a high ratio suggests it 'had legs' and stayed in the theatres for several weeks or months. *Titanic*, for example, made just 5% of its final box office in its opening weekend when 20% is considered good. It therefore had an enormous staying power in theatres. Gitesh Pandya writes, concerning this ratio: 'Recent live-action hits like *Elf* [Jon Favreau, 2003], *The Santa Clause 2* [Michael Lembeck 2002] and

How the Grinch Stole Christmas [Ron Howard 2000] all bowed in November and reached final totals that were five times their openings. Of course there have also been expensive kid-oriented duds like *The Cat in the Hat* [Bo Welch, 2003] which went on to gross less than three times its opening'.[3]

9. Time taken to reach $100million mark – How long does it take for a film to reach the industry's magical $100million mark? In a 2004 issue of *Variety*, data from Nielsen EDI is quoted for the average days needed to reach $100million between 1998 and 2003. Firstly, the article lists the number of films that achieved it within 10 days: in 1998, no films achieved this feat; in 1999, 2; 2000, 4; 2001, 9; 2002, 9; 2003, 8. (Anon. 2004: 16). Next is listed the fastest and slowest of each year to reach $100million. In 2002, for example, *My Big Fat Greek Wedding* (Joel Zwick, 2002) took 148 days, whereas *Spider-Man* took a mere three days, thereby creating a new phenomenon: the $100million opening weekend. Of course, with the yearly rise in ticket prices it becomes easier for a film to reach the $100million mark: more recent films can achieve this feat by selling fewer (but more expensive) tickets. Comparing dollar earnings therefore needs to take inflation into account. A more objective measure of a film's success is to consider how many tickets it sold.

10. Ratio between box office and budget – What is the ratio between the film's box office takings and its budget? A film's success is not merely measurable according to its box office; instead, a more accurate measure of its profitability is to calculate the ratio between takings and budget. *The Blair Witch Project* (Daniel Myrick and Eduardo Sanchez, 1999) represents the most successful film in this respect: the film grossed $140.5million at the US box office with a budget of $37,000 (excluding marketing costs).

These ten variables represent only the beginnings of box office data mining. They are nonetheless a significant advance on the media's superficial engagement with box office figures, and begin to illustrate A. D. Murphy's argument that box office figures are not mere numbers, but offer a concise and condensed representation of the audience's behaviour patterns. Other variables indicating box office success go beyond the study of one film. We can discover trends and identify how much the entire top ten earned; or chart the box office success of each studio per week or per year; or study the rise and fall of the box office attraction of stars, or the influence of Golden Globe and Academcy Award nominations/wins on a film's box office (a film that wins an Academcy Award can expect a 30% increase in its box office, for example). In the following section, however, we shall examine the box office of *The Fellowship of the Ring* using the ten criteria outlined above.

The box office profile of *The Fellowship of the Ring*

The Fellowship of the Ring was an even riskier undertaking than the typical contemporary blockbuster. The film was financed by New Line, a quasi-independent unit of AOL Time Warner which did not possess the same marketing muscle and financial resources as its parent company. *The Fellowship of the Ring*, with a production budget of $109million, was a daunting project for the studio, one that could potentially cripple them. A *Variety* article published a month prior to *The Fellowship of the Ring*'s release observed that: 'New Line has embarked on this project of unprecedented size and ambition at the exact moment that the company itself is most vulnerable' (Harris & Dawtrey 2001).

Furthermore, the film featured no big name stars and was helmed by unproven New Zealand director Peter Jackson, whose previous box office best was 1996's *The Frighteners* which grossed a modest $16.7million.[4] Though the film was based on the highly acclaimed and widely read novels, there was no guarantee the audience for the Tolkien books, supposedly much older and diverse than the pre-delivered youth audience for 2001's prior smash hit *Harry Potter and the Philosopher's Stone* would be eager to attend the film. *The Fellowship of the Ring* relied heavily on its appeal both as an adventure film and as a special-effects extravaganza.

Running Total	Engage-ments	Weekend in Box Office	Change Total	Weekly Total
Week 0 $27,917,978	3359	N/A	N/A	$27,917,978
Week 1 $117,166,830	3359	$47,211,490	N/A	$89,248,852
Week 2 $182,503,422	3359	$38,695,582	-18%	$65,336,592
Week 3 $212,119,615	3381	$23,006,447	-40.5%	$29,616,193
Week 4 $232,944,803	3381	$16,201,260	-29.6%	$20,825,188
Week 5 $250,646,197	3266	$12,473,748	-23%	$17,701,394
Week 6 $260,569,940	2703	$7,803,075	-37.4%	$9,923,743
Week 7 $267,798,522	2309	$5,704,259	-27%	$7,228,582
Week 8 $272,933,520	1706	$3,618,397	-36.6%	$5,134,998
Week 9 $279,733,224	1507	$4,701,851	+30%	$6,799,704
Week 10 $284,255,274	1510	$3,457,862	-26.5%	$4,522,050

Total Worldwide: $867.7million

Table 11: **Domestic box office figures for** *The Fellowship of the Ring*
Source: http://www.boxofficemojo.com/movies

A box office analysis of *The Fellowship of the Ring* is somewhat complicated by the fact that New Line chose to open the film on 19 December 2001, a Wednesday rather than the more typical Friday opening for most feature films. New Line opened *The Fellowship of the Ring* in 3,359 theatres, a considerable number, which qualifies it as a saturation release, though the count was not as high as that for several other blockbusters. *Harry Potter and the Philosopher's Stone*, for example, had opened in a staggering 3,672 theatres, reflecting a greater degree of certainty in the film's prospects relative to the riskier *The Fellowship of the Ring*. However, New Line's saturation release was proven justified as the film grossed $47.2million for its opening three-day weekend, then a record for a December opening (a record that has since been eclipsed by both other *Lord of the Rings* films, *The Two Towers* and *The Return of the King*). The film garnered a total of $75.1million for the opening five-day period. (See Table 11, above, for all the box office figures of *The Fellowship of the Ring*.)

The Fellowship of the Ring also held up admirably throughout its entire first week of release raking in a seven-day total of $89.2million.[5] The film's opening weekend total was therefore only 53% of its weekly take, an unusually low percentage which partially reflects the film's enduring strength, but can also largely be attributed to the fact that the first full week coincided with the Christmas holidays. There is no simple rubric which can be applied across the board to all films in a box office analysis system; specific factors such as seasonality must always be taken into account. Films released around major holidays will perform differently than films released at other times.

The raw totals, as impressive as they are, do not tell the entire story. An equally important measure is *The Fellowship of the Ring*'s performance on a per engagement basis. By this measure, *The Fellowship of the Ring* once again rates as an astounding success. The film averaged $14,055 per theatre during its opening weekend, despite the fact that audience members already had the opportunity to see it for two days prior to the weekend. Such a figure is unusual for a film opening in so many theatres, suggesting that even the considerable supply (the number of engagements) was easily matched by the demand. For the full opening week, *The Fellowship of the Ring* averaged $26,570 per engagement, a number that certainly pleased the New Line executives and alleviated any lingering doubts they had over their unprecedented risk.

The opening weekend is only the first step, though an increasingly important one in contemporary Hollywood, in determining a film's success. The film also needs to prove that it 'has legs', that it can sustain business by producing strong word of mouth and continuing to generate audience excitement even when it is no longer a brand new product. One of the best measures of this success is the percentage drop in box office from opening weekend to the second weekend. *The Fellowship of the Ring* fared exceptionally well on this front, losing only 18% in its second weekend, when it drew an additional $38.7million in revenues. If a

40% drop is generally considered normal, *The Fellowship of the Ring* beat that level easily. Once again, the figure is somewhat skewed by the holiday season; the second weekend fell between Christmas and New Year's Day. However, considering that *The Fellowship of the Ring*'s opening weekend was a then December record, the performance was still indicative of the film's considerable staying power. In fact, *The Fellowship of the Ring*'s second weekend of release placed second all-time for December weekend performances. The second weekend figures were so encouraging that New Line actually expanded the film's release by a handful of theatres, increasing the number of engagements from 3,359 to 3,381 for Week Three and Week Four. Even a modest expansion from a saturation release is relatively unusual and reflected the studio's belief in the film's continuing strength.

As a result of its remarkable opening and its subsequent strength, *The Fellowship of the Ring* reached the $100million mark in only eight days of release. At the time, only four films had reached the century mark faster. By February 2005, *The Fellowship of the Ring* was tied at 19th with nine of the ten fastest films to $100million having been released from 2002–04.[6] Perhaps no other measure more aptly demonstrates the industry's trend towards intensification: extracting as much revenue as possible in the earliest days of a film's release.

The Fellowship of the Ring's strong 'legs' can also be measured by the number of weeks the film remained in release, as well as the number of weeks it held onto the number one spot or remained in the top ten. *The Fellowship of the Ring* remained the top grossing domestic film for four weeks, an unusually long run in today's marketplace. Once again, however, we must take seasonality into account. Unlike summer blockbusters such as *Spider-Man*, *The Fellowship of the Ring* did not have to compete with weekly blockbuster releases. January is generally a tepid month for box office receipts, and *The Fellowship of the Ring* had the blockbuster market all to itself. Its only major rivals during its first four weeks of release were the Academy Award-winning drama *A Beautiful Mind* (Ron Howard, 2001) and *Orange County* (Lawrence Kasdan 2002), a comedy. *The Fellowship of the Ring* was eventually unseated in Week Five by the first major action release of 2002, Ridley Scott's *Black Hawk Down*. Nonetheless, *The Fellowship of the Ring*'s four-week run atop the charts was an unqualified success and a testament to the film's enduring drawing power. The film did not drop out of the top ten in the weekly charts until Week Seven of release. New Line also kept *The Fellowship of the Ring* in release for 35 weeks, an unusually long release. However, the film was only playing in a handful of theatres by then; perhaps a more relevant measure is that *The Fellowship of the Ring*'s theatre count did not drop below 1,000 until Week 16 of release, still a lengthy run. By any standard, *The Fellowship of the Ring* was no flash-in-the-pan or opening-week wonder.

New Line's gamble paid off quite handsomely. *The Fellowship of the Ring* finished with a total domestic gross of $314.8million,[7] ranking it 15th all-time among American films.[8] The domestic take, however, was dwarfed by the film's performance in foreign markets. New Line lacked an international distribution arm and was forced to rely on a 'guerilla campaign' of sorts which involved reliance on a network of independent distributors across the globe carefully organized through painstaking personal attention by the studio. *Variety* described the strategy as 'a handcrafted approach to marketing that would be impossible for a studio to achieve' (Harris & Dawtrey 2001). This risky approach succeeded, as *The Fellowship of the Ring* amassed $552.9million in the overseas markets, meaning that a full 63.7% of its worldwide gross of $867.7million, the ninth-highest all-time, as of February 2005, derived from its foreign revenues. At the time, this percentage was exceeded only by *Harry Potter and the Philosopher's Stone* (67.5%) and *Titanic* (67.3%) among the top fifty grossing films of all-time. Since then, such a figure has become somewhat more common, reflecting the growing importance of foreign markets in blockbuster marketing plans. In 2004, for example, *The Day After Tomorrow* (Roland Emmerich), 29th all-time worldwide, earned 65.6% of its gross in foreign markets while *Troy* (Wolfgang Petersen), 35th all-time, drew 73.2% of its revenues overseas. Even more impressive from New Line's perspective, *The Fellowship of the Ring*'s worldwide total of $867.7million places ninth all-time, but only third in the *Lord of the Rings* franchise; *The Two Towers* ranks fifth with $924million and *The Return of the King* places second, joining *Titanic* as the only billion-dollar films with a worldwide total of $1.12billion.

The ratio between a film's opening weekend box office and its final box office can also be utilised to evaluate its performance. *The Fellowship of the Ring*'s opening weekend accounted for 15% of its final domestic take. When we understand that the film set a December record for an opening weekend, we get a better perspective on just how impressive the film's staying power really was. Despite a record opening, the film held enough appeal to earn nearly seven times its opening weekend take. Generally, a 20% ratio is considered good; *The Fellowship of the Ring* exceeded even that standard. It should be noted that the figure may be skewed somewhat by the fact that the film opened on a Wednesday, thus siphoning some of the potential revenue from the three-day period of the opening weekend. This ratio provides further evidence that *The Fellowship of the Ring* had both the power to open big and had strong 'legs', a dream combination for any studio.

If Hollywood is a bottom-line business then it is obviously important to look beyond the gross revenues to a measure of profitability. One such measure is the ratio between a film's final box office to its production budget. Such a measure is only intended as a rough estimate of profitability; most notably, it does not include marketing costs, which can often equal or even exceed a film's production budget. Generally, however, a film is considered profitable if its gross exceeds 2.5 times the production budget. With an estimated production budget of $109million, *The Fellowship of the Ring* grossed 2.9 times its costs in domestic revenues alone and pulled in nearly eight times its production budget in worldwide gross. Of course, the ratio is only one measure; absolute profit is another, and one that is of greater interest to the studios. A film that earns $10million on a $1million budget will have the same ratio as a film that earns $100million on a $10million budget, but the latter will impact the studio's profits to a much greater extent. *The Fellowship of the Ring* earned $758 million more in revenue than it cost to produce.

Conclusion

The Fellowship of the Ring's extraordinary success alleviated any concerns that New Line had about this potentially risky blockbuster. The studio pursued a similar but even more aggressive release strategy with the following two *Lord of the Rings* films, experiencing increasing box office success with each installment. All three films were released domestically in December, each on the Wednesday of the last full week before Christmas. *The Two Towers* opened in 3,622 theatres and *The Return of the King* bowed in 3,703 theatres, making *The Fellowship of the Ring's* 3,359 theatre opening seem relatively modest by comparison. Each film set a new all-time December record for a three-day opening weekend; *The Two Towers* grossed $62million and *The Return of the King* grossed $72.6million. As of February 2005, the three films held the top five all-time December weekend performances among them.[9] *The Two Towers* grossed $341.8million domestically and $924.3million worldwide while *The Return of the King* grossed $377million domestically and a staggering $1.12billion worldwide. The most impressive testament to the overwhelming success of the franchise is that, as of February 2005, *The Return of the King*, *The Two Towers* and *The Fellowship of the Ring* occupied the 2nd, 4th and 9th spots, respectively, in all-time worldwide gross.[10]

This analysis only explores several of many potential possibilities for box office data mining. For example, overseas box office figures have only been analysed as a whole, but closer study based on weekly and regional performances would yield a more nuanced understanding of this increasingly significant aspect of the Hollywood blockbuster strategy. The analysis also focuses exclusively on theatrical performance, and considers dollar earnings, not ticket sales. Yet in the last several years, DVD rentals and sales have become increasingly lucrative and, in many cases, substantially augment a film's financial performance. DVD sales figures are not always as readily available to the public as box office figures. Studios still control the official releases of these numbers, though other unofficial estimates often exist. New Line did not release official sales figures for the *Lord of the Rings* DVDs. But successful releases sell millions of copies in their first week of release. *Finding Nemo* (Andrew Stanton and Lee Unkrich 2003) for example, sold 13.5million DVDs in just its first week.[11] Once reliable figures for DVD sales are regularly provided, they should be incorporated into any complete analysis of a blockbuster's financial performance.

Notes

1 We wish to thank Peter Krämer, Alison McMahan and Yannis Tzioumakis for their comments on previous drafts of this chapter.
2 All figures from http://www.boxofficeguru.com/.htm (accessed 1 February 2005).
3 Gitesh Pandya, http://www.boxofficeguru.com/11154.htm (accessed 1 February 2005).
4 www.boxofficemojo.com/directors/peterjackson (accessed 9 February 2005).
5 To be consistent with typical releases, Week 1 runs from Friday 21 December to Thursday 27 December, thus excluding the first two days of release, herein referred to as Week 0.
6 www.the-numbers.com/movies/records/Fastest100.html (accessed 9 February 2005).
7 This total includes the film's re-release in December 2003 prior to the release of the series' final installment, *The Return of the King*. *The Fellowship of the Ring* earned $313.4million in its initial domestic run, and an additional $1.4million in its two-week re-release.
8 All figures in this chapter refer to all-time rankings current as of 9 February 2005.
9 http://www.the-numbers.com/movies/record/month12 (accessed 9 February 2005).
10 http://www.boxofficemojo.com/alltime/world (accessed 9 February 2005).
11 http://www.the-numbers.com/movies/2003/FNEMO.php (accessed 9 February 2005).

Works cited

Anon. (2004) '$100 mil pix leg it out', *Variety*, 26 January–1 February, 16.

De Vany, A. (2004) *Hollywood Economics: How Extreme Uncertainty Shapes the Film Industry*. New York: Routledge.

Garvin, D. (1981) 'Blockbusters: The Economics of Mass Entertainment', *Journal of Cultural Economics*, 5, 1–20.

Harris, D. and A. Dawtrey (2001) 'Can B.O. Postman Ring Twice?', *Variety*, 27 November. Available at http://print.google.com/print/doc?articleid=g60pG45iSF (accessed 9 February 2005).

Hayes, D. and J. Bing (2004) *Open Wide: How Hollywood Box Office Became a National Obsession*. New York: Miramax Books.

Pandya, G. (2005) http://www.boxofficeguru.com/111504.htm (accessed 1 February 2005).

SECTION 2
PUBLIC RECEPTIONS

'Wellywood' and Peter Jackson: The Local Reception of *The Lord of the Rings* in Wellington, New Zealand

Davinia Thornley

Introduction

In late 1998 when Peter Jackson landed the contract for a trilogy of films based on *The Lord of the Rings*, it was hardly surprising that media reports waxed ecstatic. In August when the news was made public, the *Dominion* headline ran 'Jackson Scores the Holy Grail of Cinema' (Houlahan 1998a: 11). In December of that year, Mike Houlahan also wrote: 'It was the biggest story in New Zealand film this year. Scratch that: the revelation ... was the biggest New Zealand film news of any year' (1998b: 12). *The Evening Post* crowed about the 'colossus' *Lord of the Rings* employing five production units full time, stating 'even the smallest will have the crew of a low-budget New Zealand film' (Anon. 1998b: 40). Over a year later the buzz had not abated, according to international accounts. *The Los Angeles Times* quoted Wellington's mayor, Mark Blumsky, saying: 'My city's buzzing. We've got hobbits walking down the main street of Wellington' (quoted in Accinelli 2000: 10). By the beginning of 2001 David Cohen, *The Guardian London*'s correspondent in New Zealand, chose to focus on the city's economic gains, citing a 'multi-million dollar boom to New Zealand's capital' (2001: 16).

This chapter examines the specific reception of and opinions on *The Lord of the Rings* in one particular New Zealand location: Wellington. New Zealand's population numbers a little under four million. Wellington, New Zealand's capital city, has a population of less than half a million. Into this sheltered environment dropped *The Lord of the Rings*, a film bankrolled by New Line Cinema. Peter Jackson's project took over three years to complete, hiring over 15,000 people (the vast majority of whom were New Zealanders) and costing in the vicinity of NZ$600million (US$300million). As I will detail, according to media reports, the arrival of a mega-budget blockbuster within the emerging New Zealand film industry and the close-knit community of Wellington has had an indelible economic and cultural impact. Throughout that extended period of time, media reports were largely occupied with three main topics. The first and most predominant charted the unprecedented monetary and social impact the production had – and continues to have – on Wellington. The second highlighted New Zealand's role as a filmmaking nation, in line with other expanding production locations such as Australia and Canada. Finally, as could be expected, the various local newspapers all exhibited a single-minded obsession with what went on during filming, positioning their articles and columns as forums for *The Lord of the Rings* gossip mongering among 'regular' Wellingtonians.

However, I was interested in whether this same perspective was taken up wholesale by the regular Wellingtonians these media outlets purport to represent. Did they in fact view this interaction between the Hollywood industrial system and their town as in line with these themes? Was the cultural experience of *The Lord of the Rings* as it was hyped in the major newspapers and by institutional bodies such as the New Zealand Film Commission (NZFC), or did it prove quite a different experience for Wellington people? In order to begin answering these questions, I set up an informal email questionnaire and sent it out to various Wellington contacts, who in turn forwarded it on to others. Responses unearthed a few dominant themes, including Peter Jackson's pivotal role in the New Zealand film industry, the country's attempts to mobilise a national image within an increasingly global political economy, and the colonialist ramifications of such a move. Most importantly, however, I also discovered various levels of disjunction between media reports and respondents' everyday experiences, which this chapter will examine further.

Questionnaire design

In designing the questionnaire, my primary concern was to learn about the impact of *The Lord of the Rings* on Wellingtonians – in their own words, rather than through media channels. I therefore kept my questions to a minimum, focusing on a few in-depth questions that asked respondents to write substantial paragraphs, rather than several, more surface-level enquiries. It seemed to me that more questions would generate more ostensible 'data', but less detail about people's quotidian activities and perceptions. Therefore, I began with primarily demographic questions (name, occupation or area of study, residence, and so on) and finished with questions that dealt with *The Lord of the Rings'* impact on Wellington and individual respondents – *according to those respondents* – for a total of twelve questions.[1]

My original contacts were two friends from the Wellington area, various staff at both the Wellington and Upper Hutt city councils, and a Victoria University

(Wellington) film professor. At the beginning of the project, I hoped to contact a wide variety of people in all occupations, the majority of whom were uninvolved with *The Lord of the Rings*. Instead, simply because one of my friends and the professor were involved with the entertainment industry, I found that over half of the twenty questionnaires eventually returned were answered by people who had some kind of relationship to the production. These relationships took different forms and constituted different degrees of interaction. Jean Johnston, Project Manager for Film and Television for the Wellington Economic Development Trust, was given the (rather enviable) job of escorting a 'group of [stars] along to watch the final of the Bledisloe cup [rugby match]'. Others were extras or simply one of the thousands of locals who tried out for parts, movie theatre managers and staff – through to the Victoria University professor who wrote: 'Given a choice when writing an assignment for class, students often choose PJ [Peter Jackson] as their topic. Gets old after a while' (Harriet Margolis).

That said, I also received questionnaires from students, a hydrologist, business and research consultants, a librarian, an art gallery owner and others, all of whom were at least tangentially affected by the *Lord of the Rings* production, if only to register it as a blip on the arts landscape. Lawrence McDonald, editor of *Illusions* (a national film and theatre magazine), wrote in reply to my inquiry regarding the impact of *The Lord of the Rings* on him personally:

> *The Lord of the Rings* doesn't impinge much on my consciousness. Sure, when it opens I'll go along and I'll arrange for someone to review it. But that will pretty much be it. Like Everest, it's great that it's there and it's great that it's being climbed here in Wellington but I guess other areas of NZ film production concern me more.[2]

Regardless of the respondents' take on the project, all agreed that *The Lord of the Rings* was reaping 'heaps of media attention' (Robert Catto). However, in the questionnaire answers it became clear that there was a large disparity between this 'media attention' and the actual impact on the respondents' day-to-day lives and activities, in spite of the fact that a large percentage studied and/or worked at media-related institutions and industries.

Peter Jackson: Wellington's 'Great Man'

Several themes became apparent when looking at both media reports and the questionnaire replies. One of the most predominant was the inordinate amount of attention paid to Peter Jackson's role as the 'great man' of the New Zealand film industry, the central point from which all other film-related activity is generated. Questionnaire respondent Anton Ferrari wrote

A main differences I have noticed is the constant referring to Peter Jackson, the producer of *The Lord of the Rings*, and the influence he has had on bringing [New Zealand] to the attention of other film companies as a locality for films.

The Evening Post summed up Jackson's career to date in the following terms:

In little more than 10 years [Jackson] has rocketed from being a backyard film-maker of cult splatter films to New Zealand's premier director and the film industry's lifeblood … He has helped to provide an infrastructure for developing projects and talent, and has opened Hollywood's eyes to the economics of making movies here. (Anon. 1998b: 40)

Indeed, Jackson's story does fit easily into the rags-to-riches structure often employed in entertainment news stories. He began his career making 'splatter films', such as *Bad Taste* (1987), *Meet the Feebles* (1989) and *Braindead* (1992) in his spare time. All these films are over-the-top, cheaply made, vile gore-fests of bad-taste humour and gratuitous violence. His backyard served as a set; the friends he could get to help him when they had time off work were his cast and crew. *Heavenly Creatures* (1994), his Academy Award-nominated film based on an actual 1950s matricide, was also made on a small budget, the special effects being completed on a 'single, leased computer', a fact brought up often in media articles in contrast to the mind-boggling smorgasbord of technical equipment employed on *The Lord of the Rings* (Roston 2001). With only one medium-budget Hollywood-backed film to his credit – *The Frighteners* (1996) – Jackson won the contract for *The Lord of the Rings* and the rest, according to media reports, is national cinematic history. This larger-than-life portrait of Jackson's endeavours is bolstered by headlines that read: 'Lord of the fantasy', 'Jackson brings the action home: The king of splatter becomes Lord of the Rings', and 'Lord of the Rings – Jackson worth $20m' (Barton 1998: 15; Anon. 1998b: 40; Bedford 2001: 1).

Several of these articles discuss Jackson's firm hold on most of Wellington's film infrastructure. Not only did he land the *Lord of the Rings* contract, he also snapped up the previously government-owned Film Unit when it was in the process of being privatised and turned it into 'the most complete post-production facility in the Australia-South Pacific region' (Cardy 2000: 2).[3] The media's coverage of Jackson's prominent role in the privatisation of New Zealand's media assets had two effects. First, it normalised the privatisation process for a public wary of the country's wholesale turn towards American-styled capitalism. Second, Jackson's well-known, approachable personality is a far cry from the faceless bureaucrats normally associated with such economic adjustments and was often spotlighted on television and in the papers. Portrayed as 'one of us', Jackson's move to purchase government assets became rhetorically framed as less the constant parcelling up and selling off of New Zealand's resources and more as simply a transfer of ownership to another Kiwi (keeping New Zealand products in New Zealand, owned by New Zealanders). Margolis suggests: 'We ... feel some relief that Peter Jackson has been able to buy things the government was going to sell, and that he has thereby kept key components needed for a film industry here in local hands.'

Questionnaire responses indicated that the general feeling was of Jackson as a New Zealander – and more specifically a Wellingtonian – who had 'done good'. Alison Bartley noted:

> Peter Jackson is now a major player and is committed to living and working in Wellington and that in itself is great for the city. So many New Zealanders feel they need to travel and work overseas to make it.

This feeling may have much to do with the country's 'tall poppy syndrome': the idea that everyone must remain at the same achievement level. Those who do attempt to differentiate themselves from the rest of their fellow Kiwis tend to be 'cut down to size'. In earlier work I have touched on the 'tall poppy syndrome' in relation to the acquisition of knowledge. This syndrome is one of the reasons given for the constant one-way flow of creative and intellectual talent from New Zealand to other countries providing greater resources and opportunities (see Thornley 2000: 63). Jackson's decision to remain in New Zealand flies in the face of this trend, marking one of the main reasons why Wellingtonians are so attached to his media persona. When asked how she personally felt about the impact that *The Lord of the Rings* has had on the community of Wellington, Sara Gordon replied:

> Fabulous! It's added a bit of fun to the area. Being from Miramar myself [Wellington suburb where Jackson has a home], PJ is a bit of a hero and it's always fun to try and sneak a look in his window whenever you drive past ... Good for local confidence that someone as powerful as Peter Jackson has the world as his oyster, could travel anywhere to film anything, but chooses to bring the work home to his people.

Gordon's choice of words – Jackson as 'powerful', 'chooses to bring the work home to his people' – show solid support for Jackson's decision to remain in New Zealand. Both Bartley and Gordon recognise Jackson's importance as a central figure in the region's always fragile film industry. Indeed, most respondents realised that Jackson's decision to remain in the Wellington area had, in effect, turned the tide for the local film industry. Gordon went on to comment:

> PJ will have even more clout and be able to continue making his movies here – which creates more jobs for locals in an industry that had all but given up the ghost, with the majority of television production moving to Auckland.

There is a constant ongoing rivalry between Wellington and Auckland, as Auckland is the largest city in the country; it has expanded rapidly in the last three decades, pulling people in search of job opportunities away from other cities, which in turn undermines the infrastructure necessary for industries such as media production. In light of this rivalry, Jackson can be seen as embodying Wellington's (but also New Zealand's) struggle to carve out a discursive space for itself within the move towards increasing corporatisation, urbanisation *and* globalisation.

In line with this push to mobilise a national image within an increasingly global political economy, Jackson is seen in a favourable light by several of the respondents because of his sheer Kiwi 'down-to-earthness'. Press coverage portrays him as an unassuming figure, fairly short and rotund and usually dressed in jeans and a T-shirt, glasses hiding what little of his face an unkempt beard does not cover (Sara Gordon again: 'My husband looks a lot like him (hairy with glasses!) so that gives us hours of entertainment value!'). Several newspaper reports and magazine articles made mention of the fact that Jackson liked to roam around barefooted while production was going on (see Roston 2001: 98). Paul Emsley summed it up in his reply: 'Peter Jackson is generally regarded as an eccentric genius locally.' Respondents' replies showed that they saw Jackson as 'one of them'.

No. 8 Fencing Wire: *The Lord of the Rings* and 'Kiwi ingenuity'

It is worth investigating a little further how such modest values as Jackson displays have come to be so highly regarded and cultivated nationally, particularly in sharp contrast to America's fascination with stardom, celebrities and 'making it' in the cut-throat media environment. This preoccupation with self-effacement and social levelling has an entrenched history, with New Zealand gaining a reputation for itself as 'one of the most egalitarian countries in the world' (Bedggood 1980). New Zealanders' understandings of this egalitarianism were predicated on the type of settler that founded the nation. In the aftermath of the Industrial Revolution, many disillusioned working people flocked to the promise held up by the New Zealand Company, a venture started by London capitalists in 1838, of virtually free land for settlement. Edward Gibbon Wakefield, founder of the Company, stated: 'Possess yourselves of the soil and you are secure' (quoted in Owens 1992: 50).

These new arrivals were fleeing not from religious persecution as in America but from desperately poor backgrounds with almost no economic or political security. Once they arrived, the land had to be cultivated; a man who worked hard was admired and respected. Labourers often had to come up with ingenious ways around impenetrable terrain, lack of food and supplies, and inadequate equipment. Thus one of New Zealand's most well-known icons made its way into national myth: No. 8 fencing wire, which good Kiwi men could use to get just about any task done.[4] No. 8 stands in as a synecdoche for both the cultural metaphor of

Kiwi ingenuity and the diverse number of ways that this ingenuity manifests itself. Jackson is seen in this vein (as mentioned in relation to the Mt Everest quote; see note 2); a 'likeable, genuinely modest and unaffected' protégé of the folkloric New Zealand hero (Anon. 1998b: 40), battling on against insurmountable odds with only his energy and wits – very much like one of his hobbits in *The Lord of the Rings*.[5]

In addition, New Zealand's culture corroborates this insistence on equality at all costs by deploying an ideological tack in regards to such diverse areas as welfare, social reform, race relations, and even to how New Zealanders are understood by the rest of the world. These beliefs took root in the 1890s when New Zealand became known as the social laboratory of the world due to a spate of laws passed during that period, their intent being to improve the working peoples' lot. In reality, these laws functioned to first mask real social differences by providing a government-sanctioned 'safety net' for the less fortunate, and secondly to curb possible organised unrest due to this classed inequality. While these changes did provide some justification for the label of 'social laboratory', on the whole they have failed to institute changes of the scale imagined, to this day, in average New Zealanders' minds and reproduced in everyday discourse.

Ideological acceptance of egalitarianism, however, has continued throughout the country's history. Values of thrift, modesty, neighbourliness and equal life chances were consolidated by political rhetoric, particularly after the Depression and World War Two.[6] In historian Graeme Dunstall's article on the social scene of the 1950s, he refers to a quote from *Landfall*, one of New Zealand's most longstanding literary magazines, in order to describe the ruling idea of the post-war society – 'everyone acts the same, receives the same amount of the world's goods, everyone moves in the same direction' (1992: 453). Seen from this perspective, Jackson's meteoric rise to fame becomes discursively re-orientated: to Wellingtonians he *is* a powerful media industry player, but he is also a loyal hometown boy who gives back to the community through his financial choices and public presence. As Heidi North puts it: 'He's reported as a bit of a local hero really.'

Other public figures and respondents saw the hype surrounding Jackson as less rosy, however. They suggested that his work may overshadow other efforts at filmmaking in New Zealand, a conclusion McDonald also leaned towards with his reference to *The Lord of the Rings* and Mt Everest. Deakin University academic Keith Beattie expressed concerns that *The Lord of the Rings* was a double-sided coin – 'on the one side is the positive spin-off financially but on the other we risk displacing local films with Hollywood films made here' (quoted in Anon. 1998a: 4). Arts consultant Hamish Keith, head of a government arts and culture strategy team convened on the tail end of *The Lord of the Rings*, summed up the delicate balance between foreign and local investment that projects like *The Lord of the Rings* threaten to displace. Keith stated more research needed to be undertaken on 'the relative value of New Zealand projects, such as the Kiwi-made film *Scarfies* (Robert Sarkies, 1999), and overseas projects with New Zealand input and value to the economy, such as *The Lord of the Rings*. We need both. Both are important in giving us somewhere to be in the world' (quoted in Barnao 2000: 6).

'Wellywood': Wellington in the wake of *The Lord of the Rings*

This consideration – the incessant push and pull between imported and home-grown, big business and community – surfaces repeatedly in the media and public discourse, although depending on where you look the situation is either cause for celebration, consternation or an uncertainty located somewhere between. Many of the questionnaire responses were also divided. Some replies argued both eloquently and passionately for the positive ongoing impact of a production such as *The Lord of the Rings*. Rachel Laurenson, a Film, English and Religious Studies undergraduate, addressed a central reason why *The Lord of the Rings* should mean more respect for other New Zealand projects.

> I think it has been good to have a major feature film shot here, by a prominent New Zealand director, as there is little faith by many people in films, music or anything produced in New Zealand.

Laurenson's comment makes reference to the country's notorious 'cultural cringe', that is, the idea that anything produced nationally could not possibly be as good as those cultural products produced overseas. Many respondents see *The Lord of the Rings* as producing a quantum shift in the way that people think about what New Zealand is capable of, as respondent Catto's extended quote discusses:

> There was, late in the filming and afterwards, a period where nobody even wanted to talk about it, because it seemed the topic had been exhausted or at least badly overexposed. People were 'bored of the bloody Rings', especially in the film/TV industry, who felt badly overlooked by all the attention this one project received. But it's hard to imagine such growth in that same industry, or such international attention, without this enormous production. As lovely as Wellington and New Zealand are, we were destined at most to be an offshoot of the Australian industry, the equivalent of a small province of Canada in terms of our ability to attract major projects. Now the potential is seen to be limitless; [in] the same way a film like *Moulin Rouge* can change the industry's perception of what a country is capable of, we are pinning our hopes on Peter's masterpiece(s) being our showcase to the world.

The sheer scale of *The Lord of the Rings* gives it disproportionate weight in much public discourse. In line with Jackson's exalted role, media representations of *The*

Lord of the Rings also perform rhetorical work, weighing in on the debate surrounding New Zealand's move into the global media economy, pushing the idea that *The Lord of the Rings* is the country's ticket to national recognition. Many other respondents agreed with Catto, mentioning again the distinctions now (slowly) being made between Australia and New Zealand as separate film industries ('not just somewhere south of Australia' – Desiree Goodall), and the ongoing impact that high-profile films such as *The Lord of the Rings* will have in the minds of overseas viewers (Margolis). Others remained skeptical, sensing 'a certain amount of hype in the press about [*The Lord of the Rings*] being "good for the local economy" and "here's one for a New Zealand director taking on the Hollywood role", etc' (Paul Emsley). McDonald wrote: '*The Lord of the Rings* seems to have been used mostly by public relations people to promote the idea that there is now somewhere called 'Wellywood', in the hope that it will attract further production companies here.

Many – including Michael Baines, CEO of the Upper Hutt Economic Development Agency and a survey respondent – felt that even the various business clusters and other government initiatives set up to deal with the aftermath of *The Lord of the Rings* may not be enough. Baines writes:

> I worry about the next project, when it will happen and what will happen to the infrastructure in the interim. I believe that we need three or four major projects occurring simultaneously to ensure that we maintain the people and other infrastructural issues. If it has all been a one-off then it has been fun but it will have little ongoing impact on the region.

If long term growth is to occur – after *The Lord of the Rings* has 'done [its] job and then disappeared into the sunset with minimal direct impact on the community as a whole' as Baines put it – several respondents seemed to think this would only come with more money, more government involvement, and more widespread community support. These were all issues the local papers only infrequently touched on, let alone investigated in depth.

The Guardian London wrote that *The Lord of the Rings* 'has come as sweet relief to a domestic film business whose highly limited output to date has been described as adventurously low-budget or, alternatively, direly underfinanced' (Cohen 2001: 16). The New Zealand film industry tends to operate on a fire-fighting basis: dealing with different projects on a shaky 'as it occurs' basis, rather than providing the funding that would enable a viable industry, capable of functioning year-round. This leaves national film production vulnerable to both the internal economy and the reception of international audiences. While appearing particularly optimistic, Catto's response was also followed by the suggestion that 'a tremendous sense of local pride in the project [is] tempered with a small fear of what the reputation of the NZ film industry (along with the whole country) will be if something in the films doesn't gel properly'. 'But', he continues, 'this is never mentioned; the patriotic pride is too great to think that good ol' kiwi ingenuity won't conquer Hollywood.'

Several government websites and NZFC articles stressed the possibilities that *The Lord of the Rings* opened up for further filmmaking ventures in Wellington and nationally, although the sheer size, length and financial clout of the production often left local government scrambling to productively keep up. Reports rushed to assure the New Zealand public: Prime Minister Helen Clark was quoted as saying 'the government is determined that the enormous opportunities offered by the epic *The Lord of the Rings* project … are not lost' (NewsRoom 2001). The Wellington City Council set up Film Wellington, an arm of the council designed specifically to assist with film production in the region (SmartWellington), while the mayor made the rounds of American industry tradeshows (Saffioti 2000). Plans for a *Lord of the Rings* museum were shelved after a hasty trip to America showed government officials they were somewhat out of their league when it came to the manoeuvring required to secure the legal rights for *The Lord of the Rings* paraphernalia the city wished to be able to feature (Rendle 2001: 3). Whether promoters or detractors, however, those on both sides of the discursive fence recognised that *The Lord of the Rings* represented a 'new plateau' for the New Zealand movie industry (Margolis). It remains to be seen, however, whether and how that growth will pan out within the local media industry in the near future.

'Mexicans with cellphones': New Zealand and globalisation

As already implied, an ongoing concern for New Zealanders is their lack of visibility on the world scene – both culturally and economically. As an isolated nation, New Zealand constantly struggles to stay current with, and connected to, what is going on in the rest of the world, especially in economic centres that are geographically removed, such as Europe and America. Jane Gilbert, who started the locations arm of the NZFC in 1998, stated the following:

> Three years ago, no one knew how to get in touch with our film people, our line producers, production-servicing people, or even what the country looked like [Now,] New Zealand has become accessible. As a business, we had to minimise the tyranny of distance and show that we have an infrastructure not based on apple boxes and sheep. (Quoted in Accinelli 2000: 10)

However, this movement away from primary products and towards industries such as media and technology has not been quite as simple, or as instantaneous, as Gilbert's quote makes it appear.

New Zealand has long struggled to separate itself from a postcolonial mentality. Even though the country became formally independent from Britain in 1911, economically New Zealanders depended on trade with the motherland: they supplied meat and dairy products, Britain supplied processed goods. Britain's mid-1970s move to join the European Economic Community ended the guaranteed market for New Zealand's primary products. This change produced a domino effect, with the country's farmers and the processing, packing and transportation industries scrambling to fill the void with new forms of product and new markets. The move away from 'apple boxes and sheep' and towards high-tech industries (such as media/entertainment) and tourism indelibly altered the country's economy over the last quarter of the twentieth century. In addition, this national shift is far from complete and continues to cause sharp growing pains, as can be seen both in mediated and 'everyday' discourses surrounding *The Lord of the Rings*.

A great number of these discourses interrogate New Zealand's position within the world economy. As expected, New Zealanders want their country to be recognised for the quality of its products and the experience and industriousness of its people. Midway into *The Lord of the Rings*' filming schedule, the *Dominion* ran an editorial stating:

> It has been estimated that [international film and television] productions have contributed $400million to the Wellington economy alone over the past year. New Zealand is seen as a fresh – and cheap – place to make movies and television shows. (Anon. 2000: 12)

In line with this perception, Roderick D. Smith, vice president for motion picture production finance at Disney, stated: 'I was struck by how open and eager to help out [New Zealand] workers are. [In the States] they are so compartmentalised. A wardrobe assistant would never drive a truck' (quoted in Accinelli 2000: 10). However, New Zealand battles with an inherent set of difficulties in enacting this articulation. These include not only the 'tyranny of distance' but also a currency that has never been particularly strong and which is presently sharply devalued (approx. NZ$1.60 to US$1). Additional problems include a small labour force, intense competition from other countries with similar resources and more robust markets, and the constant 'brain drain' of talented intellectuals and artists. These drawbacks and the country's cultural invisibility also contribute to a perception – held particularly in several developed countries in the northern hemisphere – that New Zealand is simply another cheap place to make films, not all that indistinguishable from Mexico or Canada.

This in turn aligns New Zealand with other countries which have consciously or not become inexpensive labour and technology pools for places such as the United States. American industries see these countries and, by default, New Zealand as 'the loci of the production of surplus for the capitalist economics of the North' (Smith 1998: 130). New Zealand newspaper articles boasted that Jackson's studio could produce certain special effects for a fraction of the cost charged by George Lucas's Industrial Light & Magic studio (Cohen 2001: 16). Several businesses have sprung up in the wake of *The Lord of the Rings* that trade on their competitive prices, vis-à-vis American rates.[7] Both are examples of what might be termed either entrepreneurship or exploitation depending upon where a country finds itself positioned in the global pecking order.

In the case of film production – having paved the way with numerous scouting trips, legal strategising and tax write-offs – the production houses go into the country in question, hire actors, crew and technicians, film what they require, and then leave. Others were less sanguine with their choice of words regarding this 'shoot-and-run' philosophy. Gary Elshaw another of the respondents, offered the following anecdote: 'A friend who was doing camera work for the production said that many of the US production people called the [New Zealand] crew "Mexicans with cellphones" i.e. cheap labour with some technological know-how.' Here, not only are the New Zealand crew ostracised and differentiated from the American crew, but they are discursively re-orientated through a process of prolatisation. New Zealand is aligned with Mexico, a country that has found itself standing in for the rest of the underdeveloped world, largely due to the number of Mexican immigrants living in the United States and therefore constantly registering in the political and ideological framework of many Americans.

In addition, the transfer of international capital from geographical centre (America) to periphery (New Zealand) works to colonise those who seem to profit from it. That is, Paul Smith suggests that while multinational capital formations may have turned away from 'direct colonial subjugation of the subject' (at least in the case of New Zealand), 'domination occurs intensively at the levels of discourse, representation and subjectivity' (1998: 138), as can be seen in the comment just discussed. New Zealanders may not consider themselves pawns in the global shuffle towards multinational corporate exchange, but as far as their American counterparts on *The Lord of the Rings* are concerned, that is exactly what they represent. As Jane Wrightson, the chief executive of the national Screen Producers and Directors Association, stated:

> The next period for Wellington film will be important. We must not market ourselves as a cheap and cheerful option. You don't want to be Mexicans providing cheap labour because you can burn out very quickly. (Williams 2000: 11)

That the chief executive of one of New Zealand's foremost film industry associations would employ the same comparison as the American production crew shows the extent to which this ideological re-articulation has entered the national vocabulary, shaping the way New Zealanders view themselves in relation to the rest of the world.

Hobbits in the backyard? *The Lord of the Rings* and the everyday

Media sources also made much of how Wellington specifically – as the capital and the location for parts of the *Lord of the Rings* production, plus Jackson's workplace and home – was affected by the extended presence of *The Lord of the Rings*. Articles discussed large-scale changes such as the rise in housing prices (Cohen 2001: 16; Williams 2000: 11), the boost to Wellington's film industry (Cluster), and spin-off ventures involving several of the city's institutions, including Te Papa, the national museum (Barnao 2000). There were also several other changes – perhaps less sweeping and more localised – within the city. The Wellington Public Library's website provided links to *The Lord of the Rings* resources, both at their library branches and across the Internet (Wellington Government Website), while Victoria University offered a series of lectures investigating *The Lord of the Rings* and medieval literature, timed to coincide with the release of the film (Clothier 2001: 2). In addition, prolonged battles over *The Lord of the Rings* producers landing their private planes at the city airport occupied the attention of the local media columns (Wellington Government Website).[8]

Catto situates the charged relationship between residents and *The Lord of the Rings* producers regarding this issue within a wider context, whereby *The Lord of the Rings* developments, the movement of personnel and related ramifications became common knowledge among Wellingtonians as a whole:

> In some ways, it's reminiscent of David Mamet's film *State & Main* [2000] in which the locals, at first seemingly unaware of anything to do with the film, can, by the finish of shooting, quote grosses straight from the pages of *Variety* and chart the progress of a studio from birth to present off the top of their heads; no one admits to reading the fan pages online, but everyone knows everything as soon as it happens. The guy at the video shop has seen the trailer before it's on the web, the entire Miramar region knows when New Line is next going to land their Gulfstream at the airport, and my partner's grandmother in Waikanae [Wellington suburb] can comment knowingly on housing in Seatoun (where the stars were generally staying).

Catto's response, along with media reports, suggests that *The Lord of the Rings* has impacted the city of Wellington in several pervasive (if somewhat amorphous) ways; however, his response was the exception. It seems instead there is somewhat of a gap between the media and respondents' conceptions of how *The Lord of the Rings* has affected Wellington: that is, several respondents did not believe that Wellington was impacted significantly.

Figure 2: 'It's become part of the landscape really'; Wellington celebrating the premiere of *The Return of the King* – note the logo of tie-in company Burger King in the background (courtesy of theonering.net)

As example, often respondents had trouble differentiating *The Lord of the Rings* coverage from other media events, or from the ongoing activity of city life. David Moore wrote: 'In the early stages of the project there was a flurry of media interest, but that soon died away'. Laurenson agreed: 'There was probably more interest media-wise in *The Lord of the Rings* about a year ago when everything was just getting started. It's become part of the landscape really.' North added: 'It's just another thing that's been going on here, I suppose. Being such a long production, it sort of lost its glamour, I guess, and became part of what happened here.' In addition, most filming disturbances were kept to a minimum: several people said that although they had seen glimpses of sets from the highway or in certain suburbs, 'nothing has really disturbed Wellington activity' (Laurenson). On an economic level it was interesting to read Baines' comment, which acts as somewhat of a foil to Catto's:

> It has bought a level of pride to the city that such a large project has been head-quartered here, but the Wellington region has a long history of being associated with film and TV (Avalon and the National Film Unit [film studios]) and so it is much more accepting of the special needs of the industry and more blasé about its activities.

Long a 'film town' – more than other places *The Lord of the Rings* also filmed in (such as the Waikato region and the central North Island) – Wellington largely absorbed the excitement of *The Lord of the Rings'* presence. Respondent Gina Dellabarca summed it up:

> It hasn't been as big a deal as I expected. Although half the city has been involved in one way or another. In a way it has been an event that served as a bit of a talking point. Something to bind people together by giving them something besides the weather to talk about.

This dislocation from the hype surrounding *The Lord of the Rings* was even more prevalent at the level of the quotidian. Fully three-quarters of the respondents did not consider themselves personally affected by *The Lord of the Rings'* presence or believed that there had been any noticeable impact on their daily activities and the activities of those around them, such as friends or family. Although several of the respondents mentioned recognising New Zealand, or even their city, as occupying a different global position (both economically and ideologi;cally) than before *The Lord of the Rings*, this influence did not alter their routines of work, school and leisure substantially, or extend to respondents changing their daily patterns of behaviour. This is particularly interesting given the media's insistence on a connection between national ideologies and personal ideologies. The prevailing assertion was that because *The Lord of the Rings* had dominated New Zealand's economic, industrial and even political landscape for three years, it would necessarily garner the same level of attention and investment from those 'regular' Wellingtonians who supposedly represent the viewing and reading public for these media sources. If anything, the opposite occurred. The majority of respondents wrote about *others* they knew of who had been extras or got work connected with *The Lord of the Rings*. Survey participants talked about friends who had managed star sightings, or shared their concerns about acquaintances finding ongoing work, given the number of positions lost in the film and television industry in the wake of *The Lord of the Rings*. Elshaw stated: 'No, *The Lord of the Rings* hasn't affected me directly at all. It has affected a number of others who are close to me, and I do have some major concerns for their future and the NZ film industry in general.' However as far as my respondents' lives were concerned, impact was 'extremely minimal (couldn't even elaborate)' and '...not on the top of my mind on a regular basis' (Emsley; Lewellen). Dellabarca considered it 'not a big deal, no major impact', while Ferrari did not 'notice any discernable difference pre- or post-*The Lord of the Rings*'.

In effect, these responses show that there is a disjunction between media reports and peoples' everyday experiences. Although this appears an obvious statement at face value, it remains that with media inserting itself ever more indistinguishably into people's daily experiences it becomes more and more difficult to separate the two. This inability to separate peoples' 'lived experiences' from discourse occurs in commonsense understandings of the ways in which media structures our lives, but also often in academic work on the subject. The quotidian is often seen to be mediated (pun intended) to an unprecedented extent in the early twenty-first century: routines arranged around favourite television shows, film dialogue making its way into ordinary conversations, understandings of current events gleaned through front-page reports and editorials.

In contrast to this push to fuse the two, respondents carved out an everyday space for themselves separate from the overarching presence of either *The Lord of the Rings* or the media's interpretations of the trilogy's impact. I am not necessarily arguing that respondents were somehow untouched by *The Lord of the Rings* events. They may in fact have been affected in different ways or to different levels than they disclosed, ways that perhaps they were not even aware of themselves. However, I am arguing that *they perceived themselves* as having the ability to avoid the slippery slope often constructed between media representations of their lives and their actual 'lived experiences' as Wellingtonians – within the city's myriad of jobs, responsibilities, connections, passions and frustrations. This perception can be seen as a form of agency, employed on a daily basis, whereby respondents filter and select the media paradigms they wish to accept.

Conclusion

It is true that *The Lord of the Rings'* presence had substantial impact on the respondents in an important area. For the majority of respondents, this impact necessitated a shift in their understanding of New Zealand's ideological location in relation to the rest of the world. However unlike media reports persisted in suggesting, *The Lord of the Rings* did not have the same impact on people at a personal, everyday level. Peoples' lives continued on much as they would have, before production and after *The Lord of the Rings* wrapped, aside from the fun moments occasionally provided by glimpses of sets or stars. Hollywood may have stretched its tinsel arms across the globe for three years, and even deposited itself in a few New Zealand backyards, but that does not mean that those New Zealanders now set their clock by hobbit time. Rather, some of them might take their children to see the finished product – a lot of them might go to see it themselves! – but they will then return home to continue doing the things they do the other 364 days of the year.

Notes

1   I have edited respondents' comments for spelling, grammar and comprehensibility.
2   McDonald's comment is particularly interesting because of the connections between

Peter Jackson and Sir Edmund Hillary that are brought up by his reference to Mt Everest. Hillary is a New Zealander and the first white person to climb Mt Everest. Both men are exalted in popular New Zealand culture and folklore as prime examples of Kiwi ingenuity and 'the can-do mentality', national traits that New Zealanders hold dear (as I will elaborate).

3   Which is also, incidentally, 'the only facility in New Zealand with a mutimillion-dollar digital telecine' (Accinelli 2000: 10).

4   'Common myths along traditional Protestant lines include: everyone in New Zealand has the same opportunities, hard work will produce wealth, there is no real poverty in New Zealand' (Consedine 1989: 174).

5   Tom Roston (2001) mentions that Elijah Wood and his fellow actors gave Jackson a scale model of the director as a hobbit, complete with pointy ears and hairy feet, when filming wrapped.

6   Where these myths differ from those immortalised in 'the American Dream' is that there are sanctions on the accumulation and display of wealth. The rhetoric of equality works to bring the top down as well as the bottom up. That is, although it is everyone's right and, indeed, responsibility, to acquire the same standard of living as their neighbour, they should not move beyond this. In addition, the acquisition of economic resources should also be discretely managed; conspicuous consumption is frowned upon. This value perpetuates the notion of egalitarianism, making it even more difficult to identify the rich from the poor, so to speak.

7   Matthew Lewellen, one of the respondents, wrote: 'Already, there's a web design outfit called "Cyber Elves" that has started up. Their push is getting jobs out of New York. "You need the work done overnight? Let the elves do it while you sleep!" – as its daytime here, and they're half the price to boot'.

8   Margolis also wrote: 'One or two suburbs got some major charity donations from the US producers to allow some use of the airport that would normally be blocked. (Time of arrival/departure, extent of noise, flight path … can't quite remember. But the execs wanted to use their own plane at their own convenience and were willing to pay a few thousand dollars to get what they wanted).'

Works cited

Accinelli, L. (2000) 'New Zealand Making a Pitch to Filmmakers', *Los Angeles Times*, 15 March, 10.

Anon. (1998a) 'Jackson Rejects Hollywood Tag', *Dominion*, 28 August, 4.

_____ (1998b) 'Jackson Brings the Action Home', *Evening Post*, 8 October, 40.

_____ (2000) 'A Pitch for Wellywood', *Dominion*, 29 November, 12.

Barnao, P. (2000) 'Government Orders Arts and Culture Strategy', *Dominion*, 31 March, 6.

Barton, W. (1998) 'Lord of the Fantasy', *Dominion*, 29 August, 15.

Bedford, D. (2001) 'Lord of the Rings – Jackson Worth $20m', *Evening Post*, 20 July, 1.

Bedggood, D. (1980) *Rich and Poor in New Zealand: A Critique of Class, Politics and Ideology*. Auckland and Sydney: George Allen & Unwin.

Cardy, T. (2000) 'Jackson Snaps up National Film Unit', *Evening Post*, 8 February, 2.

Clothier, J. (2001) 'Lectures to Brush Up on Your Tolkien', *Evening Post*, 30 June, 2.

Cluster. 'Film Capital of New Zealand'. Online. Available at http://www.cluster.org.nz/ wbc_brochure.pdf, 6. (accessed 25 June 2005).

Cohen, D. (2001) 'Lord of the Rings Brings Riches to City', *Guardian London*, 20 January, 16.

Consedine, B. (1989) 'Inequality and the Egalitarian Myth', in D. Novitz and B. Willmott (eds) *Culture and Identity in New Zealand*. Wellington: GP Books, 172–86.

Dunstall, G. (1992) 'The Social Pattern', in G. W. Rice (ed.) *The Oxford History of New Zealand*, second edition. Auckland: Oxford University Press, 451–81.

Houlahan, M. (1998a) 'Jackson Scores the Holy Grail of Cinema', *Dominion*, 26 August, 11.

_____ (1998b) 'Rumours Run Rings around Truth', *Dominion*, 24 December, 12.

NewsRoom (2001) 'Government Mounts *LOTR* Publicity Campaign'. Online. Available at http://www.newsroom.co.nz (accessed 7 November 2001).

Owens, J. M. R. (1992) 'New Zealand before Annexation', in G. W. Rice (ed.) *The Oxford History of New Zealand*, second edition. Oxford: Oxford University Press, 28–53.

Rendle, S. (2001) 'Rings museum on back burner', *Evening Post*, 18 April, 3.

Roston, T. (2001) 'The Chosen One', *Premiere*, 14, 12, 98.

Saffioti, T. (2000) 'Lord of the Rings Dazzles at US Film Expo', Wellington City Council press release, 29 February. Online. Available at http://www.wcc.govt.nz/news/ press/2000/pr000153htm (accessed 7 October 2001).

SmartWellington. 'Film and Television'. On-line. Available at http://www.smartwellington.co.nz/smart industries/p3 7.html (accessed 17 October 2001).

Smith, P. (1998) 'Visiting the Banana Republic', in A. Ross (ed.) *Universal Abandon?: The Politics of Postmodernism*. Minneapolis: University of Minnesota Press, 128–48.

Thornley, D. (2000) 'Duel or Duet? Gendered Nationalism in *The Piano*', *Film Criticism*, 24, 3, 61–76.

Williams, P. (2000) 'Reel Picture in Wellywood', *Evening Post*, 14 October, 11.

Wellington Government Website. 'Hot Topics! Page: Lord of the Rings'. Online. Available at http://www.wel.govt.nz/path/newsubjects/hot lordrings.html (accessed 7 October 2001).

_____ 'Minutes' Eastern Suburbs Steering Committee meeting (26 July). Online. Available at http://www.wel.govt.nz (accessed 30 October 2001).

Reviews, Previews and Premieres: The Critical Reception of *The Lord of the Rings* in the United Kingdom

Ernest Mathijs[1]

The Lord of the Rings is the most popular book. *The Sun* is the most popular newspaper. Nuff said. (Humphreys 2003: 23).

Introduction: public presence and the day of release

How does the newspaper press of a country prepare itself for the release of a major blockbuster, hyped to the extreme, on the day of its release? It is like asking children what they will be doing the night before Santa Claus arrives. It is also like asking those sleep-deprived, sugar-wired children to offer an objective opinion, perhaps on waist-girth as a measure of cardiovascular disease risk, of the jolly fellow who is about to bring them presents, *lotsa presents*. On Wednesday 17 December 2003, the day *The Return of the King* was due for general release, the nine national newspapers of the United Kingdom chose different ways of readying themselves, encapsulated in 19 pieces about the film and/or books they carried between them. In so doing, they displayed an arsenal of ways to attend to and connect with the public presence of a major event.

Cleverly, *The Daily Mirror* and *The Daily Express* singled out Sky Movies One's broadcast of *The Fellowship of the Ring* as their 'film of the day' and 'today's choice' respectively, pictures and captions included (Knaggs 2003). Equally dexterous, *The Daily Express* and *The Sun* chose this day to announce that Orlando Bloom was voted *More Magazine*'s Celebrity Man of the Year (Anon. 2003b), and to report that Viggo Mortensen and Josie D'Arby went on a 'loved-up weekend' in Paris (Anon. 2003a). Similarly, *The Daily Mirror* used its front page to advertise a two-page interview with Orlando Bloom on 'life as a sex symbol' to be found inside (Webster 2003), employing the pun 'lad of the rings' – thus forwarding their apparent agenda to inject sophistication into the apathetic state of public wit. Not to be outdone, but sticking to the self-perceived profile of their broadsheet serious-ness, *The Times* and *The Guardian* chose 17 December to print news reports on, again respectively, 'The Orlando Bloom effect' – or two full pages on how women became attracted to *The Lord of the Rings* (Whitworth 2003) – and on *The Return of the King*'s chances of success at the still-two-months away Academy Award cer-emonies (Campbell 2003). Also in *The Times*, columnist Mary Ann Sieghart man-aged to mention *The Lord of the Rings* twice, strategically both in the opening and last paragraphs, in an otherwise unrelated diatribe against lists of 'ten best ever things' (2003: 3).

By far the cleverest pieces, by dint of self-reflexivity, were two letters, selected by *The Daily Mail* and *The Guardian*, that seem to represent two kinds of pop-ular observations about the public presence of *The Lord of the Rings*. The first letter addressed the assertion that the books would have never been chosen as the 'most popular book' without the enhanced visibility the films gave it – some-thing the writer happened to disagree with (Jones 2003). The second letter dryly implied a connection between the popularities of the books and the notorious tab-loid *The Sun*, suggesting their popularity is somehow symptomatically connected (Humphreys 2003).

Together, these pieces demonstrate how far-reaching the public presence of *The Lord of the Rings* was at the time of its release. It penetrated virtually every kind of discourse newspapers can offer, and it testifies to the sheer blanket reach of such a penetration within other, unrelated news stories. Importantly, it also shows how the public presence of *The Lord of the Rings* became a *perpetuum mobile*, a media machine that uses the energy it creates itself to reach a momentum through which it becomes self-sufficient. These pieces show how the story of the *release* of *The Lord of the Rings* had become as important as stories *about the film*. The public presence of *The Lord of the Rings* was worth devoting attention to because it war-ranted … public attention.

The conflation of criticism and publicity

Officially, criticism, in the form of reviews and informed discussions of film texts upon their release, has long attempted to escape connections with publicity, and claimed success in doing so. While it has been said repeatedly that such isola-tion is unattainable (as former *Cahiers du cinéma* editor Serge Daney admits, in Simons 1988: 59) or even undesirable (Mathijs 1997), it still haunts reviews and reviewers (Rosenbaum 1998), making it a pressing issue in the study of the public presence of cinema today. This chapter addresses this issue by investigating the critical reception of *The Lord of the Rings* in the national newspapers of the United Kingdom.[2] It relies upon a systematic collection and coding of all reports on *The*

Lord of the Rings and J.R.R. Tolkien in Britain's nine national newspapers between 1 October 2003 and 1 January 2004.[3] As a starting point, the chapter assumes a certain kind of unease between the traditional role of the critic as a disinterested commentator who discusses cultural products and (sometimes) links them to their public presence, and the accusation that all criticism has become futile because it has been colonised into what Jonathan Romney has called 'auxilliary PR troops' (1998: 66).

One obvious thing inviting this unease, in fact offering an argument about the complicity of the British press with the publicity efforts of the film's distributors, is the conflation between criticism and publicity in general. By far the most common attention *The Return of the King* received on 17 December was through adverts. *The Daily Express, The Daily Mail, The Daily Mirror, The Daily Star, The Guardian, The Independent, The Times* and *The Sun* all carried an identical advert, covering a column-long, outer-corner half-page with the exact same picture and the exact same slogan, 'at cinemas everywhere now' (see Figure 4, overleaf). Such adverts are arranged by other departments in the newspapers' households, and as such they escape editorial scrutiny and control. But there is something uncanny about them. All of these adverts prominently feature praising quotes from reviews of the as yet unreleased film *from the very same pool of newspapers*. The praise includes hyperbolic phrases like 'a masterpiece', 'the film of the year', 'astounding', 'unmissable', 'stupendous', all carrying the much coveted five-star rating these same papers granted *The Return of the King* in earlier discussions.

The Lord of the Rings seems to have functioned as a kind of Christmas day feast for the usually feuding press, in its capacity to unite them, like so many ornery relatives, in a flushed and fervent toast. Such is the intoxicating power of the publicity machine over editorial policies. Yet some measure of pride has been allotted to the revelers: while the range of quotes covers at least five sources per advert, thus forcing newspapers to acknowledge the public validity of their competition, the papers have apparently been allowed to put their own quotes first. So *The Times'* first quote, claiming *The Lord of the Rings* is 'the great film of our time' comes from *The Times; The Daily Star* quotes *The Daily Star* first, *The Daily Mail The Daily Mail...* and so on. There is a subtly yet decidedly incestuous aura hanging over all this co-mingling, like the one hanging over that weird candid photo of uncle Bob and cousin Nancy under the mistletoe. Apart from the fact it is perfectly reasonable for a paper to re-use its own statements, there are three remarkable elements to this quoting. The first is that they quote reviews, while the film itself is not yet released. The second is that the framing of these quotes as publicity praise in an advert re-conceptualises their value as critical statements. It seems that the review was written with this boughs-of-holly use in mind. Third, on a more general level, these two elements beg an examination of the relationships between the use of reviews and the editorial policies of the press. In tackling these elements, this chap-

Figure 3: *The Lord of the Rings* newspaper advert of 17 December 2003

ter will first discuss current trends in film reviewing, describing the conditions under which this activity occurs, and paying particular attention to previews and premieres. Next, it will systematically sketch the trajectory of the critical reception of *The Return of the King* in the UK, outlining its major characteristics. Finally, it will single out two papers, *The Times* and *The Independent*, who have been appropriating *The Return of the King* to convey moral and political perspectives, and examine how the attitudes these papers have towards its public presence correspond to their editorial policies on film reviewing.

Reviews, previews and premieres

Traditionally, criticism functions as the forum of discussion *par excellence* of aesthetics and arts. It is a form of writing dedicated to close examination of cultural products, the relationship of products to their contexts, and their social roles. Terry Eagleton (1984) places criticism firmly within the bourgeois public sphere, as a tool through which communication on the topics of society, its culture, its values and its arts can be facilitated. But Eagleton also makes note of pressures that criticism is subject to. Among the many he and others note, two stand out as most significant (also see Ciment 1998; Taylor 1999; Mathijs 2003a and 2003b). First, there is pressure to set a tone. As in all debates, whoever makes the first argument, whoever scores the first point, has an advantage. So there is pressure on the critic to make haste to ensure topicality, and to refer only to the present when discussing a product. This pressure goes directly against the necessary distance a critique requires in order to come to terms with the complexities and intentions (sometimes less than honourable ones) of the cultural product under scrutiny. Second, and partly subsequently, there is a pressure on the critic to submit to the lures and appeals of either the product or the cultural context it attains to. All products, and their makers, presenters and beneficiaries, have an interest in receiving the best possible criticism, as it will (they hope) increase the relevance of the product. Similarly, forces within cultural contexts will try their best to accommodate or oppose certain products – will try to force or prevent connections with certain values and tastes. They see the critic and his or her judgement as one that must be influenced in order to attain a desired outcome.

These pressures of topicality and disinterestedness are key to understanding contemporary film reviewing. As a challenge to disinterestedness, for instance, David Bordwell (1989) discusses the pervasiveness of 'invisible colleges', circles of professional practice and beliefs which advocate certain approaches towards reviewing film (like auteurism, or symptomatic interpretation, or linking characters to spectators) and hence limit the possibilities of interpreting films (see also Branigan 1993). Beyond Bordwell, even more stringent limits like editorial policies and formats, personal egos, partisan alignments and restricted access are recent examples of the pressure on the disinterested critic (Corliss 1990; Ebert 1990; Cook 1993; Wood 1993; Mathijs 1997). They have become so dominant that they can actually block a reviewer from doing his/her job. As a result, critics now need to both prove their independence while juggling all sorts of influences to guarantee publication – permitting the use of their language and status for publicity purposes being only one of them. Topicality, as a challenge to the critic's distance to the product, is recently often cloaked in controversy, hype and the rush towards publication. These are indicative of a marketplace rank with competition, antagonism and hyperbole. In other words, it is expected that contemporary reviewers be the first to espouse what will become the prevailing opinion, or to trumpet that opinion louder and more elaborately than anyone else, or to hold a deviating position, if the critique is to be noted at all among the many that are published. Newspaper reviewing is especially sensitive to these pressures, as it sees itself as threatened on two fronts by the fickleness of its audience. On the one hand it must compete with new(er) media like television and the internet in getting word out first. On the other it sees itself, traditionally (because of the place newspapers still hold in the public sphere), in competition with weekly and monthly publications for delineating relevance in a society. Consequently, newspaper reviewers need to be fast, and they need to be 'right'.

The two pressures and their implications have led to a curious situation in which newspaper film reviewing has pushed topicality beyond interpretation into anticipation, and disinterested distance into uncomfortably close proximity. It has led to the advent of what I propose to call 'previewing': securing access to the product before its actual release, thus being forced to guess its cultural impact (rather than observing it), getting the message out among a frenzy of publicity hyping, carefully mimicking pre-approved languages so as not to jeopardise that access for future use, and to admit that same message for re-packaging in subsequent publicity efforts. Ironically, in twenty-first-century film reviewing, previewing has become part and parcel of regular procedure. In relation to *The Lord of the Rings* the term 'previewing' has been used by Bertha Chin and Jonathan Gray (2001) in their essay on the prefiguration of *The Fellowship of the Ring*. Even though Chin and Gray mainly focus on the internet and, to some extent, on fans, their essay is nevertheless revealing in its positioning of previews:

> Amidst continuing and excited press releases, magazine articles and official website updates ... the film had already attracted numerous and sizeable organised discussion groups ... A curious situation therefore exists in which people are congregating to discuss, often in great detail, a text which does not yet truly exist. Or, to reword, 'pre-viewers' are discussing 'pre-texts'. (2001)

Chin and Gray only implicitly refer to previews as conflated with publicity, and they prefer, much like Bordwell, to see 'pre-viewers' as interpreting 'pre-texts' pretty much free from the pressures of distance and/or topicality. Nevertheless, they note the setting of this activity is 'bathed in hype' – inundated with pre-release attempts to attract viewers. I would like to extend Chin and Gray's pre-viewer to the actual preview procedure, and firmly place its interpretive act in the middle of the pre-release clangour of other agendas and activities, and see it applicable not just to the internet but to printed press as well (of both official and fanzine kind).

The earlier example of newspapers quoting their own reviews of a yet unreleased film is a perfect illustration of the preview procedure. The apparent contradiction of quoting non-existing reviews was conveniently solved by an event that took place six days before the general release: the gala premiere. Once an important aspect of classical Hollywood, the premiere had seemingly lost much of its appeal in a world of global multiplex releases. But the move, observed by Daniel Biltereyst and Philippe Meers in this volume, of making blockbusters into media events has allowed them a comeback. They not only function as a newsworthy event generating coverage, but they also, and importantly, function as crucial in generating that high-status coverage known as 'critical review', even prior to general release, so that it can be recuperated for further publicity use. On Thursday 11 December 2003, hundreds of distinguished guests, including cast members Viggo Mortensen, Liv Tyler and Ian McKellen, attended the British Leicester Square opening of *The Return of the King*. Until that day, news on *The Return of the King* had been limited to either referencing it in unrelated stories (itself a sign of its lurking presence of course), or to short blips; on the day of the premiere itself, the British newspaper press carried six pieces mentioning the films and/or the books. One, in *The Times*, was an announcement for the upcoming *Sunday Times* (promising a free poster of Legolas). Three were gossip tales, about Liv Tyler wearing no pants when filming the trilogy in *The Sun*; about Elijah Wood being unable to find a girlfriend because of his Hobbit connotations in *The Daily Star* (Purves, Brooks & Watts 2003); and the UK distributors Entertainment Films refusing displays of the books at their gala opening in *The Daily Express* (Hickey 2003)). One piece was a rant against the books' popularity in polls (including the phrase '*L*rd of the Bl*ody R*ngs*') in *The Independent* (Walsh 2003), and another, by a former student, was an account of how boring J.R.R. Tolkien's lectures were in *The Times* (Blamires 2003).

But after the premiere the number and quality of reports and stories on *The Return of the King* rose to 57, including big front-page pictures, previews with critical praise for the films in all national papers (with the exception of *The Sun*), and many special editions devoted to the film (no paper had only one piece on the film – *The Daily Telegraph* carried the lowest profile with two pieces). It is from this pool that the quotes used in the blanket publicity on the day of the general release were pulled. And the reviewers themselves were fully aware of that. To take one example: Kevin O'Sullivan in *The Daily Mirror* explicitly states that he was 'one of the privileged "elite" to attend the very first British screening' (2003: 40). And in *The Daily Mail* Christopher Tookey also seems very aware of the fact that his words will be eligible for publicity recycling. Assuming his adjectives will end up as endorsements, he decides to be witty about it and starts his discussion with words he knows are contrary to what is expected:

> Disappointing. Overblown. Anti-climactic. Bungled. These are just some of the adjectives I shall not be using to describe the third part of *The Lord of the Rings*. How about amazing, stupendous, jaw-dropping and overwhelming? (2003: 52)

There are a few exceptions to this recruitment of previews into the publicity machine. As already noted, *The Sun* did not publish a review on 12 December. Instead it chose to be true to its populist identity and chastise Elijah Wood and Orlando Bloom for not attending the premiere, stating that 'these pampered luvvies should remember who made them famous – or their careers could soon be heading for Mount Doom' (2003h: 12). Two days later, *The Sun*'s Sunday paper *News of the World* did publish a highly favourable preview. Another curious exception is that the previews published in *The Daily Telegraph*, *The Guardian* and *The Independent* did not end up in the quotes-list for the general release publicity campaign. One reason is the tone of the previews. While generous and positive, they are also less hyperbolic, more moderate. Sukhdev Sandhu's preview in *The Daily Telegraph* broaches issues such as the 'love' attraction between Sam and Frodo, or the long ending, or the 'glacially slow' first hour, and is critical of Mortensen's 'over-seriousness' and his lack of 'cadence and rousing phraseology in his battlefield speech', Sam's 'oddity,' and wishes the film had had 'some topping and tailing' (2003: 21). Similarly, Charlotte O'Sullivan in *The Independent* is cautious and insists the ending is too long and 'soppy' (2003: 5). A more likely reason is that these three newspapers did not reach agreement with the marketers for re-use of their words for publicity purposes, for reasons of integrity perhaps, or because they are less 'wanted'. For in the end, *The Guardian*, *The Independent* and *The Daily Telegraph* could be seen as being rebuked in having to carry the general release publicity with other papers' generous quotes heading the page, without even the comfort of having their own quotes displayed – a route the remaining broadsheet *The Times* did take.

A systematic view on the critical reception of *The Return of the King*

It seems, then, that previews are linked to policies. But before delving into a case study comparison between the approaches of *The Independent* and *The Times* with regard to previewing and reviewing *The Return of the King*, how well-penetrated the concept of previewing is needs to be determined. Does the example of the general release day advert mean all previews are mere accomplices of the media machine? Answering this requires a systematic view on critical reception of cinema.

Traditionally, critical reception of cinema is studied qualitatively, as I have been doing here so far. It stems from a combination of a film studies and cultural studies approach towards cinema. The film studies approach focuses on the actual activity of interpretation, and is concerned with which (and how) meanings *inherent* to film are communicated in criticism. Robin Wood, David Bordwell and Rick Altman have studied how ideology, narrative, and genre are treated in film criticism (Wood 1978; Bordwell 1981, 1997; Altman 1999). The cultural studies approach is more concerned with how (and which) interpretations are *created* by criticism. Janet Staiger, Barbara Klinger and myself have emphasised how ideology (again), style and rhetorics are evoked by critics (Staiger 1992, 2000; Klinger 1997; Mathijs 2003a). But qualitative studies of reception have never managed to convincingly prove that their observations are also representative for an entire reception. Staiger's discussion of gender and sexuality in the critical reception of *The Silence of the Lambs* (Jonathan Demme, 1991) for instance, may well refer to a very marginal discourse, one which hardly upsets the mainstream reception of the film (Mathijs 2002; see also I. Q. Hunter's chapter in this volume).

Studying the previews and reviews of *The Return of the King* thus requires an integrated approach, which attempts to combine the attention for detail of a qualitative analysis with the representativeness of a quantitative one. In this study, this has led to the adoption of a method of coding and analysing 935 newspaper publications, collected between 1 October 2003 and 1 January 2004, without losing sight of the details of their content and language. The method is similar to content analyses, and is derived from Karl Erik Rosengren's study of the Swedish literary frame of reference, Marcus Hudec and Brigitte Lederer's study of theatre reviews and Wesley Shrum's analysis of performing arts reviews (Rosengren 1984; Hudec & Lederer 1984; Shrum 1991). At its base lies the 'mention': a term or word within the print message that contains meaning, in the form of its references, allusions, opinions, indications or implications. According to Rosengren:

> A mention may be regarded as an expression of an association made by the reviewer, and … can be used as an indicator of topicality … All the mentions made in all reviews of the press in a region during a given time period (or in a representative sample thereof) may be regarded as an expression of the lexicon … available to the reviewers and constituting a central element of [their] frame of reference. (1984: 238)

In this case, all mentions of *The Lord of the Rings*, *The Return of the King* or Tolkien in all British newspapers were coded. The coding system consisted of eight dimensions: date, source, size (5pt. scale: more than a full page, full page, ½ page, ¼ page, less than ¼ page), emphasis within size (5pt. scale: feature, lead, significant attention, filler, mention), kind of report/text (8 types), key expressions, key references and notes. The eight kinds of reports are: p/review (with a subcategory

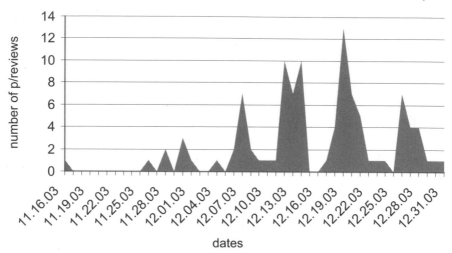

dates of publication of p/reviews (release date 17/12/2003)

Table 12: Spread of publication of p/reviews

for p/reviews of related materials like *The Two Towers* DVD), interview, news report, gossip/trivia report, advert, unrelated news report, and letter.

For this chapter only p/reviews are taken into account. Of the 935 reports, 101 (10.8%) qualified as p/reviews of *The Return of the King*. Just over half of these (51) were published before the general release of the film, confirming the impression that previews have become an increasingly important phenomenon in film criticism. As expected, peaks in publication occur around events like the gala premiere or the general release (and the weekends following these events) (Table 12).

One curious observation here is the lull of Wednesday 17 December, the 'eye of the storm' tranquility on the day of the general release; a not-altogether unexpected but still remarkable moment, and one that most accounts of media hyping fail to mention.

A breakdown per newspaper shows striking differences between certain titles. There seems to be a peculiar distinction between tabloids and broadsheets. With the exception of *The Times*, which published no less than 188 reports (an average of *two reports per day*), broadsheets carry far less reports mentioning *The Lord of the Rings* than tabloids (the lowest is *The Daily Telegraph*, which still has one report every two days in which the film is mentioned). Yet, while the tabloids have as many p/reviews as the broadsheets on average, the majority of them devote less than 10% of their coverage of *The Lord of the Rings* to p/reviews (*The Daily Mirror*'s 12.12% being the top). Broadsheets devote at least 15% of their coverage to p/reviews; a notable exception, again, being *The Times* (and the top being *The Independent* in which a fifth of all reports is a p/review).

Unsurprisingly then, the two papers that carry most p/reviews are broadsheets, namely *The Times* and *The Independent*, who each publish 18 p/reviews (given the fact there are hardly any in the first two months, this means one every five days on average). These relations are not unusual, and they largely conform to editorial policies and common sense views on the British daily press. I will come back to the anomaly of *The Times* later.

Publication	Nov. (preview)	Dec. (preview)	Dec. (review)	# p/review	# reports	% p/review
Daily Express	0	3	2	5	79	6.33%
Guardian/ Observer	0	6	3	9	60	15%
Independent	1	2	15	18	88	20.45%
Daily Mail	0	7	4	11	133	8.27%
Daily Mirror	0	6	6	12	99	12.12%
Star	0	3	3	6	115	5.22%
Sun/NW	3	4	4	11	106	10.38%
Telegraph	2	4	2	8	45	17.78%
Times	1	8	9	18	188	9.58%
Other	0	1	2	3	22	13.63%
Total	7	44	50	101	935	10.80%

Table 13: P/reviews per newspaper

When separating previews from reviews, using the day of general release as a cleavage point, there are again remarkable dissimilarities. Confirming the impression of the importance of previews, all but one of the British newspapers publish more previews than reviews. The exception to this is *The Independent*, which has a preview/reviews ratio of 1:5, completely different from any other newspaper. Most other papers have a near 1:1 ratio, which means that although there are just more previews than reviews overall, there are only small differences. In fact, excluding the one more review than preview *The Times* has, *The Independent* alone accounts for balancing the overall ratio of 51/50. The differences between tabloids and broadsheets here are less sharp than with the overall reports, but they are still remarkable. Perhaps more interesting, however, is the division along political and editorial policy lines. When all right-wing or conservative papers are grouped together (*The Daily Express, The Daily Mail, The Times* and *The Daily Telegraph* – excluding the populist *Sun* and *Daily Star*, whose ratio is 1:1

anyway), there is a 22:17 ratio of previews:reviews. By way of comparison, the progressive/left-wing papers have a ratio of 15:24. So, preceding explanations we have the fact that conservative papers seem to put more emphasis on previews and progressive papers tend to focus on reviews; a dichotomy of setting the tone for or worrying about/celebrating the upcoming event versus explaining/reflecting on the perceived trajectory of the event post-hoc. Hysteria versus history if you want.

A final general observation relates to the number of p/reviews close to the cleavage point. Separating p/reviews either way from the cleavage point by periods of a week (so 14 days and 7 days before the 17th and 7 days and 14 days after it, respectively), we find an unsurprisingly steep increase in reports near the day of general release, and an equally unsurprisingly more gradual decline afterwards.

Publication	14 days before	7 days before	Release day	7 days after	14 days after	Total
Daily Express	0	3	0	1	1	5 (5)
Guardian/Observer	1	5	0	3	0	9 (9)
Independent	0	2	0	9	6	17 (18)
Daily Mail	5	2	0	2	2	11 (11)
Daily Mirror	2	4	0	2	4	12 (12)
Daily Star	0	3	0	2	1	6 (6)
Sun/NW	1	3	0	3	1	8 (11)
Telegraph	1	3	0	2	0	6 (8)
Times	3	3	1	6	3	16 (18)
Other	0	1	0	2	0	3 (3)
Total	13	29	1	32	18	93 (101)

Table 14: P/reviews per newspaper near release day

When broken down per title, we see that the two tabloids traditionally associated with setting agendas and chasing scoops on either side of the political spectrum, *The Daily Mirror* and *The Daily Mail* are, together with *The Times*, the first to start previewing *The Return of the King*. This is even before the London gala premiere described above. In fact, when we examine the previews, we see that much is made about being the first to comment and set the tone. Until 9 December, when *The Times* announces on the top of its front page (in colour) that it is publishing 'the first review' of *The Return of the King*, all critical attention for the film is captured within the borders of collectors' packages in special editions of the paper, a promotional tool with some critical value. It seems that the news-papers themselves make a distinction in critical stamina between these 'collectors' previews', and that it is, at that point, more important to be the first one publishing any kind of critical discussion than to offer a proper 'stand alone' preview. This is certainly the case with three out of the five previews in *The Daily Mail* (all published on 7 December, in the Sunday special edition). They are highly descriptive in tone, and obviously directed towards offering as much information about the film as possible (and very little discussion). The conflation with publicity is also very clear from the explicit mentioning of sponsors like New Zealand Tourism and New Zealand Air. Significantly, next to the descriptions, the foci in the three previews are on the film's box office expectations, the New Zealand premiere event, and the special effects efforts, only dabbling in classical textual discussion.

Conforming more to the 'stand alone' discussion form are *The Daily Mirror* and *The Times* previews – if only because both actually refer to themselves as 'reviews'. *The Daily Mirror* proudly states its preview of 10 December is the 'first review of the final rings epic' (Hiscock 2003: 21). In it, John Hiscock puts considerable emphasis on the 'little man' perspective *The Return of the King* maintains, even amidst the big spectacle. 'Peter Jackson, the barefooted film-maker' has, he writes, 'hobbit-like' succeeded in keeping a balance, to 'make us care about the fates of the heroes and the little hobbits, the fallible folks fight-

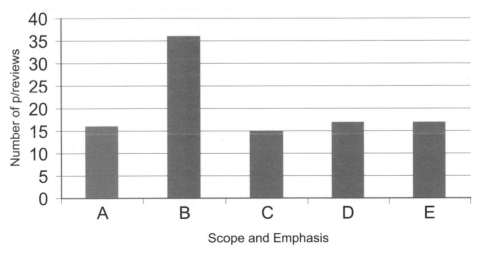

Table 15: Scope and emphasis in p/reviews

ing impossible odds' (ibid.). The odd one out here is definitely *The Times*, a well-respected establishment broadsheet (though with a tarnished blazon since its takeover by Rupert Murdoch almost twenty years ago). It beats *The Daily Mirror* by a day in publishing its 'first' preview. It is in fact, as a footnote to the text explains, 'an edited version of a review which appeared in *The New Zealand Herald*' (Baillie 2003: 17). This admission cuts both ways. It devalues the originality of *The Times'* preview as only a re-hash, not a scoop. But it also gives the preview the proper weight of a review (after all, it was published *after* a premiere!). I will come back to the content of this p/review below, when comparing it to others, but *The Times'* efforts to get its voice heard early and loud among the newspapers are a recurrent thread throughout the critical reception of *The Return of the King* in the United Kingdom.

In the 7-days-before bracket, we see an overall increase in attention, with all newspapers, except for *The Daily Mail* (which actually falls back a bit, probably because 'collectors'' scoops became less relevant so close to the actual release). As has been pointed out above, a lot of this increase is predictable, as it includes the London gala premiere, thus inviting proper p/reviews, albeit ones that are up for recuperation in the final-push publicity effort. Together with *The Daily Mail*, *The Independent* also stands out, not only because, as noted earlier, it failed/refused to get its quotes used in the subsequent poster campaign (and indeed published a lukewarm rather than hysterical p/review of the premiere), but also because it has the slowest increase. It seems *The Independent* is the most reluctant of British newspapers to follow the hype, either because of its attitude towards the hype itself, the product, or the story. I will come back to *The Independent*'s characteristics below.

On the day of the general release *The Times* is the only paper publishing a p/review, again a sign of its commitment to reporting on the film, whether slavishly following the hype or driving it. The week after the release shows the highest number of p/reviews, expectedly, though only by a small margin; the hype is now at its high point, with each paper devoting at least two reviews to the film. In itself this is not surprising, since this period includes a weekend, allowing for one review on either Thursday, the first day following the release, or Friday, the usual day for reviews (especially in Friday Review sections), and one in the Sunday edition. Among the immediate post-release coverage the broadsheets stand out. They account for 20 out of 32 reports, a notable increase, especially since they had been devoting far less attention to the film prior to its release. It leads to suggest that broadsheets conform more to the traditional template of reviewing. Especially exceptional is the high increase in reports in *The Independent* and *The Times*. For *The Times* this still seems a continuation of their devotion to the topic, but for *The Independent* it is a clear break from its reluctance. Again, I will elaborate on this below.

In the next period, running up to two weeks after the release, all papers show the expected decline in coverage: the hype is over and new topics gradually take over; an evolution also mirrored in the diminishing size of reports. Four papers, however, maintain a continuous interest markedly higher than the others. Together, *The Daily Mail, The Daily Mirror, The Times* and *The Independent* account for 15 out of 18 reviews in this period. They are a round-up of usual suspects: *The Times'* attention is to be expected by now, and *The Independent* seems to extend its recent surge in interest in the film. And *The Daily Mail* and *The Daily Mirror* were (with *The Times*) the papers that kick-started the p/reviews.

But just how much attention to *The Lord of the Rings* do these p/reviews give? In other words, how high is the intrinsic newsworthiness of the film, as perceived by the papers? Since the qualification for being included in the corpus of materials was mentioning *The Lord of the Rings/ The Return of the King/*Tolkien this could, technically, mean that all p/reviews only briefly mention them and then devote most of their argumentation and space to other issues. A look at the size and emphasis in p/reviews shows this not to be the case.

The majority of p/reviews give half a page to a full page to the topic, the regular size of a p/review – and the regular size of a publicity-sponsored special collectors' description as well. But there are some peculiarities. For one, it needs to be noted that the longest p/reviews, covering more than a page, only appear up to 18 December, the day after the film's release. This size may be not unusual for the first post-release day of a blockbuster hyped to the extent of *The Lord of the Rings*, but it certainly is for anything appearing prior to the release. When taking a closer look, these pre-release previews of more than one page are all part of special issues, collectors' editions, and so on. This pattern suggests that the size of p/reviews (as well as their formatting) is closely related to the immediacy of the actual product they are connected to (or even supposed to support). It makes the conflation between criticism and publicity even more clear. When looking at them per title, they are curiously all part of the conservative part of the political/editorial spectrum (with the exception of *The Guardian*), and most of them are tabloids (whose pages are admittedly more easy to fill). Conversely, when looking at the smallest p/reviews, they all seem to come from the progressive/left-wing press (12 out of 17), and – tied-in of course – they are mainly post-release.

Does this mean the conservative press is more easily tricked into tapping into a hype constructed by publicity machines? Or does it mean the conservative press helped create that hype? Why? Did it consciously seek an alliance with that hype, rallying around the same cause? And what is that cause: easy profit in sales, visibility, an enhanced public presence? Or is there, perhaps intangibly, a textual reason why the conservative and tabloid press appropriated *The Return of the King*, claiming it as one of theirs, and giving it a full-blown (if not overblown) endorsement? Similarly, is there something in *The Lord of the Rings* text that makes progressive/left-wing papers cringe (its politics, its popularity)? Or do they just loathe being part of a hype, hence resisting it (sabotaging it) by only offering the minimal amount of exposure, by carefully balancing praise and criticism? Or did they not even get selected by the publicity machines, not allowed on the gravy train? Paranoid as these questions may seem, they are not irrelevant. They go to the heart of contemporary synergies between media, to the heart of how the public presence of *The Lord of the Rings* is aided, resisted and managed even via such small a tool as film reviewing.

The Times versus *The Independent*

One way of getting some answers to these questions on conflation between criticism and publicity, and the complicity (or resistance) of the film press to hypes and receptions, is to isolate two symptomatic *and* representative cases, two *causes célèbres*, whose confrontation allows speculation on intentions, infights and inferences – a boxing match. Take one guess which titles best qualify for such a polarisation: Yep, *The Times* and *The Independent*; the grand ole dame and the new kid on the block. As stipulated repeatedly above, they have profiles epitomising (and taking into extremes) positions occupied by newspapers from opposite ends of the editorial and political spectrum. And although both papers have recently gone 'compact' (meaning they appear in tabloid format without adhering to tabloid practices), they display two different strands of broadsheet attitudes towards film, popular culture, art and society.

The Times and *The Independent* published more p/reviews than any other newspaper in the UK. For *The Times* it was only part of much wider coverage of *The Return of the King* (it only covered 9.58% of all their reports mentioning the film); for *The Independent* it made up a fifth of their coverage (20.45%). Among

Size/ Emphasis	Independent	Times	All newspaper p/reviews
A	0	3 (1p/2r*)	16
B	4 (1p/3r)	7 (5p/2r)	36
C	2 (1p/1r)	4 (2p/2r)	15
D	6 (6r)	2 (1p/2r)	17
E	6 (5p/1r)	2 (2r)	17
Total	18	18	101

Table 16: Size and emphasis in p/reviews of *The Independent* and *The Times*
*1p/2r = 1preview/2reviews

them, they published a third of all previews and half of all reviews. The differences in balance between previews and reviews are huge: *The Times* published as many previews as reviews, whereas *The Independent* published 13% previews and 87% reviews. When we look at the size and emphasis in these p/reviews, we see that the general pattern noted in the overall emphases is confirmed. *The Times* gives much more space to *The Return of the King* than *The Independent* and in its p/reviews the film is the sole topic of discussion.[4] Significantly, most of its full-page pieces are previews, and the two larger-sized reviews are from 17 and 18 December (so right after the release). In other words, *The Times* must be seen as either spearheading the hyping of *The Return of the King*, at least in terms of reviewing it, or as a close accomplice in that hype. Conversely, *The Independent's* p/reviews are much smaller, indicating that it sees the film as far less of a newsworthy event or product than *The Times*. The tenor of its p/reviews is actually not that different from that of *The Times*, but the smaller size shows the reluctance of the praise, as if *The Independent* is weary of being caught up (or recuperated by) the hype. Tellingly, when we look at the actual pieces, several of *The Independent's* smallest ones are *capsule reviews* from a recurring banner in its review section in which *The Return of the King* is, day after day, mentioned as one of the five best films on release. It seems, then, that whereas *The Times* hypes, *The Independent* evaluates.

The question is to what extent these attitudes shine through in the actual contents of the reviews, and in which way they are part of editorial policy. In other words, do *The Times* and/or *The Independent* p/reviews connect, as a p/review should (at least classically), film text to context, and discuss the film's cultural relevance? And does in that effort the editorial policy shine through? The short answer is they do, it does, and further even there is an interesting tension between the editors and the reviewers themselves. Looking at the previews first, and taking *The Independent's* 'first night' preview by Charlotte O'Sullivan as an example, it is clear how much previews see it as their duty to cover the event as well as the film. These are her opening paragraphs:

> From the start, director Peter Jackson said the final instalment would be the best. Hundreds turned up in the wee hours of yesterday morning, despite the rain, so they would have a good view of cast members such as Liv Tyler, Orlando Bloom and Sir Ian McKellen walk into the premiere at London's Odeon Leicester Square.
>
> Tolkien's *The Lord of the Rings* trilogy has morphed from being a quirky gamble – a fantasy adventure too frightening for kids and possibly too silly for adults – into the surest thing in town. *Harry Potter 3* did not dare take it on this Christmas. The battle for the West has been fought and Jackson, the hairy, humble New Zealander who met his wife while working on the BBC's *Worzel Gummidge*, would seem to have won. Expectations for *The Return of the King* have peaked somewhere around the Himalayas. The opening sequence leaves us giddier still. (2003: 5)

Even before the first word on the film text itself is uttered, O'Sullivan has given the reader 142 words on the event, up to a description of the weather and how Jackson met his wife, taking up about a fifth of her total space. *The Times* previews display roughly the same pattern, but with more focus on the metaphorical elements of the event. Here's how Roger Baillie ends his preview:

> Like the book, the film takes a while to find its ending but it deserves a few curtain calls. Much of the film is beyond exhilarating, and this instalment is certainly the best of the three, effectively elevating the series into the greatest trilogy in cinema history. Peter Jackson started off filming a legend. Now he is one. (2003: 17)

There is less emphasis on the event element, but at least as much on the placing of the film in an event-context, even giving it historical overtones.

In terms of actual content, the difference between *The Times* and *The Independent* previews is one of tone. Both praise the film, but in *The Independent* there is a clear reluctance to use hyperbolic language, resulting in a more moderate, careful tone, whereas *The Times* goes full-out on superlatives. It raises the suspicion that *The Times*' policy was one of full endorsement or even alignment, and *The Independent*'s was one of anxious neutrality. Even the references used fit this suspicion. O'Sullivan draws attention to *Harry Potter*, *Worzel Gummidge*, the bad teeth of Orcs, Gollum's qualities as a tourist guide and, as expected (and in line with the earlier quoted preview from *The Daily Mirror*) 'the little hobbits' who 'play a much bigger (ahem) part' (O'Sullivan 2003: 5). These are small-scale, even funny and, why not, childish references; attempts to bring the size of *The Return of the King* down to earth, and in fact resisting its epic implications. Baillie puts forward a completely different set of comparisons than O'Sullivan. Instead of acknowledging the 'small men' point of view, he sees *The Return of the King* only in terms of bravura and grandeur. The references are to King Lear, Henry V, Shakespeare and 'politics, loyalties and blood ties' (2003: 17). It gives his arguments a much heftier look, and, incidentally or not, an inference of imperialism and empire. Ironically since it was originally published in New Zealand (but heavily edited), this seems a very empire-establishment preview, quite happy to use the 'epic' trope to put forward what could be seen as aristocratic (dare I say despotic?) and feudal-sounding claims about 'loyalty' and 'blood ties' – there is no mention of the 'little man' here.

Turning to reviews, the same discourses prevail. Looking at both lengthy and capsule reviews of each paper, there are also some fascinating editorial differences within titles. Firstly, it is worth noting that the focus on the event does not wear off after the release. It is still at the centre of reviewing. *The Times Supplement* review of 18 December spends two pages (including its front page) laying out how the film taps into the original story by giving the impression it is 'a boy's tale' (Macaulay

2003: 1, 5). This is not just an argument about how few girls there are in the story or film, but one about the cultural sedimentation of *The Lord of the Rings*; a history of its relevance. And on the same day we find a capsule review in *The Independent*, describing the event element of the film as follows: '*Rings III* is that rare thing: an event movie that rises to its sense of occasion with both emotive heft and fierce spectacle' (Anon. 2003d: 14). *The Times'* review is riddled with the same references and rhetoric as Baillie's preview: the same emphasis on romanticism, mythology, 'gods and kings', respect for enlightened despotism, and an added sense of nostalgia. Sean Macaulay writes: 'Amid the rise of the anti-hero and hardboiled disenchantment, Tolkien dared to offer up a Boy's Own fairy story' (2003: 1). This nostalgia, and the emphasis on the boyishness, makes Macaulay's inferences on the story's politics slightly more democratic (meritocratic?) than Baillie's; it turns them into an 'old boys' rhetoric. But the gist is still the same; it adds to the paper's backing of the story as one with whose politics they happily align themselves.

Curiously, *The Independent's* capsule review seems much less qualified than its previews, effectively countering the moderate tone of its p/reviewers. Other capsule reviews and review pieces from *The Independent* show the same pattern. Moreover, by re-publishing them on an almost daily basis, *The Independent's* editors reinforce these capsule reviews' messages, over and beyond that of the p/reviewers' isolated, one-off criticisms. In so doing, they reveal a strange tension between editorial content and review content. Their presence and tone seems to suggest *The Independent* lets its reviewers write what they want, but it exercises strict editorial control over less authorial pieces, like the capsule reviews. And in those pieces, the editors seem as keen to endorse *The Return of the King* as much as any other paper in the business, including unqualifiedly putting it forward as a brilliant event movie. A perfect example of this is a capsule review published on 20 December under the heading 'The Week in Review', in which a digest of the week's most memorable cultural event is given. The reviews are formatted so as to give an 'overview', 'our view' and a 'critical view' which includes opinions from other papers (Anon. 2003d: 14). The 'our view' section quotes from O'Sullivan's preview, and includes the criticism about the ending, but the other sections are much more positive towards the film (with the exception of one hilariously offensive diatribe from *The Daily Mirror* which mentions 'the nerdy Tolkien talk about elves, orcs and all that crap'). In all, the capsule review's overall presence, and the sheer fact it lists the film as one of the week's major events, again counters the papers own p/reviewer.

When looking carefully at some of both *The Times'* and *The Independent's* other reviews, this tension between editors and reviewers recurs quite frequently. It is present in Rod Little's criticism of the trilogy in his review of the year's most memorable events in *The Times* of 20 December, and in Howard Jacobson's review column in *The Independent* of the same day (Little 2003; Jacobson 2003). Both writers are allowed to take whatever position they want – both call *The Lord of the Rings* childish and undemocratic – but their opinions are frequently countered by pieces much more controlled by the editors. A very peculiar example is a quarter-page review piece carrying more news about *The Return of the King*'s box office performance and the audience research project this chapter (and others in this volume) is drawing from, both decidedly more about the event than about the actual film text (Malvern 2003).

Answering the question about the balance between textual discussion and criticism of the film's public presence more carefully, then, it seems that both *The Times* and *The Independent* are less hegemonic sites of critical discourse than first assumed. They are sites of struggle over authorial control between reviewers, whose individual opinions sometimes conflate with that of the publicity machine (especially when it comes to previews), and whose independence to write what they want (especially in post-release commentary) is checked by smaller pieces under strict editorial control, and editors, who negotiate a balance between editorial policy (*The Times* aligns with the film, *The Independent* remains careful) and the undeniable newsworthiness of the event itself. Previews seem to be better controlled by editors. Reviews still tend to escape some of that control, perhaps because, and this is the irony of the whole thing, some of the reviewers are stars in themselves. They can be paraded in all their eccentricity in the pages of a paper, and it is the connection of their public presence with that of the film-event, rather than the content of their criticisms, which makes, in the eyes of the editors, all the difference. Any contrary messages can easily be corrected. Returning to the question of the general political landscape of the British press, it appears, then, that in all newspapers, film reviews of *The Return of the King* are complicit in creating, maintaining and, ultimately, serving its massive public presence in the last few months of 2003 – regardless of their political affiliation or editorial attitude, and with only minimal possibility of resistance or deviation.

Perhaps the ultimate illustration of this pattern is articulated by Jonathan Romney's review in *The Independent on Sunday* entitled 'OK Peter. Message Received'. For Romney, celebrating an event such as *The Lord of the Rings* equals celebrating totalitarian cinema, all inferences included – part of which he traces to the film text (which he sees as 'self-important', 'hyperbolic', 'ideologically overstated', 'atavistic' and 'nasty'). This is how he ends his review:

> Critiquing such a film is like critiquing a religion; you either believe or you don't. ... I can't help feeling Jackson's trilogy goes further towards absolute imaginative domination of its audience than cinema ever should. I suspect there will come a saner time in film culture, which will look back on Jackson's achievement as magnificent but futile, perhaps even as a dreadful warning. Meanwhile, some of us pray for a little calm, a little restraint – a little minimalism please in 2004. (2003: 8)

Romney's main worry is for the independence of the reviewer amidst the frantic attempts of the publicity machine to force editors and reviewers to acknowledge the size and scale of *The Return of the King*, and to create a hype, an overwhelming public presence, from which there is no fair escape, thus validating the film culturally through that public presence, rather than through its textual qualities.

Conclusion

The key word in all British p/reviews of *The Return of the King* is 'epic'. But does it refer solely to a generic quality of the film? It would seem the epic element here is the event, the management of the film's release, more than its actual form and content. This chapter has tried to demonstrate how much of the newspaper film criticism process has become part of a negotiation of such management, be it in the forms of editorial politics, of conflation of criticism and publicity efforts, and of the complicity of reviewers in hyping a film (or resisting that very hype, equally contaminating for the critical enterprise). A blockbuster like *The Return of the King* has only magnified the extent to which these processes inhabit contemporary film reviewing.

One clear finding is that, in the case of *The Return of the King* there is indeed a conflation and complicity between film reviewing and publicity, between the discussion of a film's public presence and the promotion of that film's public presence. It is apparent not only in the editorial policies of the 'usual suspects' (the tabloids, the poujadist press), but also in the broadsheets and more moderate papers. It permeates decisions about size, emphasis and timing. It has led to a situation in which previewing a film has become more important than reflecting upon it post-release; a situation in which anticipative guesses about a film's impact and relevance for culture are more likely to get published, and are better controlled, than actual critical observations of that impact. On a smaller level, it has reinstated the premiere as a key event in the public launch of a film, and (as evidenced by case studies of *The Times* and *The Independent*) it has demonstrated how reviewers struggle to juggle their actual discussions of a film and their allegiance to whomever is kind enough to allow them to review anything at all, both their editors and their suppliers.

It takes a film trilogy of the magnitude of *The Lord of the Rings* to put these mechanisms in a clear light. It remains to be seen to what degree the critical reception of smaller films, and compared to *The Lord of the Rings* everything is smaller, adheres to the patterns and mechanisms laid out here. My conjecture is that they are not exclusive to Hollywood blockbusters. They may well be everywhere.

Notes

1   I want to thank Martin Barker, Daniel Biltereyst, Kate Egan, Philippe Meers and above

all Emily Perkins for willingly commenting on earlier versions of this chapter. Some of you got to hear the rant version only. Sincere apologies.

2   The newspapers investigated are: *The Daily Express/The Sunday Express, The Daily Mail/ The Mail on Sunday, The Daily Mirror/The Sunday Mirror, The Daily Star/The Sunday Star, The Guardian/The Observer, The Independent/The Independent on Sunday, The Times/The Sunday Times* and *The Sun/The News of the World* (the first title is the daily one, the second refers to the Sunday edition).

3   This research was developed as part of the International Lord of the Rings Research Project, supported by a grant from the UK Economic and Social Research Council (ESRC Grant No. 000-22-0323) to whom we record our gratitude.

4   This may seem logical, but the UK newspaper press has a tradition of publishing 'combined' reviews in which, in the scope of one review article up to five or six films on release will be discussed. In the case of *The Lord of the Rings* all its instalments received individual reviews, which is indicative of the importance the press allocates to it.

Works cited

Anon. (2003a) 'D'Arby Winner', *The Sun*, 17 December, 20.

_____ (2003b) 'Ears to You Orlando', *Daily Express*, 17 December, 21.

_____ (2003c) 'Film of the Day', *Daily Mirror* (17 December 2003), 28.

_____ (2003d) 'The Five Best Films', *The Independent Review*, 18 December, 14.

_____ (2003e) 'Free Lord of the Rings Poster Advert' (11 December 2003), 18.

_____ (2003f) 'Lad of the Rings Advert', *Daily Mirror* (17 December 2003), 2.

_____ (2003g) 'Liv Tyler', *The Sun* (11 December 2003), 21.

_____ (2003h) 'Missing', *The Sun* (12 December 2003), 12.

Altman, R. (1999) *Film/Genre*. London: British Film Institute.

Baillie, R. (2003) 'One Film to Rule them All', *The Times*, 9 December, 17.

Blamires, D. (2003) 'The Bore of the Rings', *The Times Supplement*, 11 December, 7.

Bordwell, D. (1981) 'Textual Analysis Etc.', *Enclitic*, 10, 5/2, 125–36.

_____ (1989) *Making Meaning: Inference and Rhetoric in the Interpretation of Cinema*. Cambridge, MA: Harvard University Press.

_____ (1997) *On the History of Film Style*. Cambridge, MA: Harvard University Press.

Branigan, E. (1993) 'On the Analysis of Interpretive Language, Part I', *Film Criticism*, 17, 2–3, 4–21.

Campbell, D. (2003) 'Return of the King tipped as one film to rule them all at Oscars', *Guardian*, 17 December, 13.

Chin, B. and J. Gray (2001) '"One Ring To Rule Them All": Pre-viewers and Pre-texts of the *Lord of the Rings*', *Intensities: The Journal of Cult Media*, 2. Online. Available at http://www.cult-media.com/issue2/Achingray.htm (accessed 5 July 2005).

Ciment, M. (1998) 'The Function and the State of Film Criticism', in J. Boorman and W. Donahue (eds) *Projections 8: Film-makers on Film-making*. Londen: Faber & Faber,

35–43.

Cook, D. (1993) 'Making Sense', *Film Criticism*, 17, 2–3, 31–9.

Corliss, R. (1990) 'All Thumbs or, Is There a Future for Film Criticism?', *Film Comment*, 26, 2, 14–18.

Eagleton, T. (1984) *The Function of Criticism*. London: Verso.

Ebert, R. (1990) 'All Stars or, Is There a Cure for Criticism of Film Criticism?', *Film Comment*, 26, 3, 45–51.

Hickey, J. (2003) 'Column', *Daily Express*, 11 December, 24.

Hiscock, J. (2003) 'Hobbit Forming', *Daily Mirror*, 10 December, 21.

Hudec, M. and B. Lederer (1984) 'A Text Model for the Content Analysis of Messages in the Print Media', in G. Melischek, K. E. Rosengren and J. Stappers (eds) *Cultural Indicators: An International Symposium*. Vienna: Verlag der Osterreichischen Akademie der Wissenschaften, 273–99.

Humphreys, K. (2003) 'Letter', *Guardian*, 17 December, 23.

Jacobson, H. (2003) 'Democracy is a Fine Thing; But Not For Everyone', *The Independent*, 20 December, 17.

Jones, R. (2003) 'Why Tolkien Lords Over it All', *Daily Mail*, 17 December, 42.

Klinger, B. (1997) 'Film History Terminable and Interminable: Recovering the Past in Reception Studies', *Screen*, 38, 2, 107–28.

Knaggs, S. (2003) 'Today's Choice', *Daily Express*, 17 December, 40.

Little, R. (2003) 'Stars and Stinkers', *The Times Review*, 20 December, 8–9.

Macaulay, S. (2003) 'Everything but Girls', *The Times Supplement*, 18 December, 1, 5.

Malvern, J. (2003) 'Tolkien Films Team Trawls Net "to find fantasy"', *The Times*, 20 December, 9.

Mathijs, E. (1997) 'Namedropping en het referentiekader van de hedendaagse kritiek', *Andere Sinema*, 150, 50–5.

_____ (2002) The 'Wonderfully Scary Monster' and the International Reception of Ridley Scott's *Hannibal* (2001)', *Kinoeye*, 2, 19. Online available at: http://www.kinoeye. org/02/19/mathijs19.php

_____ (2003a) 'AIDS References in the Critical Reception of David Cronenberg: It May Not Be Such a Bad Disease after All', *Cinema Journal*, 42, 4, 29–45.

_____ (2003b) 'The Making of a Cult Reputation: Topicality and Controversy in the Critical Reception of *Shivers*', in M. Jancovich, A. Lazaro-Reboll, J. Stringer and A. Willis (eds) *Defining Cult Movies: The Cultural Politics of Oppositional Taste*. Manchester: Manchester University Press, 109–26.

O'Sullivan, C. (2003) 'I Was Stroked and Stimulated into Submission, Then Soppy Farewells Put Me on the Orcs' Side', *Independent*, 12 December, 5.

O'Sullivan, K. (2003) 'Just Orc-Some', *Daily Mirror*, 12 December, 40–1.

Purves, L, N. Brooks and A. Watts (2003) 'Frodo Frozen Out By Babes', *Daily Star*, 11 December, 12.

Romney, J. (1998) 'A Critic's Diary', in J. Boorman and W. Donahue (eds) *Projections 8:*

Film-makers on Film-making. London: Faber & Faber, 64–86.

_____ (2003) 'OK Peter. Message Received', *The Independent on Sunday*, 21 December, 8.

Rosenbaum, J. (1998) 'Untitled', in J. Boorman and W. Donahue (eds) *Projections 8: Film-makers on Film-making*. London: Faber & Faber, 45–9.

Rosengren, K. E. (1984) 'Time and Culture: Developments in the Swedish Literary Frame of Reference', in G. Melischek, K. E. Rosengren and J. Stappers (eds) *Cultural Indicators: An International Symposium*. Vienna: Verlag der Österreichischen Akademie der Wissenschaften, 237–57.

Sandhu, S. (2003) 'The Epic to End All Epics', *Daily Telegraph*, 12 December, 21.

Shrum, W. (1991) 'Critics and Publics: Cultural Mediation in Highbrow and Popular Performing Arts', *American Journal of Sociology*, 97, 2, 347–75.

Sieghart, M. A. (2003) 'The Listless Making of Lists', *The Times Supplement*, 17 December, 3.

Simons. J. (1988) 'Het maniërisme in de hedendaagse cinema. Gesprek met filmcriticus Serge Daney', *Skrien*, 159, 56–9.

Staiger, J. (1992) *Interpreting Films: The Historical Reception of American Cinema*. Princeton: Princeton University Press.

_____ (2000) *Perverse Spectators: The Practices of Film Reception*. New York: New York University Press.

Taylor, G. (1999) *Artists in the Audience: Cult, Camp and American Film Criticism*. Princeton: Princeton University Press.

Tookey, C. (2003) 'Long Live the King of the Rings', *Daily Mail*, 12 December, 52–3.

Walsh, J. (2003) 'Brought to Book', *The Independent Review*, 11 December, 7.

Webster, N. (2003) 'I Only Got into Acting for the Girls … the Money doesn't Matter to Me', *Daily Mirror*, 17 December, 24–5.

Whitworth, D. (2003) 'The Orlando Bloom Effect, Or How Sisters Are Doing It For Their Elves', *The Times Supplement*, 17 December, 4–5.

Wood, R. (1978) 'Responsibilities of a Gay Film Critic', *Film Comment*, 14, 1, 12–17.

_____ (1993) 'Critical Positions and the End of Civilization; or, a Refusal to Join the Club', *Film Criticism*, 17, 2–3, 79–92.

'Apocalyse Now in Middle Earth': 'Genre' in the Critical Reception of The Lord of the Rings in Germany

Susanne Eichner, Lothar Mikos and Michael Wedel[1]

Introduction

Raising the question of genre in relation to *The Lord of the Rings* may, at first glance, appear to be a questionable, if not outright inappropriate undertaking. Too clearly, it seems, it falls into the realm of fantasy. However, if one takes into account Christine Gledhill's recent assertion that in 'the contemporary moment of reinvention ... genre boundaries, once seemingly securely in place if sometimes disputed, are repeatedly crossed by filmmaker, critic, historian and socio-cultural analyst' (2000: 222), and consequently considers the productivity of genre analysis to consist not only in that it tells us about different kinds of films 'but about the cultural work of producing and knowing them' (ibid.), then the question of genre in relation to *The Lord of the Rings* seems less rhetorical. Understood as an index of cultural negotiation and appropriation, the practice of generic address and identification forms part of what Miriam Hansen once called 'the blockbuster gamble ... of offering something to everyone, of appealing to diverse interests with a diversity of attractions and multiple levels of textuality' (1993: 199). As a blockbuster aimed at, and thus 'gambling with', a global audience 'fragmented beyond any controllable identity' (Corrigan 1991: 23), it seems sensible to assume the *Lord of the Rings* trilogy to be characterised by more than one generic regime and a high degree of textual and interpretative multiplicity. But how exactly are different and sometimes contradictory generic signals organised in the film(s), and what kinds of culturally specific interpretative horizons are generated in the context of the trilogy's public reception in Germany?

This chapter sets out to investigate this complex negotiation process through an investigation of the 'genrefication process' (Altman 1999: 77) of *The Lord of the Rings* as a critical strategy in reviews, relating it to generic categorisations in the German critical discourse on blockbusters. Our approach to genre analysis will be a decidedly pragmatic one, understanding the formation of generic discourse as a culturally and historically specific contract between film and audience, involving production, marketing, the text itself, critical reception (reviews) and fan discourse. The underlying premise is that only a pragmatic approach which 'treats genres as a site of struggle and co-operation between multiple users' (Altman 1999: 211) can yield significant insights into culturally specific patterns of appropriation and socially symbolic acts of mediation and transcoding, recognition and understanding (Jameson 1989: 39–40, 105–6). Such a pragmatic approach comprehends genres as systems of orientation, expectation and convention that circulate between production, text and audiences (Neale 1981: 6). They are historically dynamic processes (Altman 1999: 54) and they 'indicate what kind of communication will be facilitated in specific social formations' (Berry-Flint 2004: 41). As modes of regulating production and reception/interpretation, genres 'are the product of the society – as expressed by the institution and audience expectation – and the history of the genre' (Lacey 2000: 143). They form one of the main elements of what has been called the 'viewing contract' (Mikos 1995) between a particular media product and its user, consumer or recipient. Genres, therefore, organise communication within the context of situational structures of relevance. In this sense, genres are privileged forms of cultural practice, by which the broad field of texts and meanings circulating in a given society is ordered and controlled.

It is important, before moving into the study itself, to briefly consider the status of *The Lord of the Rings* as a blockbuster. Recent attempts to relate the industrial, cultural and aesthetic phenomenon of the blockbuster to critical concepts of generic modes of address in the cinema suggest the 'big movie' to constitute a meta-genre of its own which cuts across traditional genre formations.[2] Thomas Elsaesser, for instance, neatly summarises what can be regarded as the basic characteristics of the contemporary Hollywood blockbuster:

> What characterises a blockbuster? First, a big subject and a big budget (world war, disaster, end of the planet, monster from the deep, holocaust, death battle in the galaxy). Second, a young male hero, usually with lots of firepower, or secret knowledge, or an impossibly difficult mission. The big movie is necessarily based on traditional stories, sometimes against the background of historical events, more often a combination of fantasy or sci-fi, with the well known archetypal heroes from Western mythology on parade. In one sense, this makes blockbusters the natural, that is, technologically more evolved, extension of fairy tales. (2001: 16)

Elsaesser's description seems especially apt when applied to *The Lord of the Rings*. As such, and as indicated by Elsaesser, but also by Thomas Austin (2002) and Kristin Thompson (2003), blockbusters also rely heavily on existing patterns of reception, whether through fans, or genre. By anticipating divergent patterns of reception, the blockbuster draws on a number of exploitable elements. Apart from the indispensable star appeal provided by the featuring of first-rate celebrities, the production of spectacular qualities via the use of special effects is a second element that looms large in this respect. According to Geoff King, blockbusters 'continue to base much of their appeal on the promise of providing a variety of spectacle that befits the nature of the specifically cinematic context of exhibition' (2003: 116). The twin attractions of major stars and special effect-generated sensational spectacle have long been recognised as being part and parcel in elevating the blockbuster to the higher echelons of an 'event' movie, which both as a cultural phenomenon and as a unique aesthetic experience stands out from the everyday media routine (King 2000 and 2003: 114–18; Blanchet 2003: 184–6; Krämer 2003). Sometimes underrated in recent writing when compared to the other two, but nonetheless still of major importance, is a third factor that has become exploitable for the production of an extra-audience appeal and which points us back to the question of generic regimes: it is to be found in the plotting and scattering of isolated generic motifs woven into the films to be picked up, 'extracted and commodified for extra-diegetic circulation' in newspapers, magazines, television shows and fan gossip just as the star images and special effects attractions (Austin 2002: 3).

Critics and the politics and community of fantasy

Underscoring the central role of the critic in relation to the 'genre contract', Rick Altman describes the critic as a 'shaman, interceding between the audience and the text, the society and the industry' (1999: 28). When the first part of the *Lord of the Rings* trilogy premiered in German cinemas on 18 December 2001, its critical reception was strongly marked by a fundamental uncertainty about what kind of generic identity was to be attributed to the film. Across the matrix of a wide range of generic identifications – stretching from fantasy and literary adaptation to war film, splatter-horror, action adventure and historical epic, to name only a few – the aesthetic value, cultural meaning and socio-political implications of Peter Jackson's blockbuster were publicly debated controversially and on chameleon-like shifting grounds. Generic regimes were strategically, it seems, superimposed onto the fantastic story material: the overabundance of 'generic artefacts' (Collins 1993) distributed in the films themselves was used to evoke alternative 'narrative images' (Neale 1990) which then could be read back into specific cultural and political agendas.

For many critics, the strongly-felt heterogeneity of *The Fellowship of the Ring* served as a convenient starting point to question any secure generic identity and open up a film towards re-interpretation, which was considered a 'cinematic opera mixing the genres of the fairy tale, the western, the war film, the cloak and dagger movie, the adventure saga and the epic quest' (Fischer 2001). 'What Peter Jackson has created,' another critic asserted, 'moves somewhere between *Indiana Jones* and *Braveheart, King Kong*, and *Star Wars* with occasional brushes of *Titanic* in between' (Kanthak 2002: 44).[3]

Whereas *The Fellowship of the Ring* – together with *Harry Potter and the Philosopher's Stone* (Chris Columbus, 2001) released in Germany at about the same time – was considered a 'litmus test for the unwavering popularity of the fantasy genre' (Wolf 2001), the presence of various traces of alternative generic intertexts was quickly instrumentalised to discredit 'fantasy' as a label which is applied arbitrarily to all kinds of 'culture industry garbage' and which was said to be decisively responsible for the stultification of the youth (Kirchner & Staun 2001). For most critics who approached the film from such a negative perspective, fantasy was seen as a genre that grants the pleasure of access to 'the totality of the fantastic invention' only for an exclusive circle of fans already initiated to this particular mode of make-believe. For the rest of the audience, including the professional reviewers themselves, the megalomaniacal attempt to transplant Tolkien's remote world of literary imagination into the realm of the visible has effectively blocked our fantasy. Interestingly, this verdict was also extended to Jackson himself: 'In consequence, to adapt *The Lord of the Rings* effectively means to dispose oneself of one's own fantasy' (Kothenschulte 2001). That one gets the feeling that 'the director was forbidden to draw on his own fantasy' (Allmaier 2001) is echoed in other reviews several times, thus becoming a distinct rhetorical pattern in the reception of *The Fellowship of the Ring*. In opposition to what was taken as evidence for Jackson's restrained fantasy, it was repetitively highlighted, that 'Tolkien had left his fantasy take its course' (Anon. 2001).

In the same vein, critic Peter Körte (2001), who describes the film's *mise-en-scène* as 'hopelessly wooden' and the mythology which comes with it 'musty', voices the opinion that 'even the most successful digital creatures only tell of the fact that they are successful digital creatures'. Equally critical was the reviewer of the weekly *Der Spiegel*, who showed a perfect understanding of why 'many creative people and every book-keeper in Hollywood' for such a long time had been scared off by 'the humourless story itself', which at the core evolves around nothing more than 'a confused battle between petty bourgeois small in stature, the hobbits, and various unappetising monsters, fought in a hermetic fantasy world called Middle Earth which is packed with myths, monsters and loads of infantile botch-up – and the whole expenditure because of a ring which might prove to be hardly telegenic' (Wolf 2001). 'Tolkien fans will find many things they have loved about the book,' he concluded: 'But for a three-hour film this is not enough. The hobbits, who could have used a little more character development, are in every respect the lesser evil. The worst thing is that Jackson seems to have no faith in his own story. Instead he tries to overwhelm the audience where he should have convinced it' (ibid.).

This criticism of fantasy also takes on a political tone. Michael Allmaier (2001) of the *Frankfurter Allgemeine Zeitung* would have wished for a more radical approach to the adaptation of Tolkien's book, 'even if the Tolkien-community would have stormed out of the cinemas with curses on their lips'. And the critic of the *Süddeutsche Zeitung*, with obvious enjoyment quoting *The Independent*'s speculation that Hitler would have loved the film, concludes that *The Fellowship of the Ring* appeals to 'the wrong kind of fans' (Hermanski 2001a). Only to add, a few days later, that also 'George Bush must be one of the biggest fans of the film' (Hermanski 2001b). The reviewer of the specialised film journal *epd film* also found the speculation about Hitler 'not wholly unjustified' and regarded the general design of the film to be 'somewhat *Terminator*-like' (Kanthak 2002: 43).

What emerges, is that the critical reception of *The Lord of the Rings*' first part was strongly built on a rhetorical pattern which established a strict division between, on the one hand, the community of fantasy and Tolkien fans as a particular group already initiated to the film's mode of address and therefore predestined to enjoy it; and, on the other hand, the regular cinema-goers and critics as the 'uninitiated' who would have a hard time gaining pleasure from the film unless some basic things are explained in advance, i.e. some attempt has been made to 'initiate' them to a particular mode of (non-critical, apolitical) experience and enjoyment (see, for example, Wild 2001). Gunnar Decker (2001), writing for the former official GDR-state newspaper *Neues Deutschland*, was led to the idea that *The Fellowship of the Ring* 'made a fantasy film of Martin Heidegger's *Being and Time*' to accentuate his sense that the film was definitely 'nothing for uninitiated'. Judging on the basis of its first part, the renowned academic Elisabeth Bronfen (2001) expected the projected trilogy to become a 'fantasy soap' at best. Jackson's own claim that he himself was not so much interested in fantasy but in mythology which would 'bestow onto the film a sense of historicity, not fantasy' (quoted in Bodmer 2001) was largely ignored. In the same article, the Swiss critic Michel Bodmer called *The Fellowship of the Ring* 'perhaps the most breathtaking fantasy film of all time' and thus displays a far less negative relationship to the fantasy genre than his German colleagues. For the latter, positive evaluations of the film as a piece of fantasy were often paired with an emphasis on its multi-generic qualities. Symptomatically, Peter Kroll saw *The Fellowship of the Ring* setting new standards not only in the realm of fantasy cinema, but above all as a 'furious adventure movie of unusual physical force' (2001: 25).

Genre and the auteur: *The Fellowship of the Ring* as horror

For many reviewers, the critical strategy to read the film against the grain of the fantasy genre went hand in hand with a pronounced nostalgia for Jackson's previous work in the genre context of the horror and splatter (Wolf 2001). For Bronfen,

The Fellowship of the Ring represented an experiment in marrying sub-cultural tastes with high-art sensibilities:

> On the one hand the legacy of European painting: the sublime battle scenes of Renaissance art, the fantasy creatures of the British Pre-Raphaelites or the picture puzzles with which the symbolists and surrealists translated paranoid fantasies into the realm of the visible ... On the other hand, however, we find the language of the American psycho-horror. (2001)

According to the reviewer of the *Berliner Zeitung*, the central religious questions posed by the trilogy's first part – 'How does one bear his own minimality in the face of a world which can never be fully understood? How can this existential suffering, which stems out of the pain of unsurpassable mortality, be overcome?' – referred the film back to the core element of the splatter film, through which this particular genre used to transcend 'the mere sensuality of its effects': 'What, under the all-encompassing impact of irony, this genre lost of its forcefulness in interpreting the world, *The Lord of the Rings* once more brings to the fore' (Balzer 2001). At the centre of the film, the aesthetic experience and affective potential of horror is revealed as radically exceeding the boundaries of the fantasy genre:

> In its best moments, *The Lord of the Rings* zooms in on the suffering of its heroes as closely as in the best moments of the splatter genre, e.g. in Hooper's *Texas Chainsaw Massacre* or Romero's *Night of the Living Dead*. Everywhere in this film, the process of subjectivisation works according to this model: what started out as a mythical, i.e. relatively 'shallow', character ensemble in moments of being tortured gains such an intensity of subjectivity that it completely changes the narrative genre. (Ibid.)

On the release of *The Two Towers* on 18 December 2002, the German press related just another generic cue of Jackson to the public. '*The Two Towers* is my western, somewhere between Kurosawa and John Ford' (quoted in Göttler 2002a). More or less unimpressed by Jackson's frequent and quite inconsistent remarks about the generic identity of his films, the majority of the critics perpetuated the rhetorical patterns that had been solidly established in the reception of the trilogy's first part. 'The weaknesses of *The Two Towers* are mainly due to the weaknesses of the fantasy genre', the reviewer for the specialised journal *film-dienst* wrote: 'psychologically-flat characters, black and white picture of good vs. evil, bringing the film dangerously close to what can be considered a "proto-fascist" aesthetics' (Binotto 2002: 24). He had three warnings for the general audience:

> First, for those who have missed the first part and have not read the books – they will be hopelessly lost in trying to understand what is going on. Second, for those who

rightly think that fantasy is a stupid or at least not very interesting genre – they will be confirmed in their view, since this is, and doesn't want to be anything else but, the ultimate fantasy film. Finally, for those parents who take *The Two Towers* to be a children's movie – the battle scenes of explicit violence make *The Two Towers* even less suitable for children than the first part had already been. (2002: 24–5)

For those critics mainly judging from an author-oriented perspective, the nostalgia for Jackson's achievements as director of horror and splatter movies was still playing an important role. They painted the image of Jackson as 'the creator of such unforgettable pearls as *Braindead* or *Heavenly Creatures*' whose frequently announced return to 'low-budget and splatter films' after this brief excursion into the 'hardly modest and highly moralistic fantasy epic' which at least allowed him the staging of an 'impressive bloodbath' (Lüthge 2002) was widely welcomed.[4] For Fritz Göttler, critic for the *Süddeutsche Zeitung*, New Zealand alone conjured up sweet memories of a time and place when Jackson made his splatter classics *Braindead* and *Bad Taste* as well as the 'dreamlike-murderous master piece *Heavenly Creatures*' in the happy situation of absolute 'financial and creative freedom':

One believes to see the old horror film director spooking around in the super-expensive and super-elaborate panorama shots of battle scenes – and is ready to bet that after Christmas 2003 a new Jackson zombie-film will be on the agenda. (2002a)

The critics' nostalgic re-reading of the horror concept back into the matrix of fantasy was one way of coping with and at the same time consciously appropriating what most critics saw as an utterly hermetic filmic universe, exclusively aimed at those fractions of the audience who are familiar and feel comfortable with the particular idiom of fantasy. The imaginary division between those fans of the genre on the one hand, and the regular cinema-goers on the other was once more reinforced. 'Nobody explains anything', one reviewer lamented: 'Several laws of gravity are broken. And nobody explains anything ... Which means that those who go to watch *The Two Towers* without any prior knowledge of Tolkien's world will helplessly and without the slightest sense of orientation roam through the first hour of Jackson's film, just as Tolkien's hobbits on their way to Mount Doom in the dark land of Mordor' (Krekeler 2002). The film's appeal, as the conclusion of another critic read, was neither based on rational understanding nor on sensual pleasure, but on an almost religious belief. For Peter Körte of the *Frankfurter Allgemeine Sonntagszeitung*,

The Lord of the Rings has long eluded any criticism and transformed itself into a phenomenon which in the final consequence you can only understand if at the same time you unshakeably believe in it. (2002)

Hidden generic identity: *The Two Towers* as a war film

As an adaptation of a literary work, and in stark contrast to *The Fellowship of the Ring*, the trilogy's second part was estimated to be a towering achievement, and even praised to have rendered its literary source altogether 'superfluous' (ibid.). This acclaim of *The Two Towers* as a literary adaptation was, however, paired with the conviction that only in the 'decidedly more action-packed' second part Jackson had finally 'emancipated himself more visibly from Tolkien' (ibid.). A central element of this putative emancipation process was seen in the 'stronger emphasis put on the war between good and evil' which would lend *The Two Towers* a new topicality: 'This is how one would wish war to be in reality' (ibid.).

Whereas the categorisation as 'fantasy epic' became a standard reference in reviews of *The Two Towers*, a generic attribution now passing largely un-debated and hardly any more glossed on and problematised (Bodmzer 2002; Schulz 2003), the war film emerged as the hidden generic identity of the film, and with it a number of new levels of meaning for which suitable reading strategies were suggested. Generally, Jackson's tendency to enlarge and intensify the action, fight and battle scenes in comparison to Tolkien's more functional description was taken as an indicator for this generic shift (Reden 2002). Only a minor rest of Tolkien's art of storytelling was said to have remained discernible beneath the 'massacre scenes' which have at least tripled in the trilogy's second part and turned *The Two Towers* 'above all into one thing: a giant military mobilisation movie' (Decker 2002). The critic of the *Berliner Zeitung* aptly described the starting point where the second part was to pick up the narrative from its predecessor: 'The front lines are clear, now everybody is called to arms' (Balzer 2002).

Where the first part had managed to reconcile the fantastic with the poetic, Dietmar Kanthak wrote, 'any poetic quality is now drowned in the noise battle' of the second part's action and battle scenes: 'on the monumental tableau of war which Jackson puts on the canvas, tender feelings are nothing more than occasional spots of colour ... *Apocalypse Now* in Middle Earth' (2003: 50). The film was perceived to be overabundant in its staging of the war, and the resulting feeling of déja vu mounted against its aesthetic impact, since 'the nth battle with umpteen thousand orcs can never have the same strong effect as the first one had' (Bodmer 2002). Aragorn's recruitment of allies for the battle against the tower-axis Orthanc (Saruman) – Barad-dûr (Sauron) may have originated from Tolkien's memories of World War Two, 'today, however, it reminds one of the current efforts to build an alliance against another "axis of evil"' (ibid.).

In the critical discourse, the war film emerged as the generic matrix across which the film's social symbolic could be deciphered more clearly. 'Is the Jesus-like warrior Aragorn not going into final battle with the battle cry "for the countries of the West"?', Katja Nicodemus asked the readers of the weekly *Die Zeit*: 'And do the horizon-filling armies of the black spotty Uruk-Hai not look like the Al-Qaida-nightmare of every American citizen looking onto the world from his suburban home? Indeed, the axis of evil runs through Tolkien's Middle Earth as dead straight as it runs through the rhetoric of a George W. Bush.' But, she added, 'why on earth should one blame *The Lord of the Rings* for an American president who decided to fight in the same movie?' (Nicodemus 2003). When towards the end of *The Two Towers* the Ringwraith is attacking the ruins of Osgiliath from the air, and Frodo and Sam are desperately running for shelter, the mental image of a bomb attack is inevitably conjured (Horst 2003). Again and again, distinct features of the war film genre are identified to be part and parcel of *The Two Towers* narrative design, including male bonding, kitsch and pathos as well as heavy symbolism (Bodmer 2002). In this context, the second part of the trilogy was received as a particularly obtrusive 'signal for masculinity' (Krekeler 2002). In view of the war film boom in Hollywood from the 1990s to the present day, the depressing truth, as one critic stated with a sigh of disappointment, is 'what awaits the refugee from reality in this mother of all fantasy stories? War again' (Geisenhanslüke 2002). For critic Gunnar Decker, the 'myth of encirclement' he saw returning with a vengeance in *The Two Towers* can not only be read as a metaphor for present anxieties around international terrorism, the conflict between Palestine and Israel, South and North Korea. For European viewers, he suggested, it also reflects a subconscious fear of 'the European fortress being invaded by the onslaught of poverty from outside'. The fantasy of being encircled, according to O. K. Werckmeister (1991) a prominent trope in Western film, literature and the visual arts ever since the 1970s, was interpreted of bringing back through the back door a set of motifs that have also loomed large in a particular kind of the German war film, the 'Nazi-Durchhaltefilme', i.e. war propaganda movies, of which Veit Harlan's *Kolberg* (1945) is only the most notorious example: 'Blood runs in streams. This war shows us the hero as a labourer of extinction' (Decker 2002).

In the view of the critics, Jackson's film disintegrated into different narrative paces and cinematic genres: on the one hand, the 'battle fray rapturously rolling over the beholder, the cheerful slaughter with men and monsters', on the other 'the slow-moving wandering of the desperate ring bearer' (Balzer 2002). In *The Two Towers*, however, the epic dimension was felt to be secondary, mainly serving as a recurring peripetia in a film which on the whole 'is worth watching because of the magnificent zombie-villains who zombie-director Jackson unleashes on the screen' (ibid.). Faced with the cult status and the huge fan communities of recent blockbusters such as the *Harry Potter* films and *The Lord of the Rings*, Göttler shifted the war metaphor to another dimension altogether when he wrote that 'a time will come in the not so distant future when cinema only exists in its over-dimensional form. One will go to the movies together as one once used to march into battle' (Göttler 2002b).

In a sweeping attack on the overall ideological concept of the film, cultural critic Georg Seesslen saw the war film logic radically undermine the film's status as fantasy:

> It is not so much the inevitability of war which leaves a nasty taste in the mouth but, above all, the narrative of fundamental precipitation. The most memorable contributions of the fantasy genre tell of innumerable forms of life, innumerable forms of intelligence and sensitivity, innumerable forms of culture. At the genre's magic locations all these forms intermingle and inseminate each other into a cosmic or prehistoric creolity. By the way, therein also lies the erotic of fantasy. (2002)

'The new fantasy', of which the *Lord of the Rings* films are taken as prominent examples,

> undoes the creolisation of the fantasies, it once more sets against each other the races, cultures, religions and even the sexes. From the journey into the other, one returns with clean, i.e. dirty concepts of an enemy on the safe ground of reality … This kind of cinema has only seemingly led us away from our depressing reality; as a matter of fact it only leads us in the midst of it. (2002)

To underscore and reinforce this particular generic redefinition of *The Two Towers*, several German newspapers related to its readers Salman Rushdie's view both of Jackson's film and Martin Scorsese's *Gangs of New York* (2002) as being based on the primary interest in the 'artistic staging of war action' (Kilb 2003). What Rushdie, in his original *Guardian* article, was far more careful in formulating in terms of the films' 'mutual interest in battle', Andreas Kilb's report tended to give another twist and a sharper edge, isolating and quoting at length Rushdie's initial point 'that both filmmakers share an interest in the cut and thrust of hand-to-hand fighting, of close conflict realistically depicted according to the "ancient laws of combat"'.

The generic tensions between fantasy and the war film continued with the reception of *The Return of the King*, released on 17 December 2003. Welcomed once more as a 'milestone of the fantasy genre' (Martig 2003: 25) it was said to finally have achieved a balance between 'battle scenes and more intimate moments', although the specularity and sheer grandeur of the opulent battle scenes would tend to push psychological conflict and romance to the fringes. This tendency led more than one critic to agree with special effects supervisor Jim Rygiel who referred to *The Return of the King* as a 'World War Zero' film (quoted in Martig 2003: 24; see also Kniebe 2003). As was already the case in the critical debate around *The Two Towers*, the horror intertext figured far less prominently than the redefinition of *The Return of the King* in terms of the war movie genre.[5] In this context, *The Return of the King* was lauded for offering 'twenty times as much action' (Jung 2003a: 50) as *The Two Towers* which already had been perceived to increase the share of action and battle scenes considerably when compared to *The Fellowship of the Ring*:

> Where so far ten thousand monsters, bristling with weapons, marched for attack, there are now two hundred thousand. Where so far only a few towering war elephants moved leisurely through the countryside, there are now dozens storming into battle. Where so far only a few dragons flew through the air, spying and scouting, they are now entering the action like diving fighter bombers. (Kniebe 2003)

Surprising character developments, such as Gandalf's and Sam's transformation into action heroes, were noted as carrying with them not only new patterns of identification, but endowing the whole film with a new set of generic attributes; 'More than one character undergoes a spectacular development', Andreas Jung wrote in the popular film magazine *Cinema*:

> Gandalf, the magician, mutates from a contemplative mystic into a powerful action hero, who throws himself into battle with his sword and turns out to be a most determined commander. Also the otherwise so hesitant hobbit Sam reveals undreamt-of combat strength when faced with Orcs and the giant spider Shelob. (2003b: 87)

The critical acclaim which *The Return of the King* earned in the German press was in the majority of cases based on its successful staging of physical action and battle scenes. Symptomatic is this respect is Daniel Kothenschulte's (2003) praise, presented in the form of a rhetorical question: 'Which action film, which war film ever managed to go beyond a running time of 200 minutes so elegantly?'

Judged as a war film, *The Lord of the Rings* was, however, also taken to task for missing an important affective dimension of the genre. 'Where war scenes, even in the most chauvinistic and resentful films, always carry a horror which is hard to ward off', as Claudius Seidl (2003) polemically put it in the *Frankfurter Allgemeine Zeitung*, 'Peter Jackson turns his warriors literally into butchers: the orcs are to Aragorn and his people what a herd of buffalo is to Buffalo Bill'. In this constitutive lack of empathy for the enemy, which Seidl took as the central index for what he called the film's 'synthetic racism', *The Return of the King* was seen as even surpassing the regular run-of-the-mill war picture on the latter's own generic terms. What in the context of fantasy may well have been regarded as one of the outstanding merits of the film, namely its immense and almost irresistible affective potential, was now by many reviewers re-measured against the ethics of the war film and condemned as breaking the tacit generic taboo of not giving in too readily to an 'Überwältigungsästhetik' (aesthetic of overpowering): 'It seems as if

every New Zealander was involved in a holy war over the heart of the cinema-goer',
Thomas Kniebe observed in the *Süddeutsche Zeitung*. He continued:

> And Jackson, one can hardly put it any other way, is out for overpowering the audi-
> ence in every single image. He not only celebrates the unconditioned destruction
> of evil, he also wants the unconditioned surrender of the spectator – until the final,
> tear-stricken farewell. (2003)

To Kniebe, only the cultural background of the production itself was rendering
Jackson's approach to the representation of war just about acceptable:

> Were he and his team coming from America, from a European nation with a super-
> power past, or even from Germany, one could bear neither these images nor the
> many calls for military idealism which lurk at the core of the story. (Ibid.)

In matters of the ethics of representation, cultural positioning became the crucial
factor, 'because, after all', as Kniebe remarked, 'it does matter who has put up this
war game: the heirs of peaceful Kiwi-growers and sheep farmers' (ibid.).

Seen from a German perspective, Gunnar Decker (2003) noted, *The Lord
of the Rings* trilogy presents itself 'like the ultimate film of the ideology of the
Volkssturm [whose] mendacious militant kitsch, celebrating heroic death [would]
firmly install upon its audience a "*Führer-und-Volk-Weltanschauung*"'. The critic of
the newspaper *Neues Deutschland* actually felt compelled to compare Jackson's trilogy to German film history's ultimate bad object in this respect, Leni Riefenstahl's
Triumph of the Will (1935). 'Even if they are only computer simulated', he wrote,
'the mass scenes one can witness here would have brought Leni Riefenstahl to her
knees' (Decker 2003). Via the superimposition of moral implications associated
with the war film genre onto a subject matter belonging to the realm of fiction
and fairy tale, any clear distinction between fantasy and real world was successfully made to collapse: 'Soon, very soon', Thomas Kniebe carried this point to its
extremes, 'the first suicide assassin will be on its way to the Shire'.

The blockbuster clientele: critics on the audience

In the face of the extraordinary box office success and the broad popularity the first
two parts of the trilogy had already gained in Germany at the time of the release
of the final episode,[6] the imaginary division between a community of fantasy fans
as direct addressees and a much wider blockbuster clientele, which had figured so
prominently as a rhetorical trope in the previous debates, was now seen to be set-
tled. Despite the many deviations from the novel, one critic dryly remarked that
'the sceptical Tolkien-fans love the films as much as those who have never read the

books' (Distelmeyer 2003). Solely Seidl still believed those parts of the audience who simply want to watch and understand the films without having read the books were put at a disadvantage. He thought those parts of the audience would lack the manual to the narrative and the material collection that would add resonance to the inner conflicts of the protagonists into whom the films themselves, as Seidl argued, failed to invest sufficient interest.

Critics continued to differentiate various audience segments, regrouping them into the category of the 'philologically oriented', the potentially critical fraction of readers of the books, a variety of fantasy fans (ranging from a general preference to hard-core spiritualists), popular culture consumers and media users. But all these groups were now embraced and reassembled as mutually constituting the new cross-section of 'fans and lovers of the films' (Horst 2003). The films' integrative power, Sabine Horst argued, was mainly due to a strategy of 'infinite diversity in infinite combinations', not least also pursued in terms of generic multiplicity. The trilogy's apparent success in pulling together so many divergent strings and thereby meeting so many different audience expectations all at once put Jackson back at the centre of the critics' attention. Those who had so harshly criticised the director for his lack of fantasy two years (and two releases) earlier now once more sang his praises, but this time without any trace of nostalgia for the splatter genius of the past. 'This is why these films are so good, this is why their ending is so triumphant', Jens Balzer's (2003) verdict read, 'Because there is no contradiction between the global public, at which they are targeted, and the personal fantasies of their creator'.

The incorporative power of Jackson's *Lord of the Rings* was now taken for granted, but occasionally still characterised as a forceful, even violent strategy of overwhelming the viewer whose sense perception is held under fire like an enemy in order to keep in check any critical impulse:

Of course, one is startled about oneself ... About how the sheer force of the flood of images which descends upon the viewer and without any resistance washes away even the smallest desire for critical distance and reflection. (Ibid.)

The sentiment irritating and alienating this particular reviewer the most, however, came creeping up on him from another corner: 'It is a strange and peculiar feeling: that a film assembles its audience without a trace of resistance in such an all-encompassing way as a community of believers' (ibid.).

Conclusion

The first conclusion to be drawn from our attempt to track the public status of *The Lord of the Rings* in Germany is to acknowledge that multiple generic images of the trilogy are generated and circulated in different discursive formations. Applied to this particular blockbuster movie, the answer to the question of genre must necessarily be hetero-topic and multi-dimensional. The survey of the critical reception in Germany indicates that professional film reviewers tend to conceive of fantasy as a 'super genre' (Distelmeyer 2002: 20) less defined by a characteristic and self-sufficient set of semantic and syntactic structures than by a fan community whose tastes and practices are either shared and valorised or disapproved and rejected as culturally inferior pleasures. In the majority of reviews, the 'narrative image' of fantasy itself was considered too broad a category to communicate an identifiable meaning and a stable frame of understanding to a wider audience. Rather, it served as an umbrella category for various, even divergent, generic attributes. It is on these generic micro-levels that the German press negotiated the cultural value and public status of *The Lord of the Rings*, in an attempt to break open what was perceived as a closed circle of fantasy and Tolkien fans and to arrive at a reading strategy which would be able to re-define the frames of reference in terms of alternative generic expectations. As a result, and no less a '[cross-]cultural phenomenon' (Rosebury 2003: 193) as Tolkien's work itself, the movie trilogy's exorbitant success may, in the end, be explained not so much in terms of artistic creativity and generic distinctiveness but rather be seen in what seems to be the most recognisable ability of the contemporary blockbuster: to 'simply entertain' and at the same time stir up public debates about neuralgic points and foundational principles of a given society in different national and geographical contexts. In other words, to lend itself to 'cultural processes whereby the distinctiveness of the original work is dissolved into wider cultural categories and practices' (ibid.).

Notes

1 This chapter was developed as part of the International Lord of the Rings Research Project. Its research was made possible by support of the Konrad Wolf Academy of Film and Television in Potsdam-Babelsberg, Germany, and by a grant from the UK Economic and Social Research Council (ESRC Grant No. 000-22-0323) to whom we record our gratitude.

2 Julian Stringer notes that 'size is the central notion through which the blockbuster's generic identity comes to be identified' (2003: 3).

3 All quotes have been translated from German into English by the authors.

4 The information of Jackson's future return to the low-budget horror genre originates from a review in *The New York Times* (see Anon. 2002).

5 Where references to the horror genre are still to be found, they were now explicitly and exclusively tied to Jackson as an auteur director. See Kothenschulte 2003: 'Just once, in the very beginning, one discovers the uninhibited surrealism of earlier Jackson films such as *Bad Taste* and *Braindead* in the form of a self-reference.'

6   The German attendance figures for *The Fellowship of the Ring* (11.8 million) and *The Two Towers* (10.7 million) were indeed impressive, especially when the sales of videos and DVDs are factored in (no absolute figures available). *The Return of the King* was to draw 10.4 million viewers to German cinemas.

Works cited

Allmaier, M. (2001) 'Was ist mit Seite 53?', *Frankfurter Allgemeine Zeitung*, 19 December.

Altman, R. (1999) *Film/Genre*. London: British Film Institute.

Anon. (2001) 'Hat ein Balrog Flügel?', *Der Tagesspiegel*, 17 December.

_____ (2002) 'Zurück zum Zombie-Film', *Berliner Zeitung*, 19 December.

Austin, T. (2002) *Hollywood, Hype and Audiences: Selling and Watching Popular Films in the 1990s*. Manchester: Manchester University Press.

Balzer, J. (2001) 'Ein Triumph des Kinos', *Berliner Zeitung*, 18 December.

_____ (2002) 'Der Moment danach ist am schönsten', *Berliner Zeitung*, 18 December.

_____ (2003) 'Erlöst', *Berliner Zeitung*, 17 December.

Berry-Flint, S. (2004) 'Genre', in T. Miller and R. Stam (eds) *A Companion to Film Theory*. Oxford: Blackwell, 25–44.

Binotto, T. (2002) 'Der Herr der Ringe – Die zwei Türme', *film-dienst*, 26, 24–5.

Blanchet, R. (2003) *Blockbuster: Ästhetik, Ökonomie und Geschichte des postklassischen Hollywoodkinos*. Marburg: Schüren.

Bodmer, M. (2001) 'Ringelreihen der Rekorde', *Neue Zürcher Zeitung*, international edition, 19 December.

_____ (2002) 'Glaubenskrieg um zwei Türme', *Neue Zürcher Zeitung*, international edition, 18 December.

Bronfen, E. (2001) 'Traum und Katastrophe', *Die Tageszeitung*, Berlin edition, 19 December 20.

Collins, J. (1993) 'Genericity in the Nineties: Eclectic Irony and the New Sincerity', in J. Collins, H. Radner and A. P. Collins (eds) *Film Theory Goes to the Movies*. New York: Routledge, 242–63.

Corrigan, T. (1991) *A Cinema Without Walls: Movies and Culture After Vietnam*. New York: Routledge.

Decker, G. (2001) 'Alles kreist um den Ursprung', *Neues Deutschland*, 19 December.

_____ (2002) 'Nach der Schlacht ist vor der Schlacht', *Neues Deutschland*, 18 December.

_____ (2003) 'All die toten Helden', *Neues Deutschland*, 17 December.

Distelmeyer, J. (2002) 'Zuhaus in Mittelerde: Das Fantasy-Genre und seine Fans', *epd film*, 12, 18–23.

_____ (2003) 'Die letzten Seiten sind für dich', *Die Tageszeitung*, Berlin edition, 17 December.

Elsaesser, T. (2001) 'The Blockbuster: Everything Connects, but Not Everything Goes', in J. Lewis (ed.) *The End of Cinema as We Know It: American Film in the Nineties*. New

York: New York University Press, 11–22.

Fischer, M. (2001) 'Im Reich der Ringe', *Financial Times Deutschland*, 19 December.

Geisenhanslüke, R. (2002) 'Schlaflos in Mittelerde', *Der Tagesspiegel*, 18 December.

Gledhill, C. (2000) 'Rethinking Genre', in C. Gledhill and L. Williams (eds) *Reinventing Film Studies*. London: Arnold, 221–43.

Göttler, F. (2002a) 'Leb an einem anderen Tag', *Süddeutsche Zeitung*, 14–15 December.

_____ (2002b) 'Volle Kraft voraus', *Süddeutsche Zeitung*, 24–26 December.

Hansen, M. (1993) 'Early Cinema, Late Cinema: Permutations of the Public Sphere', *Screen*, 34, 3, 197–210.

Hermanski, S. (2001a) 'Mit der Heimat verwurzelt', *Süddeutsche Zeitung*, 13 December.

_____ (2001b) 'Lichtgestalten im Kampf mit der Finsternis', *Süddeutsche Zeitung*, 20 December.

Horst, S. (2003) 'Willkommen in Bruchtal!', *Freitag*, 19 December, 52.

Jameson, F. (1989) *The Political Unconscious: Narrative as a Socially Symbolic Act*. New York: Routledge.

Jung, A. (2003a) 'Der letzte Schlacht um Mittelerde', *Cinema*, 12, December, 38–50.

_____ (2003b) 'Der Herr der Ringe: Die Rückkehr des Königs', *Cinema*, 12, December, 87.

Kanthak, D. (2002) 'Peter Jacksons Ausflug in die Hobbit-Welt', *epd film*, 1, 43–4.

_____ (2003) 'Wie war das noch im Mittelteil? Neues von Frodo und Co.', *epd film*, 1, 50.

Kilb, A. (2003) 'Bandenkrieger', *Frankfurter Allgemeine Zeitung*, 9 January.

King, G. (2000) *Spectacular Narratives: Hollywood in the Age of the Blockbuster*. London: I. B. Tauris.

_____ (2003) 'Spectacle, Narrative, and the Spectacular Hollywood Blockbuster', in J. Stringer (ed.) *Movie Blockbusters*. New York: Routledge, 114–27.

Kirchner, B. and H. Staun (2001) 'Wider die Verwichtelung!', *Frankfurter Allgemeine Sonntagszeitung*, 16 December, 50.

Kniebe, T. (2003) 'Heil den Neuseeländern', *Süddeutsche Zeitung*, 11 December.

Körte, P. (2001) 'Triple Cheese Ring', *Frankfurter Allgemeine Sonntagszeitung*, 16 December, 50.

_____ (2002) 'Wieviel Bits ergeben einen Hobbit?', *Frankfurter Allgemeine Sonntagszeitung*, 15 December, 50.

Kothenschulte, D. (2001) 'Bits und Hobbits', *Frankfurter Rundschau*, 19 December.

_____ (2003) 'Monument für Mittelerde', *Frankfurter Rundschau*, 16 December.

Krämer, P. (2003) '"Want to Take a Ride?": Reflections on the Blockbuster Experience in *Contact* (1997)', in J. Stringer (ed.) *Movie Blockbusters*. New York: Routledge, 128–40.

Krekeler, E. (2002) 'Kantersieg des Kinos über die Literatur', *Die Welt*, 16 December.

Kroll, P. (2001) 'Der Herr der Ringe – Die Gefährten', *film-dienst*, 26, 24–5.

Lacey, N. (2000) *Narrative and Genre: Key Concepts in Media Studies*. New York: St. Martin's Press.

Lüthge, K. (2002) 'Eine Frage der Zahnhygiene', *Frankfurter Rundschau*, 18 December.

Martig, C. (2003) 'Der Herr der Ringe – Die Rückkehr des Königs', *film-dienst*, 26, 24–5.

Mikos, L. (1995) 'The Viewing Contract: Genre, Conventions, and Viewer's Activities', paper presented at the 'Semiotics of the Media: State of the Art, Projects, and Perspectives' conference, organised by the International Association for Semiotic Studies in Kassel, Germany.

Neale, S. (1981) 'Genre and Cinema', in T. Bennett, S. Boyd-Bowman, C. Mercer and J. Woollacott (eds) *Popular Television and Film*. London: British Film Institute, 6–25.

_____ (1990) 'Questions of Genre', *Screen* 31, 1, 45–66.

Nicodemus, K. (2003) 'Der Bush der Ringe', *Die Zeit*, 17 December, 52.

Reden, S. von (2002) 'Digitaler Gleichschritt', *Die Tageszeitung*, Berlin edition, 18 December.

Rosebury, B. (2003) *Tolkien: A Cultural Phenomenon*. Basingstoke: Palgrave Macmillan.

Rushdie, S. (2003) 'Arms and the men and hobbits', *Guardian*, 4 January.

Schulz, T. (2003) 'Durchgeknallt in "Wellywood"', *Der Spiegel*, 1, 75.

Seesslen, G. (2002) 'Und nun beuget die Knie!', *Die Zeit*, 18 December, 52.

Seidl, C. (2003) 'Hinter tausend Kriegern keine Welt', *Frankfurter Allgemeine Zeitung*, 17 December.

Stringer, J. (2003) 'Introduction', in J. Stringer (ed.) *Movie Blockbusters*. New York: Routledge, 1–14.

Thompson, K. (2003) 'Fantasy, Franchises, and Frodo Baggins: *The Lord of the Rings* and Modern Hollywood', *Velvet Light Trap*, 52, Fall, 45–63.

Werckmeister, O. K. (1991) *Citadel Culture*. Chicago: University of Chicago Press.

Wild, H. (2001) 'Piercings in Mittelerde', *Der Tagesspiegel*, 20 December.

Wolf, M. (2001) 'Murks in Mittelerde', *Der Spiegel*, 17 December, 51.

Realising the Cult Blockbuster: *The Lord of the Rings* Fandom and Residual / Emergent Cult Status in 'the Mainstream'

Matt Hills

Introduction

Fandom is by no means an under-explored phenomenon in film, media and cultural studies (see Jenkins 1992; Hills 2002; Sandvoss 2005; Staiger 2005), and it could be argued that cult film and television fans have been over-represented within this growing body of work. Yet 'cult' status has usually been thought of as somehow antithetical to 'the mainstream' of consumer culture (Hollows 2003). 'Authentic' fans of 'underground' cult genres and texts have thus been contrasted to supposedly less authentic and frequently feminised 'consumers' of mass-market popular culture. Scholarship on fandom has displayed a marked tendency to champion certain types of fans over others (see Crawford 2004), sometimes even participating in fans' own subcultural struggles over status and authenticity (see Jancovich 2000 and 2002).

But if fans have been variously celebrated for their activities and participatory cultures – seemingly operating against the strategies and machinations of 'the mainstream' – then where might this have left fans of that most commercial of forms, the blockbuster movie? In fact, a number of critics have recently begun to take 'blockbuster fandom' more seriously (see Kirsten Pullen's chapter in this volume), refuting the constructed binary oppositions of mainstream/underground, incorporated/resistant and commercial/artistic, and seeking to explore the new commerce of auteurism as well as how distinctive fan identities have been enacted in relation to a range of 'blockbuster' films and mainstream media (Brooker 2002; Hills 2003 and 2004).

In this chapter I want to consider the specific struggles over fandom, cultural value and authenticity which have circulated around the *Lord of the Rings* films. How have 'the blockbuster' and 'cult fandom' intersected here in ways which both resemble and differ from other 'blockbuster fandoms' such as those previously surrounding *Titanic* (James Cameron, 1997), *The Matrix* (Andy and Larry Wachowski, 1999) and its franchise, and the *Star Wars* films? How have fans sought to (re)value the *Lord of the Rings* movies as 'legitimate' cult artefacts?

Cult times: anticipating, dreading and extending the blockbuster 'event'

As Sheldon Hall notes, '"Blockbuster" has entered common parlance as a term to describe the kind of cinema most readily associated with the dominant commercial forms of modern, mainstream ... Hollywood' (2002: 11). Regardless of whether a film makes gigantic profits – and the production costs often associated with these types of films means that it is entirely possible for them to 'bomb' at the box office – the term 'blockbuster' semiotically binds such texts to powerful notions of commercialism. 'Blockbuster', while perhaps not quite designating a genre, is nevertheless a way of labelling specific films as 'hyped, everywhere, "must-see" ... universal in their appeal ... undemanding ... honestly "commercial" about their wish and intention to make money' (Barker & Brooks 1998: 185; see also King 2000; Austin 2002). Such connotations mean that the contemporary 'blockbuster' has come to stand in for culturally devalued 'modes of consumption' (Jancovich & Faire 2003: 191) which are figured as lacking cultural capital and cinephilic appreciation. The blockbuster is assumed to be nakedly commercial by virtue of supposedly targeting everybody: it thus allegedly represents the lowest common denominator of mass appeal, standing in stark contrast to the refined sensibilities of 'art-house' movies (Hills 2003).

These connotations of 'the blockbuster' mean that cult status would seem to be denied, by definition, in such cases. Cultishness hinges on an assumed 'sense of distinction from "mainstream, commercial cinema"' (Jancovich 2002: 317) where the cult film's inaccessibility and exclusivity are crucial to this process of differentiation: 'One has to be in the know to even get to see' some cult films (Jancovich, 2002: 319), given that they may be censored or banned. The distinction of cult status is, on this account, heavily dependent on audience knowledge and activity, whereas the consumption of non-cult, mainstream texts is contrastively represented as not requiring audience skill, knowledge or discrimination. Cult films have to be knowingly sought out by their cognoscenti, whereas mainstream films are simply 'there' in the multiplexes up and down the land.

However, this emphasis on 'cult = anti-mainstream' neglects to consider how cult and mainstream status can intersect. Markers of cult fan activity can be preserved within such collisions, with fan audiences making distinctive readings of their favoured texts, producing secondary texts and repeatedly viewing their beloved films. These textual focal points for cult fandom may not, however, be inaccessible, exclusive or 'rare' underground texts – instead they might be found playing at the local multiplex. Cult status undergoes something of a dislocation and transformation in such cases: far from being 'underground' and so sustained by the knowledgeable consumption of obscure texts, here cult fans consume the same 'blockbuster' texts as the 'mass'/'mainstream' audience, but their 'cult' audience distinction is preserved because they continue to interpret/read these films distinctively. The difference of fan readings lies not only in their textual productivity (i.e. they create their own online reviews/responses/fictions – see Pullen in this volume) but also in the *temporality* of textual knowledge and experience that they call upon. By viewing repeatedly – often going to see a film at the cinema many times before then seeing it again repeatedly on DVD – fans begin to read for intra-textual details. But fans also 'pre-read' or 'pre-view' their favoured texts (see Chin & Gray 2001), spending many months anticipating the release of a 'blockbuster', and avidly consuming production information and tracking storyline leaks (called 'spoilers') or industry rumours.

In a sense, then, certain industry or 'mainstream' connotations of the blockbuster, that it is 'everywhere … yet at the same time evanescent' (Barker & Brooks 1998: 185), are reworked by fans when they cultify and cultivate blockbusters. For the cult audience, the 'blockbuster' does not burst onto the cultural scene and then rapidly fade away: instead its appearance is keenly anticipated over months or even years, and it then lives on through fan interpretations, debates and memories/memorialisations. This longer-term fannish 'mode of consumption' builds up great knowledge about the history and making of a beloved 'blockbuster', partly feeding into industrial notions of the blockbuster as an 'event', but also simultaneously challenging those ideas by restoring the actual production time of the film – and its cultural afterlife/intertextual citation – to consideration. For fans of cult blockbusters, seeing the film is just one moment (albeit perhaps a privileged one) within a series of textual engagements: reading about the film before its release, possibly seeing pirated copies or early/variant screening prints, and latterly viewing special editions on DVD as well as watching alongside DVD commentaries.

This reworking of the temporality of the blockbuster as it enters into cult fans' practices could, however, be analysed less as a type of 'cultification' and more as an outcome of the film industry shifting its patterns of release away from the 'primary window' of the film premiere and towards a multiple-window release pattern of film/DVD/special edition DVD. Nevertheless, viewing fan practices merely as a reflection of industry activities (see Klinger 1991) does a disservice to both industry and fan cultures, discursively positioning forces of commodification and capital as unassailable or as powerfully deterministic. Instead, we might consider cult audience practices as existing both inside and outside the parameters of commodification and consumer culture (Hills 2002), hence working to re-contextualise industry texts and strategies as well as being partly caught up within these strategies. This process of fan co-option, but also fan contextualisation and 'cultification' of the *Lord of the Rings* blockbusters has been examined by Bertha Chin and Jonathan Gray (2001) and Simone Murray (2004), and in what follows I want to briefly compare and contrast these two readings of *The Lord of the Rings* as a 'cult blockbuster'. Chin and Gray address the pre-film release online postings – at various official and unofficial websites – of what they identify as 'Tolkien fans':

> In analysing the postings, what is immediately noticeable is that all come from devoted fans *of the books*. Perhaps elsewhere, pre-viewers are congregating around stars such as Sir Ian McKellen or Liv Tyler, over cult director Peter Jackson, or over the fantasy genre in general, but here the pre-viewers all display the utmost familiarity with, and regard for, Tolkien's *Lord of the Rings*. (2001)

For these fans, the fidelity of the *Lord of the Rings* films to Tolkien's books was pre-judged on the basis of rumours and reports concerning the filming of *The Fellowship of the Ring*. Although some fans 'pre-viewed' New Line's cinematic efforts positively, others were highly negative/critical, or fell in between these extremes. All such fans made Tolkien's work their primary point of engagement with the films, whether they either keenly dreaded or anticipated the first film. And given the range of online fan comments, it is difficult to conclude that fandom was necessarily 'co-opted' into New Line's pre-release marketing strategy. Rather, this fan culture brought its own sense of textual authenticity and primacy into play, acting as a distinctive interpretive community, but also as a community which (pre-)interpreted the films intensely and intently over time.

By contrast, Murray focuses on New Line's approach to 'managing the unpredictable tides of online fan behaviour' (2004: 170), whereby what New Line characterise as 'Rabid Tolkien Fanatics' were targeted as an 'early-adopting' group whose enthusiasm could contribute to corporate publicity. Murray analyses how, rather than seeking to enforce intellectual property rights in a draconian manner, New Line instead sought to 'work with' Tolkien fans by releasing a drip-feed of pre-release information to more heavily-visited unofficial websites:

> By such means, New Line actively stokes the impetus towards one-upmanship and elaborate hierarchies of authenticity which characterise all media fandoms ... The elite inner sanctum of New Line-approved fan sites is supported by a broader programme of co-ordinated information dissemination ... Fan 'poaching' and reworking of New Line content was encouraged provided it was not hostile to the franchise in spirit or commercial in intent. (2004:19)

Although Chin and Gray emphasise online fandom as a culture set apart from (and somewhat oppositional to) the industry and New Line, the differences in these two accounts of the films' cultification can, perhaps, be resolved by noting that they regard different textual moments. Murray's analysis is of the pre-release of *The Two Towers*, whilst Chin and Gray discuss pre-*Fellowship of the Ring* fan activities: a sea change in industry/fan interactions thus seems to be caught by these two very different scholarly snapshots.

However, I want to suggest that this positivist and empiricist assumption is insufficient. To assume that online Tolkien fans simply moved from being relatively resistant to being selectively appropriated by and absorbed into New Line's marketing enterprise reduces the complexity of these cult audiences' reactions to the *Lord of the Rings* blockbusters. In defence of her argument that fandom has become a part of commercial marketing, Murray notes that 'cultural studies analyses ... may have erred in too readily accepting fans' individualist self-conception' (2004: 20) by excessively stressing the anti-commercial autonomy of fan culture. However, such analyses may also err in the other direction if they accept the self-conceptions of marketing folk, taking too seriously *their* claims to autonomy, control and 'management' of fan activities. One can hardly challenge one cultural group's self-representation (i.e. fans) but then accept another's (i.e. New Line's marketing personnel).

Instead, I would suggest that what New Line and the 'Rabid Tolkien Fanatics' struggle over 'brand' control indicates is that these fans have partly succeeded in re-contextualising the *Lord of the Rings* films within their own cult community's temporality of anticipation/dread, hence inciting New Line to reactively produce 'official' pre-release information. Rather than commodification/industry or separatist, 'pure' fandom clearly winning out, this scenario enacts a necessarily contradictory dynamic. Commercial forces appear to become more pervasive, but only by virtue of responding to a cult film experience of textual 'unfolding' and extended temporality, and moreover one which has previously been alien to the blockbuster as a typically and relatively 'ephemeral'/'mass' form.

If the blockbuster is potentially 'cultified' here by this movement away from well-disciplined consumers who only consume a text (as a bounded, symbolic entity) at appropriate points such as within its industry-led promotion and release window, then we still need to consider what this collision of 'cult' and 'blockbuster' means for the connotations of both terms. It is this that I will now move on to address.

Multiple cults in the multiplex: the 'residual' and 'emergent' cult blockbuster

The notion that 'cult' 'implies a minority' taste (Peary 1982: xiii) is actually maintained in relation to the distinctive interpretive community of 'Tolkien fans' examined by Chin and Gray, and Murray: this audience is very much a specific 'niche', centrally interpreting the films via Tolkien's original books. It could thus be argued that the *Lord of the Rings* films are a special type of blockbuster enterprise, since they are *adaptations of texts which already possess a cult following*. Rather than cult status emerging primarily around a blockbuster film, cult status here is seemingly carried from one text to another, being transferred from Tolkien's novels to the films via a sort of intertextual affective contagion (see Hills 2002; on the 'original' Tolkien cult, see Whissen 1992). Cultishness does not, on this reading, enter the 'mainstream' of the blockbuster film other than as a reflection or refraction of cult 'distinctions' residing elsewhere. To speak of the *Lord of the Rings* films as 'cult blockbusters' would thus appear to be not at all the same thing as analysing the *Star Wars* films, *Titanic*, or even the *Matrix* films as blockbusting mainstream movie 'cults'. By contrast, in these instances a sense of cult status – via fan activities such as massively repeated viewings; the production of related texts; the generation of distinctive reading protocols – is primarily produced in relation to the films themselves rather than (inter)textually and trans-medially pre-dating them (see Nash & Lahti 1999; Brooker 2002; Hills 2003). The differentiation called for is perhaps that of *emergent* cult status within 'the blockbuster mainstream' versus cult status which is *residually* carried over into 'the mainstream' for a time via the production and circulation of new versions or new media iterations of already beloved characters, narratives and, above all, diegetic worlds like Middle Earth.

Unfortunately, even this specific emergent/residual differentiation – as well as its film versus popular literature binary – partly reduces the complexity of the *Lord of the Rings* films and their 'cult blockbuster' status. For it tends to make the *Lord of the Rings* 'cult' purely synonymous with a literary 'Tolkien cult', thereby rendering invisible other non-literary-based cult audiences such as that, for example, based upon reading the *Lord of the Rings* films as moments within the unfolding career and auteurism of 'cult director' Peter Jackson. With regards to the cult status of these New Line films, both author and auteur require consideration.

As Harmony Wu highlights,

> despite the big production gloss and mainstream respectability of *The Lord of the Rings*, before this Peter Jackson was mostly known to cult audiences, at first for his 'low' splatter horror and gore films and then for his 'high' art-house film *Heavenly Creatures*. The *Rings* films are by far Jackson's biggest, most commercially mainstream productions to date – and yet, contrary to usual oppositions of 'cult' and 'blockbuster', these anticipated blockbusters, like his earlier films, are still the site of cult desire, as illustrated by … examples of fan behaviour (2003: 84–5).

Akin to my own arguments above, Wu makes fan-cultural practices of anticipation and desire – fans' interest in downloading film trailers and intently following news on the production of the films – central to establishing that these are mainstream blockbusters which have become cultivated and cultified via audience practices (see also Harper & Mendik 2000). 'Event' blockbusters (Wu 2003: 84) are thereby recontextualised into audiences' self-narrated arcs and temporalities of awaiting/forward-looking and analysing/looking-back on moments of affectively-weighted textual encounters. If film and cultural studies have paid much attention to the events and cognitions of filmic interpretation, where audiences are tacitly assumed to 'produce' readings in the instant of viewing, or across the duration of a film screening, they have paid rather scant attention to the phenomenon and phenomenology of cult audiences who project-forward a desired sense of what a text will be like, and then near-obsessively repeat and return to the present-absent limit moment of textual-aesthetic experience.

As well as (implicitly) noting the importance of fan-cultural practices and their temporalities, Wu makes Peter Jackson, rather than Tolkien *per se*, the focus of her exploration of New Line's *Lord of the Rings* cult status. She points out how the 'intersection of "cult" with both "low" and "high" texts as well as with "mainstream" in Jackson's films is a useful reminder of the need to be attentive to the nuanced articulations of cultism in a variety of [cultural] locations' (2003: 85). More than this, though, Wu's recuperation of Jackson points inescapably to the possibility that 'cult' status can, in fact, be multiply articulated in relation to any given film – working through different fan interpretive communities focused on a variety of 'cult' actors, screenwriters/authors and director-auteurs. Cult status may, therefore, be over-determined, emerging not through any singular anti-mainstream or 'high'/'low' cultural cachet, but instead forming through a range of different textual attributes (Hills 2002) and through a range of differing readings. Cult blockbusters – as well as cult films more generally – may not always represent 'singularly' cultish texts, but may instead become differently cultish for different audience fractions.

Just as the 'Rabid Tolkien Fans' read *The Lord of the Rings* through Tolkien's work, so fans of Peter Jackson read these films through Jackson's career. The discursive and narrative thread of Jackson's 'author-function' allows films of widely varying types and genres to be stitched together into an uneasy coherence, and provides a further type of 'cross-over' or transference from prior cult texts and audience fractions into the 'mainstream blockbusters' of *The Lord of the Rings*. In her analysis of Jackson's career phases, Wu argues that it is possible to discern different versions of Jackson-as-cult-auteur: one corresponding to Jackson's early gross-out/splatter/horror films such as *Bad Taste* (1987) and *Braindead* (1992) – though the intervening *Meet the Feebles* (1989) is difficult to characterise solely as gross-out, since its subversion of children's puppet films and Muppet-esque escapades already has a pronounced art-house sensibility – and another version which can be characterised as 'art-house cult', in the form of *Heavenly Creatures* (1994). Utilising the auteurist notion of a unified artistic 'career' – constructing coherence by relating different 'phases' to each other within an unfolding narrative – Wu notes:

Jackson's film career illustrates a canny ability to parlay specialised cult films, as well as both high and low films, into mainstreamed commercial viability … Jackson illustrates that a manipulation of 'cult' and both high and low aesthetics in the intersection of national/international cinemas and audiences works, paradoxically, to make possible a broader international audience, and to engender, through the capital his cult films have secured for him, more wide-scale commercial production on New Zealand soil. (2003: 104)

In this coherence-securing narrative, the cult status of Jackson's films begins as something properly 'anti-mainstream', subversive and opposed to good taste. Jackson's 'cult' status then moves through a transitional phase whereby it is articulated with less stridently 'bad taste' but still specialised and anti-mainstream art-house films, before a move into the mainstream becomes possible – albeit still in a genre which has traditionally been seen as 'childish' and geeky: fantasy. Jackson's negotiation with forms of 'cult' status, in fact, may well have marked him out as an appropriate figure to work on *The Lord of the Rings* for New Line, given that the position of his work here is relatively homologous to that of Tolkien's: a cult author's work is therefore 'mainstreamed' by a cult film auteur who, in that very act, moves his own output firmly into the blockbuster mainstream. Beyond this homology, it is also worth noting the profile of New Line itself, which as a 'major-independent'-turned-mainstream-Hollywood-industry-player has a history of supporting 'midnight movies' and cult titles such as *Reefer Madness* (Louis J. Gasnier, 1936), *Pink Flamingos* (John Waters, 1972) and *The Texas Chainsaw Massacre* (Tobe Hooper, 1974) (see Wyatt 1998). New Line, much like the cultural shifts surrounding Tolkien's work and Peter Jackson's career, has moved from connoting cult status – beginning with ' "arty and freak" films […] opened […] in a midnight screening pattern, followed by a larger theatrical release' (Wyatt, 1998: 76) – to occupying the mainstream. New Line's 1980s back catalogue is characterised by genre movies which broke out into mass, commercial success such as the *Nightmare on Elm Street* franchise. New Line's more recent cultural respectability therefore also resonates with Peter Jackson's and Tolkien's shifting cultural locations/distinctions, in what could be described as a semiotic echo-chamber or trilogy of cult-turned-mainstream movements. The 'brands' of New Line, Tolkien and Peter Jackson as a type of 'commercial auteur' (Corrigan 1991: 107) are all characterised by residual or cross-over cult identities, bringing multiple cult cachet to the *Lord of the Rings* blockbusters. At least two 'cult communities' – possibly three if we accept that fans of Jackson's *Heavenly Creatures* may constitute a different subset to the 'trash' fans of *Bad Taste* (2003: 103), or if we include genre 'fans'/followers of New Line itself – are thereby drawn into the blockbuster mainstream.

Despite Wu's suggestion that Jackson 'uniquely embodies the construct of the "cult auteur"' (2003: 102), a range of Hollywood directors have gravitated from overseeing low-budget, anti-mainstream 'cult' hits to helming mainstream block-busters. Indeed, this 'progression', in terms of escalating budgets, prestige and so on, indicates precisely that 'the trading in of low-brow horror for mainstream big-budget fantasy spectacle re-iterates a dynamic where the Hollywood model of film-making (and its good taste, polished aesthetics and bourgeois ideologies) remains on top' (Wu 2003: 93).

John Carpenter and James Cameron, for instance, were both linked to 'cult' discourses early on their careers, before then moving on to more 'mainstream fan-tasy spectacle' and thus potentially carrying their cult cachet and fan communities with them (Conrich 2004) into otherwise hyper-commercial Hollywood produc-tions such as Carpenter's *Starman* (1984) or *Titanic*. Alexandra Keller (1999) has even analysed James Cameron as a 'blockbuster auteur', constructing auteurist coherence by claiming that one of the unifying concerns of Cameron's work has been the creation of spectacle-as-capital. And for at least one 'cult community' of film fans, James Cameron's 'cult' connotations are sufficiently cemented and taken-as-read that emphasising his involvement as a writer/producer on *Strange Days* (Kathryn Bigelow, 1995) can act as a discursive strategy for supporting the 'cult classic' status of that film (see Brooker 2003: 207–8). The blockbuster and cult auteurism are, it would seem, no longer the enemies which 'art vs com-merce' binaries would assume. But the blockbuster and art have to be discur-sively stitched together, either through the route taken by Keller – seeking a unity across the auteur's films which can also be related to their 'blockbuster' main-stream apotheosis – or the path taken by Wu, where early anti-mainstream 'cult' phases can be 'parlayed' and transferred into a new career phase of mainstream filmmaking.

Conclusion

What the intriguing instance of the *Lord of the Rings* films indicates is that 'cult blockbusters' can take on their cult status in a variety of ways, and not simply through a 'residual vs emergent' cult either/or, where 'cult' is either carried over into the mainstream (from preceding cult formations) or emerges as a differential set of reading strategies within that 'mainstream'. Rather, cult status can appear through a variety of cult readings which represent multiple 'residual' cult com-munities (Tolkien fans/Jackson fans/New Line fans or followers) as well as other 'emergent' cult communities such as those valuing and reading the *Lord of the Rings* films primarily through their blockbuster special effects (Maltby 2003: 237; Pierson 2002). In this latter case, fans of the *Lord of the Rings* films can celebrate them – as connoisseur consumers – for their photo-realist CGI advances without necessarily reading as Tolkien or Jackson fans:

The growth in and diversification of cultures of film connoisseurship that we are witnessing at the present time feeds the expansion of the entertainment and consumer industries in fairly obvious ways, creating demand for ever more state-of-the-art technologies that promise to make attentive, repeat home-viewing of films more pleasurable and promoting a consumerist culture of connoisseur-collectors. (Pierson 2002: 165).

The Lord of the Rings with its grandly extended DVD special editions and publicity emphases on the realisation of, say, Gollum, could be said to have played a significant role within this industry shift towards interpellating 'consumerist/connoisseur-collectors' beyond the market of cult audiences, hence seeking to generalise the 'cult' activity of attentive, repeated viewings for a 'mainstream' audience (see Kirsten Pullen's and Jonathan Gray's chapters in this volume).

Rather than perceiving the 'cult blockbuster' as an inherent oddity or an oxymoron, and rather than viewing cult status as dependent on singular factors and singular 'minority' audiences such as 'Tolkien fans', I have argued here for the need to address cult status as over-determined, and as multiplied across different audiences. This makes the 'cult blockbuster' less of a surprise, perhaps, and more of a plural, nuanced *residual and emergent* cult(ural) phenomenon, one which calls out for case-by-case consideration rather than blanket derision or celebration. As Thomas Elsaesser has so poetically argued:

> Between past and future, between childhood and parenthood, mainstream cinema has found its cultural function as the world's time machine, with the blockbuster the 'engine' that simultaneously raises expectations, stirs memories, and unites us with our previous selves. (2001: 22)

But this affectively binding and connecting operation can not only bridge adult and child selves, it can also connect 'cult communities' to the cultural 'mainstream' in a variety of ways. *The Lord of the Rings* does not represent a mass-cultural or mainstreamed 'one cult to rule them all': instead, as a 'cult blockbuster' its cult status is multiplied by and for different cult fan audiences such as cinephiles/auteurists, Tolkienites, and special-effects-consumer-connoisseurs.

Works cited

Austin, T. (2002) *Hollywood, Hype and Audiences: Selling and Watching Popular Films in the 1990s.* Manchester: Manchester University Press.

Barker, M. and K. Brooks (1998) *Knowing Audiences: Judge Dredd, Its Friends, Fans and Foes.* Luton: University of Luton Press.

Brooker, W. (2002) *Using the Force: Creativity, Community and Star Wars Fans.* London:

Continuum.

_____ (2003) 'Rescuing *Strange Days*: Fan Reaction to a Critical and Commercial Failure', in D. Jermyn and S. Redmond (eds) *The Cinema of Kathryn Bigelow: Hollywood Transgressor*. London: Wallflower Press, 198–219.

Chin, B. and J. Gray (2001) '"One Ring To Rule Them All": Pre-viewers and Pre-texts of the *Lord of the Rings*', *Intensities: The Journal of Cult Media*, 2. Online. Available at http://www.cult-media.com/issue2/Achingray.htm (accessed 21 July 2005).

Conrich, I. (2004) 'Killing Time … and Time Again: The Popular Appeal of Carpenter's Horrors and the Impact of *The Thing* and *Halloween*', in I. Conrich and D. Woods (eds) *The Cinema of John Carpenter: The Technique of Terror*. London: Wallflower Press, London, 91–106.

Corrigan, T. (1991) *A Cinema Without Walls: Movies and Culture After Vietnam*. London: Routledge.

Crawford, G. (2004) *Consuming Sport: Fans, Sport and Culture*. London: Routledge.

Elsaesser, T. (2001) 'The Blockbuster: Everything Connects, but Not Everything Goes', in J. Lewis (ed.) *The End of Cinema as We Know It: American Film in the Nineties*. New York: New York University Press, 11–22.

Hall, S. (2002) 'Tall Revenue Features: The Genealogy of the Modern Blockbuster', in S. Neale (ed.) *Genre and Contemporary Hollywood*. London: British Film Institute, 11–26.

Harper, G. and X. Mendik (2000) 'The Chaotic Text and the Sadean Audience', in X. Mendik and G. Harper (eds) *Unruly Pleasures: The Cult Film and its Critics*. Guilford: FAB Press, 237–49.

Hills, M. (2002) *Fan Cultures*. London: Routledge.

_____ (2003) '*Star Wars* in Fandom, Film Theory, and the Museum: The Cultural Status of the Cult Blockbuster', in J. Stringer (ed.) *Movie Blockbusters*. London: Routledge, 178–89.

_____ (2004) '*Dawson's Creek*: "Quality Teen TV" and "Mainstream Cult"?', in G. Davis and K. Dickinson (eds) *Teen TV: Genre, Consumption and Identity*. London: British Film Institute, 54–67.

Hollows, J. (2003) 'The Masculinity of Cult', in M. Jancovich, A. Lázaro-Reboll, J. Stringer and A. Willis (eds) *Defining Cult Movies: The Cultural Politics of Oppositional Taste*. Manchester: Manchester University Press, 35–53.

Jancovich, M. (2000) '"A Real Shocker": Authenticity, Genre and the Struggle for Distinction', *Continuum*, 14, 1, 23–35.

_____ (2002) 'Cult Fictions: Cult Movies, Subcultural Capital and the Production of Cultural Distinctions', *Cultural Studies*, 16, 2, 306–22.

Jancovich, M. and L. Faire (2003) 'The Best Place to See a Film: The Blockbuster, the Multiplex, and the Contexts of Consumption', in J. Stringer (ed.) *Movie Blockbusters*. London: Routledge, 190–201.

Jenkins, H. (1992) *Textual Poachers: Television Fans and Participatory Culture*. London: Routledge.

Keller, A. (1999) '"Size Does Matter": Notes on *Titanic* and James Cameron as Blockbuster Auteur', in K. S. Sandler and G. Studlar (eds) *Titanic: Anatomy of a Blockbuster*. New Brunswick: Rutgers University Press, 132–54.

King, G. (2000) *Spectacular Narratives: Hollywood in the Age of the Blockbuster*. London: I. B. Tauris.

Klinger, B. (1991) 'Digressions at the Cinema: Commodification and Reception in Mass Culture', in J. Naremore and P. Brantlinger (eds) *Modernity and Mass Culture*. Bloomington: Indiana University Press, 117–34.

Maltby, R. (2003) *Hollywood Cinema*, second edition. Oxford: Blackwell Publishing.

Murray, S. (2004) '"Celebrating the Story the Way It Is": Cultural Studies, Corporate Media and the Contested Utility of Fandom', *Continuum*, 18, 1, 7–25.

Nash, M. and M. Lahti (1999) '"Almost Ashamed to Say I Am One of Those Girls": *Titanic*, Leonardo DiCaprio, and the Paradoxes of Girls' Fandom', in K. S. Sandler and G. Studlar (eds) *Titanic: Anatomy of a Blockbuster*. New Brunswick: Rutgers University Press, 64–88.

Peary, D. (1982) *Cult Movies*. London: Vermilion.

Pierson, M. (2002) *Special Effects: Still in Search of Wonder*. New York: Columbia University Press.

Sandvoss, C. (2005) *Fans: The Mirror of Consumption*. Cambridge: Polity Press.

Staiger, J. (2005) *Media Reception Studies*. New York: New York University Press.

Whissen, T. R. (1992) *Classic Cult Fiction*. New York: Greenwood Press.

Wu, H. (2003) 'Trading in Horror, Cult and Matricide: Peter Jackson's Phenomenal Bad Taste and New Zealand Fantasies of Inter/National Cinematic Success', in M. Jancovich, A. Lázaro-Reboll, J. Stringer and A. Willis (eds) *Defining Cult Movies: The Cultural Politics of Oppositional Taste*. Manchester: Manchester University Press, 84–108.

Wyatt, J. (1998) 'The Formation of the 'Major Independent': Miramax, New Line and the New Hollywood', in S. Neale and M. Smith (eds) *Contemporary Hollywood Cinema*. London: Routledge, 74–90.

The Lord of the Rings Online Blockbuster Fandom: Pleasure and Commerce

Kirsten Pullen

This is not so much a review as … praise to Peter Jackson for bringing this marvel of an epic story by J.R.R. Tolkien of good vs. evil to the screen. In these times this is a refreshing reminder that no matter how bad things can get one must always have hope that in the hearts of men there lays truth and within that truth lays good … [It] has brought people together to appreciate the concept and message behind the story. Praise to Peter Jackson and the wonderful cast and crew for bringing this treasure to life for all of us to marvel in and to take something with us that very few movies tend to provide in today's lacklustre Hollywood vibe. (Imbue 2003)

Introduction

When media studies, influenced by the arguments about popular culture and agency advanced by the Birmingham Centre for Cultural Studies, split from qualitative, sociologically-inflected communication models, fandom was a key site for mapping the limits of hegemony within mass media texts (Penley 1991; Fiske 1992; Grossberg 1992; Jenkins 1992). When the internet emerged as a technology for personal self-expression and community-building as well as commercialisation, the fan remained a model for exploring the consumption of pop culture texts and the democratisation of fan culture (MacDonald 1998; Fernback 1999; Baym 2000; Jenkins 2002; Pullen 2004). Now, as *The Lord of the Rings* recasts the rules of film production, distribution and marketing, the internet fan is a key component of the blockbuster phenomenon.

In this chapter, I will describe the traditional fan and the internet fan of *The Lord of the Rings* as a background for theorising the potential pleasures of blockbuster fandom. In important ways, *The Lord of the Rings* created the blockbuster fan, a popular culture consumer who retains many characteristics of the 'traditional' fan but is more deeply imbricated with institutional processes than its predecessors. Specifically, *The Lord of the Rings* producers and fans entered an increasingly global, linked and complex negotiation to expand a traditional and traditionally marginalised text into a blockbuster commercial and critical success. Using *The Lord of the Rings* trilogy and the website theonering.net as case study, I will describe the characteristics of the blockbuster fan, suggesting how *The Lord of the Rings* producers and fans worked together to elevate the trilogy into a blockbuster success with integrity, authenticity and a sense of community.

The pleasures of fandom

Traditional fan studies suggest that fans exploit the resistant potential of mass media texts in often liberatory, counter-hegemonic ways. Though working specifically with television texts, Henry Jenkins (1992: 277–80) identified five characteristics that all fan communities share. First, fans watch and re-watch favourite programmes, looking for meaningful details, internal contradictions and ambiguity in order to find the gaps that suggest a space for intervention. Second, fans create a 'meta-text', one that has more information about characters, lifestyles, values and relationships than the original but that derives consistency from the shared values and reading practices of the fan community. Third, fans are active consumers, writing letters about plot lines and characters, and in some cases successfully lobbying to keep their beloved television series on the air. Fourth, fans create unique forms of cultural production: zines; information about actors' appearances and production schedules; episode guides; gossip about the text; videos of moments from the text set to popular music and resembling music videos; fan artwork; and, increasingly, fan fiction. Finally, fans create an alternative social community, creating a space that is more 'humane and democratic' (Jenkins 1992: 280) than the everyday world. Brought together by their love of a particular text, these fans form alliances with others who may have different political, social and economic backgrounds but are committed to the ideals expressed by their favoured text. Within the community, fans also frequently express pleasure and relief to find others who are like them.

Traditional fans celebrated what John Fiske termed 'producerly' texts (1992: 42), texts which contain internal contradictions and ambiguities, providing opportunities for fans to fill in the gaps and make their own meaning.[1] For example, as exemplified by Constance Penley's study of female *Star Trek* fans, science fiction and fantasy offer more freedom than other genres, because these texts allow for discussion of real-life issues unconstrained by real life circumstances (1991: 138). Texts set in the future or in alternate universes are open to fan activation: the fantasy included in the original text legitimises the flights of fancy engaged in by the fans as they revise, continue and rework plot lines. Producerly texts invite fans to incorporate their own ideals and practices into the original narratives.

Further, traditional fan studies posit an ideal and particular fan, outside mainstream viewing practices. Fans are drawn to producerly texts because they see something in them that critics and the mainstream audience have missed; the fans' marginality affords a critical cachet. Fans form an alternative community which rebels against mainstream norms and creates a space for open communication of liberal, democratic ideals. Members of disenfranchised groups, such as women and the working class, find in favoured programmes a more equitable society and seek to replicate that society within the fan community. In fact, some media scholars (most notably Jenkins' and Penley's early studies) express a certain romantic attachment for fan activity, uncritically assuming that fans who rework meaning are somehow better than the average viewer. For most scholars, the pleasures of traditional fandom come from the creative reworking of texts and from membership in a select society with greater knowledge of and appreciation for their favoured (and usually obscure) texts.

Internet fans expand these categories.[2] The internet has mainstreamed fandom; according to Jenkins, 'contemporary popular culture has absorbed many aspects of "fan culture" that would have seemed marginal a decade ago' (2003: 291). *The Lord of the Rings* fans can choose from and interact with nearly 700 websites devoted to the films, novels and videogames. Most of the sites are hyperlinked to each other, often including plugs for other sites and the people who created them. In addition, many of the sites offer tips for creating webpages and offer the use of graphics to those designing new sites. By checking out a search engine and surfing the Web, even a fan new to either Tolkien or the internet can quickly find other fans and information about joining the online fan community. Most important for internet-based fan communities are the distribution and production of fan-created texts and the sense of community talking about a favoured text can impart, even to viewers separated by thousands of miles. Further, the immediacy of the internet enables fans to get a rapid response to their interpretations of a particular text or fan production, rather than waiting weeks and even months for a new zine or newsletter. Fans' pervasive presence on the internet suggests that stereotypes of the fan as a fringe obsessive have given way to views of the fan as an average internet user.

Joining an online fan community also frequently entails interacting with an official (and market-driven) website. Nearly all television programmes and films have some sort of internet presence; those directed to a youth audience are often especially interactive. Most of these websites provide the kind of information previously available only through fan clubs and fan activities such as newsletters and conventions. In addition, celebrities from all forms of media engage in live, interactive, online discussions with their fans, especially when promoting a new film, special television programme, new season, or music release. The internet, then, ties fan activity more closely to commercialism than earlier, do-it-yourself efforts.

At the same time, of course, the internet enables new opportunities for creative intervention, especially for distributing creative reworkings of the original text. Within traditional accounts, fan fiction is often suggested as the basis for creative, interventionist fan activity. Fans write and circulate stories, continuing narratives, creating alternate endings and, most frequently, suggesting romantic relationships not explicitly designated by the original text. This fiction, often with homoerotic themes, is called slash fiction, named for the '/' that separates the character names, as in fiction about a homosexual relationship between Kirk and Spock (in Penley's original study) or Frodo and Sam (*The Lord of the Rings'* most popular couple). Penley asserts that the original, polysemic *Star Trek* text explicitly invites this kind of rearticulation, and further that only texts like *Star Trek* offer the ambiguity necessary for such textual intervention (1991: 138). However, internet fan fiction suggests otherwise. The Yahoo! search engine lists nearly 1,300 fan fiction sites, many with multiple stories and multiple authors.

In addition to fan fiction, fans create increasingly sophisticated digital media based on existing texts, as both homage and critique. The *Star Wars* films, perhaps because of Lucasfilm's innovations in computer-generated imagery and special effects, have inspired several fan films. In response to the seemingly toy- and sponsor-driven narrative, juvenile writing and superfluous characters of *Star Wars: Episode 1 – The Phantom Menace* (George Lucas, 1999), long-time fans created *Star Wars: Episode 1.1 – The Phantom Edit* by removing Jar Jar Binks from the narrative and circulated this film on the internet (see Hoberman 2001: 13). *George Lucas in Love*, a film written, directed and produced by film students at the University of Southern California (Lucas's alma mater), parodies *Shakespeare in Love* (John Madden, 1997) as well as the familiar characters and narrative of the original *Star Wars* trilogy. There are dozens of *Star Wars* fan projects available (or previously available) on the internet (Jenkins 2003: 310–12). In another medium, music fans produce mash-ups, songs by different artists combined through digital sampling, such as 'Public Holiday' which combines Madonna's 1993 chestnut with Jessica Simpson's 2006 'Public Affair'. Creative fan revisions of original texts are more available and more varied because of new digital technologies.

Of course, the increased variety and visibility of fans' creative intervention may meet serious resistance from the copyright holders. If, as Jenkins suggests 'fans envision a world where all of us can participate in the creation and circulation of central cultural myths' but studios assume their 'intellectual property is a "limited good" to be tightly controlled lest it dilute its value; (2003: 289) it is unsurprising that the ubiquity of fan creation on the internet has led to increased legal action on the part of studios who view fan stories as infringing their intellectual property. But when Twentieth Century Fox threatened legal action against *Buffy the Vampire*

Slayer fansites in 1999 and again in 2001, fans were outraged. *Buffy* fans, like all fans, see their texts as inhabiting alternate universes where friendship, freedom of choice and redemption are celebrated and affirmed. Thus, the actions of Twentieth Century Fox seem to negate their positive experiences as a community. Fans of the *Star Wars* and *Harry Potter* films, novelist Anne McCaffrey, Scooby Doo, and Trekkers have also been subject to legal action because of internet-based fan activities. Though the ease of publication and circulation offered by the internet has increased the amount of fan fiction and arguably enhanced a sense of community, this increased visibility has also curtailed some fan activity that had previously existed under the radar of copyright owners.

Though most fans view producers' enforcement of trademark and copyright law as draconian,[3] the argument that fan fiction might dilute or even damage the brand seems legitimate. Lyndon Barber (2001) quotes a 'slash' Harry Potter: 'Draco eyed a sweat droplet as it ran down Harry's cheek and neck, to disappear into the collar of his robes. Every instinct suddenly cried out to follow the damp trail with his tongue…'. It is not difficult to understand why J. K. Rowling and Scholastic books want to quash this kind of homoerotic (and even paedophiliac) slash fiction, given their primary market of pre-teenagers. George Lucas is invested in maintaining ownership of the *Star Wars* universe, especially in light of negative critical and fan reaction to *The Phantom Menace* and *Attack of the Clones*. In 1999, Lucasfilm threatened legal action against *The Phantom Edit*. Though Lucas has since sponsored a contest for 'authorised' fan parodies and documentaries, Jim Ward, marketing vice-president of Lucasfilm is clear about the limits of even this activity:

> We love our fans … But if in fact someone is using our characters to create a story unto itself, that's not in the spirit of what we think fandom is about. Fandom is about celebrating the story the way it is. (Quoted in Murray 2004: 11)

Thus, the internet has both expanded (in terms of technology and media) and limited (in terms of legal restrictions) fans' creative work.

In addition to providing more outlets and opportunities for creative work, the internet also offers fan communities opportunities for real-world networking, social action and activism. As Jenkins points out, internet fandom 'becomes much more effective as a platform for consumer activism' (2002: 161). Fan communities use the internet to facilitate charity giving and volunteerism. Theonering.net supports literacy programmes in Chicago, New Zealand and Africa; the official *Star Wars* series site co-sponsored the Film Industry Art Auction for Tsunami Relief at Maverix Animation Studio on 4 February 2005. Other fan websites have ongoing charities with opportunities for direct donation as well as auctions for fan memorabilia alongside information about local volunteer opportunities (see Pullen 2004). This charitable activity seems to demonstrate the opportunities for social action the internet might offer, suggesting that fans are harnessing internet technology to move beyond merely talking about a favoured television text and the ideals it espouses to putting those ideals into practice.

Though the internet has increased fan activity and fan pleasure, its commercialism is an obvious limit to its liberatory potential. Because movie studios increasingly target a young, technologically savvy, up-scale audience, websites advertising films are becoming more visually complex and interactive in order to create fans before a film's release. Though *The Lord of the Rings* trilogy exploded this trend, it is important to note they followed an established industry pattern. Most internet fan scholars point to the 1999 marketing for the independent Artisan Entertainment release *The Blair Witch Project* (Daniel Myrick and Eduardo Sanchez, 1999) as launching a new synergistic relationship between film and the internet. By establishing an enormous internet presence, with a detailed and interactive website, Artisan created fans of the movie before the movie even existed. Many reviewers noted that the pre-movie internet buzz and film website were more interesting than the movie itself.

Creating the blockbuster fan

The blockbuster fan overlaps many characteristics of the classic and internet fan, though there are important differences, especially regarding commercialism and creative output. Like all fans, however, the blockbuster fan identifies intensely with the original text and the fan community and works to maintain the authenticity and integrity of the text as well as the fan experience. Though *The Lord of the Rings* provides a potent case study, other films, such as *X-Men* (Bryan Singer, 2000), *Spider-Man* (Sam Raimi, 2002) the *Harry Potter* series and of course the two *Star Wars* trilogies might also be examined through this lens. If the fan has always served as the extreme viewer from which other audience experience may be extrapolated, then the blockbuster fan suggests new methods for understanding audiences at a moment when global, linked mass-media entertainment proliferates across technologies, throughout industries and within audiences. Salient characteristics of blockbuster fandom are: the existence of a marginal, traditional fan base from which to draw; fans' creative work as part of the marketing process; a willingness to trade spectacular commercialisation for greater access to and influence over the production; and a celebration of the authenticity and integrity of the text, production and fan community as defined against other Hollywood products. As the following discussion makes clear, the negotiation between *Lord of the Rings* fans and producers before, during and after the filmmaking engendered the blockbuster fan.

The Lord of the Rings' production company, New Line Cinema, whose global interactive marketing senior vice-president Gordon Paddison clearly embraced the lessons of *The Blair Witch Project* and Artisan, aggressively courted (or solicitously wooed) the existing Tolkien fanbase, somewhat hyperbolically estimated at 100 million (Shefrin 2004: 265). The narrative of Paddison and director Peter Jackson's internet outreach project is nearly legendary among industry-watchers. In August 1998, before filming had even begun, Jackson was interviewed on web gadfly Harry Knowles' Ain't-it-Cool-News site because it was 'the only way [he] could imagine reaching all [the fans] in an efficient way' (Knowles 1998). Knowles helped with the efficiency; 14,000 fans submitted questions for Jackson, from which Knowles culled twenty (casting questions were off-limits). Jackson participated in a second interview in January 1999, further discussing the structure and narrative of the three films and addressing proposed changes. Paddison developed the official website in late 1999, first limited to brief announcements, but expanding over the release of the films to include trailers, interviews, behind-the-scenes videos, links to the official fan club, international versions of the website, online shopping, some of Tolkien's original material, downloadable screensavers and wallpaper, music previews and photo galleries from the film. The official site is extensive and complex and more visually interesting and interactive than most film websites.

Clearly, New Line and Paddison had an enormous advantage over earlier films like *The Blair Witch Project* because of the enormous fan base that pre-existed their project. As *Sci Fi* editor Scott Edelman made clear, Tolkien fans wanted and needed to love the films: 'my lifelong love of Tolkien had left me feeling invested in the critical success of the film in a way that just wasn't present for the average genre film' (quoted in Thompson 2003: 53). Further, these fans were already online, and already active. Simone Murray describes New Line's 'steady drip-feed of production information … to a coterie of approximately forty of the most heavily trafficked Tolkien Websites', with the top ten offered even more insider information and exclusive content to provide 'the impetus towards one-upmanship and elaborate hierarchies of authenticity which characterise all media fandoms' (2004: 19). Indeed, as a banner on ringbearer.org asked during the production of *Return of the King*, 'ever wonder why the other sites report our stories AFTER we do?' (2003), suggesting that other sites were poaching their insider information. As the oldest Tolkien site on the internet (at least according to their website), ringbearer.org was anxious to demonstrate its position within the hierarchy of fan websites.

The Lord of the Rings online fandom and theonering.net

Theonering.net,[4] because of its New Zealand presence and aggressive recruitment and even co-optation of other Tolkien sites, became the website most closely linked with the production. This site is enormous, and even years after *The Return of the King*'s release it continues to post information. Perhaps most significantly, it hosts Peter Jackson's fan club, The Bastards Have Landed, as well as the fan website for Jackson's later project, a remake of *King Kong*, a film that, though grossing over US$500 million worldwide, was a disappointment compared to the *Lord of the Rings* trilogy. The homepage features the site's banner, a grey-ink drawing of Sam and Frodo led by Golllum into Mordor with the legend 'TheOneRing.net: Forged by and for Fans for J.R.R. Tolkien' and 'Serving Middle Earth Since the First Age'. An advertising banner, usually from allposters.com, amazon.com or WETA/Sideshow sits below the title bar, and in 2005 a link to the festival schedule for the documentary *Ringers: Lord of the Fans*, about fifty years of Tolkien fandom, sits in the upper-right-hand corner. Along the left side of the page, links to chatrooms, the online store, gaming sections, archives, character information, FAQs, interviews and spy reports. On the lower right, the onering.net polls, weekly questions about the books, films, characters, casting, collectibles, DVDs and other fan topics are updated whenever a new fan votes. This enormous website, with its carefully maintained archives, multiple arenas for fan interaction, interviews with Jackson and other crew members, and downloadable photos and graphics from the production is simply more complex than any other fansite on the internet. The creation of theonering.net demonstrates how *The Lord of the Rings'* producers exploited existing fans' desire for information, as well as their desire to be the most authoritative source for that information.

The homepage of theonering.net includes headlines (updated regularly) about *The Lord of the Rings* filming, DVD releases, actors' personal appearances, related projects, fan conventions, collectibles and events of interest to the fan community culled from other internet websites, fans' cast and crew sightings, and print media. Importantly, these headlines are gathered and submitted by fans as well as webmasters; for example, the week that *The Return of the King* was released, fans submitted a transcript of Elijah Wood's *Good Morning, America* appearance, an interview with Liv Tyler and Orlando Bloom originally published in the Melbourne *Herald-Sun*, a box office report, an ecstatic fan's spotting of Dominic Monaghan at *The Return of the King* at a Hollywood cinema, and a plea for Canadian fans to nominate composer Howard Shore to Canada's Walk of Fame (2003a). The headlines are an important way for fans to interact with the site and the text. Not only can they read 'breaking news' about the production, they can also contribute news of their own. In addition, since most of this news is recycled from other sites, fans do not need to be close to the production or Hollywood insiders to contribute. Clearly, the buzz around the film was maintained at least in part by fan desire to be seen and heard on the internet.

Polls were another important way for fans to monitor the production and even influence its outcome. The first poll, posted in April 1999, asked fans who they hoped would play Gandalf. Ian McKellen was not even mentioned; Sean Connery was the overwhelming winner. In the weeks leading up to *The Return of the King*'s release, poll topics included 'Who will be responsible for the most laughs (Gimli [2003b]) or tears (Samwise [2003c])'; 'Did you dress up as a LotR character for Halloween?' (2003d); 'How are you getting your *The Two Towers* Extended Edition?' (60% planned to purchase it at the store the day it was released [2003e]); and 'The 1 week mark approacheth: How do you feel?' (respondents evenly split between 'each second feels like a thousand minutes' and 'sad it will all end soon' [2003f]). In general, the polls were fairly evenly split between questions about casting, favourite moments from the films, and reaction to DVD, VHS and collectible sales and garnered an average of 7,500 fan responses. Kristin Thompson has demonstrated that theonering.net's weekly internet polls influenced marketing for the film if not the narrative itself. She suggests that although the poll questions are solicited from fans, 'some questions clearly come from people connected with the film' (2003: 56). The polls, then, with their instant updating, offer both fans and producers a quick and easy way to gauge reaction to the trilogy production. The fans are also able to see how their interpretations of the films line up with other fans; the huge response indicates they are part of a dynamic and wide-ranging community.

Although New Line was clearly reaching out to who they called 'Rabid Tolkien Fanatics' or RTFs (Murray 2004: 17), those fanatics were reaching back. In November 1999, theonering.net created the 'LotR Movie Integrity Petition', urging Jackson and New Line to be as faithful to the novels as possible, as anything else would 'be a terrible disservice to the story that Tolkien wrote and could not represent artistic integrity in any way' (Landro 2000). Nearly 17,000 internet fans signed the petition. It is important to note that *Lord of the Rings* fans aggressively wooed New Line, arguing that their input on the film and their goodwill toward the project could be an important component of the marketing campaign. In addition to theonering.net, websites like ringbearer.org, xenite.org and tolkienonline. com were anxious to be counted as allies with the trilogy's production.

The Lord of the Rings online fan fiction

Because the blockbuster fan loves a blockbuster text, the marginality and polysemy associated with traditional fandom is less essential. The original *Lord of the Rings* trilogy, together with *The Hobbit* and *The Silmarillion*, is a relatively closed text, despite active fans. First, the lengthy appendices, including family histories, Middle Earth legends, songs and the linguistic system for Elvish (the language created by Tolkien), seem to cover most of the ambiguities usually exploited by fans. Tolkien also adamantly resisted fan interpretation of his work, rejecting the suggestion that the battle for Middle Earth was an allegory for the rise of fascism and decrying the 1960s counterculture appropriation of 'Frodo Lives!' as a slogan to express dissatisfaction with the status quo. As most readers agree, the original trilogy is profoundly nostalgic and even conservative, and in the wake of the films' visual representation of Orcs, the Nazgul and other villains, potentially racist (Kim 2004). Second, though the films themselves have some ambiguities, the video and DVD editions (fans spent just over US$800 million on videos and DVDs between 2003 and 2006 (Lee's Movie Info)) include their own appendices, deleted scenes, explanations for the changes to Tolkien's original and multiple documentaries about film production. Even though on one hand the extra-narrative material of both the original books and the film trilogy offers fans a great deal of material with which to work, it also forecloses many avenues of exploration by providing authoritative answers about the history and future of Middle Earth.

Despite the limitations of the original text, New Line was willing to allow fans to celebrate the stories the way they wanted, trading total control of its intellectual property for the free publicity websites offered. Paddison provided film stills and 'insider' information to fan websites; theonering.net had exclusive trailers and interviews; poetry, songs and stories about the members of the fellowship as well as characters who had been excised from the film version were allowed to flourish and thus tacitly encouraged. This should not suggest, however, that New Line ceded all control. Rather, the fans' creative work was harnessed by the marketing campaign. Simone Murray describes the synergistic potential of the 'elite inner sanctum':

> Hot-linking of the multitude of Tolkien and fantasy fansites to the official *LOTR* site; extensive monitoring of chat-room and message-board discussion to quell potentially hostile rumours and personal e-mailing of selected fan Webmasters to establish direct channels of flatteringly one-on-one communication. New Line also offered fans 'charter membership' of the official *LOTR* fan club, guaranteeing the names of all members would appear in the DVD credits for each film. (2004: 19)

Thus, fan creativity was directly tied to its marketing potential, and the leaks and creative control ceded to fans were an important component of New Line's marketing plan.

Moreover, fan fiction about *The Lord of the Rings* is implicated in the hype surrounding the film. According to Anna Smol, though fans created their own stories about *The Lord of the Rings* characters, slash fiction did not exist prior to the film's production (2004: 971). She continues:

> Most slash fiction imagines the characters as they are represented by the actors in the film: Frodo is usually dark-haired, blue-eyed and slender; Sam golden-haired and sturdier, clearly referring to images of Elijah Wood and Sean Astin rather than to the hobbits as described by Tolkien. (Ibid.).

Fan fiction apparently promotes the images and characterisations drawn from the films rather than the novels or the fans' imagination. Further, this slash fiction was perhaps initiated by the gossip surrounding the film. The sex lives of the actors, especially those playing the hobbits, were the subject of intense internet speculation. Ted Casablanca, gossip columnist for the network and website E! (which also posted regular reports from the New Zealand location (see Thompson 2003: 55)) included regular insinuations about the bond between the actors:

> You've heard the stories, right? All that ferocious frolicking those *Lord of the Rings* riders have been getting up to? So, let's stop in at the Hollywood premiere of *Lord*'s second installment, *The Two Towers*, and ask Elijah Wood himself, shall we? 'Pardon me, Mr. W.,' I insisted. 'Please complete the following: Hobbits who play together' … 'Make sweet love together,' Elijah responded faster than an Orc attacks. (2002)

Even slash fiction, that most transgressive fan activity, is influenced by the blockbuster.

Fan access and activities

Like most blockbuster films, especially those marketed to a youth audience, *The Lord of the Rings* depended on a secondary market for film merchandise. Authorised products included toys; card games; videogames; apparel; collectible figures from Sideshow/Weta, the films' special effects company; and global promotions through the Burger King chain of fast-food restaurants (see Raugust 2001).

Fans were willing to accept this commercialisation in order to gain unprecedented access. New Line Cinema strove to involve fans in the process, positioning themselves as better than other blockbuster producers (implicitly comparing themselves with George Lucas and the *Harry Potter* franchise) because they listened to fans. Clearly, blockbuster fandom involves negotiations between fan involvement and the widescale promotion of the text and secondary merchandise. Fans, especially those associated with theonering.net, were allowed extraordinary access to the production. For example, Erica Challis, the New Zealand-based contributor, was first served with a restraining order for trespassing on the *Lord of the Rings* set but then invited for on-set visits and meetings with cast and crew; Challis posted glowing reports so that all visitors to the site could share her experiences and knowledge. Of course, the 'steady drip-feed' of information, supplemented by fan reports and production spies, existed cheek-by-jowl with opportunities to purchase *Lord of the Rings* products. Tickets for conventions where *Lord of the Rings* actors appear (and which offer multiple opportunities to purchase memorabilia) are regularly available on theonering.net. Sideshow/Weta 'leaked' character designs, special effects images, and posted Q&A sessions with their designers on theonering.net; a banner directing visitors to their website, where *The Lord of the Rings* and other movie memorabilia may be purchased, sits directly below the title banner which proclaims that theonering.net is 'forged by and for fans of JRR Tolkien'.

Though New Line provided access to the producers, cast, images and film-making process, Jackson and other members of the production crew were adamant that they, not the fans, were in charge. In an interview on theonering.net, Jackson insisted that he 'literally' could not think of 'a moment when we had done something and then changed our minds just because of fan reaction' (Thompson 2003: 57). Though Jackson and company may not have changed the direction of the films or readjusted narratives to please fans, they did stress that their decisions were in the best interests of the film. Further, the production team seems to have managed negative fan reaction through the websites. For example, fans were initially outraged when news that Arwen, played by Liv Tyler, was given a larger role that transformed her into a warrior. That Arwen, rather than fan favourite Glorfindel, would rescue Frodo from the Nazgul in *The Fellowship of the Ring* was especially distressing:

> And now he's going to be replaced by Arwen, Warrior-Princess. He's fought a *Balrog*, for Heaven's sake, and he loses out to a GIRL! Played by Liv Tyler, no less! (Flame of the West 1999)

Despite extensive complaints, Jackson stood firm and Tyler remained as the warrior-elf. At the same time, Arwen's character change and Tyler's casting were insistently recuperated. Tyler spoke directly to fans (via internet chats) about her love of the novels, her identification with Arwen, her gratitude at playing the role: 'I see it as an honour to be one of only a few women in the picture and to bring the feminine touch to the story' (LotR Official Movie Guide). Perhaps most importantly for fans, she embraced the Elvish language, Tolkien's invented linguistic system, as 'a legitimate language... It's such a beautiful language too, it's really brilliant' (Elf Maiden Arwen) and spoke Elvish when she appeared on *Late Night with Conan O'Brien* to promote the film on 26 April 2001 (LotR Official Movie Guide). After *The Fellowship of the Ring* was released, many fans changed their minds about Tyler: '... Last but not least, LIV TYLER! "Come and claim him" indeed! ... the much-reviled Arwen definitely claimed this viewer' (John 2001). Her rescue of Frodo, when she used her Elf magic to drown the Nazgul in Anduin River, was hailed by fans as one of the most visually stunning and exciting moments of the first film:

> [The movie is] coming to me. It's coming to me as a grandiose wave of river-water lifted by the spellbinding of Arwen (Liv Tyler looks so stylish, such a timeless beauty). (Koola 2001)

Clearly, Jackson's insistence that fans did not determine the films' narrative should not obscure the extraordinary efforts made to assuage fan disapproval, nor the effectiveness of those efforts.

Despite the obvious interest in marketing, and the commercial aspects of *The Lord of the Rings* fandom, New Line and Peter Jackson attempted to downplay commerce in order to highlight the authenticity and integrity of the production. For example, the official New Line site used a .net rather than the industry standard .com as its internet address. Though some fans may be aware that any kind of site can use .org, .net or .com extensions, most associate .coms with more commercial interests; registering as .net connotes a more democratic and artistically pure website.

Fandom and location

The bucolic New Zealand location also fostered the idea that *The Lord of the Rings'* production was markedly different from most blockbusters. According to Kristin Thompson, the official sites, major fan sites, and personal websites like Sir Ian McKellen's (Gandalf) mckellen.com fostered the sense that the massive, fifteen-month, three-film shoot was

> small in relation to big Hollywood shoots … taking place in a relaxed and friendly atmosphere for cast and crew alike … happening in a beautiful and remote locale uniquely suited to being Middle Earth. (McKellen 2003: 55)

The New Zealand location, promoted through regular dispatches on theonering. net as offering important tourist and film production opportunities to a locally driven economy that just happened to be Jackson's homeland, mediated the commercialism usually associated with Hollywood blockbusters. Moreover, the incipient environmentalism of Tolkien's novels was carried over into the production; the cast and crew were good eco-citizens, and the New Zealand landscape was left undamaged, despite the massive battle scenes. Fans were invited to distinguish between Jackson's crew and the environmental damage of other Hollywood blockbusters (such as *Lara Croft: Tomb Raider's* destruction of Cambodian rain forest).

Perhaps more importantly, New Line and the *Lord of the Rings* trilogy shared its profits, albeit indirectly, with the fans, underscoring their honesty and integrity as producers. The websites in the 'elite inner sanctum' were offered premium, insider content, and used that content to increase traffic, garnering advertising sponsors such as amazon.com. The webmasters for theonering.net leveraged their status as the premier *Lord of the Rings* fan website into several business opportunities. Founder Erica Challis edited two books, *The People's Guide to J.R.R. Tolkien* (2003) and *More People's Guide to J.R.R. Tolkien* (2004). Though not bestsellers, these collections of essays that first appeared on theonering.net and written by its webmasters are available in bookstores, on amazon.com and barnesandnoble. com, and the website. Co-founder Michael Regina has upgraded his fan hobbyist status to professional film web designer. According to an article in *The Los Angeles Times*, his Montreal-based company, The One Ring Inc., 'specialises in construct- ing movie fan sites – including kongisking.net and theonelion.net, for the upcom- ing *Chronicles of Narnia: The Lion, the Witch and the Wardrobe*' (Lee 2005); clearly, his experience working for the fans has made him an expert on interactive media.

Fans and the auteur

Finally, Peter Jackson, the overweight, overly enthusiastic, overly sweaty director was an important identificatory figure for fans. His persona, as much as any other element, mediated New Line's marketing machine. From his 1998 appearance on Harry Knowles' Ain't-it-Cool-News to his 2004 Academy Award acceptance speech, Jackson strove to convince fans that he was one of them. He reportedly reg- ularly visited fan websites (Thompson 2003: 56); located his official fan club, The Bastards Have Landed, on theonering.net; filmed *King Kong* in New Zealand with much of the same crew; and appeared bearded and barefoot in television interviews to promote the films. The affectionately dubbed 'Hobbit of Hollywood' seems more approachable than other blockbuster directors like James Cameron (who famously crowned himself 'King of the World' in his Academy Award acceptance speech), George Lucas (who complains that fans are not ready for his artistic vision (see Blumberg 2002), or Jerry Bruckheimer (who is building a television franchise that focuses on law-enforcement procedure rather than character and narrative). Jackson's personal integrity overlaps the integrity of his films.

Conclusion

The blockbuster fan, the audience member who praises Peter Jackson for 'bringing this treasure to life' in a world where few films rise above a 'lacklustre Hollywood vibe' (Imbue 2003), demonstrates how the marginal activities associated with fandom shift when played out on a large scale. If the films succeeded, hobbity Jackson, bucolic New Zealand and beloved J.R.R. Tolkien, as well as the fans themselves, shared in that success. Blockbuster fandom, whose activities and iden- tifications may overlap with more traditional fandoms, demonstrates the complex negotiations between text, industry and audience that mark global mass-media entertainment. As always, fans want to believe in the integrity and authenticity of their experience; *The Lord of the Rings* demonstrates how that experience is shaped by new media technologies and new media audiences.

Notes

1 According to Fiske, all television texts are polysemic – that is, open to interpretation and requiring viewers to make their own meanings – but some texts are more polysemic than others and are thus more likely to be appropriated and used by fans. Fiske defines these texts as 'producerly'.

2 And, of course, many fan scholars have substantially revised their findings in the last decade (see, for example, Jenkins 2002).

3 Many lawyers and free-speech activists agree that lawsuit threats are an over-reaction to fan creation. Chilling Effects, a website operated by the US Electronic Frontier Foundation and students at the Harvard, Stanford, Berkeley, University of San Francisco and University of Maine law schools offers free, concise advice about how to avoid copyright infringement, much of it targeted directly to fans who use the internet to celebrate a particular text. Chilling Effects is also a free-speech watchdog group; they operate a clearinghouse for copyright cases on the internet in order to 'encourage respect for intellectual property law, while frowning on its misuse to "chill" legitimate activity'.

4 Founded by Michael Regina in Montreal, Quebec, Erica Challis in Auckland, New Zealand, Christopher Pirotta in State College, Pennsylvania and William R. Thomas in Kenosha, Wisconsin, theonering.net was created especially for the films, but the founders had chatted online about Tolkien and other fantasy texts before the film was announced. Other popular and favoured websites, like ringbearer.org, xenite.org and tolkienonline.com, predated the film production.

Works cited

Barber, L. (2001) 'Harry, the saucy boy sorceror', *The Australian*, 3 September.

Baym, N. (2000) *Tune In, Log On: Soaps, Fandom, and Online Community*. Thousand Oaks: Sage.

Blumberg, A. T. (2002) 'Attack of the Fans: George Lucas Speaks! Part One', *Cinescape*. Online. Available at http://www.cinescape.com/0/Editorial.asp?aff_id=0&this_cat=Movies&action=page&obj_id=34659 (accessed 11 June 2005).

Casablanca, T. (2002) 'The Awful Truth', Online. Available at http://www.eonline.com/Gossip/Awful/cauth/Archive2002/021219b.html (accessed 14 June 2005).

Chilling Effects (2002) Online. Available at http://www.chillingeffects.org (accessed 3 October 2002.

Elf Maiden Arwen (2005) Online. Available at http://groups.msn.com/ElfMaidenArwen/livtyleramparwen.msnw (accessed 11 June 2005).

Fernback, J. (1999) 'There is a There There: Notes Toward a Definition of Cybercommunity', in S. Jones (ed.) *Doing Internet Research*. Thousand Oaks: Sage, 203–20.

Fiske, J. (1992) 'The Cultural Economy of Fandom', in L. Lewis (ed.) *The Adoring Audience:*

Fan Culture and Popular Media. London: Routledge, 30–49.

Flame of the West (1999) Online. Available at http://neil.franklin.ch/Usenet/rec.arts. books.tolkien/19991008_Arwen_And_Eowyn_in_movie (accessed 11 June 2005).

Grossberg, L. (1992) 'Is There a Fan in the House?: The Affective Sensibility of Fandom', in L. Lewis (ed.) *The Adoring Audience: Fan Culture and Popular Media*. London: Routledge, 50–65.

Hoberman, J. (2001) 'I Oughta be in Pictures', *New York Times*, 15 July, 13.

Imbue (2003) 'Ringer Review', theonering.net. Online. Available at http://www.theoner-ing.net/movie/rotkreviews (accessed 14 June 2005).

Jenkins, H. (1992) *Textual Poachers: Television Fans and Participatory Culture*. London and New York: Routledge.

_____ (2002) 'Interactive Audiences?', in D. Harris (ed.) *The New Media Book*. London: British Film Institute, 157–70.

_____ (2003) 'Quentin Tarantino's *Star Wars*?: Digital Cinema, Media Convergence, and Participatory Culture', in D. Thorburn and H. Jenkins (eds) *Rethinking Media Change: The Aesthetics of Transition* Cambridge: MIT Press, 281–312.

John (2001) 'Ringer Review', theonering.net. Online. Available at http://www.theonering. net/movie/reviews/review.php?id=8598 (accessed 12 Jun 2005).

Kim, S. (2004) 'Beyond Black and White: Race and Postmodernism in *The Lord of the Rings* Films', *Modern Fiction Studies*, 50, 4, 875–907.

Knowles, H. (1998) 'Peter Jackson Interview', *Ain't-it-Cool-News*. Online. Available at http://www.aint-it-cool-news.com/lordoftherings.html (accessed 10 June 2005).

_____ (1999) 'Peter Jackson Interview', *Ain't-it-Cool-News*. Online. Available at http://www. aint-it-cool-news.com/lordoftherings2.html (accessed 10 June 2005).

Koola (2001) 'Ringer Review', Online. Available at http://www.theonering.net/movie/ reviews/review.php?id=8061 (accessed 12 June 2005).

Landro, L. (2000) 'Hobbits in cyberspace', *Wall Street Journal*, 20 March, 8.

Lee, C. (2005) 'New kids on the blog', *Los Angeles Times*, 12 June.

Lee's Movie Info. Online. Available at http://www.leesmovieinfo.net/Video-Sales.php?y= 2002&type=3 (accessed 14 June 2005).

LotR Official Movie Guide. Online. Available at http://www.theonering.net/movie/cast/ tyler.html (accessed 13 June 2005).

MacDonald. A. (1998) 'Uncertain Utopia: Science Fiction Media Fandom and Computer Mediated Communication', in C. Harris and A. Alexander (eds) *Theorizing Fandom: Fans, Subculture, and Identity*. Cresskill: Hampton Press, 131–52.

McKellen, I. (2003) 'The White Book', Online. Available at http://www.mckellan.com/ cinema/lotr/wb/index.htm (accessed 11 June 2005).

Murray, S. (2004) '"Celebrating the Story the Way It Is": Cultural Studies, Corporate Media and the Contested Utility of Fandom', *Continuum: Journal of Media & Cultural Studies*, 18, 1, 7–26.

Penley, C. (1991) 'Brownian Motion: Women, Tactics, and Technology', in C. Penley and

A. Ross (eds) *Technoculture*. Minneapolis: University of Minnesota Press, 135–61.

Pullen, K. (2004) 'Everybody's Gotta Love Somebody Sometime: Online Fan Community', in D. Gauntlett and R. Horsley (eds) *Web Studies*. London: Arnold, 80–91.

Raugust, K. (2001) 'Licensing hotline', *Publishers Weekly*, 2 July, 19.

Ringbearer.org. (2003) Online. Available at http://www.ringbearer.org (accessed 11 June 2005).

Shefrin, E. (2004) '*Lord of the Rings, Star Wars,* and Participatory Fandom: Mapping New Congruencies between the Internet and Media Entertainment Culture', *Critical Studies in Media Communication*, 21, 3, 261–81.

Smol, A. (2004) '"Oh … Oh … Frodo!": Readings of Male Intimacy in *The Lord of the Rings*', *Modern Fiction Studies*, 50, 4, 968–76.

Star Wars Official Website. Online. Available HTTP: http://www.starwars.com/community/news/charity/news20050203.html (Accessed 10 June 2005).

Theonering.net (1999) Online. Available at http://img-www.theonering.net/images/old_polls/poll416.gif (accessed 20 June 2005).

_____ (2003a) Online. Available at http://www.theonering.net/archives/main_news/12.15.03-12.21.03 (accessed 21 June 2005).

_____ (2003b) Online. Available at http://www.theonering.net/cgi-bin/poll_SSI.cgi?keyword=hardeharhar_20031030 (accessed 21 June 2005).

_____ (2003c) Online. Available at http://www.theonering.net/cgi-bin/poll_SSI.cgi?keyword=wahhhhhhhhhhh_20031018 (accessed 21 June 2005).

_____ (2003d) Online. Available at http://www.theonering.net/cgi-bin/poll_SSI.cgi?keyword=hallerweener_20031109 (accessed 21 June 2005).

_____ (2003e) Online. Available at http://www.theonering.net/cgi-bin/poll_SSI.cgi?keyword=ploop_20031120 (accessed 21 June 2005).

_____ (2003f) Online. Available at http://www.theonering.net/cgi-bin/poll_SSI.cgi?keyword=approacheth_20031218 (accessed 21 June 2005).

Thompson, K. (2003) 'Fantasy, Franchises, and Frodo Baggins: *The Lord of the Rings* and Modern Hollywood', *Velvet Light Trap*, 52, 45–63. Online. Available at http://80-muse.jhu.edu.ezproxy.lib.ucalgary.ca:2048/journals/the_velvet_light_trap/v052/52.1thompson.html (accessed 15 January 2005).

'This is What it Must Look Like': *The Lord of the Rings* Fandom and Media Literacy[1]

Judith E. Rosenbaum

Introduction

Paying large sums of money to attend the premiere of *The Lord of The Rings*, attending so-called 'elf fairs' dressed up as Legolas or Arwen, and engaging in endless arguments about the qualities of the books versus the movies. These are all examples of fan behaviour, ones that cause outside observers to wonder at the fans' dedication to re-creating and living in the world presented by the movies, as well as at their ability to perceive the movies as a fictional construction.

The dichotomy between fans' desire to perceive the world created in their favourite programme as real and their aspiration to understand its construction, both on a narrative and on a technical level, has been discussed in various studies into fandom (see, for example, Brooker 2002; Jenkins 1992a). None of them, however, have established the extent to which fans are able to extract themselves from the world created by their favourite text, and adopt the more distant and critical perspective advocated by many scholars (for example, Buckingham 2003).

Thus, this chapter will address the following two issues. First, how do fans' abilities to perceive the *Lord of the Rings* movies as a fictional construction compare to non-fans' abilities to do so? Second, the notion that fans live in the world created by the trilogy suggests that they are unable to adopt a critical distance towards the text – this study will explore this notion by assessing whether there are qualitative differences between fans and non-fans in the way they think about *The Lord of the Rings*. I will use the concept of media literacy to answer these questions about fans' and non-fans' appraisal of *The Lord of the Rings*.

Media literacy and fandom

The first discussions about people's ability to critically appraise the media, also known as media literacy, came about in the early 1930s, when the radio had become the first mass medium (Buckingham 1998). Ever since those first publications, the media have grown and expanded until they have become omnipresent in almost every individual's life. At the same time, academic and educational interest in media literacy has increased exponentially. There are a large number of ways in which media literacy can be defined. In this chapter, however, I use the definition proposed by David Buckingham (2003) who argues that in order to be considered media literate people need to have an understanding of the four key concepts of media: production, language, representation and audience. The reason for working with his definition is two-fold. First of all, its key concepts overlap with various definitions of media literacy, such as the one developed by the British Film Institute and the National Leadership Conference on Media Literacy (see Bazalgette 1989; Bowker 1991; Alvardo & Boyd-Barrett 1992; Aufderheide 1997). Secondly, Buckingham's definition is extremely extensive. It provides a detailed description of each key concept, unlike many other definitions of media literacy which generally contain little elaboration or explication. This comprehensiveness renders this definition very suitable for translation into an interview guide and instrument of analysis. Below is a brief summary of each of the key concepts.

Production: This key concept centres on the awareness that media texts are the result of a complicated production process. Understanding media production means knowing about the different factors that influence the construction of media messages, such as the economic interests that can be at stake, the technologies and professional practices used in the production process, and the regulations that guide production. Buckingham also claims that media literacy means knowing about the circulation and distribution of a message and how a product can be sold through different channels (for example, releasing a movie on DVD).

Language: As Buckingham explains: 'every medium has its own combination of languages that it uses to communicate meaning' (2003: 55). Verbal and written language are an example of such a language, but so are moving images and sound. The latter two use conventions that most people understand, such as soft music to express romance. Media literacy means that one is aware of the languages used in media content, and how these languages can be used to convey meaning.

Representation: The third key concept refers to the way in which the media present the 'world out there' to their users. The media do not present a window on reality, but create a subjective view of people, places and events (Entman 1989). Buckingham claims that people need to know what kind of image of the world the text presents, how realistic this image is, and how they and other people might experience this image.

Audiences: The notion that audiences are easy-to-manipulate masses was rejected decades ago. Subsequently, Buckingham contends that media literacy includes knowing how audiences are addressed and targeted, and how different groups use, enjoy and interpret media texts.

Why is it particularly important that fans are media literate? As mentioned earlier, media literacy is important because of the large role that the media play in people's lives; fans (Fiske 1992; Brooker 2002) and non-fans (Papper *et al.* 2004) alike. A second reason why many researchers believe people should be media literate is because of the socialising potential of the media. All media users need to be critical towards media content because it shapes their ideas about, for instance, norms, values and acceptable behaviour (Brown 1998; Rosenbaum & Beentjes 2004; Silverblatt 2004). Fans, however, spend so much time with one text only that they, contrary to non-fans, are socialised by mainly one set of values and ideas (Brooker 2002). This implies that a critical attitude is especially important for fan communities.

Is there, then, a difference in media literacy between fans and non-fans? Are fans critical of the texts that they enjoy? Larry Grossberg commented on this question by describing fandom as a dichotomy: fans are either seen as 'easily manipulated and distracted ... passive, ignorant and non-critical', or as 'actively appropriating the texts of specific popular cultures, and give them new and original significance' (1992: 51–2). Existing literature on fandom reflects this dilemma. On the one hand, there is indirect evidence that fans are in fact media literate concerning their favourite text. First, there are those activities that, according to Henry Jenkins (1992a, 1992b) lie at the core of fandom: the production of fan fiction, consumer activism and critical interpretation. Although Buckingham (2003) does not explicitly refer to these activities as part of media literacy, various other authors do (Aufderheide 1997; Hobbs 1998a, 1998b; Thoman 1999; Potter 2004). Furthermore, John Fiske (1987) suggests that extensive knowledge of intertextual references helps the reader activate the polysemy of a text. In other words, an awareness of texts related to the primary programme or movie aid in reading against the grain, and adopting a more critical attitude. Keeping in mind that fans are in general more aware of texts related to their favourite programme or movie than non-fans (see Gwenllian-Jones 2003), this suggests that fans can be media literate regarding those texts.

On the other hand, the extent to which fans are able to adopt a media literate attitude towards their favourite texts can be questioned. First, there is the fact that media education (teaching media literacy) is very difficult when students enjoy the texts used in class (Buckingham 1998). This point is underlined by a study on the effectiveness of a media education project regarding Disney's *The Little Mermaid* (Ron Clements and John Musker, 1989), which proved that it is impossible to render the fans' attitudes towards the movie more critical (Sun & Scharrer 2004). Secondly, various studies have shown that fans are unable to walk away from their favourite text when new storylines or movies disappoint them tremendously. These fans continued their sometimes life-long attachment to the programme or movie despite their own disenchantment (see Brooker 2002; Jenkins 1995). Thus, these studies imply that fans assimilate their favourite text into their lives in such a way that taking a step back and critically surveying the text becomes almost impossible.

All this raises the question as to how critical fans are of their favourite text. In the remainder of this chapter I will try to provide a tentative answer through presenting the findings from an explorative study into the level of media literacy of Dutch fans and non-fans of the *Lord of the Rings* trilogy.

Researching *The Lord of the Rings* fans

There is a particular reason why this study focuses explicitly on the *Lord of the Rings* saga. To begin with, it has an impressive one fan base, which is probably only matched by those of *Star Wars* and *Star Trek*. Additionally, the *Lord of the Rings* fan base is different from other fan bases in that it existed prior to the release of the three movies since the books, published in the 1950s, had already assembled an impressive array of active fans; and in that the *Lord of the Rings* fan base is the only fan base which was, reportedly, actively included in the production of the movies (Shefrin 2004).

The distinction between fans and non-fans, a necessity for this study, immediately raises the question of establishing how and when someone is a fan. The problem is that there are a myriad of definitions, and not all of them agree with one another. Henry Jenkins and John Tulloch (1995), for instance, make the distinction between fans and followers. Fans are active participants who experience a shared social identity, while followers do not experience a larger social identity. Will Brooker and Deborah Jermyn define fandom as going beyond simple active participation: 'rather than simply create their own meanings in the home or cinema, fans characteristically make cultural artefacts of their own, travel across the country to meet their idols or fellow fans' (Brooker & Jermyn 2003: 167). Conversely, Matt Hills (2002) points out that it is impossible that all fans are producers, and that it is incorrect to claim that fans who do not create their own fan fiction are not fans. This large collection of, at times contradictory, definitions makes it very difficult to decide when someone qualifies as a fan, a follower or a non-fan. In order to avoid any confusion, I decided to interview people who defined themselves as fans. As it turned out though, all of the self-defined fans engaged in several of the activities outlined in the previous paragraph.

The data for this study were gathered through interviews with fans and non-fans of *The Lord of the Rings*. I collected information about the level of media literacy of fans and non-fans through group-interviews with both. The group interviews were preceded by a viewing of two scenes from *The Lord of the Rings: The Fellowship of the Ring*: 'Balin's Tomb' and 'Bridge of Khazad-Dûm'. There were several reasons why I decided to use group interviews. First, most people, but fans especially (cf. Jenkins 1992b), share the experience of a movie such as *The Lord of the Rings*, either through watching or discussing it with others. If I would have conducted individual interviews, I would have run the risk of missing out on ideas and opinions that are the sole result of group interaction; i.e. notions that make up the shared stock of knowledge (Bloor *et al.*, 2001). Furthermore, I would have not been able to witness the process through which meaning and ideas are created, a process which grants in-depth insight into what exactly people mean with certain answers (cf. Greenbaum 2000). Finally, by conducting group interviews preceded by a viewing of selected scenes from *The Lord of the Rings*, I aimed at reconstructing a natural viewing situation as much as possible, thus taking away many of the inhibitions usually experienced by respondents.

A total of four group interviews were conducted in December 2004. Two interviews were held with fans of the *Lord of the Rings* trilogy, and two with people who had seen most of the three movies, but did not consider themselves fans. The groups consisted of people who all knew each other very well, and had watched most of the trilogy together. The number of respondents in each group ranged between two and four. All participants were between the ages of 21 and 32, and all of them were either in the process of obtaining or had completed at least an undergraduate degree. All the interviews were taped and transcribed. The questions used to assess the respondents' level of media literacy were developed using Buckingham's (2003) four key concepts of media literacy (see appendix). Buckingham divided each concept up into seven aspects which were each explicated using several questions, and for the purpose of this study, these questions were adapted to the *Lord of the Rings* movies.

The correct answers to the questions, i.e. the answers that would display a high level of media literacy, were in part derived from Donovan Jacobs (2003). He discusses *The Lord of the Rings* by outlining the answers to the five core questions of media literacy (developed by the Centre for Media Literacy). These five core questions cover almost all of the four key concepts advocated by David Buckingham. The only key concept that is not covered by Jacobs is 'language', a concept that refers to people's understanding of the codes and conventions used in the media. In this study, this key concept was discussed in regard to the two scenes from *The Lord of the Rings* viewed by the respondents. Whether an answer given by the respondents was correct was assessed in two different ways. First, there were questions which addressed the meaning the producer was trying to convey using these scenes. The assessment of these answers was based on the extent to which respondents were able to elaborate on their answer. Second, a series of questions addressed the conventions used in the scenes. The correct answers were determined using Maria Elizabeth Grabe, Shuhua Zhou and Brooke Barnett's (2001) work on the meaning of conventions used on television.

Findings: understanding *The Lord of the Rings* as a fictional representation

Overall, the study showed that both fans and non-fans are able to see and describe *The Lord of the Rings* as a fictional construction. The main differences lie in the manner in which the different groups discuss the trilogy. The findings regarding the differences in media literacy between fans and non-fans will be discussed per key concept.

Production

In the description of this key concept, I outlined various aspects which, according to Buckingham, affected the production process. First of all, in regard to the circulation and distribution of the movie and the DVDs, the fans, as opposed to the non-fans, knew that the three movies were released once every year between 2001 and 2003, and that they were digitally revised, i.e. that the visual effects used in the movies were updated using the most recent technologies, between each release. Both the fans and the non-fans were also aware of the release of a regular and a special edition DVD. Second, with regard to the professional and technological practices, both fans and non-fans appeared to be equally aware of the technologies used to create the trilogy. However, with regard to professional practices, fans were better aware of who exactly produced and directed the movies, while non-fans were unable to give names. On the other hand, one non-fan group gave a very accurate description of the production process, making it apparent that perhaps knowing names is not essential in determining one's level of media literacy:

> S (non-fan group 2): The book of course needs to be transferred to a film script. So someone probably had the idea, hey, that's a nice book, maybe we can turn it into a movie. And maybe that person isn't a scriptwriter, so he'll find someone who is, and ask them to turn the book into a script. Or maybe the person with the idea is a scriptwriter, and once he's written the script, he'll ask a director to become involved, or maybe it was a director who had the idea to turn the book into a movie. And once the script is written, they'll need ask people to help work on the movie … And because so many people participate in making this movie, it will be very important that everyone knows what the movie is supposed to look like … So there must be one person who has the final responsibility, someone who sits in with the computer people and tells them, this is what it must look like.

The description of how the idea of the movie originated is very close to reality (Ain't it cool news 1998). As for economic interests, both fans and non-fans understood that a studio financed the production, and that that studio as well as the director received profits. Interestingly, non-fans pointed out that the studio took a large financial risk producing a movie as expensive as *The Lord of the Rings*, and that it was therefore 'logical' that they would receive most of the profit.

Buckingham also includes an awareness of the connections between the media under 'production'. In the case of *The Lord of the Rings*, this aspect refers to merchandising and the relationship between the movies and the books. Both fans and non-fans were aware of the enormous merchandising effort that surrounded the release of the three films. However, the fans were better able to describe the relationship between the books and the movie. Having read all of the books multiple times, and discussed them in great detail, the fans were able to explain not only the differences between the books and the films, but also the reasons for the changes that the director had made. As one of the fans pointed out:

> G (fan group 1): They definitely made the movie more commercial than the book, but they also took the fans' ideas and wishes into account

Another fan pointed at another reason for some of the differences:

> G (fan group 2): He [the director] left parts out, because the book was like 3,000 pages long … you have to maintain a certain pace in the movie, otherwise people will start falling asleep…
> B: For instance, that scene where they are chased on horseback, with that elf Arwen, where she brings him to safety when he is stabbed. In the book that's a man.
> *I: Why did he change that?*
> G: Because she is his [Aragorn's] girlfriend, and in the book that doesn't become apparent at all, except that it's mentioned once or twice that she is his girlfriend.
> R: A movie is just a different medium. A marriage is something romantic that needs to be put in because it's a movie aimed at a very large audience. So you add in a little romance for the average viewer, so they get it too.

Finally, neither fans nor non-fans were able to explain the influence that media regulations can have on a movie such as *The Lord of the Rings*.

Language

This key concept refers to the techniques used to convey a message. Before the questions regarding this concept were posed, all respondents watched the two scenes described earlier. During this part of the interview, a few interesting differences between fans and non-fans became apparent. One difference is that fans tended to refer to texts outside *The Lord of the Rings* to explain their point; either the original books, or other movie cycles such as *The Matrix* (Andy and Larry Wachowski, 1999–2003) or *Indiana Jones* (Steven Spielberg, 1981–89). Furthermore, whilst watching the two scenes, the fans either expressed dismay when the DVD was stopped, or used the scenes to discuss all sorts of role-games they were involved in, while the non-fans did not make such extensions. One non-fan even expressed relief when the scenes came to end.

Nevertheless, both fans and non-fans were equally capable of explaining the meanings that the two scenes are intended to convey, and the techniques used to express them. Both elaborated on what the director is trying to make the viewer feel in these two scenes:

S (non-fan group 2): I think you really sympathise with the members of the group, you want them to survive, so you're all excited and tense, like, come on, run, run, run.

L: Yeah, they seem like a real group. When one of them gets hurt, the other two immediately attack that monster or beast to revenge, so it really presents this group-feeling.

I: *And what do they do to make you feel like that?*

S: Music, and silences. At one point it's completely silent, and then one person hears something, and then the orcs show up, and it's chaos with music and sound all over. So you think, oh jeez, what's going on.

M (fan group 2): I think the scene is trying to convey suspense. So you're glued to the screen, wondering what will happened next. They're in a tough spot, so … and especially that pounding, that spells trouble, that those bad guys are coming. So when you hear that first pounding, you think, oh dear … and well, the character's faces betray the same feeling.

G: Yeah, and they're in a really confined space, and then that kid drops the corpse, and that is how the suspense is built up.

Moreover, both fans and non-fans drew upon film-style languages to explain features and meanings, such as when they agreed that close-ups were used to draw the viewers into the emotions felt by a character. Both groups were also aware of the fact that techniques such as close-ups and slow-motions are essential to achieving the kind of involvement with media content that the viewer experiences with these two scenes, and that other techniques might not be as successful.

Additionally, Buckingham (2003) claims that media literacy includes being aware of how the technologies used to create a media message can influence the meaning of that message. The non-fans mentioned that the use of special effects added to the unique character of the trilogy, and probably some of its success. One group of fans concurred with this point of view, while the second group disagreed. They contended that it is possible to create the same kind of movie using less technology:

B (fan group 2): There are many ways to express these emotions. You may need to add a little more psychological depth to the characters, but the suggestion of something creates a great deal of suspense as well.

R: And the movies made in the 1950s and 1970s were just as suspenseful as this one ... Hitchcock managed to create a lot of suspense too, and his movies are scary even today.

So although this group disagreed with Buckingham's perspective, they do make a valid point.

Finally, people need to be able to discuss the film's genre in order to be media literate. Both fans and non-fans were able to do so, arguing that *The Lord of the Rings* belongs to the fantasy genre. Both fans and non-fans alike gave good reasons why this is so: the movie focuses on imaginary creatures, has a fairy tale-like nature, takes place in a non-existent world, and so on. A difference between the two groups was that fans referred to other movies to explain their choice of genre, while non-fans limited themselves to the trilogy.

Representation

This third concept of media literacy refers to the image that the media, in this case the *Lord of the Rings* trilogy, create of the real world, as well as the impression that this image can leave on people. In terms of how realistic the *Lord of the Rings* trilogy is, both groups realised that although the trilogy qualifies as fantasy, it does have some realistic elements, especially the human emotions and relationships. The fans and non-fans also pointed out that a movie needs to be realistic if people are to identify with its characters and storylines.

F (non fan group 1): It's a little like a plug and an outlet. If you're too far away from reality, you can't connect to the story, and so you won't be involved in it.

However, while non-fans only discussed which aspects of the movie they thought were realistic and which were not, the fans debated the themes portrayed by *The Lord of the Rings*. One fan group discussed how Tolkien wrote his books as a metaphor for World War Two (cf. Jacobs 2003), while the other group elaborated on how the cutting of trees to make way for machines in *The Two Towers* addresses the dangers of industrial expansion. Although this does not necessarily relate to the fans' level of media literacy regarding realism, it does show that they have a greater insight into the meaning of the movies than non-fans do. A second aspect is the awareness of the norms and values portrayed by the text. All groups, both fans and non-fans, were able to reflect on the different kinds of norms expressed by *The Lord of the Rings*.

The next aspect that Buckingham discusses concerns the presence and absence of certain groups of people and stereotyping. When asked about the representation of different races in *The Lord of the Rings,* all groups mentioned that there were no races present other than white people. When explaining the reason for this, the fans referred back to the original:

> A (fan group 1): I don't think the book mentions that they're all white, because that wasn't part of his [Tolkien] world. I'm not even sure if he'd ever seen a black person when he wrote it, they didn't really play a role in society back then...

Fan group 2 added that the only non-white people in the movie are the bad guys, namely the Orcs and the Uruk-Hai, and that the latter were played by the only non-white actors in the movie, the Maori. The non-fans, on the other hand, ignored the movies' roots in the books. One non-fan group mentioned people's expectations of mythical figures:

> K (non-fan group 1): Have you ever looked in a children's book and seen a black dwarf or a black elf? ... The director just took people's expectations into account.

The other non-fan group took a different approach:

> S (non-fan group 2): I don't think you can compare it, I mean, it's a totally different world, so what you would call races here, Asians or something like that, whites, blacks, however you want to call them, over there it's more about tribes, so elves, dwarves, hobbits and humans.

Although both groups provide a reason for the lack of racial diversity in the movies, the fans showed more insight into the production process of the movie, where the script was closely based on the books and fans' ideas of the novels. Both fans and non-fans also noticed that the movies showed very few women, displaying an equal level of media literacy. There is again a noticeable difference between fans and non-fans; only the fan groups elaborated on the original books. These contain few women, and are the reason for the movies showing mainly men. The fans claimed that Tolkien was an old-fashioned man, who could not relate to women:

> G (fan group 2): But it could be that he [Tolkien] created that old-fashioned image of women on purpose, because he's trying to connect to the old Celtic myths, where women are women at a distance.

The non-fan groups mentioned two different reasons for the lack of women in the movie. One of the non-fan groups claimed that the movie takes place in the past, when women simply were inferior to men. The other non-fan group states the movie merely reflects people's beliefs of men and women:

> S (non-fan group 2): When you think of soldiers you automatically think of men, it's a little stereotypical, and I do think the movie is doing that too much, but it is a fact that people like that are most often men. So the movie is realistic in that sense … because men are stronger than women, they are better at fighting, and that is why this movie is about a group of men.

The next aspect of media literacy is an awareness of how audiences think about the norms and values presented in *The Lord of the Rings*. People are media literate when they can consider what the morals presented in the movies mean for them and others. In this case, both fans and non-fans were able to do that, both for themselves and for others:

> K (non-fan group 1): Everybody looks at this movie in their own way. There are people who are absolutely crazy about these movies … their norms and values are more in line with those in the movie. Whereas we're more down to earth about it, for us the movies are merely entertainment, that's it.

Finally, this concept also includes knowing to what extent *The Lord of the Rings* has influenced its audience. Although the direct influence such a movie can have on people is debatable, denying that there is no influence whatsoever is also incorrect. Both groups gave an accurate description of how the movies could influence other groups. However, both fans and non-fans initially denied that the trilogy influenced them. Only after some probing did the fans admit that they were influenced in some way:

> M (fan group 2): You acquire a certain kind of knowledge that you recognise in other fantasy stories.

But besides this admission, fans and non-fans remained adamant that the movies did not really influence them. So the different groups are not very media literate when it comes to discussing the influence that media content can have on their own lives.

Audiences

The final concept of media literacy refers to the audience in terms of targeting, media usage and interpretation. First of all, in order to be media literate, people need to know what type of audience the media content targets at, and how this becomes apparent through the content. Both fans and non-fans realised that the *Lord of the Rings* trilogy was meant for as large an audience as possible. Both groups were also able to reason how this becomes apparent from watching the film.

> R (fan group 2): Because your average audience wants suspense, action, humour and romance, and all of those elements are present in the movies.

Interestingly, only the fans mentioned that the romance was added in to draw a larger, more female, audience. Since the non-fans had not read the books, they were not aware of the lack of romance in the original novels.

The second aspect centres on an awareness of how people use a specific media message; i.e. how many times they have seen the *Lord of the Rings* movies. Both fans and non-fans can make accurate estimates of how often they have seen the movies. Additionally, there is no difference in how fans and non-fans describe other people's viewing of the trilogy. Next, Buckingham argues that media literacy also includes an awareness of what a media message can mean for them and others. Once again, there is no difference between fans and non-fans. Both were equally capable of reflecting on the meanings that *The Lord of the Rings* holds for them and others. Of course, the meanings are different. Non-fans described the trilogy as mere entertainment, whereas one fan claimed the following:

> A (fan group 1): Fantasy means a lot to me, you know, all those things, the books…

Non-fans also experienced no problems in describing what the trilogy could mean to others who liked the movies more than they did:

> K (non-fan group 1): To them, it's like an extension of their imagination, something on TV they usually only have inside their own heads.

Furthermore, in terms of how people from different socio-economic backgrounds experience *The Lord of the Rings* differently, both fans and non-fans showed a similar level of media literacy. Both argued that a different background is cause for a different interpretation:

> S (non-fan group 2): Like in Japan, they're much more about that whole group-thing. So that group-feeling that we see throughout the whole movie may not be that obvious to them, because they're more used to it than we are.

> R (fan group 2): The point is, in regard to ethnicity, if you are a Maori, and you're in a disadvantaged position, and you see this movie, I could see how you would find it disturbing, the implicit implication that you are somehow part of an evil race.

Finally, Buckingham (2003) argues that people also need to be able to explain what pleasure they and others derive from a text. Once again, both fans and non-fans were able to reflect on their own and others' pleasures.

Conclusion

This chapter has looked at the differences between fans and non-fans of *The Lord of the Rings* from the perspective of media literacy. Specifically, it addressed two issues: the ability to perceive the trilogy as a fictional construction, and the manner in which fans and non-fans think about the movies. Although the results from this study are merely tentative, they do provide some insight into the relationship between fandom and media literacy. First, there are very few differences between fans and non-fans with regard to their awareness of the *Lord of the Rings* trilogy as a fictional construction. Both groups did equally well on the key concepts 'audience' and 'language', and there were only some differences between fans and non-fans regarding the remaining key concepts 'production' and 'representation'. Thus, the fans, just like the non-fans, realise that the movies are fiction, and are able to describe how the movies were constructed. This finding is in contrast with results from a study on *Star Wars* fans (Brooker 2002). Those fans experienced the beliefs presented by the movies as a guide to their own lives, using them to shape their future. Conversely, the fans in this study realise that *The Lord of the Rings* is a fictional artefact, and describe the morals as good, but unrelated to their daily lives.

The second question addressed the issue whether there were any qualitative differences between fans and non-fans. Although both fans and non-fans are equally capable of extracting themselves from the world created by *The Lord of the Rings*, the fans are much more elaborate in their responses than the non-fans are. They use various intertextual references to explain their answers, such as *Indiana Jones* and *The Matrix*, while the non-fans never venture outside the material presented by the trilogy. Moreover, the fans use the questions to discuss the themes presented by the trilogy, such as World War Two and the dangers of industrial expansion. Conversely, the non-fans merely answer the questions.

So, are fans more media literate than non-fans? The answer to this question concerns two dimensions. On the one hand, in terms of correct and incorrect answers, this study shows little difference between the two groups. This could be because all the respondents were highly-educated. It is possible that education, rather than fandom, is a determining factor in one's level of media literacy. Another reason for the lack of difference might be that *The Lord of the Rings* was widely advertised, using not only trailers and posters, but also documentaries shown on many television stations. Many of the non-fans were exposed to these messages, and thus made aware of how the movie was created and financed. On the other hand, there is a difference in the way in which the two groups answer the questions. The fans use a much richer discourse than the non-fans. Their answers include all sorts of references to events, incidents and people both outside and inside the *Lord of the Rings* text. This suggests that the fans have spent more time thinking and talking about the text, and linking it to other parts of their lives. The text thus seems to be more meaningful to fans than it is to non-fans. In short, the fans in this study seem to possess the understanding of media content advocated by media literacy scholars, and are a far cry from Grossberg's (1992) 'cultural dopes'.

Appendix: Interview Guide (based on Buckingham's (2003) key concepts)

Production

Technologies
What technologies were used to make these movies?
Professional practices
Who were involved in making these movies?
Why were they involved?
Who took care of which aspect of making these movies?
Industry
Can you tell me something about the financing of these movies?
Did they make a profit?
Who received the profit?
Connections between media
Can you tell me something about merchandising?
Can you tell something about the sale of DVDs?
Can you compare the books and the movies? Why were they different/the same?
Regulation
Can you tell me something about media laws and the production of LotR?
Did the producers keep these laws in mind when making the movies?
Circulation and distribution
Can you tell me about the release of the movies?
Why did that happen the way it did?
How about the release of the DVDs?

Language
this topic was preceded by a viewing of the two scenes

Meanings
What are the producers trying to convey through these scenes? What do they want the viewer to experience?
Why do you think so?
Combinations
What does the producer do to convey that meaning? What sort of techniques does he use?
Does he use multiple techniques to convey meaning?
Choices
In the scenes you just watched there were a number of close-ups, why did they use them?
Conventions
In these scenes, specific techniques (e.g., music) are used, why do you think the director used those?
Are there specific techniques you use to convey a certain message?
Codes
Is it possible to convey the same message using different techniques? How?
Technologies
Is it possible to convey the same meaning using less technology?
Genre
What kind of genre is LotR? Why do you think so?

Representation

Realism
Is LotR realistic? What is realistic or unrealistic about it?
What did the producers do to make the movie seem realistic? Why is it important that these movies are realistic?

Bias & Objectivity/Telling the truth
What sort of norms and values does LotR represent?
What kind of ideas about people does it convey?
Does it contain a moral?
How do the producers try to express these ideas and norms?

Presence and absence
Can you say something about the ratio men-women in LotR? How does this ratio relate to reality? Why is it different/the same?
Can you say something about the presence of different races in the movies? Does this represent reality?
Is there a group in this movie that makes all the decisions? Why is that so?

Stereotyping
Do you think that LotR contains stereotypes? What makes you think so?

Interpretations
What do you think about the ideas presented by LotR?
What would other people think of these ideas? Why?

Influences
Do you think that LotR has influenced you in any way? How?
Do you think other people have been influenced by LotR? How? Can you think of an example?

Audiences

Targeting
What kind of audience was LotR made for? How can you tell?

Address
If we assume that LotR was made for a certain audience, what were the producers' ideas about this audience? How can you tell?

Circulation
How did the intended audience find out about the existence of LotR movies?

Uses
How many times and where did you see the LotR movies? Can you answer this question for other people as well?

Making sense
What does LotR mean to you? What role does it play in your life?
Can you say something about the role LotR could play in other people's lives?

Social differences
Does people's background (education, ethnicity etc.) influence their ideas about LotR?

Pleasures
What is your opinion of LotR? Why?
How do others think of the movies? Why? How and why are their opinions different from yours?

Note

1   I would like to thank Hans Beentjes and Ruben Konig for their valuable contribution to this study.

Works cited

Ain't it cool news (1998) 'Peter Jackson Answers the Geeks: 20 Questions About Lord of the Rings'. Online. Available at http://www.aintitcoolnews.com/lordoftherings2.html (accessed 12 January 2005).

Alvarado, M. and O. Boyd-Barrett (eds) (1992) *Media Education: An Introduction*. London: British Film Institute.

Aufderheide, P. (1997) 'Media Literacy: From a Report of the National Leadership Conference on Media Literacy', in R. Kubey (ed.) *Media Literacy in the Information Age. Current Perspectives: Information and Behavior* (vol. 6). New Brunswick: Transaction, 79–88.

Bazalgette, C. (1989) *Primary Education: A Curriculum Statement*. London: British Film Institute.

Bloor, M., J. Frankland, M. Thomas and K. Robson (2001) *Focus Groups in Social Research*. London: Sage.

Bowker, J. (ed.) (1991) *Secondary Media Education: A Curriculum Statement*. London: British Film Institute.

Brooker, W. (2002) *Using the Force: Creativity, Community and Star Wars Fans*. New York: Continuum.

Brooker, W. and D. Jermyn (eds) (2003) *The Audience Studies Reader*. London: Routledge.

Brown, J. A. (1998) 'Media Literacy Perspectives', *Journal of Communication*, 48, 1, 44–57.

Buckingham, D. (1998) 'Media Education in the UK: Moving Beyond Protectionism', *Journal of Communication*, 48, 1, 33–43.

_____ (2003) *Media Education: Literacy, Learning and Contemporary Culture*. Cambridge: Polity Press.

Entman, R. M. (1989) *Democracy Without Citizens: Media and the Decay of American Politics*. New York: Oxford University Press.

Fiske, J. (1987) *Television Culture*. London: Routledge.

_____ (1992) 'The Cultural Economy of Fandom', in L. A. Lewis (ed.) *The Adoring Audience: Fan Culture and Popular Media*. London: Routledge, 30–50.

Grabe, M. E., S. Zhou and B. Barnett (2001) 'Explication Sensationalism in Television News: Content and the Bells and Whistles of Form', *Journal of Broadcasting and Electronic Media*, 45, 4, 635–55.

Greenbaum, T. L. (2000) *Moderating Focus Groups: A Practical Guide for Group Facilitation*. Thousand Oaks: Sage.

Grossberg, L. (1992) 'Is There a Fan in the House? The Affective Sensibility of Fandom', in L. A. Lewis (ed.) *Adoring Audience: Fan Culture and Popular Media*. London: Routledge, 50–65.

Gwenllian-Jones, S. (2003) 'Histories, Fictions and *Xena: Warrior Princess*', in W. Brooker and D. Jermyn (eds) *The Audience Studies Reader*. London: Routledge, 185–92.

Hills, M. (2002) *Fan Cultures*. London: Routledge.

Hobbs, R. (1998a) 'Democracy at Risk: Building Citizenship Skills through Media Education', in M. Salvador and P. Sias (eds) *The Public Voice in a Democracy at Risk*. Westport: Praeger, 57–76.

_____ (1998b) 'The Seven Great Debates in the Media Literacy Movement', *Journal of Communication*, 48, 1, 9–29.

Jacobs, D. (2003) *The Lord of the Rings: A Media Literacy Review. Applying the Five Key Questions to Frodo and Friends*. Online. Available at http://www.medialit.org/reading_room/article645.html (accessed 12 January 2005).

Jenkins, H. (1992a) *Textual Poachers: Television Fans and Participatory Culture*. New York: Routledge.

_____ (1992b) '"Strangers no more, we sing": Filking and the Social Construction of the Science Fiction Fan Community', in L. A. Lewis (ed.) *The Adoring Audience: Fan Culture and Popular Media*. London: Routledge, 208–36.

_____ (1995) 'Out of the Closet and into the Universe: Queers and *Star Trek*', in J. Tulloch and H. Jenkins (eds) *Science Fiction Audiences: Watching Doctor Who and Star Trek*. London: Routledge, 208–36.

Jenkins, H. and J. Tulloch (1995) 'Beyond the *Star Trek* Phenomenon: Reconceptualizing the Science Fiction Audience', in J. Tulloch and H. Jenkins (eds) *Science Fiction Audiences: Watching Doctor Who and Star Trek*. London: Routledge, 3–24.

Papper, R. A., M. E. Holmes and M. N. Popovich (2004) 'Middletown Media Studies: Media Multitasking ... and How Much People Really Use the Media', *The International Digital Media and Arts Association Journal*, 1, 1, 1–57.

Potter, W. J. (2004) *Theory of Media Literacy: A Cognitive Approach*. Thousand Oaks: Sage.

Rosenbaum, J. E. and J. W. J. Beentjes (2004) 'Reconceptualizing Media Literacy', in K. Renckstorf, D. McQuail, J. E. Rosenbaum and G. Schaap (eds) *Action Theory and Communication Research: Recent Developments in Europe*. Berlin: Mouton de Gruyter, 141–63.

Shefrin, E. (2004) '*Lord of the Rings, Star Wars* and Participatory Fandom: Mapping New Congruencies Between the Internet and Media Entertainment Culture', *Critical Studies in Media Communication*, 21, 3, 261–81.

Silverblatt, A. (2004) 'Media as a Social Institution', *American Behavioral Scientist*, 48, 1, 35–41.

Sun, C. F., and E. Scharrer (2004) 'Staying True to Disney: College Students' Resistance to Criticism of *The Little Mermaid*', *Communication Review*, 7, 35, 35–55.

Thoman, E. (1999) 'Skills and Strategies for Media Education', *Educational Leadership*, 56, 5, 50–5.

Sacred Viewing: Emotional Responses to
The Lord of the Rings

Anne Jerslev[1]

Introduction

It is extremely difficult to answer questions as to our immediate film experience. Very general statements such as 'good', 'fabulous', 'boring', 'bad', 'impressive' most often come to mind. The words and sentences are expressing a general experience of the film; the sum of the many different emotions felt in the course of watching the film tentatively put into appropriate words by respondents. What respondents actually write may, thus, not at all be a true expression of what was actually felt. What we get in responses is not a description of the actual experience at any one time during viewing but a verbalised condensation of the many different emotions in another form and at another level of expression. The words function as a representation of emotions but not necessarily the exact emotions felt during viewing.

Yet, even though the terms are very vague in the sense that they are not meant to label specific emotions related to specific scenes, there is no question that when people are asked to sum up their response to a film, their experiences are centered around *emotion* and they try to give expression to *an unusual film experience* that comes from *an intense emotional engagement*. The joy of watching the film or the pleasure derived from it has to do with *experiencing strong emotions*. Thus the enjoyment of film may come from the extremely successful fulfillment of the expectations of emotional gratification from going to the cinema (Carroll 2003).

Asked in The Lord of the Rings Research Project questionnaire, part of a twenty-country study of the launch and reception of the the final part of the *Lord of the Rings* trilogy,[2] to mark what they thought of *The Return of the King*, 91% of Danish respondents gave it the highest marks; 63% found the film to be 'extremely enjoyable' and 28% 'very enjoyable'.[3] An explanation to the marking follows in a question where respondents are given a maximum of a hundred words to 'sum up your response to the film in your own words'. The 1,496 Danish answers to the question provide quite a large and rich qualitative material which I shall analyse in this chapter, asking what kind of experience the answers are trying to express. In the first part I shall illustrate how the variety of responses may be condensed into five different categories according to the kind of explanation the viewers give to their experience. Then I go on to discuss in a more theoretical way the emotional involvement in the film, and in the final section I shall briefly draw on responses to one of the last questions in the questionnaire where respondents are asked: 'For some people, seeing a film like this is a social event, an experience to be shared with other people. Was this true for you? Can you say in what ways?'

Since I am primarily interested in discussing what it actually means to audience members who agree to label their experience of the film 'extremely enjoyable', I am excluding a little less than a third of the answers. Even among the very enthusiastic 68% there are respondents who have critical interventions;[4] I am not going further into those either. My discussion will not lead me to conclude anything about the Danish *Return of the King* audience; although from a limited and inconclusive angle – as I am here only going in-depth with the answers to this one question – it might, however, provide some explanations of why the film to a large part of the audience is so extremely enjoyable.

Emotional Engagement with *The Lord of the Rings*

In general, it seems that the different descriptions of the emotional engagement can be divided into two main categories. Overall, emotions are attached *both* to the fictional universe *and* to the making of it. Furthermore, emotions in relation to the fictional universe are *both* attached to the unfolding of the narrative and engagement with characters *and* to *mise-en-scène*. Thus the emotional attachments to *The Lord of the Rings* may be illustrated like this:

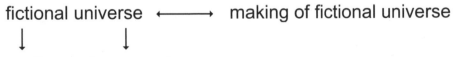

Figure 4: Emotional Attachments in *The Return of the King*

Respondents are, for example, either referring to impressive (special) *effects* or to parts of the film that are *visually* impressive. Thus, using the word 'effects' ('Very very good special effects e.g. Smeagol/Gollum' as one respondent answers) points towards feelings attached to the making of the film and 'visual' to *mise-en-scène* and the diegetic world ('An emotional and visual high and the perfect climax to the saga') even though respondents may be talking about the same thing like, for example, the grand battle extreme long shots. But descriptions of what is 'visually' grand like the magnificent sceneries (either landscapes or armies) relate to *mise-en-scène* most often. And then there are of course examples where it is impossible to tell what the respondent is actually talking about, like: 'A magnificent end to the trilogy. Beautiful images. Fabulous battle scenes.'

However, no matter whether respondents are talking about the fictional universe or the making of the fictional universe they are describing an *emotional* experience. Experiencing non-diegetic matters is just as emotional as talking about characters or plot developments. Either they do it by means of two of the most recurrent word in the material 'fantastic' (the Danish word 'fantastisk' means in English both 'fabulous' and 'extremely') and 'grand' or by means of other words that may be used to transmit a strong feeling of *being immersed in* – a kind of *being-lost-in a fictional universe* that is in every sense overwhelming – the story, the images, the scale of the project, the technical skills:

> Grand, fantastic, grippingly beautiful – I was completely absorbed in the universe and wanted to be there myself. Brilliant escape from the everyday.

It seems that to many viewers knowledge of the production of the film reinforces the emotional absorption both in the story and the images, and, likewise, the mere scale of the battle scenes and the scenery heightens the absorption in the narrative unfolding.

In the entire material the most recurrent adjectives for emotions are (and this comes I think as no surprise): spellbinding, impressive, magnificent, fabulous/extremely (as both adjective and adverb), beautiful, touching, overwhelming, spectacular, exciting, incredible/unbelievable.[5] What may be more surprising is that the word 'entertaining' is only used on very few occasions; it seems that 'entertaining' is much too weak an expression to describe the overall emotional feeling of having had an exceptional experience.

In all, it is possible to distinguish between *contextual* explanations, explanations related to *themes*, explanations related to *formal features* and explanations related to the *viewing situation*. Thus the material may be organised in the following categories and sub-categories:

1. 'Immediate' emotional responses
2. Contextual explanations of emotional responses:
   – explanations related to the book
   – explanations related to expectations, i.e. after viewing the first two films
   – explanations related to the director
3. Thematic explanations to emotional responses

4. Formal explanations to emotional responses
   – explanations related to trilogic structure
   – explanations related to narrative and style
   – explanations related to the visual pleasure
5. Explanations related to the viewing situation.

1. Immediate emotional responses – One large sample among the respondents answers very shortly and powerfully and often does not develop upon their choice of labels. They often write a number of single words side by side neither dividing the words by comma or full stop and there are several capital letters and exclamation marks. Thus their staccato listing of words may in itself communicate their overall emotional impression of having had an experience of their lives:[6] 'Grand'; 'Emotionally sublime sincere unparalleled'; Very beautiful film ...Tearjerker!!! Incredibly fantastic'; 'Exciting spellbinding touching captivating disturbing loving cruel. In short it holds every human emotion and we can recognise ourselves and our reality in it'; 'Overwhelming emotional technically superior authentic inspiring this-cannot-be any-better-feeling (well except for the extended dvd)'; 'An overwhelming visual tour de force which was both spellbinding and exciting. A real adventure'. The remainder of the respondents insert their emotional expressions into one or more of four different kinds of explanatory or descriptive frames.

2. Contextual explanations of emotional responses – While there are, in theory, numerous options to use the films' context to explain or elaborate on emotional responses, only two occur frequently: the books, and the notion of personal prior expectations. Scattered throughout these two types, Peter Jackson also regularly appears as some sort of explanation, though the status of his mentions is far from clear. The word 'book' appears in many descriptions, not surprising since 54% of the respondents name the book as the main reason for watching the film.[7] Since the book has such a prominent position in these answers, the film is referred to as an *interpretation* or *adaptation* and it is evaluated in terms of its faithfulness. In Danish 'tro' may mean both 'accurate' and – more formally – 'faithful' or 'true' and the word is used in both these manners: 'A very good adaptation'; 'Incredibly well manufactured. Faithful towards the book'; 'A visually impressive universe and true to the spirit of the book'. Similarly, a very common way of expressing emotional experience is by explicitly comparing the film to the book and often also emphasising how well the film fitted in with the viewers own imagination of the universe: 'It was perfect and it fitted perfectly in with my own imagination'; 'It lived up to the expectations I had from reading the book'; 'The film is wonderful but the book is even better';[8] 'Mind-reading how on earth did Jackson know my imagination'. One more recurrent contextual evaluation is by means of *prior expectations*. Here of course the book and the two first films in the trilogy are referred to, and the film

provides emotional satisfaction if it fulfills prior expectations or even exceeds them: 'An aesthetic masterpiece with unequalled effects and landscapes. My expectations from the equally wonderful and admirable two previous films were fulfilled. A worthy end to the trilogy'; 'It fulfilled my expectations and maybe it is the best of the films. I think it is a worthy filmic retelling of the books'; 'Even though there is so much missing compared to Tolkien's masterpiece I feel that Peter Jackson has managed to transform the book into a film that is destined to write film history. In my view he has created a film true to Tolkien's universe'.

3. Thematic explanations to emotional responses – Some respondents express their emotional experience by referring to themes in the film, even though thematic explanations are not a very frequent occurrence. However, when they do, primarily two themes seem to pop up, the one being *good vs. evil* and the other *friendship*.[9] Here are just a couple of examples: 'For once I was allowed to dream of being in a place where boundaries are clearly demarcated and differences obvious and unambiguous – also between good and evil'; 'The film provided me with a wonderful feeling of escape from reality being there in the darkness of the movie theatre at the same time as there are so many things in the film that I can recognise from my own everyday life. Friendship doubt sorrow joy, well I could go on forever. To me the film is at once high-class entertainment and a reminder of the values of life and how fragile we all are'.

4: Formal explanations to emotional responses – The expression of the emotional response through formal evaluations of the film may be divided into three different elements: as part of a trilogy, through the structure and style of the film, or through the aesthetic pleasure experienced. There is frequent overlap between these three types. When respondents experience the film as *part of a trilogy*, they explain the level of emotional engagement by pointing out that they have reached closure of one film in three parts: 'An extraordinarily visually wonderful experience. A perfect end to the trilogy'; 'The joy of expectation is almost always larger but the film met almost all my expectations. Mostly I think that I looked forward to once more being part of the film's completely unique universe and meet my characters once more – side with the good and curse the evil. Pure delightful escapism. Look at how it all ends and at the same time lament that the trilogy has definitively ended with *The Return of the King.* It will leave a void.' Furthermore, respondents evaluate the film with respect to *mise-en-scène*, the *acting* or the *production*. They think that the film was 'well done' or 'extremely impressively done'. They show immense enthusiasm with its *spectacular sceneries.* They enjoy the scale of the whole production and they enjoy the special effects, both because they are impressive as filmic effects and because they offer spectacles, the viewer thinks he or she has never seen like before: 'There are some really good animations and effects'; 'A fabulous filmic experience mainly because of the combination of unparalelled landscapes and computer-generated effects combined with a thrilling story centered around the battle between good and evil (and then different wavering characters in the middle)'; 'It was magnificent. The computer-generated effects were so impressive so that they rarely resembled computer effects but rather the images of my dreams and nightmares'. Or respondents merely describe feelings of intense visual pleasure: 'A completely fantastic spellbinding film especially visually'; 'A fabulous visual experience'; 'It is primarily a visual orgasm. I left the theatre feeling immensely joyful and with a sense of physical wellbeing. Though at the same time I was sad because it is over now and I won't experience the joy of looking forward to next Christmas in the same manner'.

5: Explanations related to the viewing situation – Finally I come to expressions of the emotional engagement in *the viewing situation*. Many respondents try to express a joyful feeling of being *immersed* in the film, something that, to some extent, was already becoming visible in the explanations of visual pleasure. One way of giving expression to this is by using the words 'universe' and 'world': 'Everything was perfect and as such one of the largest experiences of completeness on film. Almost a larger-than-life experience where you felt sorry to leave the cinema and the universe which covers the large concepts of mythology history life death power and love'; '*The Lord of the Rings* trilogy is one of the best films I have ever seen. I think that seeing the films is being admitted to a completely fantastical world where orks and other creatures fight against each other'; 'I saw all three films on a trot during eleven hours. That was great. I became completely absorbed by the entire universe to a degree that I didn't experience in the same way by just seeing one of the films. The story is fantastic and yet it is in a sense completely archetypical. The impossible fight between good and evil. But it is the creation of the universe that makes the story unique'. Even though there may be other explanations to the use of these words, I think they point to a feeling of encountering a space that one can enter and be part of – a simulation of being there which is extremely emotional. Another way of describing the feeling of being completely taken in by the film is to refer to empathetic emotions like *tears* and *crying* or bodily reactions like 'being all goosy' or 'shivering all over', of being spellbound or of being absorbed in the film: 'One is absorbed by the film … and you completely forget the world around you'; 'The film was so good so that I cried at least ten times. Not only because it is sad but because it is so sad to realise that there will be no more films'; 'It is more than just a film. It is an experience, a state of mind. You fly away from the chair and disappear into the screen and you fight against orks and Uruk-hais and cling to the side of a mountain and fear the Nazguls'; 'Putting aside your everyday life and allowing yourself to be completely absorbed in another world where you can use the whole emotional spectrum. Emotions that you neglect in your busy daily life'.

Fiction emotions and artefact emotions

What do these emotions and their explanations mean? In order to reach a more elaborate understanding of the emotional responses to *The Lord of the Rings*, it seems that cognitive film theory provides a useful tool. With the exception of laboratory experiments (cf. Zillmann & Bryant 1985; Weaver & Tamborini 1996) this area of film theory has not been interested in empirical reception analyses, but rather in conceptualising the diversity of emotional experiences that narrative films construct for the viewer. Nevertheless scholars like psychologist Ed Tan (1996), Murray Smith (1995) and Torben Grodal (1997) have found it important to stress cognitive activity in film viewing, expanding on formalist theories of how viewers construct narrative meaning (Bordwell 1985). After having read the many descriptions of the joy of being absorbed in *The Lord of the Rings*, I think that Torben Grodal (2001) may be very right in assessing that *'first person' simulations* of being immersed in a fictional world, sharing a character's feelings and simulating his or her actions, are crucial in film viewing.

Grodal's argument is part of a critical reflection upon what he calls 'distant observer' theories of experiencing films. His opponents are here Noël Carroll and Ed Tan, but he also emphasises that empathetic emotions as theorised by Tan are important elements in film viewing as well. I will not go further into this debate here, but since a very conspicuous defining element in the responses when respondents express their (emotional) attachment to the film is equal attention given to narrative and *mise-en-scène*, it may nevertheless be fruitful to reflect upon the different answers to question two with reference to Tan, who distinguishes between what he calls *fiction emotion* and *artefact emotion* (F emotion and A emotion).[10] Tan finds fiction emotions and artefact emotions in every narrative film, though realised in different ways according to, for example, genre. Thus in 'spectacle films' like for example the *Lord of the Rings* films artefact emotions may be more important than in, say, a melodrama. Tan's emphasis that a film's 'surface structure' (1996: 33) may be enjoyable and emotional *in its own right* is an important point when we discuss emotions and film experience – not least in relation to *The Lord of the Rings*, which is often referred to as exactly an artefact, a 'project'.

The artefact character of the film is emphasised again and again in our responses, and Tan's concepts helps us realise that an awareness of the film as artefact should by no means only be distanciating but may, on the contrary, contribute to and even reinforce the emotional engagement. When Tan says that 'in a general sense, it may be that the more intense the emotion, the greater the likelihood the viewer will realise that this is a special experience and be aware of what he or she is seeing is indeed an artefact' (1996: 65), he emphasises that emotional intensity and a kind of metafictional sensibility can go hand in hand.

The fruitful point taken from Tan's differentiation between artefact emotions and fiction emotions seems to be that metafictional awareness needs not have anything to do with disclosing the fictionality of the film and being placed in a position of Brechtian intellectual reflection. On the other hand – and this may point to the explanatory limitations of Tan's cognitivist emotion theory – my material shows that the emotional experience of the film is not only related to the film as a powerful audiovisual object but also to different contextual practices such as the construction of the very act of going to the cinema to watch the film as a ritual or an event.

I pay somewhat more attention to artefact emotions than Tan actually does himself, though. Instead of fiction emotion and artefact emotion, he at one point talks about 'involvement and artefact appreciation' (1996: 35), implying that artefact emotions are not as intense as fiction emotions. However, it seems obvious from the above cited expressions of respondents' emotional experiences of *The Lord of the Rings* that artefact emotions are as strong and intense as fiction emotions; further explorations of the qualitative responses to other questions in the questionnaire may illuminate how the two kind of emotion are mutually enhancing.

Sacred viewing

The metafictional sensibility put forth by so many respondents, produced both by the impressiveness of the film, by the feeling of having never seen anything like it and having never seen anything so technically elaborate and magnificent, seem to these enthusiastic respondents to produce a kind of *awesome viewing*. Explicit expressions of feelings of worship like 'I watched in awe' or 'I was breathtaken with the awesome special effects' are not common; however there is a recurrent use of a kind of solemn and respectful language in expressing the emotional experience and often attached to the film as an artefact. A recurrent comment is for example that the film is 'a *worthy* end to the trilogy' or that it is '*true* to the book'. Thus it seems that despite the diversity of descriptions and explanations in the material, there is a recurrent expression of veneration in experiencing the film as an artefact which makes the experience different in degree to the experience of other touching and impressive films. The strong enjoyment of the film is framed within a semi-religious discourse where not least the metafilmic sensibility contributes to the construction of the trilogy as an object of 'worship'. This discourse may express how viewing the film forms an almost cultish experience to many of the most enthusiastic respondents.

It is essential to make a distinction with fan and cult viewing here. Many respondents refer to themselves as fans but no one refers to their experience as a cult experience when trying to sum up their response to the film. By cultishness I do not mean 'a marginality constructed against the tastes and practices of the "mainstream"' (Hills 2002: 83); this is a precise definition of a cult film experience which the experience of *The Lord of the Rings* is obviously not. I use cultishness with reference to Matt Hills' condensation of both Peter Berger and Thomas Luckmann's discussions and Emile Durkheim's reflections upon the changes from socially organised to individualised and non-institutionalised religious formations in modern societies. Thus Hills claims that the

> production of sacredness, then, depends precisely upon the everyday and proximate form of the 'profane' world ... It is the very arbitrariness of the 'sacred' which produces the force of social convention. This arbitrary nature of the 'sacred' allows for the possibility that, historically, new sacred forms may emerge from new socio-historical contexts and objects. Emergent neo-sacred spaces may be split apart from what was previously 'profane': indeed, a multiplicity of such 'sacred themes' may be generated by the interlocking of individual/subjective and social/objective projects (e.g nascent fan cultures and socially-organised fan cultures). (2002: 128)

Thus, the articulation of an awe-inspired relationship to the film can be regarded as an example of this 'neoreligiosity' as Hills puts it – a profane space which is also in a certain sense 'sacred', the construction of the film as a unique object to be given unusual attention.

However, Hills' underlining of the arbitrariness of the 'sacred' is not completely in accordance with the respectful, even awesome, reception of *The Lord of the Rings* in the sense that this specific object is absolutely not 'arbitrary'. The reception of the film is framed from the very beginning by the cultish admiration of Tolkien's novel – hence the recurrent remark that the film has been awaited for years. Just as important, the film itself is saturated with religious and spiritual themes – i.e. the whole idea of The Eye as an evil force being able to penetrate everything and thus the dissolution of distinctions between matter and spirit, the idealistic story of sacrifice, and the symbolic voyage by ship at the end that like the voyage across the river Acharon takes the Jesus-like Frodo to his death.

The artefact, the fiction, and the beautiful-sublime

Empathy is Ed Tan's key word to understanding emotion in film reception. Thus he argues that fiction emotions (F emotions) in narrative films are empathetic, for example feelings of pity, hope, joy or sorrow for a character – what Grodal would name 'third person' feelings. Non-empathetic emotions, on the other hand, are emotions related to the spectacle, 'the continuing or intensified enjoyment of the spectacle, rather than the prospect of increased understanding or any improvement in the chances of the protagonist' (Tan 1996: 176). This kind of emotion, for example the pure enjoyment of landscape as spectacle, are still fiction emotions in Tan's terms, whereas artefact emotions (A emotions), which are mostly non-empathetic, means both being taken by the spectacularity of the extraordinary full-screen views and admiring the technical skills and the mere ability to produce the magnificent spectacular views.

It seems that when respondents refer to the overwhelming and breathtaking sight of the landscapes or the battle scenes, they are describing non-empathetic fiction emotions, whereas when they mention the impressive special effects used in creating full-screen shots of thousands of orcs that 'you don't even think of as computer generated', they are expressing admiration and wonder at a non-empathetic artefact level. We may thus elaborate on the simple figure from before:

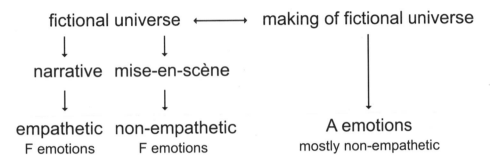

Figure 5: Emotional attachments in spectacle films[11]

Empathetic emotions are related to the absorption in plot development and the destiny of characters. Non-empathetic emotions are not related to plot development or characters but follow from the loosening of the emotional attachment to narrative action in order for the viewer to be more passively taken over by the senses and surrender to the spectacular quality of the visual style.[12] However, non-empathetic emotions are both fiction emotions and artefact emotions; they are both at least to a degree emotionally detached from the first-person simulation of the actions of the protagonist(s).

Of course Tan regards 'tour de force' visual style (for example 'spectacular special effects') as manifestations of the film as artefact. But knowledge of *the telling of the story* (1996: 65) is another example of this kind of awareness and again this may enhance the enjoyment of the film. This last example may also help us to understand the viewers' emotional engagement with *The Lord of the Rings*, as awareness of the film as being narrated is so prominent to very many spectators so that they, when asked to sum up their response to the film, start out by making comparisons with the book; 71% of all Danish viewers have already read or are reading the books and the word 'book' or references to Tolkien appear in almost one out of five responses. The mentioned use of the words 'adaptation' and 'interpretation' and the attention given to expectation (either in relation to the book or the two previous *Lord of the Rings* films) may add further to the overall impression that *A emotions are very strong for many respondents.*

How might we then finally characterise the expression of the emotional response to the film given by the many respondents who thought the film was extremely enjoyable? A suitable term for describing the highest level of emotional response to *The Lord of the Rings* explained by respondents with reference to the grandeur and power of the film could be to borrow the important eighteenth-century aesthetic term *the sublime*. The concept originates with Longinus in the first century A.D. who claims that sublime passages 'exert an irresistible force and mastery' and 'even throws an audience into transport' (cited in Dorsch 1965: 107). The sublime in rhetorics 'uplifts our souls' he claims; thus, with Longinus, the sublime is the noble speech of noblemen. Joseph Addison reflected upon the pleasures gained from 'the sight of what is great, uncommon, or beautiful'. Even though Addison does not use the word he also talks about the sublime when he refers to 'unbounded views' and 'the largeness of whole views' that flings us 'into pleasing astonishment', like

the prospects of an open champaign country, a vast uncultivated desert, of huge heaps of mountains, high rocks and precipices, or a wide expanse of waters, where we are not struck with the novelty or beauty of the sight, but with that rude kind of magnificence which appears in many of these stupendous works of nature. (Cited in Ashfield & De Bolla 1996: 62)

This notion of greatness contains many of the elements connected to the sublime in later writing, as Samuel H. Monk states: 'the aspiration of the imagination to grasp the object, the preordained failure, and the consequent feeling of bafflement, and the sense of awe and wonder' (1935: 58).

After Addison, both Edmund Burke and Immanuel Kant define the sublime as an ambiguous feeling of pleasure and pain. 'It is the strongest emotion which the mind is capable of feeling', says Burke. It is a delight which 'I have not called pleasure, because it turns on pain, and because it is different enough from any idea of positive pleasure'. Sublime is 'what ever excites this delight', and 'astonishment is that state of the soul, in which all its motions are suspended, with some degree of horror' (Burke, quoted in Ashfield & De Bolla, 1996: 132). Astonishment is not connected to beauty in Burke's thinking and likewise in Kant, the sublime and the beautiful is of a different order. Kant regards the sublime as related to the infinity and the uniqueness of the object. The sublime is an aesthetic experience, a state of mind arrived at by the experience of the immeasurability of natural phenomena:

Bold, overhanging, and, as it were, threatening rocks, clouds piled in the sky, moving with lightning flashes and thunder peals; volcanos in all their violence of destruction, hurricanes with their track of devastation, the boundless ocean in a state of tumult; the lofty waterfall of a mighty river, and such like. (Kant's *Critique of Judgment* XXVIII, cited in Adams 1992: 390)

However, this state that elevates the mind is a contradictory state of pain and pleasure where our imagination of the non-imaginable, on the one hand, and reason, on the other, clash. The imagination is occupied with 'something absolutely great' but in Kant's thinking, reason is what must necessarily come to the aid and lay the pain and fear in the sublime to rest by making us aware that the faculty of reason is able to provide us with an awareness of a superiority of mind in relation to nature 'even in its immensity'. There is no tension in beauty and aesthetical judgments of the beautiful is '*restful* contemplation', whereas the 'mind feels itself *moved* in the representation of the sublime in nature' (Kant, quoted in Adams 1992: 390–1). However, in Kant's (pre)romantic understanding, the sublime emotion is not necessarily inferior to aesthetical judgments of the beautiful; more contemporary interpretations of Kant have tended to emphasise the interesting ambiguity and transgressive power in the sublime and thus to devaluate the concept of beauty; Longinus's expression of being 'thrown into transport' might actually be more in accordance with a contemporary critical cultural interest in the sublime.

There are many similarities between, on the one hand, Kant's and Burke's descriptions of the romantic sublime nature and, on the other, the images in both *The Return of the King* and the two previous films – the volcano, the threatening rocks, the rough mountains, the heights and depths. But even though there are reminiscences of the essential classical understanding of the fear and pain in the sublime in the many elaborate expressions of being overwhelmed and taken by the film – for example 'The experience of being *all goosy* watching such a grand and magnificently made film' or 'it gave me *the shivers*'– it seems that *the awesome artefact emotion* that is represented everywhere in the responses and the continuous expressions of an outstanding, uncommon and unique experience, the expression of the magnitude of the film and the expressions of a rather immeasurable experience; also the experiences of the breathtaking views of not only nature but also of the battle scenes may be labelled expressions of the sublime. This sublime emotionality is supported by the saturated spirituality of the film that may, again, be a further reason for the strong expression of artefact emotion in the responses.

Compared to the use of other words for expressing strong emotions the word 'beautiful' is rather infrequent in the responses. Thus a term in-between the beautiful and the sublime as conceptualised by Kant and other eighteenth-century thinkers could be useful in trying to understand the intense emotional engagement described by the most enthusiastic viewers; a kind of beautiful-sublime experience of this grand popular cultural epic trilogy.[13]

Social event and closure

I have primarily been interested in analysing just one of the qualitative questions in the questionnaire – while also discussing the responses with reference to theoretical points about emotion and narrative film. Let me close by emphasising that cognitive emotion theory like the one presented here may contribute to our understanding of the many levels of emotional engagement with *The Lord of the Rings*. However, the whole question of the way contextual elements – like class and gender, or the production of expectations and social rituals surrounding the film – contribute to the emotional engagement and experience cannot be adequately dealt with from this theoretical point of view.

There is a very outspoken awareness among the enthusiastic respondents that *The Return of the King* is the narrative closure of a grand epic narrative. In many answers there is also a sad awareness that this is the end of a unique emotional experience: 'A fantastic visual and emotional experience that reaches beyond the screen and embraces you. At the same time it is an impressive closure to maybe the largest and most ambitious trilogy ever (maybe if we exclude *Star Wars*)'; 'I was so moved when the film ended as if something was just never going to come again'.

Finally, there is an awareness in part of the responses that this is the end of a particular *social* experience. The feeling of emptiness described in the first of the two quotations above is also connected to the ending of the rituals of seeing the film with one's family or the same crowd of friends and making a Christmas event out of going to see the film. There is thus a large group of respondents who thinks that part of the experience of watching a unique film like this is sharing it with others. The film is too grand and magnificent to grasp all by oneself, it is stated.

In one of the last questions in the questionnaire respondents are asked whether 'seeing a film like this is a social event, an experience to be shared with other people'. To different degrees the larger part of the respondents describe the social event of watching the film much like Randall Collins (1988) defines *social rituals* as an assembly of a group of people with a common focus, being in a common mood and directing their attention toward a 'sacred' object in order to experience strong emotions. This applies – although to different degrees – to all groups, it seems, no matter whether they consist of friends, role players, members of a Tolkien society or a family group. But there is also another and much smaller group of respondents who claim that they go to see the film with friends and they like to talk about it afterwards but, basically, it is an experience that one cannot put into words. It is 'an individual film' as one respondent put it. This group of respondents thinks that exactly because the film is so magnificent is it impossible to share the experience with others.

Whereas the largest part among the respondents regard the film as something you have in common and frame within social rituals and you enjoy talking about the film because 'like a myth in old times it is a good story and educational at the same time', another and much smaller part of the respondents go the see the film with friends but they are not very interested in participating in social rituals and want their experience to remain private.

Conclusion

The responses given by viewers who took the opportunity to sum up their reactions to *The Return of the King* in their own words provide us with important insights into both the diversity and the depth of the emotional experiences of the film. These experiences range from short and powerful statements to more elaborate responses where the film is, for example, compared to the books, respondents express their enjoyment by referring to the first two films in the trilogy, or they delve at length into the magnificent sceneries of landscapes and battles. Ed Tan's distinction between fiction emotions and artefact emotions gives us a tool to understand the experience of spectacle film of this scale. The immense enjoyment of the filmic universe and the narrative unfolding is reinforced by the spectacularity of the scenes and this enjoyment becomes even deeper in appreciation of the elaborate special effects. A feeling of *being taken* by the filmic universe and admiration of the film as an artefact seem to unite the many and diverse experiences of the film that may altogether be summed up under the heading of a *sublime* experience.

Because so many think that it matters a lot with whom you watch this final part of the trilogy, the emotional experience of the film is firmly connected to the whole movie-going arrangement. This warrants further analyses and an insight into the pleasure of watching *The Lord of the Rings* through emotion theory could fruitfully be combined with broader cultural analytical positions. It is a step waiting to be taken.

Notes

1 I would like to thank professor Torben Grodal, Department of Film and Media Studies, University of Copenhagen for many valuable comments to an earlier draft of this chapter.

2 This chapter was developed as part of the International Lord of the Rings Research Project. Its research was made possible by funding from the Danish Research Council for the Humanities, and by a grant from the UK Economic and Social Research Council (ESRC Grant No. 000-22-0323) to whom we record our gratitude.

3 Compared to the world average there is, however, a difference in the sense that more Danish viewers marked the next highest category than the world average where 70.8% thought the film to be 'extremely enjoyable' and 20.9% thought of it as 'very enjoyable'.

4   The critical comments to the film from respondents who had given the highest and next highest marks in their response were i) the ending ii) that something from the book was missing, iii) that either the ending or the whole film was too long and drawn-out, or iv) that it resembled the two previous films too much. Let me also stress that I do not use the term 'enthusiast' with reference to Nicholas Abercrombie and Brian Longhurst's (1998) distinction between enthusiasts, fans and cults.

5   Of the 1,496 Danish responses 466 were written in English. This makes it a bit difficult to be precise in counting emotion words.

6   Another explanation to this use of words may be that it mimes what many respondents know from film advertisements where words from reviews are decontextualised and put into the ads.

7   Answering a question regarding what they used as a main source to base their expectations on, 54% put their cross at 'the books' and 37% at 'the first two parts of the film'; 67% of all respondents say that they have read all three books at least once and only 20% have not read the books at all.

8   Whenever there are negative or less enthusiastic evaluations of the film the argument takes as its point of departure the books; the film is good but it is not as good as the books or it has omitted or changed crucial parts of the book.

9   Interestingly enough there is almost no evaluation with reference to genre and fantasy as a genre. Whereas a quite common reason for watching the film in question number four is that respondents 'love' or 'like' or 'is fan of' fantasy.

10 I shall here not go into Tan's discussion of witness emotions and the discussion of the differences between 'distant viewer' positions and simulation positions. I just want to refer to Torben Grodal (2001) who argues convincingly against the distant viewer position which in his discussion includes Ed Tan and Noël Carroll.

11 I have delimited the model to refer to what Tan calls spectacle films even though, again, I think that his film historical sensibility is a bit old-fashioned: to Tan, spectacle films are 'science fiction, historical extravaganzas with numerous crowd scenes films à la *Spartacus*, (1960), disaster films, costume dramas and fantasy films' (1996: 175). The term is appropriate for *The Return of the King* not because it is fantasy but because of its tribute to the film as artefact. Also, in his use of the term 'cinephilia' Tan seems a bit out of touch with contemporary film viewing. He suggests that 'appreciation of the film as artefact can be measured. Our own research has shown that film viewers can be divided along a dimension that we call *cinephilia*' (1996: 34). It seems a rather misleading word that implies that appreciation of the artefact belongs to a specific film-educated audience. Quite the contrary is the case: from the point of view of appreciation of the film as an artefact I think that the average (younger) cinemagoer is today a 'cinephile'.

12 I here use 'passive' a little different than Grodal (2003) who considers passive emotions to be emotions attached to specific genres (for example, melodrama) and narrative incidents caused by the overwhelming forces of destiny more than voluntarily conducted acts on the part of the protagonists.

13 Cynthia Freeland also discusses the sublime and Tan's emotion theory only in relation to art films like Carl Theodor Dreyer's *Joan of Arc* and Werner Herzog's *Aguirre: The Wrath of God*. She misses Tan's double understanding of artefact emotion though, probably because her examples are art films: the computer-generated production value of contemporary popular cinema that makes the 'grand scale' views possible both to make and to contemplate.

Works cited

Abercrombie, N. and B. Longhurst (1998) *Diffused Audiences: Sociological Theory and Audience Research*. Thousand Oaks: Sage.

Adams, H. (ed.) (1992) *Critical Theory Since Plato*. Orlando: Harcourt Brace Jovanovic.

Ashfield, A. and P. De Bolla (1996) *The Sublime: A Reader in British Eighteenth-Century Aesthetic Theory*. Cambridge: Cambridge University Press.

Bordwell, D. (1985) *Narration in the Fiction Film*. London: Methuen.

Carroll, N. (2003) *Engaging the Moving Image*. New Haven: Yale University Press.

Collins, R. (1988) 'The Durkheimian Tradition in Conflict Sociology', in J. Alexander (ed.) *Durkheimian Sociology: Cultural Studies*. Cambridge: Cambridge University Press, 107–28.

Dorsch, T. S. (1965) *Aristotle/Horace/Longinus: Classical Literary Criticism*. London: Penguin Classics.

Freeland, C. A. (1999) 'The Sublime in Cinema', in C. Plantinga and G. M. Smith (eds) *Passionate Views: Film, Cognition, and Emotion*. Baltimore: Johns Hopkins University Press, 65–84.

Grodal, T. (1997) *Moving Pictures: A New Theory of Film Genres, Feelings and Cognition*. Oxford: Clarendon Press.

____ (2001) 'Film, Character Simulation, and Emotion', in J. Friess, B. Hartmann and E. Müller (eds) *Nicht allein das Laufbild auf der Leinwand: Strukturen des Films als Erlebnispotentiale*. Berlin: Vistas Verlag, 115–29.

____ (2003) *Filmoplevelse*. Copenhagen: Samfundslitteratur.

Hills, M. (2002) *Fan Cultures*. London: Routledge.

Monk, S. H. (1935) *The Sublime in XVIII-Century England*. New York: Modern Language Association of America.

Smith, M. (1995) *Engaging Characters: Fiction, Emotion, and the Cinema*. Oxford: Clarendon Press.

Tan, E. (1996) *Emotion and the Structure of Narrative Film: Film as an Emotion Machine*. Mahway: Lawrence Erlbaum Associates.

Weaver, J. B. and R. Tamborini (1996) *Current Research on Audience Preferences and Reactions*. Mahwah: Lawrence Erlbaum Associates.

Zillmann, D. and B. Jennings (eds) (1985) *Selective Exposure to Communication*. Hillsdale: Lawrence Erlbaum Associates.

SECTION 3
ANCILLARY CONTEXTS

Framing Tolkien: Trailers, High Concept and the Ring

Erik Hedling[1]

Introduction

Recent years have seen an increase in the attention for trailers, the short adverts for upcoming releases screened before main features in theatres. They are a highly commercial form of framings for artworks, yet also commodities of popular culture. Trailers are in theoretical terms instances of 'paratexts' (Genette 1997), and more specifically 'epitexts', that is, 'a paratextual element not materially appended to the text within the same volume' (Genette 1997: 344). But trailers are also, as Lisa Kernan claims in her rigorous study *Coming Attractions*, 'metatexts', because of 'their heavily quotational aspect and the way they rhetorically reconfigure scenes from the film, endowing them with persuasive content' (2004: 7).

Thus, the film trailer is both similar to and different from the film that it is promoting; Kernan actually calls trailers 'a unique form of narrative film exhibition, wherein promotional discourse and narrative pleasure are conjoined' (2004: 1). Sequences and sounds from the forthcoming film are employed, but to that are added carefully chosen verbal rhetoric as well as a montage of graphics, moving images and sounds from the film.[2] As a framing device, accordingly, the trailer is both textual and contextual, though leaning towards the former, and at the same time intracompositional and extracompositional, though leaning towards the latter.

This chapter studies a striking example of modern movie trailer rhetoric, an example which also happens to be intermedial, taking into particular consideration how the framings 'frame' the work, how they create cognitive schemas to guide the audience's understanding of the ensuing films, all in order for the producers to promote the film effectively before its theatrical release. My examples here are the three trailers for *The Lord of the Rings*.

The aesthetics of High Concept

Before attending to the trailers proper, I need to make some general remarks regarding modern, commercial filmmaking, particularly as represented by Hollywood. It is essential to bear in mind the scale of *The Lord of the Rings*, three films shot back-to-back in 1999 and 2000. The trilogy has become the most financially successful of all times. Each of the three films grossed nearly or more than ten times its production costs at the international cinema box office, netting around $3billion in total.[3] Adding to that the profits from DVDs, videos and various types of merchandise – computer games, T-shirts, posters, cups, action figures, miscellaneous memorabilia – the films will undoubtedly prove to constitute one of the most overwhelming industrial media ventures so far in the twenty-first century. This success is not so extraordinary in terms of well-established American strategies for making blockbuster movies. In fact, it is a logical outcome of marketing techniques employed since the mid-1970s, or more specific since the release of *Jaws* (Steven Spielberg, 1975), the film that changed Hollywood history in terms of marketing strategies as well as aesthetics (Schatz 1993; Shone 2004). According to Justin Wyatt, himself a former market research analyst within the film industry, films with ambitions to make large financial profits – or as they are usually called, 'High Concept' movies – try to conform to three basic qualities which can be briefly summarised as 'the book', 'the look' and 'the hook' (1994: 20–2).

The first quality is 'the book'. This dimension is represented by the fact that the film should ideally be based on an already widespread narrative, since there has to be a strong force raising curiosity and attracting audiences to an otherwise unknown product. This could, as is indeed the case with *The Lord of the Rings*, be a widely circulated novel, here, J.R.R. Tolkien's mega bestseller. The reputation of the book alone, along with the pure commercial power of the film medium, induced young cult audiences to camp outside the cinemas for several days in order to obtain tickets for the premiere. It is a fact that nearly half of all films made are based on popular novels precisely for this very reason, that is, the more knowledge the potential audience have of a story, the more likely they will be to go and see it as a film in the cinema.

The basis for cinematic adaptation could also, however, be a successful Broadway musical, as in the cases of *Evita* (Alan Parker, 1996) or *Chicago* (Rob Marshall, 2002), or legendary historical events such as, say, *Saving Private Ryan* (Steven Spielberg, 1998), *Troy* (Wolfgang Petersen, 2004) or, most famously, *Titanic* (James Cameron, 1997), the single bestselling film of all times, netting nearly $2billion worldwide (that is, in cinema admissions – the videos, laser disks, DVDs, CDs and the merchandise have most likely tripled that sum). What I wish to point out is that very few people in the world who saw *Titanic* were unaware of the eventual outcome of the story, how the ship was doomed to go down into the ice-cold Atlantic. Of utmost importance for the High Concept film in order to fulfill the quality of 'the book', then, is the overall creation of intertextual recognition, to make the audience feel part of a commonly-shared social and medial space by means of, for instance, intertextual allusions to films, books or events, well-known star actors, or strong generic markers. A story no one knows the outcome of is, although not necessarily by strict logic, quite likely to be Low Concept. Particularly if there are no stars in it.

Pertaining to *The Lord of the Rings*, no expensive movie stars in the, say, twenty-million-dollar league – for example, Mel Gibson, Tom Cruise, Julia Roberts or Arnold Schwarzenegger – were really needed to create the desired intertextual recognition. In his biography of Peter Jackson, Ian Pryor discusses 'whether Jackson planned to concentrate on big-name actors or unknowns. Jackson's answer was: unknowns' (2004: 259). Tolkien's novels, however, had enough intertextual star value in themselves and as expected some of the actors appearing in the film subsequently have become major and attractive film stars, as illustrated by the ensuing careers of Viggo Mortensen, Liv Tyler or Orlando Bloom. Mortensen has since starred in *Hidalgo* (Joe Johnston, 2004), Tyler in *Jersey Girl* (Kevin Smith, 2004), and Bloom, before *The Lord of the Rings* a virtual unknown but by now obviously the most profitable of them all, in blockbusters like *Pirates of the Caribbean* (Gore Verbinski, 2003) and *Troy*.

The second quality is 'the look', which indicates a certain overall stylistic design and narrative pattern. In the High Concept film this concerns a strong match between music and striking imagery, thus dividing the film into montage sequences which can be apprehended more or less like individual music videos. Narrative and character, in the classical period up to the end of the 1960s often considered to be the particular aesthetic strength of Hollywood cinema (Bordwell, Thompson & Staiger 1985), are by now often greatly simplified. Indeed, narrative complexity or character development are often exchanged for spectacular action, both in terms of time and space. Film scholars have not entirely without justification compared the modern cinemagoing experience – of blockbuster movies, that is – to visiting an amusement park: you start with the big wheel, then you walk slowly to the dodgem car, then pause again before finishing in grand style with the roller coaster.

Regarding *The Lord of the Rings*, one has in terms of character psychology, for example, typically omitted one of my personal favourite sequences from the novel. In the last part of *The Lord of the Rings* trilogy, *The Return of the King*, Tolkien dwells with tragic ambiguity on the character of Saruman, the evil Grand Wizard, by describing how his spirit, in the shape of a cloud, tries to turn West after he has been murdered in the end by his own henchman Grima Wormtongue. The cloud, however, is dissolved by a sudden wind. The metaphorical meaning in Tolkien's novel seems to indicate that there is still something good left in Saruman, his spirit aiming to fulfill his destiny, to go West, to the land of the blessed, in order to enjoy eternal life, but that divine justice prevents him. Although it would be far too facile to complain about Peter Jackson, Philippa Boyens and Frances Walsh, all of them Tolkien-experts, and their art of adaptation – some scenes will inevitably have to be lost as a consequence of cinematic condensation – this is still typical of the High Concept aesthetic. Whereas Tolkien's Saruman appears hauntingly complex in character, Jackson's Saruman is more or less plain Grand Wizard and villain, however brilliantly played by the cinematic vampire *par préférence*, Christopher Lee. Jim Smith and J. Clive Matthews write: 'The on-screen Saruman is more dynamic than the literary one, a war leader played by a great star, but he is also much less complex' (2004: 178). And in a religious study of the films, Greg Wright states: 'Tolkien did not write *Fellowship* as a stand-alone novel, and his villain, Sauron, comes into play only in the full scope of the "trilogy". Jackson's movie, however, must work as stand-alone entertainment, and so it must have a viable villain' (2004: 66). That villain, accordingly, must be Saruman, who is, in other words, and particularly as he is hauntingly incarnated by Lee, much more literal and subsequently more High Concept. That Lee's stardom was considerably enhanced by the films is underlined by the fact that his is one of the distinct voices who welcomes visitors to *The Lord of the Rings* homepage on the Internet.[4] Ideally, then, the style and narrative of a High Concept film should even be able to be 'summed up' and sold in a single sentence – indeed the expression 'High Concept' derives exactly from this kind of linguistic condensation – although it would be grossly unfair to claim that *The Lord of the Rings* is a High Concept specimen in its purest or most negative sense.

The quality of 'the hook', finally, pertains specifically to the marketing of the film, that is literally to catch as many customers as possible by using advertising in a long line. A High Concept film today spends many millions on marketing, in the case of *The Lord of the Rings* considerably more. The hook is represented by the actual aesthetic strategy for integrating the product with the marketing and merchandising, made possible by the development of new media, such as cable TV, the Internet and DVD, and the concurrent ownership changes within the film industry, turning the studios into fully-fledged globalised, multi-medial conglomerats. It is this aspect of the hook that I want to explore further, in relation to the films' trailers.

Framings

One important way of hooking up with the intended audience is to successfully 'frame' the film for the audience before its cinematic release by ways of marketing. The most important framing, in literal terms, is the trailer; that is, the two-and-a-half-minute montage sequence that is exhibited in advance in cinemas, on DVDs, on the internet and on TV in order to effectively advertise the films. The importance of trailers cannot be overestimated since, as Kernan maintains, they are very 'cost-effective since they utilise approximately 4.5% of the advertising budget of a given film, while generating at least 20% of the film's box office revenue' (2004: 32). If that is true, it would mean that in the case of *The Lord of the Rings* the trailers were worth as much as a staggering $600million.

The trailers were under all circumstances specifically designed to raise advance audience curiosity for the otherwise mostly unknown product, despite the fact that the films were adaptations of one of the most well-known novels of the twentieth century.[5] Once the frame, the trailer, was firmly established, the product – the film – could be successfully launched. As was proved by *The Lord of the Rings*, the film works as yet another framing, *mise-en-abyme*-like, this time for both the next installment, or sequel, in the series, and also for the extended version of the film – often substantially augmented with new sequences from the novels – released on DVD some ten months after the initial cinematic opening (the theatrical version came out on DVD much earlier, and devoted fans, like myself, were thus 'forced' to buy two indvidual boxed DVD sets).

In the case of *The Lord of the Rings* trilogy trailers did not only function as framing future film releases but also, in a sense, as individual works of art or as framing the spectacular film medium as such. Unlike other film trailers, they were heavily advertised in themselves in the press as attractions at the cinema. Thus, one could read in newspaper ads that along with the new great film by or with so and so, the trailer for the forthcoming *Lord of the Rings*-film would also be screened. And the DVDs and the internet put special emphasis on them as major events. Regarding DVDs each release contained several different cinematic trailers or TV-spots.[6] And on the internet they stimulated intense debate among Tolkien readers regarding how they indicated the overall interpretation of the novel by the filmmakers. The fact is, as Ian Pryor states, the announcement of the making of *The Lord of the Rings* stirred enormous activity on the internet already in 1999 'with half of the world's Tolkien fans standing by on the internet' (2004: 258). In the terms developed here, however, the trailers were all specifically designed – framed – to fit and market the High Concept aesthetic, 'the book', 'the look' and 'the hook', albeit in ways particularly suitable for the launch of an adaptation of a bestselling cult novel.

The Fellowship of the Ring trailer: commercial pleasures of High Art

In the first trailer, *The Fellowship of the Ring*, released several months before the world premiere of the film in December 2001, many ingredients underlining the ensuing movie as High Concept are presented. We have here, for instance, a focus on the spectacular setting in New Zealand mountain landscapes and the striking computer-generated imagery applied to the landscape by the special effects company Weta. Thus, as Ian Pryor states: 'Some of the trilogy's most spectacular landscapes ... are testament to movie magic more than actual locations. The Weta wizards cut and pasted a number of photographic elements to create such imaginary landscapes' (2004: 263). Still, or even perhaps because of this manipulation,

> the trilogy's use of local scenery would later be mined extensively to promote both the movies themselves and New Zealand as a prime location for tourists and film-makers. Special maps showing where sections of the trilogy had been shot were much in demand, and a detailed pocketbook that helped fans pinpoint each location became a national bestseller. Yet for Jackson, the obsession with spot-the-location occasionally felt a little contrary to what the movies were about. He said that seeing *Fellowship of the Ring* with the film's real-life locations in mind 'defeats the purpose of a film like this'. (Ibid.)

It certainly does not defeat the purpose of profitability. By means of this strategy, landscape itself is turned into a commodity, framed effectively by the trailer, and later by the film itself, and it subsequently works perfectly to create the desirable synergy effects. That is: the landscape promotes the film, the film promotes the landscape. This way of going about things, in fact, epitomises the High Concept.

In intermedial terms, one of the most interesting aspects of *The Lord of the Rings* as literary adaptation is the emphasis put on actress Liv Tyler playing the character of the elven princess Arwen Evenstar. Her part, much more subdued in Tolkien's novel, is substantially increased in Jackson's adaptation, in the trailer exemplified by the fact that we see that it is she who in a dazzling action sequence dramatically saves the severely suffering Frodo during the final journey towards Rivendell. She even challenges the evil Ring Wraiths of Sauron at the passage by menacingly uttering 'If you want him, come and claim him', raising her sword. In the novel, it is the elven prince Glorfindel's horse that carries Frodo to Rivendell.

The reason for this augmentation of Arwen's/Liv Tyler's role is to me quite obvious. In a film specifically designed and financed to reach millions one cannot stick to Tolkien's one-sided focus on the masculine. There will often have to be objects of female alignment – that is, female characters – in order to attract women in large numbers to the cinema, not speaking of the aesthetic pleasure derived from men looking at women, a central aspect of Hollywood cinema most famously theorised by Laura Mulvey (1975). Smith and Matthews write regarding the comparison of Arwen to Lúthien, the most beautiful woman on earth or Frodo's claim never to have seen or imagined anything so lovely as Arwen:

> This is a lot for any actress to live up to, for how can any real person be more beautiful than anything the audience has ever imagined? Whether or not the then 22-year-old Liv Tyler comes close depends on each indvidual viewer's own predilections, but the fact that she had already established herself as an international

sex-symbol through films such as *Armageddon* (Michael Bay, 1997) and modelling work before the films were cast certainly lends authority to the general idea that Arwen is impressively beautiful. (2004: 120)

But I would also argue that the casting of Tyler still is done in order to promote codes relevant to the literary 'seriousness' surrounding the whole project. It is not only *Armageddon* that has made Tyler famous. She also has a status as a 'thinking man's sex symbol', representing more literary-oriented values, with her particularly strong background in art films or 'films d'auteur' (Low Concept) like Bernardo Bertolucci's *Stealing Beauty* (1996), Martha Fiennes's Pushkin-adaptation *Onegin* (1999) or Robert Altman's *Dr T and the Women* (2000). These connotations of High Art are, of course, further enhanced by the strong emphasis on the received pronunciation of Gandalf in the voice-over narrative in the trailer, played as he is by Sir Ian McKellen, Britain's foremost Shakespearean actor in the late twentieth century, or on Galadriel, played by the highly esteemed Australian character actress Cate Blanchett, whose role here clearly alludes to her generally hailed performance as the glamorous queen in the British blockbuster (albeit at a somewhat smaller scale) *Elizabeth* (Shekhar Kapur, 1998).

Trailers are, according to Lisa Kernan, generally characterised by the rhetorics of story, genre and stardom. McKellen's vital role in the trailer – even more so than his part in the film – can be illustrated by her notion that

> the rhetoric of story utilises such a trailer 'narrator' – and often a flesh-and-blood voice-over narrator as well – to promote filmic narrative. Trailers typically redouble the phenomena of narrator and narrative (a trailer narrator tells the trailer's own narrative about the film narrative) resulting in condensed layers of storytelling about storytelling that inevitably withhold more than they reveal – and the with-holding can be just as revealing as what's shown or told. (2004: 55)

What is particularly revealing in the present trailer, however, is that it is typically McKellen who reads the voice-over, who is the narrator at the beginning of the trailer, that is, before the logo of New Line Cinema appears. Then there is a cut to one of his lines of dialogue in the film. Thus, he goes from extradiegetic narrator to intradiegetic, something he does not do in the film itself, where his role is exclusively intradiegetic. Besides the pure action spectacle, the sheer beauty of the sets and the general excitement, the film is accordingly also framed for the audience as 'Shakespearean', as connected to McKellen's actor image, as adding strong notions of culture and sophistication to commercial entertainment. This is indeed emphasis, quite literally, on 'the book'.

High Art is employed here as a commodity adding to the High Concept, just as we are likely to hear Pavarotti sing opera over the speaker system in an airport lobby, or watch a reproduction of a Vermeer painting in the underground station. As a high-end cinematic product, *The Lord of the Rings* contains everything expected of it; it also, however, needs differentiation in order to cover the whole spectrum of potential audiences, hence the manifested 'artness', a term wittily suggested by Peter Wollen to represent a certain aura (1998: 156–7). Another applicable term is certainly 'actorliness', coined by John Hill as a description of a peculiarly British film acting style, strongly connected to cultural status and based on 'overtly theatrical performances which clearly announce their status as performances' (1999: 82). This style pertains to both McKellen and Christopher Lee.

Finally, also very much stressed in the trailer is the framing of generic features, that is, *The Lord of the Rings* is typically what I would call a family adventure spectacle, the most commercially attractive of all kinds of narrative, as is shown by films like *Jurassic Park* (Steven Spielberg, 1993) or *Star Wars* (George Lucas, 1977) with actors and actresses of different age groups being able to attract universal audience interest. Hence the presentation of the hobbits as transgressors of age, that is, they will most probably be pereceived as children by other children.

The Two Towers: the trailer as attraction

The second trailer, *The Two Towers*, marks a change of emphasis. Howard Shore's musical score, with its different thematic motifs, is much more underlined than in the first trailer since it is by now widely recognised by the audience. The CD of the score was released with the first film in order to create the always desirable synergy effects which means that just as the film markets the music, the music will market the film. Thus, strong effects of recognition were created for the audience.

Liv Tyler's physical beauty is yet again put at the core of developments even if she does not even take part in Tolkien's second novel on which the film is based. In the film the inclusion of her, without violation of the literary source, is accomplished through a sophisticated web of flashbacks, inserts and parallel montages, all generously present in the trailer where she appears in several different shots. Indeed, to a certain extent the trailer frames the film to be understood as a traditional love story between Aragorn and Arwen, which, of course, is not really the case even if the love story is duly, but sparingly represented in the film itself. (Needless to say, the concept of 'boy meets girl' is one of the 'highest' of them all.) Tyler's role here is to generate romantic interest as well as female alignment, a part where she eventually receives more than apt assistance from actress Miranda Otto as Éowyn, the niece of the Rohan king Theoden. Audiences, however, were not yet aware of the central part that Otto was to take as female heroine in the ensuing films. Thus, the somewhat false emphasis on Tyler.

Interestingly enough, Smith and Matthews claim that there were rumours about plans for Arwen to actually become an action heroine, even participating actively in the Battle of Helm's Deep, contrasting drastically with the role assigned to her by Tolkien (2004: 121–2). In that way she would have been tying in nicely with the archetypical, modern female gunslinger and fistfighter in High Concept films like *Lara Croft: Tomb Raider* (Simon West, 2001), a common and very popular generic type, described by Yvonne Tasker as mobilising a 'symbolically transgressive iconography' (1993: 132). These rumours were stengthened by the fact that 'shortly after the first film in the trilogy, tie-in merchandise became available, including life-sized replicas of her sword and action figures … in battle poses' (Smith & Matthews 2004: 122). These plans, however, were quite obviously disregarded, most probably to the great pleasure of Tolkien fans who debated any differences from their own interpretations of the book vigorously on the internet.

In terms of narrative content, *The Two Towers* is more advertised as a pure action movie, without the ostentatious flirting with High Art of the trailer for *The Fellowship of the Ring*. Nor does the trailer really depend very much on the rhetorical device of 'story'. Instead, focus is on the rhetoric of 'genre'. By now the audience was targeted – or, so to say, hooked – and the trailer could draw more on traditional High Concept spectacle for guaranteeing the financial success of the film. Here, the trailer fits perfectly Kernan's notion of trailers as similar to films described by Tom Gunning's famous concept of 'cinema of attractions', that is, prenarrative cinematic practice up until 1906 (see Kernan 2004: 7). Gunning writes that:

> the cinema of attractions directly solicits spectator attention, inciting visual curiosity, and supplying pleasure through an exciting spectacle – a unique event, whether fictional or documentary, that is of interest in itself. The attraction to be displayed may also be of a cinematic nature … in which a cinematic manipulation … provides the film's novelty. Fictional situations tend to be restricted to gags … or recreations of shocking or curious incidents … It is the direct address of the audience, in which an attraction is offered to the spectator by a cinema showman, that defines this approach to filmmaking. Theatrical display dominates over narrative absorption, emphasising the direct stimulation of shock or surprise at the expense of unfolding a story or creating a diegetic universe. The cinema of attractions expends little energy creating characters with psychological motivations or individual personality. Making use of both fictional and non-fictional attractions, its energy moves outward towards an acknowledged spectator rather than inward towards the character-based situations essential to classical narrative. (1990: 58–9)

Even if Gunning is describing the cinematic experience of nearly a hundred years ago, his description still fits the way movie trailers often work as framings for coming attractions in the modern cinema. At least as is the case with the trailer for *The Two Towers*. Bearing in mind the marketing purposes of the trailer, it is thus typical that the part dealing with Frodo, Sam and Gollum's lonely march into Mordor, which constitutes half of the book as well as nearly half of the film, is given so little framing space. But this part deals too much with 'non-attractive' elements such as psychological character development, which is much more difficult to market than epic and suspenseful battle scenes. Instead, as Kernan claims, 'contemporary trailers trumpet the pleasure of generic spectacle even more than did earlier trailers, often consciously appealing to audiences in terms that evoke nostalgia … for the classical era' (2004: 203). Accordingly, *The Two Towers* could be claimed to be framed as 'meta-cinema', a cinema which here is exclusively devoted to 'the look'.

The Return of the King trailer: desirable film stars

The final trailer focuses mainly on the character of Aragorn, often in close-up. I would claim that the trailer metaphorically outlines actor Viggo Mortensen's metamorphosis into a major film star, one of the world's most desirable market commodities, thus corresponding closely to Kernan's characterisation of the common rhetoric of 'stardom' in trailers. Also here, Kernan stresses the nostalgia:

> Trailers appealing to audience interest in stars in the contemporay era demonstrate a return to formula in the context of a Hollywood economy dominated by High Concept marketing. Star appeals are increasingly integrated with those of story and genre in high-tech contemporary trailers that fluidly weave these appeals together using multiple grids and sophisticated applications of music, sound effects and dialogue overlaps, along with graphics and text that cue viewers to the key art of the overall campaign. (2004: 205)

This promotion of Mortensen's stardom is achieved by means of showing how he gradually claims the throne of Gondor: his being given the re-forged royal sword, his role as responsible politician, charismatic war leader, and, not least, erotic lover. Thus, he marries the beautiful Arwen Evenstar and Liv Tyler is once again lavishly but not very faithfully (neither to the ensuing film nor to the novel) represented in the trailer, all for reasons dwelt upon above. Mortensen was a most suitable star to emerge from *The Lord of the Rings*, with his connotations of 'artness', being, as Pryor notes, an art photographer and a published poet (Pryor 2004: 268). Mortensen is also given the extreme privilege of addressing the audience (in the ensuing film, of course, also to the armies of Rohan and Gondor outside the gates of Mordor) in an ideologically charged monologue, in the trailer heard partly as voice-over against a montage of various imagery from the film. Here, he exclaims:

'I see in your eyes the same fear that will take the heart of me. A day may come when the courage of men fails, when we foresake our friends and brake all bonds of fellowship. But it is not this day. This day we fight.'

In terms of dramaturgy, this is clearly a descendent of Henry the Fifth's famous Agincourt address – 'We few, we happy few, we band of brothers' (*Henry V*, IV: 3). This kind of address has been recurringly employed in post-1991 High Concept blockbusters as a vehicle for, for instance, the American president, as in *Independence Day* (Roland Emmerich 1996) and, albeit with very different political connotations, in *The Day After Tomorrow* (Roland Emmerich 2004). As far as I can see, the reason for including so much of this address about the necessity of fighting against evil *must* have been to try to profit from assumed sentiments among primarily American audiences regarding the situation in the world at the time of the trailer's release in 2003 (the 'war against terrorism'). Anyhow, the first two films had elevated Mortensen to stardom and, accordingly, the trailer for the third film could profit generously from it. He was to be employed as bait, or indeed as 'the hook'.

This does not mean that the focus put on Mortensen excludes the other actors, or rather by this stage, 'stars'. Instead, the trailer is heavily engaged in what Kernan also claims to be typical for contemporary trailers: 'star pairings' and the 'interconnection of multiple stars', all in order to maximise the commercial desirability of the product (2004: 71). Regarding the character of Éowyn and her part in *The Two Towers*, Smith and Matthews write:

> The expansion of Éowyn's character in the second film serves to make her far more memorable than she is in the book. She not only has a far greater physical presence, but she is also shown practising swordplay (preparing the audience for her confrontation with the Witch King of Angmar), she is given expository dialogue that belongs to Éomer or Theoden in the book, and she has a far more apparent romantic interest in Aragorn. (2004: 189)

This preparation for the cinematically attractive duel is obvious in the trailer for *The Return of the King*, since we get a couple of shots of Miranda Otto in full armour. Thus, she takes on the role which apparently was originally accorded to Liv Tyler as the warlike Amazon, the action heroine, raising considerable female interest in the film, at least, I surmise, among younger women. Tentatively, I would have thought that this strategy worked well in commercial terms and even better than the filmmakers originally thought, at least judging from the fact that Tyler receives much more attention in the trailer than Otto. In the ensuing film, it is the other way round.[7]

Conclusion

The trailers framing the *Lord of the Rings* trilogy for its potential audiences firmly situated the films within the High Concept aesthetic and they did subscribe heavily to the Hollywood marketing strategy of 'the book', 'the look' and 'the hook'. That is, they put their emphasis on special effects instead of on more traditional narrative, as in the spectacular digitised battles, they foregrounded music and image in the shape of Howard Shore's bombastic and much publicised score, they contained close-ups of desirable stars, like, for instance, Viggo Mortensen as Aragorn, or Liv Tyler as Arwen, they presented an attractive and heavily-designed world, and they contained intertextual allusions in order to make certain the audience's recognition of a by now well-known medial space. They also adhered to typical aspects of movie trailer-making in employing the combined rhetorics suggested by Kernan: story, genre and stardom.

As framings of cinematic Tolkien adaptations, I would claim that they, unsurprisingly, emphasised grandiose form more than subtle content. They were, quite plainly, advertising in the High Concept mode, stressing the 'bigger, longer, better' aspects of the Hollywood product. There was no outspoken ideological reading of the book at work, as, for instance, commented on by Greg Wright who claims that Tolkien's Catholic vision was lost in the films (2004: 172–84). That does not mean that the films, or trailers, were devoid of ideological content: I have already mentioned the speech of Aragorn in the trailer for *The Return of the King*, but one could also mention many biased expressions of class, ethnicity and even gender. But that is a different story from the one I have told. Besides guaranteeing the financial success of the movie worldwide, the trailers also managed to create a so far unheard of interest for themselves, confirmed particularly by the alleged production of a six-minute supertrailer, a superframing for the whole trilogy. This could frame future re-releases of the trilogy but also stand as a monument for the elevation of paratextual framings into a kind of framed texts on their own.

Notes

1   A different version of this chapter also appears in W. Wolf & W. Bernhart (eds) (2006) *Framing Borders in Literature and Other Media: Studies in Intermediality 1*, Amsterdam and New York: Rodopi.
2   As Kernan notes, trailers may sometimes contain shots not included in the finished film, as in the famous case of Jack Nicholson in the trailer for *As Good as it Gets* (James L. Brooks, 1997) (2004: 11).
3   See http://www.boxofficemojo.com/alltime/trilogyww.htm for further information.
4   http://www.lordoftherings.net.
5   In 2003, viewers of the BBC's literary programme *The Big Read* voted *The Lord of the*

Rings 'The Nation's Favourite Novel' of all time (see Smith & Matthews 2004: 4).

6   Kernan stresses that it 'should be noted that while the rule is still a single trailer produced per film, this can be misleading in that earlier and later versions of trailers, produced for different phases in a film's ad campaign, often coexist' (2004: 238). Here I have reviewed what is labelled as trailer number one for each film, assuming this to be the initial and most widespread version, though there was no version documentation on the DVDs. However, the DVD trailers generally corresponded with my memories from the cinema. Also, they are identical on the above-mentioned site on the internet.

7   I am speculating about female audience interest in Otto's characterisation of Éowyn. Answers to this riddle, however, will undoubtedly be provided by the forthcoming publications connected with the impressive *The Lord of the Rings*-project, a survey of world audiences for the films led by Martin Barker at the University of Aberystwyth, Wales.

Works cited

Bordwell, D., J. Staiger and K. Thompson (1985) *The Classical Hollywood Cinema: Film Style and Mode of Production to 1960.* London: Routledge.

Genette, G. (1997) *Paratexts: Thresholds of Interpretation.* Cambridge: Cambridge University Press.

Gunning, T. (1990) 'The Cinema of Attractions: Early Film, Its Spectator and the Avant-Garde', in T. Elsaesser (ed.) *Early Cinema: Space, Frame, Narrative.* London: British Film Institute, 56–62.

Hill, J. (1999) *British Cinema in the 1980s.* Oxford: Oxford University Press.

Kernan, L. (2004) *Coming Attractions: Reading American Movie Trailers.* Austin: University of Texas Press.

Mulvey, L. (1975) 'Visual Pleasure and Narrative Cinema', *Screen*, 16, 3, 6–18.

Pryor, I. (2004) *Peter Jackson: From Prince of Splatter to Lord of the Rings.* New York: St. Martin's Press.

Schatz, T. (1993) 'The New Hollywood', in J. Collins, H. Radner and A. Preacher Collins (eds) *Film Theory Goes to the Movies.* New York and London: Routledge, 8–36.

Shone, T. (2004) *Blockbuster: How Hollywood Learned to Stop Worrying and Love the Summer.* New York: Free Press.

Smith, J. and J. C. Matthews (2004) *The Lord of the Rings: The Films, The Books, The Radio Series.* London: Virgin.

Tasker, Y. (1993) *Spectacular Bodies: Gender, Genre and the Action Cinema.* London and New York: Routledge.

Wright, G. (2004) *Peter Jackson in Perspective: The Power Behind Cinema's The Lord of the Rings.* Washington: Hollywood Jesus Books.

Wollen, P. (1998) *Signs and Meaning in the Cinema*, third edn. London: British Film Institute.

Wyatt, J. (1994) *High Concept: Movies and Marketing in Hollywood.* Austin: University of Texas Press.

Bonus Material: The DVD Layering of *The Lord of the Rings*

Jonathan Gray

Introduction

Between the grandiose achievements of screening one of the last century's most popular tales, creating cinema's first fully realised CGI character, winning multiple Academy Awards, revolutionising battle sequences with its Massive computer program, and grossing equally massive box office receipts worldwide, New Line's *Lord of the Rings* trilogy is notable and historic for many cinematic reasons. Meanwhile, however, it has also contributed significantly to laying new groundwork for another medium, that of the DVD. Since the DVD player's emergence in 1997, DVDs have gradually been created with more and more 'bonus material', ranging from interviews, deleted scenes or alternative endings, to cast and crew bios, subtitles and making-of documentaries. However, the *Lord of the Rings* trilogy Platinum Edition DVDs have upped the ante.

Thus, for instance, the *Two Towers* DVD set comes in an attractive 'Elven'-designed box set with four discs. Not only do these discs offer approximately one hour of extra footage, but all scenes are worked seamlessly into the cinematic text, complete with visual and sound effects, and scoring by the film's composer Howard Shore. Moreover, viewers can also sit through four full four-hour commentary tracks, or watch the thirteen documentaries amassing over seven hours in total, view any of the 1917 photographic stills (219 of which come with commentaries), or play with several of the interactive splitscreen, map- or audio-based features. With a crew of 163 and a total of 113 members of the cast or crew interviewed, the *Two Towers* DVDs open up the film and its production to viewers as few other artistic works in history have, creating well over thirty hours of bonus textuality, just as the *Fellowship of the Ring* DVD set did before it.

This chapter argues that with such an abundance of bonus materials in existence, and especially given the huge success of the DVDs (Snider 2003), it becomes important to see exactly what is added to 'the text itself', and, by extension, what DVDs are doing to textuality, or the concept of text, in this new age of bonus materials. To speak of textuality, though, is also to speak of textual criticism and of how we as analysts study texts. While no longer as in vogue (since the cultural studies boom in reception studies), close reading remains perhaps textual criticism's favoured tool. However, following F. R. Leavis, close reading often takes 'the text itself' as a fetishistic object of fascination, placing it in a vacuum, and raising it up to the status of a single ring of power. What is overlooked or denied by such an act is the crucial role of other entities – other rings – in constituting the text, in giving it power, and even in creating it. Media studies has therefore rightfully turned to many of the other rings – to reception, production, technology, political economy – to explain the status of a text. And while such work into synergy and convergence, for instance, has intricately illustrated the matrices of economic and commercial intertextuality into which many contemporary texts enter, still relatively little work examines the numerous ways in which many contemporary intertexts feedback into the very meaning, interpretation and understanding of the text. As such, in order to improve our understanding of contemporary textuality, of the DVD's 'effects' on it, and of the cultural entity that is the *Lord of the Rings* trilogy, this chapter will close read *The Two Towers* bonus material, examining how its multiple rings/discs *inhabit* the *Lord of the Rings* text, what power they hold over it, and how they add layers of meaning to the one text. In doing so, the chapter argues that the bonus material layers and enriches the quest narrative; it actively constructs an aura around the films that hearkens back to a pre-culture industries vision of art and, in doing so, creates a fantasy realm of cinematic production and reception into which producers, cast, crew and fans alike can enter.

DVD and text

Being one of the new media kids on the block, DVDs have yet to receive much academic examination, especially as regards their effects on the ontology and phenomenology of the text as perceived and received object. Thus, for instance, in Dan Harries' *The New Media Book* (2002), various authors study the DVD as it relates to intellectual property rights and piracy issues (Thomas 2002), myths of interactive cinema (Lunenfeld 2002), technological innovation (Friedberg 2002) and multimedia synergies (Caldwell 2002), but there is no dedicated discussion of the medium's effect on what the text is and on how it works. However, P. David Marshall offers the hint of a theory of DVD textuality, by studying new media's entrance and contribution to an intertextual matrix 'designed to encircle, entice and deepen the significance of the film for the audience' (2002: 69). Being on

Figure 6: The bonus material adds layers of meaning to the one text: Brothers Faramir and Boromir meet in the special edition of *The Two Towers* (Courtesy compleatseanbean.com)

one level a comment on the DVD's participation in contemporary inter-media networks of intertexts created so as to saturate the public sphere with ads for and references to a cultural product, Marshall's suggestion that DVDs might 'deepen the significance of the film' goes beyond the more common academic interest in how such intertexts deepen the pockets of the film's producers (see Englehardt 1986; McAllister 1996) to ask after depths of *meaning*. Certainly, intertextuality is never just about networking profits and capturing audiences; rather, it is also a powerful force of signification and semiotic creation (as seen by Barthes 1977; Kristeva 1980), making meaning as much as money.

Drawing on the dialogic theory of Mikhail Bakhtin, John Fiske (1989) has offered that intertextuality opens up a text, allowing it to be constructed and made sense of from outside its perceived borders, not just from inside, at the level of 'the text itself'. Similarly, numerous works in media studies examine how it is possible to create meaning *before* arriving at the text, to enter the cinema with dense intertextual matrices already activated. Martin Barker and Kate Brooks (1998), for example, illustrate how different viewing groups activated intertextual and extra-textual understandings of Sylvester Stallone, science fiction, action films or *2000 AD* comics to make sense of the *Judge Dredd* film (Danny Cannon, 1995). Bertha Chin and Jonathan Gray (2001) studied how, prior to the cinematic release of *The Fellowship of the Ring*, many Tolkien fans already had a firm sense of how they would react to the films; and Tony Bennett and Janet Woollacott (1987) observe that 'James Bond' accrues meaning across his various films, books and ads, to the point that any audience member of a newly-released Bond film has effectively begun decoding this new text and assigning meaning to it even before buying a ticket. As this latter example shows, though, these intertextual constructions work across time, modifying with each new text, advert or incarnation. What is more, there seems to be no statute of limitations of re-decoding, as evidenced by Annette Kuhn's work with elderly 'enduring fans' of 1930s films, who regularly watch favourite films as many as sixty years on, still finding and creating new meaning, as 'further layers of inter-textual and extra-textual memory-meaning continuously accrue' (1999: 145).

Fiske's version of intertextuality chaotically allows a seemingly 'anything goes' world of polysemy, whereby one can read *The Lord of the Rings* with the help of *Star Wars* (George Lucas, 1977) as much as with *Dog Day Afternoon* (Sydney Lumet, 1975), a move that, while feasible, focuses largely on intertextuality as an intensely individualistic process, never repeatable for another viewer. However, intertextuality contains within it not only these polysemic powers. Michael Riffaterre in particular has written of intertextuality as strictly *limiting* readings, taking the reader out of the text but to a definite and precise terminus, ensuring what he rather heavy-handedly calls 'proper interpretations' (1981: 227). Following on from Riffaterre, Gerard Genette (1997) notes that such regulatory intertextual relations often conglomerate around 'paratexts', textual shards that surround a text with the primary purpose of facilitating its discussion. Writing of books, Genette gives the examples of covers, prefaces, postscripts, reviews and interviews, but shifting to the screen, we could easily designate DVD bonus material as amassing its own paratextuality. Far from 'opening up' a text to endless meanings, though, this paratextuality is offered to viewers as a specific gateway for the text. If, as Henry Jenkins proposes (1992), we always create a 'metatext', or an idea of what a text is, means and does, paratexts such as DVDs can powerfully engage with and sway that metatext towards or away from certain areas. Acting like an 'airlock' to the text, as Genette proposes, paratexts can set the climate control for a reading or re-reading.

Ultimately and paradoxically, then, this airlock acts as more than an airlock, actually becoming *part of* the text, not solely a gatekeeper. After all, if a text is whatever we come to decode it as, any paratexts that can inflect that decoding hence enter the text proper. Will Brooker (2001) has helpfully offered the metaphor of textual 'overflow' to discuss the proliferation of texts into websites, clothing lines, fan discussion, CDs and the like, but again, paratexts stand to flow into their texts and not just serve as receptacles for outward flow. Meanwhile, Robert C. Allen arguably takes this process as more powerful than it is, reversing flow completely, by suggesting videos and paratextuality have overtaken, consumed and wholly become the primary text, leading to the 'last chapter of the history of Hollywood cinema and its audience' (1999: 128), as a film is now reduced to nothing more than 'the inedible part of a Happy Meal' (1999: 123). Certainly, we could all point to given instances when films appear little more than ads for their toys or computer games, but considerably more likely are the instances when text and paratext work together to create meaning across different fronts and media. It is with this in mind that media and film studies could pay more attention to paratexts and particularly DVDs and bonus materials, to see what meanings the producers are adding to the text, and, by extension, to see what role the DVD plays in actually constructing the text as meaningful object. Given the sheer density of the *Lord of the Rings* DVDs, their immense success, and the high level of public awareness of them, the *Two Towers* DVD is therefore an excellent site for us to study not only the paratextual/textual communion, but also a likely site of creation for many audiences of their (meta)texts.

Expanding the Fellowship

If *The Lord of the Rings* is an epic tale of an unlikely group of heroes who, through comradeship, resilience and compassion, manage to overcome the odds and triumph in the face of immense adversity, the *Two Towers* bonus material replicates the narrative continuously, superimposing it onto the cast, crew, director, Tolkien and New Zealand. Lending the production of the three films considerable more gravitas and mythic resonance, and following on from their work on *The Fellowship of the Rings* DVD, the DVD's producers paint a picture of multiple other fellowships, innocent and struggling hobbits, charismatic rangers and sage wizards. Most notably, the cast often transpose their filmic roles onto their own personage, or have the act performed by others. Thus, for instance, Orlando Bloom talks of how much of a privilege it was to come out of drama school and work with the likes of Ian McKellen, who, he notes, brought his 'wise old wizard' ways to the cast, becoming a real-life Gandalf of sorts. Likewise, numerous cast and crew members discuss Viggo Mortensen's charisma and leadership, as the stuntmen claim that his hard work and dedication on the gruelling Helm's Deep set inspired them; we learn of his personal pull in convincing cast and crew alike to camp out the night before a dawn shoot; he is talked of as an earthy, nature-loving man (a ranger); and Second Unit Director John Mahaffi even declares, 'If I was going into battle and I needed someone to be on my right shoulder, it would be Viggo.' Meanwhile, and most consistently, Dominic Monaghan and Billy Boyd provide much of the DVD's comic relief, clearly replicating their roles as the cheeky, prankster hobbits. In the cast commentary, they constantly toy with the film's register of reality, joking that one dreary, rocky scene looks just like Manchester, for instance, or that the Balrog never bought a round when at the pub with them; and they admit to frequently being confused for one another by crew members. Indeed, whereas most

Figure 7: Transposing filmic roles into commentary: Second Unit Director John Mahaffi declares: 'If I was going into battle and I needed someone to be on my right shoulder, it would be Viggo' (Copyright © New Line Cinema)

of the fifteen cast members contributing to the commentary were recorded individually, Monaghan and Boyd are recorded together, hence allowing their back and forth banter. Interestingly, too, while Elijah Wood and Sean Astin were recorded with them for the *Fellowship of the Ring* commentary, and similarly joked around as carefree hobbits, the *Two Towers* commentary separates them from Monaghan and Boyd (placing them with Gollum's interpreter Andy Serkis). Paralleling Frodo and Sam's path into darkness, their commentary takes on a slightly more pensive, sombre nature.

In the *Fellowship of the Ring* commentary, the cast repeatedly referred to the bond between themselves as their own 'Fellowship', and once again, the *Lord of the Rings* vocabulary is used and mirrored in the *Two Towers* DVD. Monaghan notes it was strange to be split up from the others for the filming of *The Two Towers*, an act which Wood describes as a 'literal breaking of the Fellowship'. Yet they and the DVD producers are at pains to describe how much of a complete team they were. Frustrations are downplayed, laughed away or (likely) cut, as instead we are offered the picture of a group who all respect each others' work incredibly, enjoyed and relished each other's company and are sad to be apart now. We are even told of a bizarre habit of headbutting one another that developed between the cast and stuntmen, and are shown footage of Mortensen and Sala Baker headbutting at a premier, hence suggesting an intimate, almost ritualistic shared bond between all. What is more, cast and crew remind us over and over again of the hard work and dedication that all gave to the project. Bloom, Mortensen and Brett Beattie suffered broken ligaments or bones and yet foraged on, we are told; Serkis braved a frozen river in only a lycra suit; many extras and cast worked countless nights under rain machines in damp prosthetics for the Helm's Deep scenes; Brad Dourif shaved his eyebrows off five times; and all faithfully returned to New Zealand months later for pickups. The bonus material, in other words, insists on the cast becoming their own Fellowship, united by compassion, respect and dedication, and determined to succeed in their own gruelling quest.

But the tale of The Little Hobbits Who Could plays out on multiple other levels, too, as Peter Jackson particularly is raised by all commentators to a peculiar amalgam of the sage Gandalf, the charismatic Aragorn, the bumbling Merry or Pippin, and the erstwhile Frodo. The DVD depicts a rather hobbit-like man with frizzy hair, no shoes and no film school training, whose childlike simplicity and honesty left him open to practical jokes (strategically placed weta beetles, or faked amputated fingers) or the odd tumble into a bog, and yet whose energy, enthusiasm, easygoing nature and mastery of vision successfully helmed one of cinema's boldest projects to completion. The design team, meanwhile, is given the role of the rag-tag group of hobbits, dwarves, elves and humans who make up the armies and foot soldiers who repel Sauron. Conceptual Designer John Howe, for instance, talks of how Weta Workshop Creative Supervisor Richard Taylor assembled a hardworking group who cared not for the fame, but who just loved the work and were dedicated to the cause. As one might imagine, much of the DVD bonus material studies the great feats of computer programming, set design, artwork, costuming, and so on that made *The Lord of the Rings* such a lavishly rich project, and we are often hit with remarkable numbers and information: Edoras took eight months to build for eight days of filming, only to be completely dismantled afterwards, while Helm's Deep's set creation was preceded by three months of moving concrete and rock alone. True to *The Lord of the Rings'* democratic interest in all the 'little' people who make up the grand front, the DVD introduces us to many of these crew members who contributed to making it all possible, as the entirety of the Fellowship is fleshed out. From groundskeeper to foley artists, we are shown how huge this Army of the Ring is. Anyone would do anything, so says the DVD repeatedly. As Wood enthusiastically declares, 'everyone put in everything they had' for the sake of the quest.

Throughout the documentaries, this multi-layering of quests is left not only to cast and crew discussion, though, as music from the trilogy's soundtrack is also cleverly used to embed and evoke certain themes. It is illustrative to focus briefly on the 'J.R.R. Tolkien: Origins of Middle Earth' documentary, to see how Howard Shore's compositions are employed to welcome Tolkien himself to this Fellowship, and to depict his act of writing the trilogy as its own grand quest against publishing norms, academic suspicion and other historical obstacles. The documentary begins by telling us of Tolkien's friendship with C. S. Lewis and their common commitment to a different mode of storytelling, and in the background, the soft, inspiring flute of Shore's Hobbit theme plays. Then we are told of these writers' shared experience of World War One, and as several stills of the war are shown, the harsh and throbbing warrior Uruk-Hai theme accompanies them. Later, after Brian Sibley grandiosely describes the completion of the trilogy and its delivery to the publisher as coming 'like lightning out of a clear sky', the trilogy's Fellowship theme, or quest music, cues in the background. This piece is again utilised when Jude Fisher describes how the one book was divided into three. Thus, at these four points, musical themes are used to underline, respectively, the camaraderie and nostalgic traditionalism of Lewis and Tolkien, the cruelty and terror of war, and, in the last two instances, the birth of a great epic. At the same time, though, the music serves to *equate* Tolkien's struggle to those of his characters, and in literal concert together, they parallel his very life to the trilogy's quest. As in countless other moments in the documentaries (as, for example, when any cast or crew tomfoolery is accompanied by the light and playful music from Shore's 'Concerning Hobbits'), the DVD producers propose that we view all manner of events and characters associated with the film production predominantly through diegetic *Lord of the Rings* glasses, superimposing Frodo and company's quest, travails and ultimate victory onto Tolkien, Jackson the cast and the crew.

Even New Zealand and its inhabitants are painted with a *Lord of the Rings* brush. As the title on one feature, 'New Zealand as Middle Earth', suggests, the DVD engages in a certain degree of conflation. Commentary track discussion often insists, for instance, 'that's really there' and New Zealand's landscape is imbued with all of the magic of Middle Earth by cast and crew alike, serving as a veritable if unofficial travel agent, and interrupted only by the few occasions when locations are revealed to be parking lot constructions or matte paintings. Meanwhile, from the notable presence of a local accent on many of the crew, combined with little information on their previous (if any) work; to the noted 'discovery' of a local acting talent, such as Karl Urban; to the use of cricket fans to record Uruk-Hai chanting for Sauron's Nuremberg-like rally; and to the relatively-unknown director himself, regional content in the DVD is often presented with considerable pride, almost with the suggestion of hobbit-like recluse in the world, mixed with remarkable resourcefulness. Finally, in the DVD's closing documentary, '"The Battle For Helm's Deep is Over..."', Philippa Boyens solidifies the link between the cast, crew, New Zealand and Middle Earth when she remarks that 'anytime you get back together with the cast and other crew, it's great and special ... especially in Wellington'. Boyens thus declares New Zealand as the rightful home of this magic alliance between cast, crew and diegetic world.

This multi-layering results in a formidable 'stacking' of the narrative of the film, so that in addition to being a tale of Frodo, Aragorn and Middle Earth, it is also the cast's quest, the crew's quest, Jackson's quest and New Zealand's quest.

Remembering that the *Two Towers* DVD was released prior to the cinematic release of *The Return of the King*, this stacking imbues the final chapter of the trilogy with significantly more meaning: no longer would we just be seeing Frodo's victory, but also the cast and crew's multi-year quest would come to an end, Jackson's quest would end, and New Zealand and a coded partly-local film would triumph in the almost Mordor-like world of Hollywood. Indeed, for many who have seen the *Fellowship of the Ring* or *The Two Towers* DVDs, *The Return of the King's* eventual Academy Award monopoly would seem only just and deserved, since the DVDs (and, it should be added, surrounding hype) added more levels and mythic resonance than any competitors could muster. Of course, individual viewers may choose not to care about the multiple quests, and may refuse to actualise the DVDs' proposed multi-layering, but the offers are tantalisingly calling to the viewer. If primed to accept, though, this is also due to the DVD's masterful act of bathing itself in aura.

The aura of the Ring

The multi-layering of the *Two Towers* text by the DVD bonus materials contributes to the steeping of the text in a significance and richness that tries to announce its difference from quotidian Hollywood fare. Indeed, taken as a whole, the bonus materials conduct a large-scale project to surround the text with aura. Of course, as Walter Benjamin famously declared, the age of mechanical reproduction supposedly killed aura (1969). However, the *Two Towers* DVD hearkens back to an age of aura. Housed in an attractive high-quality box, the discs are filled with explicit and implicit grabs at the title of Work of Art. Certainly, the sheer volume of information, explanation, interpretation and extra footage suggests an excess of artistry from the cinematic release, as if there was too much to fit into a mere three hours. As such, for example, in the commentary track, Wood explains how much time and work was put into one scene, and yet, 'as our luck always is ... it didn't end up in the theatrical edition'. At other points in the cast commentary, actors express delight and excitement at seeing a scene returned to the text, often expostulating at length the virtues of the scene. They also occasionally discuss the rewards of seeing certain (uncut) scenes in the theatre, separating themselves and their involvement with the film to marvel at its artistry. Meanwhile, the cast and crew alike positively gush with praise for one another's performances and work. John Rhys Davies speaks generally of how excited everyone was to watch one another on set, while Dourif and Bernard Hill, for instance, express amazement at Miranda Otto's concentration, and Wood tells Serkis, 'You're an absolute blessing to that character [Gollum],' continuing that 'It's just, uh, it's a marvel, Andy.' Similarly, the design team is credited with inspiring many a scene, especially through Howe's artwork, Serkis throws praise towards Fran Walsh's writing and directing, Wood expresses awe at the miniature work, and many of the design and effects documentaries are interspersed with testimonials from the cast on how remarkable the work was.

Beyond merely telling us how great the work was, though, in an entertaining if exhaustive manner, the galleries and documentaries *show* us how superb a job everyone did. Revealing painstaking attention to detail in every portion of the film, and the immense amount of work put into getting any one element 'right' for example, the galleries present literally hundreds of stills of sculptures, paintings, sketches, and so on, many with accompanying genealogies by their artists. While allowing the viewer to effectively slow down the film to study its minutiae, these galleries become televised versions of museums or art galleries with audio tours, rendering not only the individual works as gallery-*worthy* art, but, by extension, the entire film as well. At the same time, the documentaries include film of all of the artists at work, and information on the technologies and artwork, how they work, and how the crew revolutionised the forms. Indeed, the DVD teaches a significant amount of production literacy, familiarising audiences with the vocabulary of pickups, foley work, mime passes, second units, matte painting and key frames, even while creating new language, such as Big-atures. Much as an art gallery's audio tour or an art history class may, then, the DVD works to give us the information and to teach the appreciation for the very work that it shows us. It also aims to impress with tales of individual artists' creation values. Thus, Howe in particular is depicted as a lifelong Tolkien fan dedicated to getting everything as right, as detailed and as realistic to Middle Earth as possible, whether this meant working from archaeological finds from Sutton Hoo to closely approximate a suitably Tolkienesque culture, or placing the stables at the top of Edoras to reflect Rohan's love of horses. Howe recounts that the cast joked that the only way to stop him would be to break his fingers. Yet, here, his tireless dedication to his art is by no means uncommon, as the DVD also tells us of the groundskeeper's circulation of a memo, 'Rules About Trees', to the Fangorn creation team; Hill discusses the process of determining what sort of shoes Theoden would wear; and the stuntmen describe how Helm's Deep's door was at first built so well that they were unable to ram it.

Interestingly, and almost surprisingly, though, for all the big budget effects that in many ways characterise the film, neither the documentaries nor the commentaries paint the film as primarily an effects bonanza. Rather, the primacy of 'the story' and 'the way Tolkien wrote it' are often held up as central, and frequently with a flourish of the Fellowship theme underscoring the sentiment. As described above, the DVD likens the movie to Frodo's quest, and given the nostalgic simple English countryside ethos this valorises, especially in the face of Sauron and his dark post-industrial world ethos, the cast and crew often highlight the human's presence in, and placement above, the film's effects. The Gollum documentaries and discussion, for instance, talk at length of how all the computers and programs at Weta could not bring life to the character (or to his opposites in scenes) until Serkis arrived. Similarly, we are frequently told of how 'simple' and more 'natural' answers were used for design dilemmas instead of technical, CGI ones. And, of course, the aforementioned Fellowship narrative of cast and crew working together as one for three years suggests its own adherence to an 'older, better' way of doing things. In other words, with hobbit music in hand, the DVD depicts *The Two Towers* as an organic project, natural in all possible ways, and very human. This too, then, contributes to setting it apart from other Hollywood films (as does its very location of filming), and to its obvious desire to be seen as Art in the pre-mechanical/digital sense.

As part and parcel of this construction of, or insistence upon, aura, the DVD is keen to offer us an Author. To a certain degree, it actually offers two, as Tolkien and his intentions are used as a mantra of sorts. All cast and crew pledge enormous fealty to Tolkien and his wishes, as Christopher Lee and Sean Astin particularly talk of wanting to capture specific scenes' Tolkienesque essence, and all diversions from Tolkien's text are met with apologia, in which it is usually explained that the diversion was either necessary, or designed to remain true to the 'spirit' of the books. Beyond Tolkien, though, Jackson is lionised as a true director. Most cast and crew at some time or another glow about how he kept 'his own vision' throughout, as Elijah Wood states. We are shown and told how Jackson would retain last say on seemingly everything, checking in on second units or post-production via phone or satellite; acting as final judge on all artwork, prosthetics, costuming, and so on; and managing time to discuss decisions with all cast and crew. Bernard Hill also tells of how for one scene he doubted Jackson's direction, and yet was deeply impressed by the final product. Jackson is shown to be a democratic director who listened to and valued the opinions, ideas and creativity of all, and we even hear this in commentaries, as multiple individuals are given the chance to present their own interpretations of characters and scenes. As for his intentions, we are often offered them, itself a powerful sign of the DVD's (and of many DVDs') adherence to a pre-Death of the Author world. Moreover, Jackson's stated intentions are all artistic, as neither he nor others (even the producers) violate this claim to Authority by framing him as a man with a set 'job' in yet another product of the money-seeking culture industries. Likewise, the DVD bonus material is happy and keen to make the film Jackson's, not New Line's or Time Warner's.

Once again, then, the DVD engages in a nostalgic layering of the text, whereby even its production process claims to draw upon a golden age of artistic creation. Pushing against the studio, for instance, the DVD includes several moments when Jackson or others describe battles between New Line's narrow-mindedness and interferences and Jackson's bold vision, such as when Jackson says of New Line's early desire to have less of Gollum, 'it's tough to deal with that, really, because they don't quite have the imagination or vision of what's going to be there that we do, so you just have to ignore it simply'. Meanwhile, the very act of including extra scenes, and the general happiness with which they are welcomed back by the cast and crew in the commentaries implies a dissatisfaction with the way New Line 'made' Jackson cut the film. Many of the additional or extended scenes are from the books, too, and so the DVD not only allows Jackson as Author to overcome the studio/Hollywood system's desires, but seemingly allows Tolkien as Author more presence as well. Characters that were missing from the theatrical version rejoin the film, scenes return and Jackson and Lee's Tolkien scholarship is offered in commentaries to fill in gaps with Middle Earth lore and legend. In many ways, the DVD suggests that, as good as the theatrical version may have been, the DVD offers the Real Work of Art as ordained by Jackson and Tolkien. Certainly, *The Two Towers* was in a unique position in film history, seeing that the *Fellowship of the Ring* DVD had conditioned viewers to know that the Real, full-length, Author's version of *The Two Towers* was to be found on the DVD, not in the cinematic release. One might also note that this division of textuality is in keeping with the nostalgic picture of artistic creation that the DVD revels in, for whereas a cinematic release is a true event and experience (Barker & Brooks 1998), the DVD allows personal *ownership* of the text. Much as an art collector could hang an acquisition in his or her own living room, the DVD better suits this image of austere art in allowing the freedom to see it wherever its 'owner' would like.

The return to celluloid Hobbiton

We could be amply justified if we regarded this manoeuvre of conjuring aura cynically, seeing in it and the multi-layerings of the text a deft yet sly move of the culture industries. After all, with very few exceptions, film budgets and big-bucks Hollywood visual extravaganza comes no bigger than *The Lord of the Rings*. Peter Jackson may have been a reasonably unknown director handed a huge and daring project, but he was hardly forced to produce it as he did his first picture, *Bad Taste* (1987), baking effects in his parents' oven and starring in it with friends to deal with a tiny budget. *The Lord of the Rings* fits comfortably in a reasonably long line of effects-driven blockbusters with big-name actors and the full force of one of the world's richest industries firmly behind it. Thus, to coyly pretend that it is a film from yesteryear, and an old-style artistic work, aligning itself with the simplicity and wholesomeness of Hobbiton and Frodo Baggins seems a rather garish ploy to efface its production history, and, pre-eminently, to act as that which it is not. From a marketing standpoint, this is a coup: with the *Two Towers* DVD acting simultaneously upon release as an ad for the then-upcoming *The Return of the King*, it offers the viewer multiple sentimental and nostalgic reasons to 'support' it and its supposedly humble quest by going to the cinema, maybe even multiple times. Likewise, in this day of multi-media synergy, every part or incarnation of a text can be used to advertise another and to invest it with meaning, and so the DVD offers a general semiotic schema suggesting that *The Lord of the Rings* represents a return to Real and Authentic Art, and respect for the craft as it was meant to be practiced – a reading its marketers no doubt hoped would attach itself to all *The Lord of the Rings* products, from film to toys to posters to Burger King meals. On one level, then, the DVD fully illustrates how networks of intertextuality and paratextuality can be employed by multi-media corporations to brand their products and increase the salience and depth of their meanings across the synergistic spectrum. Doubtlessly, studio executives have discovered of late the powers that DVDs hold.

Nevertheless, to chalk up the *Lord of the Rings* DVDs as solely marketing tools or ammunition would be to crudely posit multi-media corporations as Sauron-like all-seeing eyes calling to their directors, cast, crew and viewers as the Palantir to Pippin, or the ring of power to Frodo. Thus, while this level of analysis tells part of our tale, it does not tell it all. Rather, we must also recognise the utility and *attraction* of the *Two Towers* DVD's artistic creation myth to the creative personnel and to the viewers. After all, if *The Lord of the Rings* risks being just another Hollywood item fresh off the conveyor belt, not only does the studio want us to believe it is truly extraordinary in standing above and beyond other films, but the entire crew would surely also like to believe that they are involved in something special, and the audience that they are more than the supposedly average, spectacle-awed, brainless bread-and-circuses crowd. Certainly, the DVD often plays with notions of different audiences and posits its own audience as a more knowing, savvy, aesthetically atuned and sensible lot. At multiple points in the commentaries, cast or crew refer to being aware of Tolkien fans' high standards, but never shirk these off, instead speaking of them with great respect. Thus, Sean Astin, for instance, recounts how important it was for him to capture Sam's reaction to seeing oliphants after reading a fan letter that spoke of how much meaning that scene in the book had to the writer. Even the inclusion of Jackson's extended explanations of why he cut certain scenes from the books belie the assumption that DVD watchers will be aware of their exclusion; and the insistence on how much attention to detail went into the project, along with the declarations and 'outings' of Tolkien fandom amongst the cast and crew, could be read as presentation of credentials to Tolkien fans and discerning cinephiles.

Conclusion

The last and arguably most important Fellowship is forged as the cast and crew ally themselves with the viewers, setting themselves against other filmmakers and audiences (including some theatrical version audiences) as members of a small, elite band. Frequently, the DVD shares intimate 'secrets' of the filming and similarly shares jokes, pranks and gossip from the set, so that, for example, we learn that John Howe would sword-fight other designers at lunch, that Viggo Mortensen fell for a beard-wearing stunt-woman, and we see most of the cast and crew playing around in the various documentaries. Hence, the DVD welcomes us as viewers into the Fellowship, even to the point of adding a final track to the credits that lists all *The Lord of the Rings* official fan-club members. The DVD, as such, fosters an intimate bond between cast, crew and audience, one that combines with its construction of the film as Work of Art, and with its construction of the DVD audience as discerning and requiring Art aficionados, ultimately cloaking the entire circuit of production, text and consumption in an aura of artistry and excellence. In effect, the DVD allows an elaborate role play for director, cast, crew and audience that they are transporting themselves back in time to an age of true art, pre-mechanical or digital reproduction, and thus pre-loss of aura ... or better yet, that this age has been recovered.

It would be easy to see this role play as a ruse, ironically befitting its fantasy text's genre. We should be no means underplay or underestimate the political economic ramifications of such DVD branding, nor should we forget the industry's control over the rings of power that are the *Lord of the Rings* DVDs. However, this role play also shows us the degree to which both aura and Author are not necessarily dead. Granted, as Walter Benjamin (1969) and Roland Barthes (1977) have detailed, aura and Author have changed. But perhaps in a digital era, and curiously under the rubric of new media, we are witnessing an earnest struggle to create a new variety of aura and author, and to return to older models of creation and viewership. Meanwhile, with the DVD playing, or *attempting* to play, a decisive role in influencing and/or determining the meanings of a text and the relationships between its cast, crew and audience, we should recognise the power of new media 'extensions' such as DVDs to write back to the text and play a primary role in the creation of sense and meaning. This process is all the more evident in cases such as *The Lord of the Rings*, where the *Two Towers* DVD was released prior to *The Return of the King*'s theatrical release, hence contributing to an ongoing and active diegesis, but since any text is always potentially open for re-decodings and new meanings, we need not have a trilogy for DVDs to become a vital part of the text. In this chapter, I have illustrated how the *Two Towers* DVD layers the text, so that *The Lord of the Rings* is an even more epic tale, but other close readings of the same DVD could well reveal further and equally rich meanings. In studying texts, it becomes an open trap for us to examine 'the text itself', its political economy and its audiences alone. This chapter, though, has shown how there are other rings of power, and while in the world of Middle Earth one ring can rule them all, in today's media environment, these other rings – or paratexts – can control the one ring of the text itself, and can guide the ring, creator and wearer group of text, producer and audience.

Works cited

Allen, R. C. (1999) 'Home Alone Together: Hollywood and the "Family Film"', in M. Stokes and R. Maltby (eds) *Identifying Hollywood's Audiences: Cultural Identity and the Movies*. London: British Film Institute, 109–31.

Barker, M. and K. Brooks (1998) *Knowing Audiences: Judge Dredd, its Friends, Fans and Foes*. Luton: University of Luton Press.

Barthes, R. (1977) *Image/music/text*, trans. S. Heath. Glasgow: Fontana-Collins.

Benjamin, W. (1969) 'The Work of Art in the Age of Mechanical Reproduction', in *Illuminations*. New York: Schocken Books, 217–51.

Bennett, T. and J. Woollacott (1987) *Bond and Beyond: The Political Career of a Popular Hero*. London: Macmillan.

Brooker, W. (2001) 'Living on *Dawson's Creek*: Teen Viewers, Cultural Convergence, and Television Overflow', *International Journal of Cultural Studies*, 4, 4, 456–72.

Caldwell, J. (2002) 'The Business of New Media', in. D. Harries (ed.) *The New Media Book*. London: British Film Institute, 55–68.

Chin, B. and J. Gray (2001) '"One Ring to Rule Them All': Pre-viewers and Pre-texts of the *Lord of the Rings* Films', *Intensities: The Journal of Cult Studies*, 2, Online. Available at http://www.cult-media.com/issue2/Achingray.htm (accessed 03 June 2005).

Englehardt, T. (1986) 'The Strawberry Shortcake Strategy', in T. Gitlin (ed.) *Watching Television*. New York: Pantheon, 68–110.

Fiske, J. (1989) 'Moments of Television: Neither the Text nor the Audience', in E. Seiter, H. Borchers, G. Kreutzner and E. Warth (eds) *Remote Control: Television, Audiences, and Cultural Power*. London: Routledge, 56–78.

Friedberg, A. (2002) 'CD and DVD', in. D. Harries (ed.) *The New Media Book*. London: British Film Institute, 30–9.

Genette, G. (1997) *Paratexts: Thresholds of Interpretation*. Cambridge: Cambridge University Press.

Harries, D. (ed.) (2002) *The New Media Book*. London: British Film Institute.

Jenkins, H. (1992) *Textual Poachers: Television Fans and Participatory Culture*. London: Routledge.

Kristeva, J. (1980) *Desire in Language: A Semiotic Approach to Literature and Art*. Oxford: Basil Blackwell.

Kuhn, A. (1999) '"That day *did* last me all my life": Cinema Memory and Enduring Fandom', in M. Stokes and R. Maltby (eds) *Identifying Hollywood's Audiences: Cultural Identity and the Movies*. London: British Film Institute, 135–46.

Lunenfeld, P. (2002) 'The Myths of Interactive Cinema', in. D. Harries (ed.) *The New Media Book*. London: British Film Institute, 144–54.

Marshall, P. D. (2002) 'The New Intertextual Commodity', in. D. Harries (ed.) *The New Media Book*. London: British Film Institute, 69–81.

McAllister, M. (1996) *The Commercialization of American Culture: New Advertising,*

Control, and Democracy. Thousand Oaks: Sage.

Riffaterre, M. (1981) 'Interpretation and Undecidability', *New Literary History*, 12, 227–42.

Snider, M. (2003) 'Theater releases boost DVD sales', *USA Today*, 26 December. Online. Available at http://www.usatoday.com/life/movies/news (accessed 30 August 2004).

Thomas, D. (2002) 'Innovation, Piracy and the Ethos of New Media', in. D. Harries (ed.) *The New Media Book*. London: British Film Institute, 82–91.

Playing the Ring: Intermediality and Ludic Narratives in the *Lord of the Rings* Games

Jon Dovey and Helen W. Kennedy

Introduction: Computer Game Studies

This chapter evolved from the study of computer games. It is informed specifically by observations and conversations made during a research workshop which we ran in February 2004 in which we compared the experiences of playing a *Lord of the Rings* board game, a *Lord of the Rings* computer game and watching a *Lord of the Rings* film.

The research project was originally designed as a way of investigating the conflicting conceptual frameworks being disputed between what were described as 'narratologists' and 'ludologists' in the burgeoning field of Computer Game Studies. The difference between these approaches has had sufficient force for James Newman to describe it as a major 'schism' (2004: 91; see also Eskelinen 2004, Moulthrop 2004 and Jenkins 2004 for summaries of the major positions). This debate represents a significant 'fault line' in our initial mappings of digital culture. Scholars from existing disciplines of film and media studies have brought concerns about narrative, representation, meaning and ideology to the study of the computer game. However, ludologists, drawing on psychology, game theory, human/computer interface design and cybertheory, have argued that a computer game is not a conventional text at all, but an activity more akin to play or sport. Their methodological innovation has focused on attempts to understand the formal characteristics and specificities of computer games. Within the ludological approach the conventional tools of textual analysis are seen as inappropriate when the dominant experience of the computer game player will be determined not by its narrative, fictional context or storyworld, but by its rules. So for instance we find and Espen Aarseth, Solveig Marie Smedstad and Lise Sunnana (2003), Aki Jarvinen (2003) and Jesper Juul (2003) all concentrate on the structural rule base of games in competing attempts to create a typology that will account for our experience of game play. It was our view that neither narratological nor ludological approaches accounted sufficiently for players' actual experiences. In a reformulation of an old problem for Cultural and Media Studies the embodied subject was elided in academic turf wars which concentrated on textual structure as a way of explaining experience. We wanted to investigate directly the relationships between our *experience* of 'story' and 'rules' across different media platforms and activities.

Our concentration upon experience *across* different platforms has in turn led us to consider how the relative engagements with 'rules' or 'story' function within conditions of intermediality. By intermediality we refer to the contemporary market-driven form of intertextuality in which texts and activities may refer to the same fictional 'world' despite presenting themselves as different media (Lehtonen 2001). Our focus therefore is not primarily upon the film texts of Peter Jackson's trilogy, the specificity of the film text here becomes absorbed into a web of different but interrelated engagements with the *Lord of the Rings* 'storyworld'. Despite this the films continue to exert a very powerful presence at the centre of this web of engagements; only one of the eight young people in our research project had ever read Tolkien's novel, for the others their primary point of contact with the *Lord of the Rings* storyworld was through the films or film-related advertising, products, reviews or discussions.

The Lord of the Rings and computer game cultures

We begin with a note on the particular resonances set up by studying computer game forms through a *Lord of the Rings* case study. *The Lord of the Rings* has played a key role in the development of computer games, both in designers' adaptation of its topographical narrative structures as well as in its huge influence on the individual cultural tastes of many game designers. Many senior game industry figures found their predispositions toward games and complex controllable systems were originally satisfied by paper and tabletop role play gaming usually in the form of the *Dungeons and Dragons* format: 'It is almost impossible to overstate the role of *Dungeons and Dragons* in the rise of computer gaming, even if the game itself was originally all pen, paper, dice and notebooks' (King & Borland 2003: 4). In turn the *Dungeons and Dragons* 'worlds' were heavily influenced by Tolkien's writings. The narrative structure of Tolkien's work is deeply embedded in the intensely imagined topography of Middle Earth. The story content is based upon epic journeys in which challenges are met and overcome; the recent cinema adaptations expose this topographic narrative in all its simplicity. An engagement with highly realised topographic worlds is characteristic of Role Play Game worlds and especially of their online adaptations in the Multi-User Domains (or Dungeons), and now in the 'persistent worlds' of the Massive Multiplayer Online Role Play Games such as *EverQuest* (Sony Online 1999). This culturally determined attachment to the topography of imaginary worlds can be found deep at work in the design and manufacture of computer games to this day. A game level is designed through the twofold documentation of text and map. The text describes the ideal player's progress through the level, the map visualises the level. The map is highly realised in terms of topography, features and enemy spawn points (places in the level where enemies are regenerated by the code of the game engine). This map then becomes the basic building block of the level, it is scanned and becomes the first blueprint from which artists and programmers actually build the level in paint and render programmes.

The common root in fantasy role play is a dominant narrative with two immediate outcomes for computer game cultures. The first is the movement from a predisposition towards a gaming sensibility that is 'trained' in the mathematics of game mechanics through the operations of paper, pen and dice. Mathematically calculated game mechanics based in sprawling rule books were perfectly adaptable to the algorithms of computer programs.

The second outcome of a common taste for fantasy role play is the continuing appeal of 'sword and sorcery' imaginary worlds in computer game content. Computer games turned initially, and with continuing appeal, to the archaic fantasies of the *Dungeons and Dragons* world.

Intermediality and economics

In the contemporary moment of intermediality all media texts have a tendency to bleed into one another, and distinctive media borders and definitions begin to break down. This intermediality is not merely a technological given driven by digitisation, it also concerns the social practice of a medium. Film narrative for instance, once experientially confined to a large darkened auditorium, now leaks out of its institutional setting via laptops, DVDs, mobile phones, the internet and so on (Grusin 2002). Media texts of all kinds work in increasingly close symbiotic relationships with other media texts – *The Lord of the Rings* exists as novel, board game, films, several computer games, online trailers, DVDs with new material and new ways of navigating/experiencing the film, plus a range of war gaming toys and other merchandise. (This before we even begin to consider fan production as alternative points of entry to the *Lord of the Rings* storyworld.) The world of the film/book is 'remediated' in other platforms. In this sense, the blockbuster-franchised computer game has to be understood as representing a logic of remediation in which texts are repurposed in other media technologies to build storyworlds with multiple points of access. As the points of entry to these storyworlds proliferate so the relative strength or weakness of narrative form alters; the narrative experience of reading *The Lord of the Rings* as novel, watching a DVD on your laptop on a train, or playing a computer game, will be different in each case. The single text of book or film is replaced by a commonly-branded storyworld with a number of different platform-specific points of entry.

Other commentators have also drawn attention to the imperatives of political economy driving intermediality. Henry Jenkins for instance identifies intermediality as one of the key characteristics of emerging new media landscapes; there are, he argues, powerful 'economic trends encouraging the flow of images, ideas and narratives across multiple media channels and demanding more active modes of spectatorship' (2002) He suggests that these trends are altering 'the way media consumers relate to each other, to media texts, and to media producers' (ibid.). In these conditions storyworlds become franchises – quoting the total revenue attributed to *Star Wars* products *The Observer* newspaper claimed, 'If *Star Wars* was a country, its $20bn would place it 70th in the World Bank's rankings of countries according to gross domestic product' (Smith 2005). The computer games console market has become a leader of intermedial blockbuster promotion for particular economic reasons. Competition within the market has increased faster than its overall expansion. In 2001 there were 270 games available for the three main consoles (Playstation, Xbox and Nintendo). This figure jumped to 750 in 2002 (Anon. 2003a: 8). It has been estimated that whilst development costs have doubled sales have only increased by 50% (Anon. 2003b: 8). Therefore developers now look to publishers to bear the risk of production investment and publishers find themselves minimising risk by opting for titles with a proven track record, thus reducing the space for innovation (see DTI/Spectrum Consultants 2002). Consolidation has been driven by the games publishing sector, where it is estimated that the top ten publishers internationally control 65% of the marketplace (ELSPA 2003: 7). The publisher-led consolidation of market sales has occurred through 'blockbuster' titles which often derive from film licensing deals such as Electronic Arts' hugely popular *Harry Potter* and *Lord of the Rings* titles. Electronic Arts Games, the publishers of the *Lord of the Rings* computer games, are by far the most dominant publisher in the global games market.

The intermedial text

The *Return of the King* (Electronic Arts 2003) console game has significant markers of intermediality within the 'text' itself. Obviously the game invites the player into Tolkien's fantasy world through its design, packaging and *mise-en-scène*. The introductory notes claim, 'In this final chapter of *The Lord of the Rings* the fate of Middle Earth is in your hands'. The game is structured through fifteen levels which represent the narrative timescale of the *Return of the King* film; each level notionally represents an episode in one of the film's three journey narratives. For instance a single player enters the story as Gandalf arriving at the critical moment at Helm's Deep, but in co-operative mode the players begin as Aragorn, Gimli or Legolas on the Paths of the Dead through the mountain, and are required to defeat the King of the Dead before progressing. The remainder of the game levels are divided between The Path of the King, The Southern Gate through the Black Gate, Pelennor Fields to Mordor's Crack of Doom. At different levels the player may chose to play as key members of the fellowship, namely Gandalf, Aragorn, Legolas, Gimli, Frodo or Sam. The game genre is action-adventure, 'hack 'n' slash', with the gameplay emphasis on navigation and enemy slaying – each character has different fighting characteristics which can be amended through the use of experience points accumulated through fighting. Players are required to remember and to master particular control combinations in order to dispatch the endlessly respawning followers of Sauron in the shape of ghosts, orcs and so on.

This series of computer games goes to great lengths to emphasise its relationship with its cinematic forbear. Levels in a computer game often begin with a 'cut scene', a short full-motion video non-playable sequence which sets the scene for the subsequent gameplay. In the *Return of the King* game these cut scenes are re-edited sequences from the original movie; cut and narrated like cinema trailers they offer a powerful evocation of the cinematic spectacle of the film. Compared to the cut scenes in other action-adventure computer games these sequences are long and very lavish. On first and second encounter they are genuinely forceful in offering the player an anticipatory sense of *participation* in the cinematic spectacle.

Enormous care has been taken in the cut sequences to make the move from non-playable to playable sequence almost invisible. The designers have elected to dissolve from cinema image to graphic render in the 'smoothest' ways possible so that the player has the sense of suddenly finding oneself *in* the scene as the avatar becomes playable. The dissolve from film image to graphic-rendered image is often made on sweeping camera moves thus disguising itself in the dynamic of the changing screen space. The original film dialogue or narration also continues *over* the transition, thus further reinforcing a sense of flow *into* the game space. Once in playable mode the avatars have lines from their film dialogue mixed into the game soundtrack. The flow of the gameplay itself is often disrupted by the designers' insistence on our participation in the cinematic storyworld. The graphic action often dissolves back out to the cinematic image for a few moments for a character to comment as the game moves us on to another location. Virtual camera angles too have been designed with cinematic point of view rather than gameplay fluency in mind. The convention of most avatar control in third-person computer games has been that we push the avatar away from us with the console controller as we navigate the game environment. Here, however, we are often required to reverse this procedure, 'pulling' the avatar towards us and the virtual camera lens in ways that insist on the game's remediation of the film rather than ease of gameplay.

The *Lord of the Rings* board game, designed by Reiner Knizia and released by Hasbro in 2000, offers a different set of readings into intermediality. Here the emphasis is not on cinema/gameplay remediation but on the ways in which the narrative structure of the novel can be adapted as an agonistic game structure. The narrative themes of the novel are retained but refashioned as probability, so that the players pit themselves against odds encoded within the game structure. Knizia's game design solutions offer useful insights into the relationships between narrative and rule structures. His aim, he claimed, 'was to stay within the spirit of the book so that the players would experience something similar to the readers of the book' (2004: 22). One of his original decisions was to have the players com pete not against each other but against the game system itself, with the necessity of deep co-operation and self-sacrifice built into the structure. In the board game we play as a team of up to five hobbits. The overall game state is controlled by a summary board containing a 'corruption line', which begins with a Sauron figure at one end and the hobbits at the other. As the events of the game unfold hob-bits and Sauron move closer to one another, hobbits die if they land on the same square as Sauron: 'So over the course of the game the players would gradually slip toward the dark, creating a sense of claustrophobia and impending doom – just as in the book (Knizia 2004: 24). If the ring-bearer hobbit dies the game is over. Players therefore have to 'look after' the ring-bearer keeping him as far away from Sauron as possible. The game progresses through four scenario boards, each based (like the computer game) on one of the locations in the book; in this case Moria, Helm's Deep, Shelob's Lair and Mordor. Each of the four scenario boards contain four paths which the players represented by board tokens have to complete. One of these is an 'events path' that instructs the players on the consequences of various events over which they have no control – thus the game reflects Knizia's percep-tion that 'Tolkien's hobbits were rarely in control of their situation' (ibid.). At any one point in the game players are monitoring five different game pathways thus reflecting the multi-stranded journey structure of the novel. However, as each path also has its own array of resources and threats their interplay creates the effect of putting the player in a complex dynamic simulation with many possible emergent states. This structure, together with the array of card- and token-based resource management of the game, ensures that the process is extremely collaborative with a great deal of negotiating around strategic planning.

Play as research

In order to further investigate these phenomena and the shifting status of narrative which they represent we set up a small study in which we recruited eight young people between the ages of 12 and 16 as our co-investigators. Because we have also been interested in researching differently-gendered game play we set up an all-female and all-male group. The participants were chosen on the basis of existing familial and social networks; in the case of all but two of the young women they had met before. Each team met for a day in a private house, with comfortable seating, plenty of snacks and food laid on in an effort to create as social an atmosphere as possible. We began by playing the Reiner Knizia/Hasbro board game which required full group participation, a great deal of concentration and collaboration – having this game as the first activity of each day worked extremely well as an icebreaker for each of the groups. All then played the *Lord of the Rings: Return of the King* Xbox computer game, and then finally watched the *Lord of the Rings: The Two Towers* DVD. We made video tape recordings of each day's play and viewing, as well as using a questionnaire to establish some background on the participants. We also conducted hour-long interviews with each of the participants at the end of each day. Obviously, we as researchers played a significant role in framing the event through the kinds of questions we asked and concerns we voiced both in recruiting our participants and in our interactions over the two days. This framing of the event and the activities undertaken should not diminish the role that the participants had as our collaborators in working through the issues arising from the competing claims of gameplay and narrative in intermedial experience. The rich and often contradictory discourse which emerged through our observations and conversations with the participants offers some fruitful ways of re-conceptualising some of the leading theoretical positions in the debate.

Take JH, for instance, a 15-year-old boy. He said in relation to story in the computer game:

JH: Well in the computer game it [story] wasn't necessarily important 'cause I didn't like the computer game that much, I was a tad … just a tiny bit bored.'

Later when we return to the same topic his position appears to have shifted:

Q: So what did the story of Lord of the Rings add to the computer game? If the rules and the form of game play was exactly the same what does having the Lord of the Rings story there add to it?
JH: Well it's such a good story and it's such an amazing film they've made, I think it just makes you want to do what the film does or what the books do, so you wanna get to the end and destroy the ring or use your special powers…

On one hand the story in the computer game is not that important, on the other 'it's such an amazing film they've made it just makes you want to do what the film does'. In fact, in the film-viewing session JH identified himself through his behaviour as an 'expert viewer', explaining parts of the story, special effects and DVD features to the rest of us, suggesting a high level of investment in New Line's cinematic *Lord of the Rings*. The contradiction here seems to us significant, expressing something of the slippage involved in intermedial experience; at the level of computer gameplay Tolkien's story is irrelevant; yet it somehow, in a more general way, informs our pleasurable anticipation and consumption of the product. A 16-year-old female participant, EA, shared some of the same vague sense of gameplay enhancement:

> In the video game I don't think you do need it [the story] but like it's always fun when you know where they are and if you know what you're doing 'cause if you've seen it in the film it's kind of better to know ... what you're doing and where you're going and what you're heading to, 'cause that's the aim of those kind of games to get to the end.

JS, a 13-year-old male participant and expert gamer reinforces the point that narrative in a computer game becomes more meaningful on completion than it does in gameplay:

> On one level it doesn't have much effect but completing the game and doing all the levels one after the other makes the storyline, makes it better. Well it's just like ... if you've got like one chunk of something it doesn't really mean much, something just happens, but all together they make up a whole story and that story interests you in the whole game.

This comforting sense of a storyworld 'wraparound' for the gameplay experience has been well expressed in Henry Jenkins' idea of 'evocative narrative', as a feature of what he argues is 'narrative architecture' in computer games: 'In the case of evoked narratives spatial design can either enhance our sense of immersion within a familiar world or communicate a fresh perspective on that story through the altering of established details (2004: 129). His sense of 'evocation' is palpable in this response from MD, a 15-year-old male research participant:

> *Q: What did it [the LotR story] add? Did it bring anything?*
> MD: Well the stuff like choosing the characters and stuff. It brought huge realism and imagination, like it provoked your imagination because you're there because you've seen the film and stuff, you feel like you're part of it which is what it added.

MD's remark about film knowledge influencing avatar choice was widely shared in our conversations with the participants, though again with a good deal of contradiction. HL, a 16-year-old female participant, actually summed up a classic ludological position about characters in computer games: 'It's not characters it's what they do.'

In a ludological approach to computer games character becomes capability – what can this avatar do that another cannot? How will this avatar serve me at this level of a game? Does this avatar have the right combination of weapons and moves to allow me to progress through the game? James Newman argues that the in-game character is in fact just a piece of game equipment, 'a set of capabilities, techniques and capacities that the player can utilise'. (2004: 143) However, most of the other participants felt that varying aspects of their relationships with the game avatars were being 'intermediated'. For instance, 16-year-old female participant JeS:

Yes. I think so because your knowledge of them, from the film so say you had a favourite character in the film you'd then want to play that person in the video game because that's how you would think of them.

MD shared this perception:

You got all the stuff to do with the characters and why you chose the character because you like that one from the film and what they do and what you've seen.

In fact in the computer gameplay we observed when offered a choice of playing as Legolas, Aragorn or Gimli only the first two were ever chosen, despite the fact that Gimli's axe-wielding capabilities are just as effective as the swordplay of Aragorn or the bowmanship of Legolas. In fact, especially amongst the boys, the Gimli avatar often became the object of humour ('Where's the little fat guy?') in ways that more or less directly echo his character construction in the films. Here, then, the participants' common knowledge of the films can be seen as directly influencing the way they enter into the computer game as well as being part of their in-game conversational exchanges.

On the other hand, whilst knowledge of the film clearly provides important 'contextual' orientation toward the computer game, we found just as much evidence that in the moment by moment experience of the computer game the story was of less importance than immediate challenges. Fourteen-year-old male gamer JF observed: 'Well I don't think you really require the story to be able to know what enemies to kill.' SP, a 16-year-old girl player expressed her experience in an even more ludological way:

The computer game is kind of more based on the story than the board game, but not as much as the film, because it [the computer game] is just an outline of locations and *pure events that happen*.

Her expression 'pure events that happen' echoes Markku Eskelinen's understanding of temporal relations in computer games as opposed to narrative:

The dominant temporal relation in (computer) games is the one between user time (the actions of the player) and *event* time (the happenings of the game), whereas in narratives it's between story time (the time of the events told) and discourse time (the time of the telling). (2001)

'Pure events that happen' is also a formulation that is as close as any to describing the immediacy of computer game play. In talking about the different qualities of attention required by each of the day's three activities, JH commented: 'I don't think there's much thinking involved with the computer game. if you got hit you're like 'oh no, no, no, kill, kill him!', kind of got your heart pumping a bit.' EA describes something similar: 'The video game was like, when we had a tiny bit of life left and you've go to fight for survival and it's like 'c'mon!! c'mon!!' For 16-year-old-girl SP, referring to the Paths of the Dead level, the computer game offered her most excitement during the day:

> You are more involved in what's happening because you don't have to take it in turns so you are there and you are fighting so its more exciting … it's all very high speed and you need to always be looking out and be ready to fight when the dead people come.

The immediacy of the computer game play experience was in the main sharply contrasted with participant accounts of their board game play. In most cases the board game was reported as the most popular activity during the day, principally because it required high levels of social interaction combined with concentrated strategic planning. The board game produced excitement and immersion for our players but in a very different register from the immediacy of the computer game. Thirteen-year-old boy JS commented: 'probably the board game [was most exciting] because we were all working together, so we could all get worked up together because of the whole tension of not wanting to die'. For 15-year-old female EA the board game was most exciting: 'I don't really know why, I suppose … it was more of a tactical thinking for the board game, and the video game was more for thinking in a less tactical way.' Fourteen-year-old male gamer JF describes the simulation qualities of the board game with some accuracy:

> Strangely, compared to the computer game … it did seem very busy having all these three aspects of the board game going all at once; which is a bit surprising … you had to think really hard about how your actions would affect the other areas of the game and how those areas would affect your area at the moment, you got to concentrate quite a lot and that's what made the atmosphere so tense … thinking really hard about what you were gonna do.

We noted above that players' relative investment in the *Lord of the Rings* story-world in relation to the computer game was variable. This variation is mirrored in the way they articulated their experience of the *Lord of the Rings* story in the board game. Two of the young women for instance were firmly of the opinion that it added little to the experience; SP observed:

> the board game … is just an outline of the characters and locations but what they do is not based on the story so much. The board game just gives you the characters and locations so you don't have to worry about anything, the story is in the book, you just follow the locations and do the events which don't happen in the book.

EA was more dismissive:

> [the board game] didn't really have anything to do with the story line … In the board game there was no need for the storyline at all 'cause you play Monopoly and that doesn't have a film with it, and you go along with it and people enjoy that. It's kind of the same thing with that board game.

On the other hand the boys in general displayed a greater investment in the story-world in the board game; 15-year-old JH argued that the story was important:

> I wanted to get to the end and destroy the ring and everything. So yeah it was important to me. Maybe not the story but the object of the game was important which was the story basically.

Narrative closure and game goal are again here identified as coterminous. Designer Reiner Knizia's aim to 'stay within the spirit of the book' appears to be realised in JS's comment that

> the board game was the story of *The Lord of the Rings* as well, so it wasn't just the simple board game, there was a story of it all with the ring and if you get dragged too far to the dark side you die and like Sauron is slowly advancing on you and you can use special powers or things to help you get further away from him…

For MD the story provides a motivating context for the board game: 'It's vital really because otherwise you're just gonna give up on it. It just gives you the motivation, it helps a lot to understand what's going on.' These strong statements of the boys' investment in narrative as a critical aspect of the board game experience is somewhat at odds with the 'common sense' notion that girls are more likely to be interested in narrative and that boys will be more interested in 'action'. This dominant notion of distinctly gendered play preferences and gendered investments in play is reinforced in many of the essays included in the collection edited by Justine Cassell and Henry Jenkins (1998). Perhaps if the storyworld has already been culturally coded as masculine, already has the fascination of complex fantasy worlds, boys find it more acceptable to relate their play to story.

A final aspect of our co-players' responses that is worth noting here is their awareness of storyworld as branding. We would not want to overemphasise this aspect of their experience; it is not an issue which we set out to address in our conversations and was never the focus of the discussion. However, it did come up several times, most notably through SP, commenting on the board game: 'If I hadn't played it before and I saw it in the shop I would be tempted to buy it because of "*The Lord of the Rings*" on it.' More tellingly she commented that she had had the computer game given to her as a gift: 'I had it bought for me for Christmas; easy present really.' Her formulation of the *Return of the King* XBox game at Christmas as an 'easy present' seemed to us a really accurate and fruitful way of understanding storyworlds as branding. The volume of marketing generated in conditions of intermediality around particular blockbuster film titles offers us all the prospect of an 'easy present' – a gift which can be automatically assumed to be both familiar and desirable. This 'assumption' of desirability is perversely pointed up by 15-year-old MD's 'secret' negative response to the film:

> Basically its just a bit of an effort that film, proper effort … I'm not the biggest fan,
> I think they are good but I could say that they are slightly overrated but if I said that
> in front of my friends I'd probably be shot.

The film text functions here at the centre of a web of intermedial possibilities, its huge marketing spend creating anticipation and desire for related products.

Intermedial narrative

In such a small-scale experiment any conclusions arising are limited and contingent. We found both narratological and ludological frameworks reflected in the player's discourse – the cinematic narrative clearly functioned for *some* of the players as an evocative enhancement to both computer game and board game play. Equally, other players felt that story was irrelevant to the experience of playing the computer game, to the immediate challenge of dealing with 'pure events that happen'. Disappointingly for those more interested in polemics than enquiry these findings suggest a dialectic resolution of the narrative/game debate in so far as *both* elements make up the computer game experience when dealing with those examples which, like *The Return of the King*, already have a high 'intermedial profile'. This suggests that even though the representative content of a computer game may only be an interface to the simulation of the game engine, even though action might be more significant than connotation, even though the textual meaning of the representation is secondary to the compulsive engagement with improved game performance – despite acknowledging all this most games *still use representation*. However, the significance of narrative as an organising principle of this representation is different in conditions of intermediality. Our players clearly had interpretive responses to game worlds based on something very close to Jenkins' sense of 'evocative narrative'. Participants' interpretive pleasure of a clearly boundaried narrative was less important than it would be in a novel or film and required a different kind of 'interpretive repertoire' that facilitated shifting easily through a number of intertextual connections in their experience of the storyworld. In this sense the ludologists' argument that narrative in games is mere 'packaging' for the game play is also true – yet another way to describe 'packaging' is context. Cultural and Media Studies scholars understand as a first principle that context is an important determinant of experience and of meaning.

Ludologists have also argued that the rule set of a game system is a central determinant of the gameplay experience. We did not find any evidence in the computer game that the player's experience was being determined by the underlying rule set of the game; on the contrary the 'system rules' or the game mechanic were of far less importance to our players than the immediate demands of the 'navigate, annihilate, accumulate' logic of the action-adventure genre. This was not, however, the case in the board game play; here clearly learning and negotiating the complex rule set *was* the gameplay. This might argue that transferring theoretical paradigms developed for understanding traditional 'board games' from 'Go' to 'Monopoly' may not always be the most useful way to understand a computer game.

Tastes and technicities ·

In considering user/text relations by using this form of participatory observation we, of course, found ourselves thinking about our users as much, if not more, than our texts. In particular we have been struck by the rich inconsistencies in their conversations with us, around the relative importances of story, or which activities they found most pleasurable. Their experiences, pleasures and difficulties were all very much socially mediated by the group context and by the different tastes and abilities of the other group members. Some of the group dynamics seemed to reflect superficial gender differences; however, at an individual level experiences proved far more various. We want to propose the idea of 'technicity' as a way of understanding different taste preferences and experiences in intermedial spectatorship.

What do *we* mean by technicity? This term has a particular history within cyberculture studies. David Tomas (2000) draws on the work of cultural anthropologist Lee Drummond in order to account for the new kinds of social and cultural relationships being formed through the use of technology. The significant aspect of our use of the term 'technicity' is to encapsulate within it the connections between an identity based on certain types of attitude, practices, tastes *and* the deployment of technology and a technological 'edge' in the construction of that identity. To be subjects within the privileged twenty-first-century first world is to be increasingly caught up in a network of technically and mechanically mediated relationships with others who share the same attitude/aptitude, tastes, pleasures and preferences.

For instance the internet itself enables the formation of particular kinds of social bonds based on a position towards and facility with technology. This technicity does not bring about the disappearance of other types of ethnic identities or communities but extends them with a particular type of 'technologically creolised cultural laminate with a different set of ethnic-type rules of social bonding' (Tomas 2002: 185). This historical moment produces technological competence as a key marker for success as a participant in the modern culture. However, technicity might also offer us a useful clue into understanding the different pleasures discovered by our participants in their experience of intermedial storyworlds.

Thinking about the different 'technicities' of our players therefore becomes a way of understanding apparent inconsistencies. Sixteen-year-old SP, for instance, was in fact the most experienced computer game player amongst the girls' group – this might explain her comment that playing the computer game in co-op mode was rather difficult when paired with a less experienced player.

> Sometimes it was a bit more of a hinder 'cause you needed to check where the other person was, how they were doing, and if they needed to get the life, they needed to go and get it, as oppose to working together to win successfully.

On the other hand SP was in fact the only participant who had read the novel of *The Lord of the Rings*, so her previous cultural exposure plus her computer game play experience might explain her experience of the computer game as just 'pure events that happen', or of the board game as 'just an outline of the characters and locations but what they do is not based on the story so much'. She was also one of the few participants to offer us any detailed sense of engagement with the film as narrative experience; in response to a question about which characters she cared about in her viewing and playing, she replied:

> Aragon, because he had both the physical side that he could get injured in battle or something, and at one point he did when he fell over the cliff, and also with Arwen because he obviously really loves her, and her dad's trying to split them up. It's a very sad moment for me. I don't think I particularly cared about any character in the video game because you can always restart...

Here we can see a particular combination of taste (for fantasy literature) and technicity (as computer gamer) informing an 'expert' commentary on gameplay and story.

Similarly amongst the boys the social performance of play was mediated through particular kinds of taste and technicity producing particular kinds of expertise. JF for instance, through his gameplay, viewing and commentary, identified himself as an expert gamer with a very sophisticated grasp of rule sets and game strategies. Here he is discussing what he is thinking about in computer game play:

> Yeah you're also thinking about what you'd do in the later level compared to what you've managed to do now, so if you had low health and you're playing co-operative you'd think more about making the player with more health walk ahead and maybe protect you, and you talk about how to get across obstacles such as drawbridges and how you'd go about that with enemies around, would you try and make the drawbridge go down fighting the enemies or would you kill all the enemies first and then make the drawbridge go down.

JS on the other hand has a completely different play style; at one point in the computer game play he identified a 'jump back' move that appealed to his more subversive sense of play; when in co-op mode with JF he repeatedly made the 'jump back' move for his own amusement, much to the irritation of JF. 'Play' is not the same thing for two players in the same game.

'Technicity' can therefore be seen as a key marker of a subject's ability to exercise the flexible repertoire of interpretive responses demanded by increasingly intermedial cultural landscapes. The cinematic text is now diffused in a variety of locations on a variety of platforms. In these conditions of intermediality our responses to such texts will crucially be dependent on our technicity, that combination of taste and competence that determines our ability to access a storyworld as well as our individual style of interactions with it.

Works cited

Aarseth, E., S. M. Smedstad and L. Sunnana (2003) 'A Multi-Dimensional Typology of Games', *Level Up: Digital Games Research Conference Proceedings*. University of Utrecht, 48–53.

Anon. (2003a) *Edge Magazine*, 120.

____ (2003b) *Edge Magazine*, 129.

Cassell, Justine and Henry Jenkins (eds) (1998) *From Barbie® to Mortal Kombat: Gender and Computer Games*. Boston: MIT Press.

DTI/Spectrum Consultants (2002) 'From Exuberant Youth to Sustainable Maturity – Competitiveness Analysis of the UK Games Sector'. Online. Available at http://www.

tiga.org.uk (accessed 24 March 2004).

ELSPA (Entertainment and Leisure Software Publishers' Association) (2003) 'The Cultural Life of Video Games'. Online. Available at http://www.elspa.com (accessed 22 February 2004).

Eskelinen, M. (2001) 'The Gaming Situation', *Game Studies: The International Journal of Computer Game Research*, 1, 1. Online. Available at http://gamestudies.org/0101/eskelinen (accessed 19 July 2005).

_____ (2004) 'Towards Computer Game Studies', in N. Wardrip-Fruin and P. Harrigan (eds) *First Person: New Media as Story, Performance and Game*. Cambridge, MA: MIT Press, 36-44.

Grusin, R. (2002) 'The Cinema of Interactions', unpublished paper, Bill Douglas Centre University of Exeter.

Jarvinen, A. (2003) 'Making and Breaking Games: A Typology of Rules', *Level Up: Digital Games Research Conference Proceedings*. University of Utrecht, 68–79.

Jenkins, H. (2002) *Interactive Audiences: The Collective Intelligence of Media Fans*. Online. Available at http://web.mit.edu/21fms/www/faculty/henry3/collective%20intelligence.html (accessed 19 July 2005).

_____ (2004) 'Game Design as Narrative Architecture', in N. Wardrip-Fruin and P. Har-rigan (eds) *First Person: New Media as Story, Performance and Game*. Cambridge, MA: MIT Press. Online. Available at http://web.mit.edu/cms/People/henry3/games&narrative.html (accessed 21 Nvember 2005).

Juul, J. (2003) 'The Game, the Player, the World: Looking for a Heart of Gameness', *Level Up: Digital Games Research Conference Proceedings*. University of Utrecht, 30–47.

King, B and J. Borland (2003) *Dungeons and Dreamers: From Geek to Chic*. McGraw Hill: San Francisco.

Lehtonen, M. (2001) 'On No Man's Land: Theses on Intermediality', *Nordicom Review*, 1, 71–83.

Moulthrop, S. (2004) 'From Work to Play: Molecular Culture in the Time of Deadly Games', in N. Wardrip-Fruin and P. Harrigan (eds) *First Person: New Media as Story, Performance and Game*. Cambridge, MA: MIT Press, 56–69.

Newman, J. (2004) *Videogames*. Routledge: London.

Knizia, R. (2004) 'The Design and Testing of the Board Game – *The Lord of the Rings*', in K. Salen and E. Zimmerman (eds) *Rules of Play: Game Design Fundamentals*. Cambridge, MA: MIT Press, 22–7.

Smith, D. (2005) 'Star Wars Empire Strikes Gold', *Observer* (15 May), 3.

Tomas, D. (2000) 'The Technophilic Body: On Technicity in William Gibson's *Cyborg Culture*', in D. Bell and B. Kennedy (eds) *The Cybercultures Reader*. Routledge: London, 175–89.

Cooperation versus Violence: An Ethnographical Analysis of the *Return of the King* Video Game

Mariano Longo

Introduction

Video games have only recently become an object of academic investigation, and that within a variety of different theoretical and disciplinary approaches.[1] The academic relevance of video games has raised a number of questions: What is a video game? And which is the most adequate approach capable of providing a scientific background for its analysis? By saying that a video game is a cultural object (Grinswold 1994), we make a far too simplistic statement. Yet it is a relevant one, since it underlines the important fact that a video game, far from being an autonomous item, should be analysed as the output of a variety of factors, including individual ludic needs, industrial strategies of late modernity, and specific structural and narrative characteristics. This means that video games, being cultural objects, have to be understood as social objects as well (Carzo & Centorrino 2002: 57–89).

A video game is not only the result of social processes; it is also able to produce a separated reality, the structure of which is determined by informatical elements, narrative genres and game strategies. Video games are formal systems with their own rules, their specific ways of representing reality, their specific forms of interactivity (Crawford 1984; Kasvi 2004). The structure of the video game marks a boundary, within which a space endowed with its own logic is available for the player. Applying Niklas Luhmann's system theory, we could say that a video game is less a communication medium than a system able to define by itself a distinction with the environment (see Walther 2003). From a phenomenological perspective this implies that video games produce a separate world: the game experience is an estranging one, since it takes place in a finite province of meaning, separated by the experience of everyday reality (Schutz 1967: 230). Playing is a lived experience, the characteristics of which depend on the structure of the game. It is an intense activity as well, able to produce a cognitive shock, which separates the process of playing from the normal stream of everyday events.

This brief review linked to video games as objects of scientific interest shows how numerous and complex the questions are. Confronted with this complexity, I leave untouched both the ontological question (what is a video game?) and the disciplinary problem (which academic approach is best suited to study video games?). Indeed, general problems linked to video games as a social and cultural phenomenon are here replaced by a more concrete scrutiny devoted to a video game in particular: *The Lord of the Rings: The Return of the King* (Electronic Arts, 2003).[2] My focus will be on the video game as a quasi-social setting, against which I would like to test a number of sociological concepts. This approach enables me to adopt the role of the ethnographical observer, in order to detach a number of elements useful to understand the complex architecture of the game (in both the ideological and ludic dimensions).[3] Video games in general can be understood as hyperreal contexts, within which many aspects of reality are amplified and deformed (Carzo & Centorrino 2002: 49–53). Some of these aspects (action, interaction, violence, the representation of the enemies, time and space) are here analysed through a qualitative approach to content analysis (Altheide 1996).

By reducing the range of my interest, a number of important elements are likely to fall outside my analysis. In particular, I will not pay due attention to the relation between the video game and both the novel and the movie; I do not intend to analyse the interactive dimension of the game, that is, the relation between the player and the game; I will give a limited account of the complex game structure, with its rules and the strategies the player has to adopt in order to reach the final level. Indeed, academic investigation is always selective, which means that only a limited section of reality can be subject to intellectual scrutiny. The selection I propose should enable the understanding of the implicit meanings of the game, which consists of a stock of representations of reality, endowed with a sense of their own. Adopting a sociological perspective should enable me to treat what happens on the screen as an actual social situation, regardless of the fact that it is a simulated one. This intellectual device, artificial as it is, affords the opportunity to understand the game from an eccentric point of view, whose collateral purpose is to show the potentiality of sociological imagination when it is employed outside the boundaries of its usual field of investigation.

Narrative premise: the logic of cooperation

Gandalf, now Gandalf the White, comes to help the people of Rohan at Helm's Deep. That is the moment in which the introductive trailer, synthesising the complex plot of the novel, fades into the game: movie images are replaced by the unnatural corporeity of *computer graphics*. A complex symbolism connotes the arrival of

Gandalf: the light opposes itself to the grey shabbiness of the attacking enemies, mankind resists monstrosity, and the strength of reason contrasts unreasonable strength. Already at the first level of the game a unifying element emerges: the logic of cooperation. The overwhelming number of enemies makes the coordination of different characters' actions essential. Gandalf does not struggle alone: on the contrary, he incites his fellows, helps them, and endowes them with courage until ultimate success.

In the introductive trailer to subsequent levels, Gandalf explains to the player the strategy linked to the logic of cooperation: the war fought by men, elves and dwarfs is nothing more than a diversion in order to distract the eye of Dark Lord Sauron from Frodo, the little hobbit whose hands carry the destiny of Middle Earth. A quick look at the structure of the game and the relation of the different levels shows how essential the logic of cooperation is to understand the meaning of the game. The introductive level ('Helm's Deep') is fixed: the player has to succeed in it in order to continue the game. The player accustoms himself with the skills required to play (for example, moving a third-person character in the virtual space,[4] making him fight against his enemies) as well as with the complex narrative structure. Once Gandalf has accomplished his task (destroying a bridge using some catapults) the level comes to its end with little difficulties for the player.

The player can then choose among three narrative lines, all of them converging at the final level, where Frodo struggles for the ring against Smeagol:

1) The Sorcerer's Path, articulated in three levels ('Road to Isengard'; 'Minas Tirith – top of the walls'; 'Minas Tirith – southern courtyard'[5]), the main character of which is Gandalf.
2) The Hobbits' path where Frodo and Sam, led by Gollum/Smeagol, try to reach Mordor ('Escape from Osgiliath'; 'Shelob's Lair'; 'Cirith Ungol').
3) The King's path where Aragorn, Legolas and Gimli contribute to the final victory, fighting against a variety of enemies ('Path of the Dead'; 'Southern Portal'; 'Pellenor Fields').

The Sorcerer's Path and the King's Path converge at the penultimate level ('Black Gate'), where Gandalf, Aragorn, Legolas and Gimli fight again side by side, their task being to distract Sauron from Frodo and Sam approaching Mount Doom. The brief description of the different game narrative lines shows how much the final solution depends on the confluence of the outputs of the actions of the different characters: the fellowship of the ring can win the war only if each of its members will mutually cooperate. Unlike in the real world, the video game action does not have unintended consequences: there is no contradiction between the acquired skills and the outputs of simulated action, due to the informatically precodified set of possibilities of virtual action. When the player understands the logic of cooperation and once he has acquired the necessary game abilities, there is no doubt that his simulated actions will produce the expected results.

Cooperation and solidarity have a series of functions, some of which are ludic, some ideological (for a sociological analyses of solidarity see Zoll 2003). Ludic functions are linked to the internal logic of the video game, which the player has to assimilate in order to come to the final solution: the allies will only defeat the enemies if mutually supportive. Solidarity sets itself opposite to the strategically ineffective action of the enemies: thanks to solidarity it is possible to find inter-mediated tasks, ultimate goals, apparently uncoordinated lines of action, linked together by intrinsic rationality.

Ideological functions are more difficult to detect, since they are connected less to strategies than to social representation. They are active in the process of identify-ing the player with his heroes, as well as in the opposite process of differentiation with the enemies. Men, elves, dwarfs and hobbits are cooperative since they are rational beings, hence intrinsically moral. The rational and moral capability to distinguish between good and evil enables them to detect tactics to stop the enemy, within the overall strategy aiming at the final goal. The moral characteristics of cooperative action enable us to make a first, clear-cut distinction with the enemies: the rivals are advantaged by their capability to oppose rationality with violence, morality with strength. The enemy has only embryonic attitudes to coordinate action, to cooperate, to share a common goal. That makes him weak, giving at the same time the rational rival the opportunity to oppose effectively.

The ideological dimension is the one that links the video game to the movie, and the novel. The video game is inspired by both (by the movie in particular), although it develops a narrative consistent with the game logic. Yet it appears sim-plistic in relation to the complexity of the novel and lacklustre in comparison with the spectacularity of the film. Although the movie and the video game are further steps in the direction of the reduced complexity of the novel, solidarity is, as it were, a structural *trait d'union* since it provides the different cultural products with what one could call an *ethical substratum*. The fellowship, although established for a concrete goal, is not an instrumental group. On the contrary, its members have a number of relationships based on respect, friendship and mutual support: values connect people, creating individual and collective identities. They are never seen as social products devoid of any substantial content, as is often the case in actual social interactions. In that sense, the video game incidentally represents values in a way which is consistent with part of contemporary sociological thought (especially Parsons and the structural functionalist tradition). This simplistic representation of value is easy to explain: shared values give concreteness to the simulated reality of the game, creating a world where complexity has already been systematically reduced. In this uncomplicated world, the character (hence the player) can always distinguish good and evil, friends and rivals, right and wrong.

The logic of contraposition: violence

Whereas the interaction between allies is characterised by what I have called the logic of cooperation, the relation with the enemy is fractionised in an endless series of fights. The player tests his acquired skills, takes his bearings in a hostile (virtual) environment, faces his opponents, and avoids them, in order to put off the fight. Violence marks the boundaries between opponents and allies, since it defines the *social* space of the game. Significantly, no member of the fellowship can strike against any of his allies. Weapons are indeed effective only against foes. The game pre-defines the characters against whom weapons work, and that is not casual: to the player, violence is a tool to understand the complex network of relationships, antagonism and friendships.

Paraphrasing Wolfgang Sofsky, one could say that fighting is a way to define the fields of contending actors. A fight is, as it were, at the same time a social fact and the negation of any sociality. Its *unsocial sociality* produces significant effects in the advancing of the game only when the player is able to accumulate victories: the characters (hence the player, in all his possible personifications) can complete a level only by wiping out enemies whose strength is not based on any particular skill, but on their overwhelming numbers. In order to win, the player has to turn the fight into a slaughter, into a systematic annihilation of the enemy who is always able to reproduce a series of attacks, due to his numerical superiority. While in a real social setting, hostility can result in its own dissolution (Sofsky 1998: 121), the game goes on only if violence is able to reproduce itself, by constantly reactivating the logic of contraposition. Nonetheless, there are interesting convergences between virtual and real situations, in the sense that the game strategy reproduces characteristics of a real fight. That is why the analysis of Sofsky, originally designed to understand a real fighting situation, is surprisingly appropriate to the virtual fight in the game (1998: 122). The player has to adopt this strategy of sheer contraposition, if he wants to complete the level, contributing to the advancement of the game.

In spite of the constant reproduction of virtual fights, *The Return of the King* represents violence in its own particular way. As compared to other successful video games, violence has few realistic connotations: there is no splatter element (blood, bodies torn to pieces, and so on) so typical of some of the most fashionable video games. In *The Return of the Ring*, one may notice a significant *domestication* in the graphic representation of violence, which is actually coherent with the ideological characteristics of the game. To the heroes, indeed, violence is a means, not an end in itself, and as a means it is rationally employed in order to reach specific goals. The use of violence is legitimated in accordance with superior values: that means that there is no morbid exaltation of violence, since it is justified only as a necessary means to restore peace, order and normal life, no matter that any order and normalisation (that is, any power) have inscribed in themselves the germs of their originating violence (Benjamin 1962). Shared ideals and values justify the heroes and, at the same time, enable the player to employ violence which will eventually turn into institutional order and legitimate power (Balibar 1997: 52–7). Among the enemies, the absolute lack of ideals turns violence into cruelty, making even more evident the gap between the rationality of good and the absurd irrationality of evil.[6]

The enemy

The representation of the enemy is a dichotomical one. Brutality of violence is set against the harmony of cooperation, deformity against moral and physical beauty, disgust against sympathy, the indifferentiation of the enemies against the individualisation of the main characters. Following the adventures of the fellowship of the ring, the player gets used to the sophisticated articulation of tactic and strategies that is the logic of cooperation. Cooperation has a double finality: on the one hand a practical one, in the sense that the player has to understand its logic in order to come to the final solution; on the other an ideological one, since cooperation transmits a positive image of the heroes.

The enemy, on the contrary, is characterised by an almost absolute lack of coordination and that is why one may apply to him the Durkheimian concept of 'horde'. Within a horde, coordination is impossible since there is no differentiation: the actions of its members consist in the constant repetition of the same muster. According to Emile Durkheim (1971: 185), a horde is a protoplasmatic society, situated in the realm of the undifferentiating: that means that there is neither role distribution, nor any incipient form of specialisation.

The reference to the concept of horde enables us to explain, from a sociological point of view, the incapacity of the enemies to adopt any strategy, since their only simplistic tactic is connected to their overwhelming numerical superiority. Anyway, the virtual horde does not appear in its pure form. In the different levels of the game, one can witness a sort of evolution of the qualities of the enemies. They become, indeed, more and more equipped with abilities and power. The player may fight against monsters with or without shields (the first being of course the stronger); he may face great ogres (better to be avoided) and struggle against monsters endowed with a surplus of energy (which have to be struck a number of times in order to be destroyed). Nonetheless, we are not here confronted with any form of *virtual* differentiation, in the sense that the strongest enemies are indeed the potentiated reproduction of the usual model, consisting of the replication of the summing up logic of physical strength. That is probably why the enemy seems always to be sacrificable: he has no value in himself, since he is indeed the undistinguished, void of any individuality. His value actually lies in the fact that he is an undifferentiating part of a horde, so that the hero may destroy him without any moral consequence. The sacrifice of the enemy has to be connected to the fact that he is not a character, but a mere ludic and ideological function. Tellingly, the corpses of the enemies do not accumulate on the ground, since they disappear a few moments after their death. Once killed, he has accomplished his function (that is to give the player the opportunity to train his skills) and he may now disappear, leaving the ground clear for further fights. Even when the enemy may be typified as a boss, there is little or no differentiation. According to my gatekeeper Giorgio, a boss is a skilled enemy, *appearing in important moments of the game, whose strength is useful for the hero to acquire new tools and for the player to develop new abilities.* That means the boss has a series of functions, both ludic and narrative:

1) he gives the player the opportunity to face a difficult enemy, training his acquired abilities;
2) he activates new weapons;
3) he is a link to the subsequent phases of the game.

A boss emphasises typical characters of the enemies, that is why he does not contradict the idea according to which the concept of horde should explain the coordination of virtual action among the antagonists. A boss may take the form of a monstrous spider, emphasising the animality of the enemy, and the lack of rationality in his actions (see the 'Shelob's Lair' level); a boss may appear as a being endowed with superior powers, fighting alone against Aragorn ('Black Gate'). In this case, he posesses no differentiated function as a leader: he is, as it were, fighting his own solitary battle. Only once (in the 'Paths of the Dead' level) does Aragorn fight a character with his own differentiated function: the king of the dead is actually a king, with a status, which distinguishes him from the other ghosts. In this case, the enemy is to be converted into an occasional ally. The contenders will eventually make common cause with the heroes, and that is possible only because the two parts have at least a minimum number of shared values, which makes mutual trust possible, and the belief that the agreement will be kept reasonable.

Interacting with the enemy

What are the characteristics of the interaction with the enemies? How does the video game simulate the relationship between contending groups? Is it possible to find in virtual interaction a model, to be explained in terms of sociological theories? Let us bring in Norbert Elias's figuration theory to answer this. According to Elias, a figuration consists of a chain of interdependent relations among individuals, based on a more or less stable equilibrium in the power of the participating actors. Figuration has to be understood neither as an autonomous reality, nor as the product of individual action. It is indeed independent from the single actors, able as it is to condition their conduct. At the same time, it can only be considerd as the output of a number of interconnections among individual actions. Elias (1990: 86–90) introduces game models the function of which is to show that, the more complex and structured the chains of interdependence become, the more difficult it is for the single player to control, within the figuration, the consequences of his own actions. Before analysing the different types of games, Elias describes the primary game, that is, a model of interconnected actions within which the actors belonging to different groups share neither values nor norms: in that case, interaction depends only on the physical capacity of contrasting the enemy. Whereas the horde may be adopted as a collective concept to describe the protoplasmatic sociality within an undifferentiating social group, primary game is a collective concept likely to give sociological representation to the protoplasmatic interaction among groups. Members of the fellowship and enemies may condition one another only by exerting mutual violence: there is in fact no room for shared values, norms and communication. Only conflict determines interaction, which means that only through violence do interconnections become possible. In his analysis of primary games, Elias shows that the absolute strangeness of the enemy does not prevent interaction, which takes the form of a conflicting physical clash. If we apply the idea of figuration to the game, we may notice that within the virtual space interaction with the enemy is only possible in the form of virtual annihilation. There is, however, an important difference, dependent on the fact that the game predefines the ideological representation of the contenders. The player experiences a pre-codified world, where the imputation of right and wrong is also predefined. Virtual representation of the conflict has a physical component and an ideological one: the conflict is a clash between value and lack of values, between the rationality of good and the irrationality of evil.

Time

How does time work in the video game *The Return of the King*? Is it possible to detect one or more temporal dimensions? To answer these questions it is necessary, first of all, to distinguish between the narrative and the ideological element in the game temporality.[7] The narrative element has to do with the way in which time structures the game, making it possible for the player to complete different levels, conducting the heroes along the predefined course of the game. From a structural point of view, narrative time has two main characteristics. It is linear, since it proceeds from the starting level to the ultimate solution. It is also cyclical, in two distinguishable ways: the player can always start again, but he faces as well a number of recursive situations, characterised by the same *summing up* logic of physical struggle. Linear time refers to the fact that the player has to successfully complete a number of levels, which imposes the logic of *first things first* (Schutz & Luckmann 1974: 47–8). In order to arrive at the final level, one has inevitably to follow a defined path, that is a temporal sequence, which is able to determine and, at the same time, is determined by the actual playing. In that sense, the virtual time of the game appears to be inescapable: it is, as it were, a structural element, able to influence the action of the characters on the screen, defining the strategic priorities of the player.

In the game *The Return of the King* linear time acquires a complex narrative structure which, by simulating the contemporaneity of actions, does not subvert the logic of *first things first*. That is to be connected to the overall organisation of the game, characterised by the presence of three converging narrative lines. From the first level ('Helm's Deep') the player can move to three different paths (as described above). In each path, the levels follow a temporal *continuum*: in order to get to the next level, the player has to succeed in the previous one. That means that by following just one of the paths, the player anticipates events and situations, which, on the narrative level, should be postponed. The player can choose to follow a zigzag temporal sequence since he can go back to a narratively coherent event, starting up new linear paths. Differently from what happens in most action video games, in the *Return of the King* narrative time and play time do not overlap, since here narrative time has a much more complex structure than play time. The narrative pre-exists the game, linked as it is to a literary and filmic model. Which means that the plot is somehow independent from the act of playing, and indeed the player, during his play time, has to go back and forward in the narrative temporality, in order to accomplish his task and reach the final solution.

As in the novel and in the film, in the video game temporal levels are intertwined within a variety of narrative lines which converge at the final solution. Linear time has to be connected to the ideological component of temporality: indeed, the quasi-contemporaneity of the three narrative lines seems to be the temporal equivalent of what I have above called the logic of cooperation. Temporal levels intertwine since the actions of the heroes have to as well. The heroes' time is, as it were, the time in which different deeds have to converge toward a common task. That is why the different narrative lines, whether activated or not by the player, coexist in a shared present, in which the heroes fight for the common victory. Heroes' time is time for strategy, time for procrastination, time for intermediated goals: it is the time of rationality. Once again, one can differentiate on the temporal level the hero from his enemy. To the enemy, time is momentary and irrational since it is not structured in reference to any strategy, but it consumes itself in a variety of acts of violence.[8]

The first evident element of cyclical time is linked to the obvious fact that one can always start again. The player may either save a game, starting anew from the exit point, or begin a new game, testing his acquired abilities (Juul 2003). The player has also to start a new game if the necessary skills have not been adequately implemented. The second element of cyclical time is to be connected to what I might call a sort of virtual *dèjá vu*. In each level the fighting situations are constantly repeated, up to a point where the game moves to a next stage and the graphical background changes. This virtual *dèjá vu* refers only metaphorically to cyclical time, since the constant reproduction of fights can occur only within play time: it is indeed in the linear temporality that the player can make progresses, approaching the final phases of the game.

Space

Sociological theory is by now aware that space can be understood as a social construction. Sociologists do not deny the evident fact that space is a physical dimension, within which physical (but also social) events actually occur. Nonetheless, space is socially constructed in a plurality of ways, connected both to its anthropisation and to its social representation. Summarising the complex theoretical and empirical implications of an interesting sociological debate, one could say that physical space has always a symbolic component, since the way space is socially structured and represented tells the observer something about the society that produced those structures and representations (Löw 2000). The idea of space as a social construction can be easily applied to so-called virtual space. Generally speaking, virtual space is a graphical simulation of spatiality, able to produce a social context for new forms of socialisations. With regard to the internet, virtual space may be understood as a sort of *nowhere* within which a number of socially and individually relevant activities become possible (see Benshop 2004; Izzi 2004). Generally speaking, video games make a different use of virtual space: it is a simulation of spatiality made possible by the use of three-dimensional graphics. From a merely technical point of view, simulated space is the output of software, in which operates a historically specific, highly sophisticated and rational form of representation of space relations, that is perspective. Should we restrict our understanding of virtual space to its technical construction? Or should we take into account both the dynamic and interactive dimension of virtual space (a space experienced by a player), as well as its cultural component (virtual space as a specific representation of reality) (Taylor 2003)?

In our perspective, space is a component of the overall meaning of the video game. By focusing our attention on a single video game, we may detect how space plays an important role in the construction of a plurality of meanings, connected to both ideological and game functions. As in most video games, the player of *The Return of the King* has to get used to the virtual representation of space: he has to learn a series of skills and prompts in order to lead the character within the virtual space. The game adopts the so-called third-person vision: the player observes the whole figure of the character, which prevents strong forms of identification (see Taylor 2003 on forms of identification). If we typify the representation of space in *The Return of the King*, we may find at least four main types:

1) *The boundary* is the spatial limit which must not be crossed in order to avoid physical fights: it reproduces, on the spatial level, the opposition between the heroes and the subhuman world of the enemies (for a sociological analysis of the concept of boundary, see Cassano 1996). Crossing the boundary means physical proximity, hence violence, no matter if *limina* are violated by the heroes or by their enemies. In the first case ('Helm's Deep', 'Minas Tirith – top of the walls' and 'Minas Tirith – southern courtyard') the enemies besiege cities or fortifications, and the task of the heroes is to resist, and defend their own vital and strategic space. In the second case ('Road to Isengard', 'Black Gate') the heroes attack, producing the numerically overwhelming reaction of the enemies. Nonetheless, going through the boundary imposes proximity between the struggling parts, making more evident physical and moral differences. The anthropological space of rationality and planning belongs to the heroes. It is a stylistically consistent space, structured as a place suitable for civilised living. By violating that space, the enemy profanes the sacrality of reason. On the contrary, the places where the enemy lives (one should think of the wasteland of Isengard, of Cirith Ungol, of the Black Gate and Mordor) are places devoid of any order, their only logic being devastation of physical (virtual) space and moral inadequacy.

2) *Nobody's land:* this is a wasteland through which the heroes pass after the defeat of their allies. The boundary has now disappeared (there is no fortification to be defended, no separating walls) and that produces a space devoid of any limit and rationality. The heroes have to learn anew how to find their bearings in that hostile and irrational space, because physical devastation has produced the destruction of their *modus vivendi* (the *bonum vivere par excellence*). The enemies have by now substituted their hordalic inability to manage the space for the regularity so typical of any civilisation ('Southern Portal', 'Pellenor Fields', 'Escape from Osgiliath').

3) *The journey:* the journey ties the descriptive element of spatiality to the narrative element of temporality. By connecting different places and levels, journey is the narrative device, which makes the evolution of the game possible. The hero has to go through hostile environments ('Road to Isengard', 'Cirith Urugol'), in order to arrive at the places where the most sanguinary battles are being fought. Sometimes, the journey takes the form of a Dantesque journey to hell ('Path of the Dead', 'Shelob's Lair') when the hero goes through a gloomy and claustrophobic environment, characterised by subterranean grottoes and paths, expecting an important fight with some sort of powerful enemy. The Dantesque journey reproduces once again the opposition between the heroes and his enemies, this time as a dichotomy between the luminosity of good and the obscurity of evil.

4) *The arena*: this is a circular space, within which the hero faces an antagonist endowed with extraordinary skills (a so-called 'boss'). Fighting a boss requires unusual spatial organisation. It is neither the space where the hero fights in order to defend his territory, nor a dangerous area infested by unknown enemies. On the contrary, the final objective of the fight is to defeat a single particularly irksome opponent. That is why the spatial representation presents neither boundaries nor escapes: space is now a circular arena, the perfect stage for a single combat. In the arena there is no sudden change in the representation of the antagonist. Indeed, it is less a fight between even opponents than a physical clash in which the hero faces a monster summarising all the characters of the enemies. The antagonist does not share the same nature as the hero (he belongs to the realm of the dead – 'King of the Dead'; he is less than human – 'Shelob's Lair'; he may be a synthetic representation of the power of evil – 'Black Gate'). Graphically, he shows his overwhelming superiority (he is stouter than the hero); ideologically, he is the unfair opponent, helped as he may be by weaker monsters that help him fight against one of the protagonists. The theatrical space of the arena is not the space of the encounter. Physical proximity does not help to make the gap separating the antagonist smaller: on the contrary, the differences become more evident in a graphical context within which the value of the hero is exalted, as opposed to the total lack of value of the antagonist.

Conclusion

The Return of the King is, at the same time, a typical and unique game. That is of course a tautological statement (any video game is at the same time typical and unique), which needs explanation. Its typicality is connected to the fact that it is possible to qualify it employing one or more categories taken from the typologies now available on the market of ideas (Carzo & Centorrino 2002: 158). It is an adventure video game, connected to fantasy, with symbolic and magical elements. Its uniqueness is related to the complex cultural and marketing ties the video game has with other products, all the outputs of the rediscovery of Tolkien and his characters caused by the launch of the trilogy. More deeply, the uniqueness of the game has to be connected to its ludic and narrative structure, originating from the necessity to translate in a non-simplistic way the symbolic and cultural references of both the novel and the movie. That is probably why one of the topoi typical of fantasy as a video game genre, that is the opposition between good and evil, acquires here a greater structural complexity which produces what I have called the logic of cooperation. That logic makes the dichotomy allied/antagonists not trivial, based as it is on the distinction between rationality/irrationality, strategy/tactic, morality/amorality. Moreover, the video game presents the dichotomy in a politically-correct way: brutal violence against the enemy is motivated by superior ideals, which have a pedagogical aspect (good is an example to follow) as well as a legitimating component (violence is aimed at the achievement of moral goals).

It is a risk to generalise starting from empirical material. Nonetheless, one is tempted to underline a convergence between the dichotomy allied/enemy as presented in the video game and the present strong opposition between the Western world and those who are not inclined to conform to our peculiar vision of rationality and morality. American video games in the Bush-era are more and more influenced by the ideological (and official) representation that the United States is trying to transmit of themselves and their international role. And that is in opposition to the representation of the enemy, a degraded stranger, connoted as a Muslim and terrorist. New media, and video games in particular, are becoming powerful instruments for a new kind of propaganda, in which interactivity makes the player an active fighter in the struggle for Western values. A number of video games are now available, in which the player may assume the role of an American soldier ready to fight against those who personify alternative ideals (Pennacchini 2004). In *The Return of the King* there is no direct reference to present-day events. Yet many of the characteristics of the game seem not to be in contradiction with actual conflicts in the contemporary world. That is, of course, only a hypothesis, which does not take into due account the fact that the dichotomy allied/enemy is deeply rooted in the work of Tolkien. Nonetheless, exaltation of rationality, strong opposition between worlds and values, legitimating processes of politically-correct Western violence, as well as the attempt to degrade Islamic violence, reminds us of the video game *The Return of the King*; of its ideology, with a probably casual mirroring effect, but nonetheless a meaningful one.

Notes

1 The first online journal devoted to the academic study of video game was born in 2001. Its title is *Game Studies: The International Journal of Computer Game Research* (http://www.gamestudies.org). Other sites about games and video games are *Games, Gamers and Gaming Cultures* (http://www.knowledge.hut.fi/projects/games/gamelinks.html) and *Game Culture*, a site where an online review is also available (http://www.game-culture.com/journal.html).

2 The video game runs on PC, with a very complex set of prompts involving the use of mouse and keyboard.

3 I thank Giorgio Vileda, my *gatekeeper* to the game. Being unable to go through its increasingly difficult levels, I asked a young family friend to let me observe him playing. His skilled patience has allowed me to analyse the complex set of meanings of *The Return of the King*.

4 It is the so-called objective (or third-person) vision, opposed to the subjective (first-person) vision. For the implication of the different perspectives in connection to the

process of identification with the characters see Taylor 2003.

5   The version of the game used was Italian, hence all translations of levels are approxima-
tions which do not necessarily correspond with English-language versions.

6   By adopting an idea of Georges Sorel, one could distinguish between force (a controlled kind of violence, legitimated by authority) and violence (the unmotivated violence,
justified only by its manifestation) (see Héritier 1997: 17).

7   I am here not interested in the play time, that is the time of the player playing the game.
I focuses my attention only on the event time, that is the structural time of the game.
For an analytical interconnection between play and event time see Juul 2004.

8   In some levels, the relation between linear time and the logic of cooperation is more
evident: see the penultimate level of *Heroes' path*, where the struggle of the heroes has, as
its goal, the rescue of Eowyn and Merry, but see also the last level of the *Sorcerer's path*,
where Gandalf tries to save, in due time, 100 women in the city of Minas Tirith.

Works cited

Altheide, D. (1996) *Qualitative Media Analysis*. London: Sage.

Balibar, E. (1997) 'Violenza: idealità e crudeltà', in F. Héritier (ed.) *Sulla violenza*. Roma:
Meltemi, 44–65.

Benjamin, W. (1962) 'Per la critica alla violenza', in *Angelus novus*. Torino: Einaudi, 5–30.

Benshop, A (2004) 'Peculiarities of Cyberspace: Building Blocks for an Internet Sociology'.
Online. Available at http://www2.fmg.uva.nl/sociosite/websoc/indexE.html (accessed
23 July 2004).

Carzo D. and M. Centorrino (2002) *Tomb Raider o il destino delle passioni. Per una sociologia del videogioco*. Milano: Guerini e Associati.

Cassano, F. (1996) *Il pensiero meridiano*. Roma-Bari: Laterza.

Crawford, C. (1984) *The Art of Computer Game Design*. Berkley: Osborn/McGray.

Durkheim, E. (1971) *La divisione del lavoro sociale*. Milano: Edizioni di Comunità.

Elias, N. (1990) *Che cos'è la sociologia*, Torino: Rosenberg e Sellier.

Grinswold, W. (1994) *Culture and Society in a Changing World*. Thousand Oaks: Pine
Forge Press.

Héritier, F. (1997) 'Riflessioni per nutrire la riflessione', in F. Héritier (ed.) *Sulla violenza*.
Roma: Meltemi, 12–43.

Izzi C. (2004) 'Dallo spazio geografico al cyberspazio'. Online. Available at http://www.net-
sociology.org/sezione3/spazio_geografico_cyberspazio.htm (accessed 23 July 2004).

Juul, J. (2001) 'Game Telling Stories? A Brief ote on Games and Narrative', *Game Studies.
The International Journal of Computer Game Research*, 1, 1. Online. Available at http://
www.gamestudies.org/0101/juul-gts/ (accessed 26 June 2004).

_____ (2004) 'Introduction to Game Time', in N. Wardrip-Fruin and P. Herrington (eds)
First Person: New Media as Story, Performance, and Game, Boston: MIT Press, 131–
42. Online. Available at http://www.jesperjuul.dk/text/timetoplay (accessed 29 July

2004).

Kasvi, J. J. J. (2004) *Not Just Fun and Games: Internet Games as a Training Medium*. Online. Available at http://www.knowledge.hut.fi/people/jkasvi/NJFAG.PDF (accessed 3 July 2004).

Löw, M. (2000) *Raumsoziologie*. Frankfurt: Suhrkamp.

Pennacchini, S. (2004) 'Propaganda e politica nei Videogame', *C : cube. Cultura: comunicazione: consumo*, 2, 5, 80–4.

Schutz, A. (1967) 'On Multiple Realities', in *Collected Papers I: The Reality of Social Reality*. The Hague: Martinus Nijhoff, 207–59.

Schutz, A and T. Luckmann (1974) *The Structure of the Life World*. London: Heinemann.

Sofsky, W. (1998) *Saggio sulla violenza*. Torino: Einaudi.

Taylor, L (2003) 'When Seams Fall Apart: Video Game Space and The Player', *Game Studies: The International Journal of Computer Game Research*, 3, 2. Online. Available at http://www.gamestudies.org/0302/taylor/ (accessed 25 June 2004).

Walther, B. K. (2003) 'Playing and Gaming: Reflections and Classifications (1)', *Game Studies: The International Journal of Computer Game Research*, 3, 1. Online. Available at http://www.gamestudies.org/org/Walther (accessed 25 June 2004).

Zoll, R. (2003) *La solidarietà: Eguaglianza e differenza*. Bologna: Il Mulino.

Fixing a Heritage: Inscribing Middle Earth onto New Zealand

Stan Jones

Introduction

Elen Sila Lumen Omentielmo Endore Aotearoa
May a star shine upon our meeting here in Middle Earth Aotearoa

This is a greeting Ian Brodie uses to open his talks on his *Lord of the Rings Location Guidebook* (Jones & Welle 2003).[1] He derives it from Tolkien's invented language, Elvish, and the indigenous name of his homeland, so that its hybrid identity reflects the project of the *Guidebook*, which in turn reflects the filmic adaptation. The success of Peter Jackson's trilogy, and the overwhelming acceptance of its cinematic verisimilitude in depicting Middle Earth, means that the significance of Tolkien's epic narrative has changed. Because of the way the films' producers promoted the film by feeding fansites and subsequently through the commercial 'spin off' from the trilogy, it has taken on a further identity as the source of the film. And it has also added the identity politics of New Zealand to the global discourse on Tolkien and his work, already well established in studies, associations and websites.

Now that the film trilogy has had its global first run, its extended DVD editions and TV showing, it has entered film/media history. In New Zealand, the media, tourism and related institutions are displaying a second phase of adapting and applying the fantasy of Middle Earth. Through the trilogy, it identifies this place as a cultural product to be acknowledged by others, who do not live there, and then goes on to offer the reader/viewer/fan a further role as an agent or 'performer' in permanently maintaining the fantasy-as-process. That role attaches to a physical location, which is simultaneously an idea. As James Hay puts it:

> Places are designated and mediated discursively. They become signified and signify-
> ing frames of reference for social subjects. Models and myths of places do become

a basis upon which social relations are imagined, fetishised and refashioned (albeit from particular sites and though particular technologies and modes of circulation). (1996: 372)

This chapter illustrates such an interaction between real and virtual places by using four main examples: Brodie's extended *Guidebook* and Hobbiton; the only remaining film set; a television documentary; and the *Lord of the Rings* exhibition organised by the New Zealand national museum, Te Papa. The first two cater to visitors, whilst the others are for both locals and visitors. Their local perspective shows popular modes of media and media-combinations seeking to inscribe the film as phenomenon on New Zealand. They also illustrate how local media already define place and location against a global background – the post-trilogy view of this place from overseas needs another study of its own, as evidenced by an international research project into the lauch and reception of *The Lord of the Rings*.[2] This chapter will explore their common proposition of a 'real' or an 'authentic' virtuality as applied to New Zealand/Aotearoa.

The motivation for this process can appear ironic, as in Sean Cubitt's description: 'In short, Jackson's film does not depict these few South Pacific islands, but uses them as a springboard to picture a utopian and imaginary terrain forged – in every sense of the word – from the articulation of the local and the universal' (2005: 8). This means that we are offered access to Middle Earth as a place that can only exist through conscious imagining, through constructing a myth via narrative (cf. Hall 1995: 14). This process naturally attaches New Zealand's physical remoteness, as it predisposes this place, both for locals and visitors, to envisaging as the goal of a particularly long journey. Accordingly, a New Zealand site promotes tourism by co-opting a voice from the film, that of local actor Karl Urban (Eomer) to pitch the imagined goal in its most extreme form by declaring over a scrolling map merging actual geography with Middle Earth sites: 'Of course, we New Zealanders are lucky enough to live in Middle Earth all of the time' (Home of Middle Earth 2004). The slogan 'Home of Middle Earth' is the final stage of an articulation which has already seen *The Lord of the Rings* place names applied to New Zealand geography, such as the 'Hobbits' Tunnel' on State Highway 43 from Taumuranui to Stratford, the unsuccessful suggestion from the 1970s of naming peaks in the Southern Alps after Middle Earth and the long-established commune, 'Wilderland', on the Coromandel peninsula. The wider history of this process of is clear from Thierry Jutel's four categories:

> First the discourse around New Zealand is firmly grounded in the imperialist projection upon the colonised land. Second, as a postcolonial society, Aotearoa produces multiple and often contradictory discourses about the landscape. Third, the landscape of New Zealand has come to represent a transposable 'otherness'; and

finally, New Zealand, especially as it is recognised as Middle Earth, offers its land as a commodity, which inscribes it in the forces of the global economy. (2004: 55)

The four examples show how indigenising the myth entails shifting the implied scale of this place, which extends Jutel's remarks on the way: 'the production of space ... virtualises the geography of the country' (2004: 64) towards the question of the sort of pleasure such a process offers – and to whom.

Such identity politics can be seen as reversing the flow of what Arjun Appadurai calls 'imagined worlds' (1990: 306) through global media and communications. The New Zealand market for media products shows that this country consumes far more from overseas than it produces locally. With the trilogy the direction is ostensibly reversed. Even though the production originated legally, as intellectual property, and financially in Hollywood, and locating it in New Zealand depended on the state underwriting its costs via a tax break, the second phase seeks an identity that can claim much of the myth's origins. This claim may reflect in permanent film and media production here and is an aspect of New Zealand identity that still needs further study in the light of Peter Jackson's *King Kong* project.

The Lord of the Rings Location Guidebook

The *Guidebook* displays Ian Brodie's personal identification with it. He immediately saw his book as part of the lore surrounding both novel and now film:

> And it's because I am such a fan, and I have enjoyed it now for almost thirty years ... when the book arrived and I could see an image of Middle Earth, Gandalf and my name all in one place, this was, I would have to say, the proudest moment of my life. (Jones & Welle 2003)

Above all, the *Guidebook* celebrates spectacular, epic landscapes, as it adds images and significantly enlarges existing ones. Many display the way the filmmakers adapted such landscapes as settings, either by showing production techniques or using stills direct from the film itself. Two revisions add further insights into the trilogy's production history through accounts from three of the main players (Peter Jackson, Barrie Osborne, the principal producer, and Richard Taylor of Weta Workshops), of finding and using locations and of their favourites. Brodie himself figures in the 'Extended Edition' with an account of 'performance', being an extra for *The Return of the King*.

Brodie's book presents indigenous localities as a montage to display their multiple significance. It thereby offers the visitor multiple viewpoints for experiencing this place and its immanent 'genius loci'. The cover of the first edition, for instance, combines a production shot of Gandalf striding across New Zealand high country under the film's familiar titling format with the book's title and author superimposed over the landscape. The inside cover is then the direct reverse of such a layered image. It presents a standard, simplified relief map of the North Island as a two-dimensional diagram connoting no more than actual physical relations in space. It then develops this counterpoint more elaborately by paralleling explanatory text photographs of sites and landscapes. Some are straight records by the author, some come from tourism public relations, and they complement the other major visual element, the diagrammatic maps to certain locations. Other photographs shift towards the virtual, the film's fiction, as they are production stills from the film's photographer, Pierre Vinet, from designer Alan Lee, and images from New Line's publicity. And in one particular case, one of the stars, Viggo Mortensen, contributes a form of 'commentary' on the landscape in a moody shot of Lake Taupo under a storm. Further levels of correspondence appear as marginal 'commentary' from other stars and from Jackson to parallel the physical descriptions and instructions, and others imply Tolkien's original text. Another means through which the virtual reality of the film is inferred from the locations where it was generated is through Brodie's quotes of *The Lord of the Rings* lore. However, Tolkien's exact words do not figure, because the *Guidebook* 'is published with the permission but not the approval of the Estate of the late J.R.R. Tolkien' (Brodie 2004: 4). The second edition keeps the format of the first, but follows the release of *The Two Towers* by substituting on its cover Aragorn, Legolas, Gimli and Gandalf as riders contemplating Edoras from amid the tussock. The 'Extended Edition' drops the overall maps and embraces digital graphic fantasy for its cover, with a small figure of Gandalf riding to the impossible citadel of Minas Tirith.

The book's enlarged format shifts towards the well-publicised identity of 'scenic New Zealand', with new sections describing areas, such as the Mackenzie Country or Mount Cook, which are purely tourist destinations without film locations. Similarly, the only urban imagery, of Wellington, is also 'scenic' but cannot, of course, display production or stills. Some of the stills hint at pixilation and thus reflect the trilogy's increasing use of CGI and indicate its overall aesthetic in treating its New Zealand scenery as a graphic material applied in layers for its effects. Such a function prompts questions about what Marcus Doel and David Clark call 'real virtuality', which 'is not duplicitous, but multiplicitous – it is an immanent manifold, the consistency of which depends, precisely, upon one's point of view' (Doel & Clark 1999: 267). The *Guidebook* underpins the inscription of 'Middle Earth' by quoting coordinates generated by Global Positioning Satellites (GPS), on the threshold of space. It is meant for first-time visitors, who are viewers before readers. They can be sure that, with the right high-tech in actuality, they are in the authentic location as origin of the virtual reality they experience. But such accuracy only works because it derives from a system capable of determining location relative to the entire planet. The specific locations in New Zealand are, therefore, simultaneously global references and hence locate the entire country globally. This in turn connotes, although not overtly, the place visitors started from. So the book facilitates the imaginative process through charting for people from overseas a journey/adventure allowing performance of your own – retrospective – imaginings from home, or at least your point of departure, through a montage of inner and outer correspondences laid across New Zealand, both in space and time. And this in turn offers a site for gratifying a touristic 'homesickness', a form of doubled nostalgia combining the desire to experience what you conceive of as your own home with the desire to find aspects of that home confirmed abroad. Seen historically, it is the fourth phase of the reception process which began in the 1950s with the cult around Tolkien's original text, continued with its adaptation into film and the viewers' response to culminate in the wish to insert oneself into physical locations as correspondences to fantasy.

This activity corresponds to one aspect of Betty Weiler and Colin Michael Hall's definition of 'special interest tourism' as exercised by people who share a profession or a hobby (1992: 5). Although it is essentially individualistic, it parallels fan websites. It connotes a search for an identifiable community, albeit one that has no particular site but exists only in the conviction that others have sought a range of precisely the same sites out of the common experience of the films. Brodie explains the imaginative process thus: 'That would be a lifestyle that I would enjoy, that's a lifestyle that I would like – so I will make that landscape here so I can imagine that I'm there' (Jones & Welle 2003). His book so structures the individual correspondences that it generates a New Zealand/Aotearoa, which shares some aspects of what Michel Foucault (1986) called a 'heterotopia'. It appears here through Bruno Genocchi's interpretation of 'a discontinuous but socially defined spatiality, both material and immaterial at the same time ... they also function as powerful sights of the imaginary' (1995: 38). Where the correspondences are lacking, as with Northland, Auckland, the Coromandel, Taranaki or Southland, then the book's form of heterotopia is discontinuous, but where it caters for 'the imaginary', it prompts a form of dialectic, as John Rykes points out when quoting Foucault: 'even to imagine another order/system is to extend our participation in the present one' (2002: 30). Seekers after Middle Earth can use the *Guidebook* as a sort of staging-post between actual physical reality and their experience of the film, the virtual reality they have brought with them, thus indicating that New Zealand/Aotearoa actually denotes the origin of their imaginings.

The *Guidebook* and pilgrimage

Seeking Middle Earth does not mean wandering, but a form of 'grounded pilgrimage'. That is, there and back again between home and very distant goals already visualised with a technical precision which then, on your return, confirm you visited the recognised sites. Visitor/fans seeking out such correspondences confirm a German film critic's comment on the ironic relation of fantasy and meticulousness in Jackson's film:

> This irrational world, however, behaves completely rationally, for there is nothing in fantasy, and, as it seems, for its aficionados too, that is as important as rules, roles, formulas, ciphers and constructions. These are instruments of the early Renaissance, which have been integrated into the fantasy worlds: the map, the encyclopaedia, the incantatory recounting of history; you go through the fictive world with the exactitude of a chronicler. (Seesslen 2002: 37; author's translation)

One practical example extends the cultic potential of New Zealand/Aotearoa as Middle Earth. Brodie relates the GPS capability to an extreme fan as anachronistic 'pilgrim':

> It's just the practical means of finding a place. And a logical way because it's so simple. So simple to use. I know of a case of a German that emailed me that he said, he is coming to see me, he is flying in to Auckland, he is walking the length of New Zealand, going to every one of those locations in the book … in medieval clothing, with a replica of the One Ring round his neck, but with a GPS! He said, you will recognise me when I come to see you because I will be dressed like that, I am 6ft 4 [laughter] … I just have this mental image of this medieval-dressed person with the One Ring round his neck with a very complex piece of digital equipment in his hand (Jones & Welle 2003).[3]

This pseudo-medieval traveler navigates what is for him the Antipodes using global digital technology. The *Guidebook* holds out to him, beyond its practical advice, the possibility of experience. He is not, therefore, looking for actuality but for what he needs to find here, a suitable setting for role-playing. He illustrates the *Guidebook*'s ground theme: access to Middle Earth using an 'out of frame' New Zealand on offer just beyond the film's images.

This pilgrim can, therefore, construct himself as an avatar because the physical location of his destination has declared itself coterminous with the fantasy he desires. This can figure as a bizarre example of what migrants have always done, as Jutel points out above, but now New Zealand/Aotearoa shifts from the periphery to the centre, at least for the sort of imaginings promoted by the global media. This process is related to what David Morley calls 'indigenisation': 'different locales are made though a process of indigenisation of originally foreign materials' (2000: 195).

To support the way it charts the sites for imagining, the *Guidebook* offers several examples of the process from within the production history. As each account interprets actuality through retrospection, they also legitimate the reader/viewer/tourist's activity by offering precedents from figures with cultural and creative authority. The first two reflect the indigenous identity of New Zealand. Jackson moves towards an account of the production history by tracing a journey through the imported myth, taking him out from his consciously indigenous sensibility and back again. He remembers how reading the book on a train journey transformed the familiar landscape, which: 'all of a sudden looked like Middle Earth' (quoted in Brodie 2004: 6). His imagining culminates in his assertion that

> hard work and enthusiasm, combined with fantastic locations and computer enhancement technology all came together in a special way which gives our movies a special feel – different from the Hollywood blockbusters we're used to seeing. (2004: 7)

Invoking Hollywood for comparison means assuming the common context, the global film market in which to mark off your indigenous difference.[4] The book includes a similar remark that widens the viewpoint on what Ian McKellen calls the director's 'back yard' (2004: 74), where Jackson discerns 'a familiar yet slightly fantastical appearance' (2004: 119). For the 'Extended Edition', he described 'the location hunting process', where the prime directive is 'does this feel like it came from the pages of Tolkien's book?'(2004: 15). How faithfulness to the text generates authenticity appears where he stresses the visual appropriation of landscape by defining scale as a quality from the location chosen for Rohan:

> Whenever you can put a camera down, and literally see 50km in one direction, and have no power poles, no houses, no roads, it's just expanse, it suddenly gives the film that kind of epic John Ford western quality of tiny figures in this big landscape. (2004: 16)

The location's authenticity derives subtly from its correspondence not just to the dimensions of the fantasy required by Tolkien's source text, but also to a filmmaker's intertextual memory of epic quality.

Barrie Osborne also contributes insights into the 'making of' by citing the pre-production stage of the art-design contributed by Alan Lee and John Howe to confirm local authenticity. Seeking what Osborne calls the 'texture' of Middle Earth (2004: 23) meant engaging expensively and laboriously (and now ironically for a production noted for its effects) with remote locations, such as those used for Rohan or Edoras. Osborne finally justifies the effort:

> Sometimes it felt like these remote places were just waiting to double as Tolkien's Middle Earth. Tolkien's descriptions were right there in front of us in their three-dimensional glory, waiting to grace the camera with their natural beauty. (2004: 25)

The authenticity of the adaptation from the source derives, then, from a Romantic sense of a landscape, whose authenticity lies in its spirit as perceived through its correspondence to that of the imported myth. By contrast, Richard Taylor stresses the project's materiality by recalling his satisfaction at Edoras: 'I stood in another world – one created by a bunch of New Zealanders on the top of a mountain in the middle of nowhere, and it felt utterly real' (2004: 18). He remembers anticipating the verisimilitude of the fantasy in the camera's eventual illusion. One step further, and Brodie recounts performing as an extra and finding his book itself inserted in that: 'and then afterwards discuss the *Location Guidebook* with Bernard, Miranda and Viggo. I pinch myself – is this really happening?' (2004: 29). Via star-aura, the 'making of' the book now enters the film production narrative, becoming part of the sort of authentic account it offers to its readers.

For comparative contrast, the definitive indigenous identity of this place as Aotearoa comes from Chris Winitana, who relates the Maori creation myth, beginning with Ranginui and Papatuanuku and ending with Kupe naming the created land. As Winitana tells it, its origins lie in a heroic account from a warrior culture, not unlike the myth of *The Lord of the Rings*, suggesting that the land always possessed a 'genius loci', a system of correspondences between physical reality and transcendent significance, suited to creating a Middle Earth.

Where these are the viewpoints of 'insiders', Alan Lee stresses his 'outsider' perspective on the historical scale of correspondences:

> It's a young land, primeval in places, still flexing in the aftermath of its creation. I can imagine Britain in a much earlier age, with higher peaks and the clearer light that illuminates Tolkien's pages, might have had a similar quality. (2004: 22)

His account of producing Middle Earth indicates the complex creative imagining involved and is inevitably ironic. It means making a place both primeval, in that it represents a previous stage of your home territory, and younger – 'lacking the accumulated and overlaid evidence of thousands of years of continual habitation' (2004: 19) – seem older.[5] Where New Zealand is still primeval, as with the volcanic plateau used for Mordor, the wilderness has history applied to it via digitally-generated allegorical imagery for the destruction wrought by evil on Nature. By contrast, Lee's own indigenous sensibility explains his pleasure in the similarity of the finished Hobbiton to Devonshire. The filmmakers removed the location from the postcolonial present and made it correspond to an imagined prehistory of the settler-culture origins. This process becomes extreme with Rivendell created in Kaitoke Regional Park. A form of natural environment preserved for the use of a mainly urban population becomes the last site and sight of beings whose disappearance will signal the beginning of human history.

How coterminous the book's 'out of frame' New Zealand has become with the film stands out from the photograph from Kaitoke Park (2004: 65) which shows a 'Rivendell' now attached to original signage. The 'out of frame' New Zealand identified through overlaying of the natural landscape with the imported myth is also authenticated by reference to a well-established 'virtual' version of it: Samuel Butler's novel *Erewhon* (1872). Brodie quotes from this to open his description of the Edoras location, in the Erewhon Valley off the Canterbury Plains (2004: 92). The applying of a foreign, literary imagining to New Zealand over a century ago serves to locate and depict the place where an example of this century's indigenous imagination has repeated the process for cinema.[6]

A further opportunity for visitors to 'perform' their role comes where the book extends the function of the stars. In a parallel to the introductory accounts of imaginings sited here, it cites places where the leads have already been observed outside of moviemaking and ostensibly sharing aspects of everyday life. Not surprisingly, this tends to cluster around Wellington as the trilogy's headquarters, naming and showing entertainment locales. But surfing, an iconic New Zealand sport, also appears: 'The Hobbits found another means of relaxation at Lyall Bay … Within hours all four could be seen riding the waves' (2004: 73). Given the significance of the sea in the novel, this must be the most whimsical inscription of its myth onto New Zealand. Similarly, the reference to another 'sport', bungy-jumping, specifies Orlando Bloom sampling its delights (2004: 111), a marked contrast of the actual person with the way his character almost transcends gravity in action scenes or on snowdrifts. Such references ultimately legitimise the 'pilgrimage', as the star persona functions not only as a major image in the construction of the Middle Earth sought, but also as the exemplary 'visitor', who is both virtual and actual and links that quality to the book's locations.

The television documentary, Hobbiton, Te Papa and the travelling exhibition

The *Guidebook* is not the only way in which locations were used to create heritage. Television New Zealand deployed one of its genres to seek local identity by commissioning an hour-long documentary, 'The Real Middle Earth', in 2004. It personalises the entire phenomenon by generating a 'making of' narrative to inscribe its title on its place by intercutting footage of the shoots, with clips from the trilogy, picturesque landscapes, accounts from non-celebrity New Zealanders and the well-known faces of Jackson, Osborne, Taylor or Elijah Wood. It looks backwards out of the project's historical climax, the rapturous premiere for *Return of the King* in Wellington in December 2003. Jackson then appears as the definitive New Zealander in control and narrative authority to declare: 'We managed to find just about everything described in the book reasonably well in New Zealand.' Stressing faithfulness to the original text and its lore, the documentary illustrates its ground theme of the authentic New Zealanders behind the fantasy imagery. It shows extras from Matamata recounting the real experience of Hobbiton, the weaver of the Hobbits' cloaks, the park warden who literally carpeted the mountain slopes used for Mordor to protect their sensitive flora, or the local calligrapher who drew the maps and penned 'There and back again'. The most ironic comment on the entire process comes from a casting director, Miranda Rivers: 'The army is trained to fight, what they haven't learned yet is the art of make-believe', a remark confirmed by three soldiers who recall destroying quantities of prop-weapons in their enthusiasm for the mêlée. And to reinforce the project as authentic to New Zealand, one unknown extra declares of the director: 'He treated everybody the same,' confirming Jackson's talent for egalitarianism as a major factor in its success. On the digital manipulation of the locations, Brodie's authority, by dint of the *Guidebook*, points to the locations and certifies the composite images of Isengard or the first encounter with a Ringwraith as completely faithful to the source. The documentary's final phase involves various tour organisations in the South Island displaying their territory and commenting on how the production has benefited their business. Over a standard panorama shot of the South Island high country, the commentator attributes the success of the project to the talents of the many 'little people' of New Zealand, who contributed, like the original Hobbits, and, therefore, now own of share of its identity.

The *Guidebook* and the documentary, therefore, contribute to the creation of a heritage. They are, however, *per se* finished aspects. Hobbiton, the only remaining film set, is still developing. It became a tourist attraction in 2003 and is the most material, local example of the *Lord of the Rings* phenomenon as intellectual property. It took more than six months negotiating with New Line over the display, with the studio retaining the copyright on the structures to which a farmer grants visitors access. However, guides to the site certify its authenticity through cultural retrospect from elsewhere: three academics, who had known Tolkien, apparently arrived from England, and, on seeing the location, declared that the master must have visited New Zealand (Jones 2004)! This reversal of the 'genius loci' as influence on the source is the most fantastical extreme in the film's identity politics, but the venture's commercial success, with 30,000 visitors in the first half of 2004 (ibid.), bears out the power of its myth as inscribed on New Zealand by this site. Displays of stills indicate correspondences to the film and in turn allow visitors to produce their own record of having been there by mimicking the filmmakers' point of view in their photographs of the surrounding farm and the Kaimai Range in the background. Although the entire project developed by a combination of happy chance (the weather delayed demolition) and persistent tourist enquiries, the organisers stress the permanence of the site: 'It's not just the Hobbiton set, it's the entire surrounding', particularly as it attracts as many declared readers as film fans: 'That was one of the indications that we had a product that could actually survive beyond the theme of the movie' (ibid.). The nearby town of Matamata has adopted Middle Earth imagery into its permanent townscape and already figures in a huge number of media reports from overseas as a site for the myth (up to three crews per week in the first twelve months). In one sense, Hobbiton represents the location in New Zealand where the 'making of' circle closed, as New Line has apparently sent out its own trainees to film the tourist development of the location. Should the tour operators obtain permission from the studio to make the set permanent then perhaps it will also become a physical site acknowledged globally as New Zealand heritage.

The Travelling Exhibition opened concurrently with the release of *The Two Towers* in 2002 and is still touring globally. It was easily the most popular event yet staged by the Te Papa Museum and it was also the first time that the museum has sent anything further afield than Australia (Jones 2003). Questions of copyright, intellectual property and confidentiality dominated the project, as New Line had no experience of such exhibitions. The studio was, together with the filmmakers in New Zealand, also keen that nothing displayed should be pirated or anticipate the launching of *Return of the King* in December 2003, while the Tolkien Estate apparently refused any connection to the source texts. Hence, in complete contrast to what is offered to visitors at Hobbiton, no one was allowed to document their own experience of the exhibition and its correspondences to the film or to New Zealand by recording any images from it. The film workshops also produced custom objects, such as Argonath statues or a particular Gollum figure, whilst post-production work in Wellington meant other artefacts had to go back and then might return in a new version – or not at all. Hence, the version of the exhibition, which got to Sydney in December 2004, includes material from *Return of the King* which was not available in Wellington. As Te Papa is a prime site for constructing New Zealand identity, the trilogy's artefacts gained its aura, and then had that aura confirmed by visitor response. Yet the exhibition leaves open questions of authenticity and originality, which derive from the different aesthetic understanding of the objects themselves between filmmakers and curators, as Te Papa's communications manager put it:

> People from the film industry realised the objects were beautiful, were really proud of them themselves, but, no, they were only props ... so the treatment of them, the whole sort of change in philosophy of the treatment of them, from being a film prop to being an obect, an exhibition object, that had to be cared for in the same way that we would care for a Hotere,[7] we would care for these objects. (Quoted in ibid.)

Here is another understanding of the materiality of the entire *Lord of the Rings* production history, as emphasised in the 'making of' accounts. To these, the museum

also added a particular dimension reflecting its basic purpose: an educational programme to illustrate the film's production. Yet for the curators, involvement with
The Lord of the Rings illustrates 'new museumology in actually giving exhibitions in
terms of popular culture'(ibid.). That means not so much conservation of unique
objects, although some of the *Lord of the Rings* props are such because of their
association with particular stars, but participating in the entire phenomenon as
an event. The museum's own sampling of visitors confirms the exhibition's success deriving from its usual clientele, namely about 40 per cent from overseas,
with slightly less from New Zealand, followed by residents of Wellington and
the Wellington region, and, not surprisingly, the overall profile shows a slightly
younger age range than average (Harvey 2003). Given that each overseas location
has adapted Te Papa's template to its local conditions, it may be worth eventually
comparing any available data from each to assess the exhibition's inter-cultural significance. Its local popularity outlasted expectations and means the museum's *Lord
of the Rings* shop is still offering the trilogy's merchandise.

As to their exhibition's eventual fate, the curators said: 'It would need to take on
different meanings … if it was to come back here and become a permanent thing,
the whole exhibition basis would need to be looked into' (Jones 2003). It would
lose the New Line promotional aspect and become much more a focus of cultural
identity to be integrated into other such sites in this country. As yet, the possibility
remains 'in the air', as Tania Rodgers of Weta Workshops put it: 'At this stage the
idea of a permanent museum for *The Lord of the Rings* is still only an idea. One day
in the future we hope it will become a reality' (2004). In this way, the *Lord of the
Rings* phenomenon and the related New Zealand identity would escape the contin-
gency of global media production to become physical sites for popular memory. In
this sense, they would complete Morley's process of 'indigenisation'.

Heritage and the tradition of the epic

As local aspects of the film's global reception, the *Guidebook*, the documentary,
Hobbiton and the exhibition illustrate a cinematic tradition as defined by Vivian
Sobchack: 'Most Hollywood historical epics not only repeat the narrative *within*
the film through a doubling narration but also repeat that narrative *outside* of the
film – if within its cinematic discourse' (1995: 293). As all four examples declare
New Zealand/Aotearoa suitable for Middle Earth because of its relative lack of
history compared to England, it is ironic that they contribute to shifting this place
further into global cinema history. Perhaps this compensates, in the New Zealand
context, for what Sobchack sees as a 'fear of pastlessness' (1995: 301) which moti-
vates the Hollywood epic and arises from a fundamental aspect of the national
identity of the US. How Jackson's film qualifies as an (historical) epic, particularly
in fixing national identity through cinema history, is too wide a topic for discus-

sion here. But this chapter's examples follow the tradition of the cinematic epic to negotiate the potential conflict between New Zealand's local and global identities by proposing the 'Home of Middle Earth' as part of a 'heritage'. That process is not straightforward because it seeks to establish a myth through narrative: this place's identity existing as a form of heterotopia defined by Raymond Gozzi as an 'oxymetaphor' (1999: 33). This indicates a term, which may be contradictory in itself, such as 'global village', but which does manage to secure the discursive currency of a definition denoting a range of existing circumstances, even as far as becoming a cliché.

Whether Jackson's film will become a national epic for this country is still an open question. On its long-term impact, the New Zealand filmmaker (and producer of an as yet unreleased three-DVD documentary of the 'making of'), Costa Botes speculates:

> It'll be interesting to see how long interest stays high in *The Lord of the Rings*. Personally, I think regardless of its immediate mass-market profile, there will always be a long-term fascination with the work, the film and its many artifacts. If a museum were created that was up to the standard we'd all hope for, I think it would eclipse Te Papa both in Wellington, and nationally. In fact, it could be a Disney scale attraction. (2004)

Whilst the material scale of a Disneyland, with its perceived potential for pleasure, might be desirable, the Disney scale and range of fantasy could scarcely support the sort of heterotopia capable of an authentic myth, that of the 'genius loci' suggested by New Zealand's physical reality. Yet a physical site would counteract the instability, and potential for dis-pleasure, in a 'heritage' constructed as a simulacrum without any tangible evidence. That way also lies the uncanny, which could inscribe a very different identity on this place through its potential for subversive perspectives on perceived reality. A material site would also counteract some implications inherent in promoting New Zealand/Aotearoa as a site for film locations because it presents 'the world in one country'. If the landscapes can look like anywhere else, successive layers of resemblance and mimicry laid across them suggest their identity depends not on difference from an Other but on resemblance to it. Where this Other is the film's imagery itself, comparison risks collapsing the myth and any possibility of 'heritage'. This effect appears in a travelogue report from a fan who followed Brodie's *Guidebook* as a self-declared scholarly investigation and experienced dis-pleasure in the tension between real and fantasy. When he sought the location of the trilogy's Dimrill Dale, he found that

> it shows how the portrayal of New Zealand in the films can be deceptive. When you are watching the films you are not watching New Zealand, you are watching Middle

Earth and it is important to note that difference when you are huffing and puffing in frustration and exhaustion at the top of a mountain (Keramidas 2004: 19).

While the report affirms the film's verisimilitude for the fan as viewer, for the fan as traveler, the physical location is not authentic. It has failed as an experience of 'real virtuality' because it fails the fan approaching it with Georg Seesslen's 'exactitude of a chronicler'. It does not correspond to his present memory of the film or to its imagery he recalled on the spot from a DVD. The search for exact correspondences fails because it seeks the authenticity of the fantasy in the actual, which cannot match the way the trilogy's layered images invite repeat viewings. Yet this can offer pleasure in landscape, as Claudia Bell and John Lyall put it:

> Our pleasure, being the pleasure of surprise, is very like the pleasure derived from the plot of a story, the unfolding narrative, in a novel or a movie. A second visit or rereading reveals other layers of meaning. (2002: 35)

For the second phase of New Zealand/*Lord of the Rings* identity politics, this means detaching identity from the present, or from a mimesis based on any given position in space and time, to suggest the permanent possibility of Doel and Clark's 'immanent manifold' as a heterotopia conceived in the 'future perfect' tense. Readers and viewers already well-acquainted with the texts and their myths can then find pleasure akin to what Ginette Vincendeau defined for the historical epic film:

> It's a circulation of what might be called 'memories of history'. As *Cahiers du cinéma* famously noted, all historical films are set in the 'future perfect' tense, setting up questions the spectator already knows the answer to. (1995: 35)

Instead of this country being fixed historically as the site of the trilogy, its existential scale of identity expands by becoming the permanent origin of a process both capable of looking backwards and forwards simultaneously and with the potential for a wider 'out of frame' reality than the actual.

Even for non-viewers and readers, what is on offer is a virtuality beginning with physical reference but depending on recursion via a range of correspondences, cultural, geographic aesthetic and so on, both to any number of memories connected with the trilogy and to the repeated anticipation of recreating them by finding the right place for your imaginings, even as far as the melancholia inherent in Tolkien's narrative. As Mitsuhiro Yoshimoto puts it, 'in the new global space, the dichotomy of the real and the imaginary plays a far less important role than that of the plausible and the implausible or the actual and the virtual' (1996: 111–12). The identity of New Zealand /Aotearoa resists the closure implicit in a culture of global perspectives and becomes, forever, the once and future Middle Earth.

Notes

1 The *Guidebook* has gone to three editions, with a larger format 'Extended Edition' appearing in August 2004. All references will be to this latest edition. It has been remarkably successful with over twenty weeks as New Zealand's best-selling book and over 250,000 copies sold.

2 This chapter was developed as part of the International Lord of the Rings Research Project. Its research was made possible by research grants from the Faculty of Arts and Social Sciences, University of Waikato, and by a grant from the UK Economic and Social Research Council (ESRC Grant No. 000-22-0323) to whom we record our gratitude.

3 My wife and I sighted him in Central Otago in January 2003.

4 Perhaps the most extreme example of Morley's 'indigenisation' process from the production history is the anecdote about Jackson getting the crowd at a Wellington cricket match, suitably between England and New Zealand, to chant the 'Black Speech' of Mordor for his battle scenes (see Brodie 2004: 55).

5 Layered historical identity becomes particularly obvious in the location chosen for Lothlorien, Fernside House in Featherstone, where the gardens used were designed in 1924 by the 'English garden designer Gertrude Jekyll' (Brodie 2004: 62).

6 And a further narrative level applies to the location, as Ian Brodie explained: 'Mt Sunday of course is in the valley of Erewhon and in the late 1890s and early 1900s the shepherds and farm workers would have Sunday off and climb up that hill and drink beer. So it became Mt Sunday because that was their drinking place and they always did it on a Sunday' (Jones & Welle 2003).

7 The reference is to the celebrated New Zealand artist Ralph Hotere.

Works cited

Appadurai, A. (1990) 'Disjuncture and Difference in the Global Cultural Economy', *Theory, Culture and Society*, 7, 2–3), 295–310.

Bell, C. and J. Lyall (2002) *The Accelerated Sublime: Landscape, Tourism and Identity*. Westport and London: Praeger.

Botes, C. (2004) Email correspondence with the author, 22 December.

Brodie, I. (2004) *The Lord of the Rings Location Guidebook*, extended edition. Auckland: HarperCollins.

Cubitt, S. (2005) *EcoMedia*. Amsterdam: Rodopi.

Doel, M. and D. Clark (1999) *From Pastiche City to the Screening of the Eye? or, Geographies of a Diegesis: Postmodernism, Hyperspace and Simulation in the Screening of Blade Runner*. Leeds: University of Leeds Press.

Foucault, M. (1986) 'Of Other spaces', *Diacritics*, 16, 1, 22–7.

Genocchio, B. (1995) 'Discourse, Continuity, Difference: the Question of "Other spaces"', in S. Watson and K. Gibson (eds) *Postmodern Cities and Spaces*. Cambridge: Blackwell, 35–46.

Gozzi, R. (1999) *The Power of the Metaphor in the Age of the Electronic Media*. Cresskill, NJ: Hampton Press.

Hall S. (1995) 'Introduction: Who Needs Identity?', in S. Hall and P. Du Gay (eds) *Questions of Cultural Identity*. Thousand Oaks: Sage, 1–17.

Harvey, M. (2003) *The Lord of the Rings Motion Picture Trilogy: The Exhibition Visitor Research Findings from Exit Interviews and Observations,* unpublished paper, 11.

Hay, J. (1996) 'Afterword', in L. Grossberg and E. Wartella (eds) *The Audience and its Landscape*. Boulder and Oxford: Westview, 359–78.

Home of Middle Earth (2004) Online. Available at http://www.newzealand.com/travel/homeofmiddleearth (accessed 22 December 2004).

Jones, S. (2003) 'Interview with Paul Brewer (General Manager, Communications and Marketing Te Papa) and Anne Blyth (Senior Manager, National Services Te Papa), 30 April.

_____ 'Interview with Henry Horn (Sales and Marketing Manager, Rings Scenic Tours Ltd), 10 July.

Jones, S. and A. Welle (2003) 'Interview with Ian Brodie', Wanaka, New Zealand, 26 January.

Jutel, T. (2004) '*Lord of the Rings*: Landscape, Transformation and the Geography of the Virtual,' in C. Bell and S. Matthewman (eds) *Cultural Studies in Aotearoa New Zealand,* Oxford: Oxford University Press, 54–65.

Keramides, K. (2004) 'Where am I standing?' Online. Available at http//www.nyu.edu/classes/bkg/tourist/keramidas (accessed 7 January 2005).

Mason, D. (2004). *The Real Middle Earth*. DVD F12607-9, Wellington, Television New Zealand and Rustic Rd. Productions.

Morley, D. (2000) *Home Territories*. London: Routledge.

Rodgers, T. (2004) Email correspondence with the author, 22 December.

Rykes, J. L. (2002) *Land/Seascapes of Exclusion*, unpublished PhD thesis, University of Waikato.

Seesslen, G. (2002) 'Und nun beuget die Knie!', *Die Zeit*, 18 December, 52.

Sobchack, V. (1995) '"Surge and Splendour": A Phenomenology of the Hollywood Historical Epic', in B. K. Grant (ed.) *Film Genre Reader II*. Austin: University of Texas Press, 280–307.

Tolkien, J.R.R. (1969). *The Lord of the Rings*. London: George Allen and Unwin.

Vincendeau, G. (1995) 'Unsettling Memories', *Sight and Sound*, 5, 7, 30–2.

Weiler, B. and C. M. Hall (1992) *Special Interest Tourism*. London: Belhaven Press.

Yoshimoto, M. (1996) 'Real Virtuality', in R. Wilson and W. Dissanayake (eds) *Global/Local*, Durham: Duke University Press, 107–18.

Musical Middle Earth

K.J. Donnelly

Introduction

The conclusion of *The Lord of the Rings* film trilogy ends with a bizarre sonic occurrence, or rather, at least the DVD version of *The Return of the King* does. Demanding the utmost in stamina from its audience, those who commit themselves to watching, and more to the point, listening to the whole of the lengthy end-title credit sequence, will be rewarded. Momentarily, the music changes character to quote the theme for Siegfried from Wagner's *Ring of the Nibelungen* cycle. Is this simply a musical joke? It is ambiguous. Does it refer to the distinct similarities between Wagner's cycle and Tolkien's, or does it refer obliquely to the troubling racial imaginary of Tolkien's world and Peter Jackson's trilogy of films?

The Lord of the Rings has always had music attached, from its first appearance as a book to each manifestation or partial-manifestation. Upon reading *The Lord of the Rings* as a child, I imagined the music in a particular way. The Elven (and Elven-inspired) songs I imagined would sound something like the Celtic mysticism of Seán Ó Sé's recordings for Gael-Inn records in the 1960s, particularly songs such as 'Príosún Chluain Meala' or 'Táimse im' Chodhladh' (recorded more recently by Brian Kennedy). Perhaps these Celtic imaginings reflected more the sort of music I had been exposed to rather than the more Saxon and Norse reference points that are highly evident in the books. However, my own imaginings reflected the situation of a marginal music that was also not sung in English, as good a model as any for unfamiliar Middle Earth music. I also imagined that their character might have something mixing the oriental and the occidental, in the manner of Edmund Rubbra's song cycle *The Jade Mountain* for harp and female vocals (Op.116, 1962).

This chapter will look to how the book and films have been translated into and accompanied by musical permutations and how these musical versions have articulated aspects of the original text, or, indeed, added to them. A key part of this will note what has been foregrounded and what has been marginalised, looking for a musical 'centre' to *The Lord of the Rings* as a literary, cinematic, aural and musical object in the public's mind. Since the advent of Peter Jackson's film trilogy, there has been an explosion of musical activity. This has been inspired directly by the film, with many disc releases attempting to exploit the prominence of the film; some have been inspired to provide their own versions in contrast to the film's musical profile, while others simply have been re-released and rediscovered to tie in with the sustained interest in the subject matter inspired by Jackson's films.

Middle Earth music

In 1967 sheet music was published of songs written by established songwriters Donald Swann and Michael Elvin that set Tolkien's words to music. Swann had been one the most famous British songwriters since the Second World War, having forged a particularly successful partnership with Michael Flanders. These were simply a manifestation of some of Tolkien's 'songs' as they appear in the *Lord of the Rings* books, and consist of: 'In Western Lands', 'Namarie', 'I Sit Beside the Fire', 'Errantry', 'The Road Goes Ever On and On' and 'Upon the Hearth the Fire is Red'. These are not 'representations' of the book as such. They are piano and vocal versions of the book's songs, made for home consumption in the 'parlour'. In the book, on the other hand, they are in the vast majority sung as unaccompanied songs. Of course, it is possible that these songs might be conceived as having 'parlour' versions that might be sung to piano accompaniment by Hobbits and Elves in their homes or inns. Thus the versions sung in the book are rough and ready unaccompanied versions, and the sheet music (and recordings) allow for a better version, a more polished version. 'In Western Lands' includes a section of piano alone, suggesting a radical shift from the solo vocal manifestation of verbal cultures evident in *The Lord of the Rings*. However, Tolkien sanctioned Swann's materialisation of the songs from the books, even going as far as singing some to Swann as a general guideline. This, apparently, was the case for 'Namarie' (Hargrove 2005), the least conventional-sounding song in the collection, which has much in common with poetic chanting, hitting a monotone pitch as a basis and retaining a repetitive rhythm based on the song words. Hobbit songs such as 'I Sit Beside the Fire' and 'The Road Goes Ever On and On' bear direct resemblance to fairly recent British folk songs, most notably in terms of their structural divisions and simple melodies.

In 1970, Gail Aldrich released *Music from J.R.R.Tolkien's The Fellowship of the Ring*, which largely realised the songs in the book, in a folk music idiom. American composer Alan Horvath began writing music for a Lord of the Rings concept album in the early 1970s, which was released on CD by Akashic Records in 2004. Called

Figure 8: *The Lord of the Rings* and heavy metal (from top left): Led Zeppelin's 'Ramble On' (1969), Rush's 'Rivendell' (1975), Running Wild's 'Mordor' (1985), Isildur's Bane's 'Tom Bombadil', Attacker's 'Battle at Helm's Deep' (1987), Galadriel, Stratovarius's *Tolkien* (1999)

The Rings Project, its musical pieces mostly share titles with chapters from the book and use a folk rock idiom, featuring acoustic guitar, mandolin and dulcimer. The second track on the album is 'The Adventures of Tom Bombadil' and most of the music depicts incidents from the first book of the trilogy, *The Fellowship of the Ring*. In this manner, it remains close to Tolkien's depictions in the books. In the 1970s, Australian jazz musician John Sangster recorded music that was re-released in the wake of the films: *Lord of the Rings, vol. 1* (Move Records, 2003), which was cut from his original triple-LP release of seven-hours' length.

Recordings of pieces that emanate from the world of 'legit' music, the 'serious' classical concert hall, include Johan De Meij's *Lord of the Rings*, with its five movements – 'Gandalf', 'Lothlorien', 'Gollum', 'Moria' and 'Hobbits'. This Dutch composer produced some epic but very traditional-sounding music for wind ensemble (recording by the Ensemble Vents et Percussion de Quebec, released on Atma Classique in 1998). Another composer using a traditional orchestral sound was American Craig Russell, whose *Middle Earth on Rhapsody for Horn and Orchestra* was released on a recording by Naxos in 2003 (Michael Nowak conducting the San Luis Obispo Symphony). These 'sound pictures' included depictions of Galadriel, Gollum and Gandalf. Perhaps the most bizarre was Sir James Pitton-Smith's *Lord of the Rings Trilogy* (Dressed to Kill, 2001), which was a symphony in three movements ('Overture', 'Legend of the Hobbits', 'March of the Dark Lords'). Again, this had an epic but traditional orchestral sound, but the CD itself came with a poster map of Middle Earth adorned with prominent pictures of nude women.

In 1970, Bo Hansson, a Swedish multi-instrumentalist and synthesiser player, produced a concept album called *The Lord of the Rings* which directly depicted events and images from the book. It forms a narrative that depicts the successive events in the books, starting with 'Leaving the Shire'. This piece sets the tone for the album, an impressionistic jazz-rock that bears a certain resemblance to some of German experimental group Popol Vuh's contemporaneous work. 'The Old Forest and Tom Bombadil' remains an instrumental, despite the episode in the book being saturated with singing. It is premised upon an energetic bass organ *ostinato*, mixed with wind instruments and guitar, sounding very much like the sort of folk-rock that Jethro Tull were producing at the time. The music for Tom Bombadil eschews the sort of British folk-singing that is his characteristic in the book, but instead this sound picture attempts to capture his spirit rather than his sounds. 'The Black Riders' sounds something like contemporaneous exotic music, such as Manfred Hübler and Siegfried Schwab's for the film *Vampyros Lesbos* (Jesus Franco, 1970), conjoining a rock beat on bongos with a strident trebly organ solo and distorted, overdriven electric guitar. 'Shadowfax', a paean to Gandalf's horse, involves trebly electric guitar over a galloping beat, and is reminiscent of some of Mike Oldfield's instrumental work in the 1970s. Perhaps surprisingly, Hansson's music for the Elves does not bear the hallmark of anything more exotic than we have already experienced on the album. 'Dreams in the House of Healing' comprises an organ solo, while 'At the House of Elrond and the Ring goes South' has a repeated guitar arpeggio with high organ notes over the top, and 'Lothlorien' aims for atmospheric evocation through repetition rather than relying on melodic aspects.

Generally speaking, Hansson's album uses spare musical textures, avoiding conventional sounds, apart from one or two cases where the music sounds like a band in full flight. It is dominated by jazzy organ and electric guitar. Indeed, it is more textural than melodic or rhythmic. The melodies are not supposed to be tremendously catchy, but instead the music works as an invocation of a particular atmosphere, in a way not dissimilar to some incidental music in films. Hansson's *The Lord of the Rings* certainly appears to be related to other contemporaneous musical reference points: Mike Oldfield, Popol Vuh, Manfred Hübler, Jethro Tull; this is not to suggest that it is derivative, merely that it is very much a product of the musical interests and priorities of its time.

A decade later, the BBC made a radio adaptation of *The Lord of the Rings* (1981), as 26 half-hour episodes. It included music composed and conducted by Stephen Oliver, featured David James as singer and adapted some of Tolkien's songs, including 'The Road Goes Ever On and On'. Its incidental music consisted of a small amount of music written for a small chamber ensemble, dominated by strings, including a melodic title theme that reappears as a transition for shifts in location.

Before Christopher Lee's engagement as Saruman in *The Lord of the Rings* trilogy, he had already been involved in a musical project with The Tolkien Ensemble. They released *Evening in Rivendell* (Classico, 1997), *Night at Rivendell* (Olufsen, 1999) (brought together in one collection as *24 Songs from The Lord of the Rings* (Classico, 2001), and were followed by *The Lord of the Rings: At Dawn in Rivendell* (Decca, 2003), all of which featured Lee as both a narrator and singer. These recordings realise many songs and poems from the book, and clearly aim to be faithful to Tolkien's original ideas. They include Tom Bombadil's 'Hey Dol! Merry Dol!' and 'The Song of the Ent and the Ent-Wife' – both of which are marginalised (indeed absent) in most musical incarnations of *The Lord of the Rings*. The Ensemble was founded by Caspar Reiff and Peter Hall, using mostly Danish musicians, many of them classical ensembles from Copenhagen along with more rustic-sounding guitar, accordion and mandolin. The style runs from folk songs to *a cappella* choral pieces and parlour songs with piano accompaniment, and the project appears to realise all of the poems and songs that appear in Tolkien's book trilogy.

There have been plenty of instances of pop and rock songs being inspired by *The Lord of the Rings*. Musical genres that are particularly well represented in this respect include progressive rock, folk-rock and heavy metal. Some famous hard rock groups referenced Tolkien, such as the Led Zeppelin song 'Ramble On', which has lyrics that discuss 'Gollum, the evil one', although there is no sustained focus on

Tolkien's world. Later in the 1970s, Canadian group Rush included a track called 'Rivendell' on the album *Fly by Night* (1975). Rock groups were named after both Gandalf and Aragorn. Progressive heavy metal group Stratovarius released an album called *Tolkien* in 1999. It included an instrumental piece called 'The Lord of the Rings' that mixed piano and acoustic guitar sections with repetitive guitar riffing in the classic heavy metal manner. Another group, Isildur's Bane, derived their title from a name for the one ring itself, and produced a song called 'Tom Bombadil' that aped some of this character's singing in Tolkien's book, along with a fairly incongruous background of clean jazzy rock. Heavy metal group Blind Guardian's *Nightfall in Middle Earth* (1998) includes spoken-word narration along with operatic heavy metal with catchy choruses. It is based directly on Tolkien's *The Silmarillion*, which tells of events earlier in the history of Middle Earth. Most manifestations of *The Lord of the Rings* were in the progressive rock or heavy metal vein, although an example from more marginal music was the Cold Meat Industry record label act Morthound, who produced a track called 'Mithril' on the album *Death Time* (1991). Sometimes this artist was known as 'Morthond', derived from a Middle Earth character, Gondorian Derufin, the son of Duinhir of Morthond.

Films of the Rings

Apart from the music inspired by and preceding *The Lord of the Rings*, the actual film music itself has some interesting characteristics, especially in how it tries to evoke the original world of the books (through songs).

The first film version of *The Lord of the Rings* was the animated film directed by Ralph Bakshi and released in 1978. The film's incidental music, by Leonard Rosenman, broadly conformed to the strictures of traditional Hollywood film scores while at times bearing the signature of Rosenman's interest in more austere musical language of twentieth-century concert music. There are a few instances of diegetic songs sung by characters, usually following the book. However, at Rivendell Sam narrates a poem about Tinúviel with diegetic musical backing including a harp. This does not occur in the book, although after the company have left Bree Strider chants about Tinúviel ('The leaves were long, the grass was green/The hemlock umbels tall and fair' (Tolkien 1966: 208–9)) and in the book shortly afterwards Sam sings for the others' entertainment: 'Troll sat alone on his seat of stone/And munched and mumbled a bare old bone' (1966: 223–4). This latter song is lost, conflating the two incidents in a different location. Films by necessity have to condense material when adapting books, and indeed the adaptation of books as extensive as Tolkien's could doubtless never be filmed without such reduction. Nevertheless, this musical poem retains something of the original flavour of the song sequences that have been lost.

In that there are few diegetic songs in the film, the incidental music dominates the sonic character of *The Lord of the Rings*. Rosenman's score includes a jocular theme for the quest, firstly used for the band of Hobbits and then for the journey of the fellowship of the ring itself. Rosenman reserves his more characteristic discordant and atonal music for the forces of darkness, most notably for Saruman's Uruk-Hai, and their associated battle scenes. Rosenman's career as a composer for films had started with *Rebel Without A Cause* (Nicholas Ray, 1955) and taken him to some modernist art music-style scores for *Fantastic Voyage* (Richard Fleischer, 1966) and *Beneath the Planet of the Apes* (Ted Post, 1970). His score for *The Lord of the Rings* is a middle ground between his more sonorous but dissonant earlier scores and his more traditional (and less challenging) sounding music for *Star Trek IV: The Voyage Home* (Leonard Nimoy, 1986). In the final analysis, Rosenman's score has little that marks it out as distinctively about Middle Earth, relying on traditions of music (including film music) more than any specific attempt to paint a musical picture of the different lands and peoples of Tolkien's imagination. A good example of this is in Lothlorien, where we hear a choir of children sing a song about Gandalf (whom they call 'Mithrandir'). This is the 'Lament for Gandalf' that marks what appears to be his passing. While one might expect some musical exoticism for the unfamiliar, magical yet curiously ambiguous culture of Lothlorien, instead the song is remarkably familiar in style. Indeed, it appears in a quite traditional Western idiom, with diatonic melody making short consonant leaps in pitch and broadly following a form that has been common in both Western popular and art music. Generally speaking, Rosenman's score tends to use a musical language that is not directly inspired by the material on screen. It uses the sort of music that could have been written for other film worlds. It is more interested in helping to articulate images on screen rather than being a central part of the film's depiction of the world on screen.

Jules Bass and Arthur Rankin Jr made an animated version of Tolkien's *The Hobbit* for television in 1977 and an animated version of *The Return of the King* in 1980, both for ABC. The latter was something of a sequel, albeit a rather differently-toned one, to Ralph Bakshi's film. *The Return of the King* had incidental music by Maury Laws and included the singing voice of folk singer Glenn Yarborough as a minstrel, narrating the story's events through song. These are more downmarket products than the Bakshi film and this is highly evident in their music.

When Howard Shore came to score Peter Jackson's *The Lord of the Rings*, he was faced with a history of music tied to the film as well as distinct requirements for the music derived from the book's description. In addition to this, he was also compelled to follow the exigencies of current large-scale music for expensive Hollywood blockbusters. Shore chose to score the series of three films using distinct leitmotivs, themes that represent different aspects of the narratives. This technique was prominent in the classical Hollywood cinema. Perhaps the prestige scores of Erich Wolfgang Korngold provide the best example, with their succession of reappearing themes, with *The Adventures of Robin Hood* (Michael Curtiz, 1938) containing a massive number of individual themes for different characters or situations. The common use of the leitmotiv in the classical film score was derived from Richard Wagner's earlier use of such thematic building blocks as a way to unify his large-scale operas. It is worth noting that there are some similarities between the stories of *The Lord of the Rings* and Wagner's *Ring of the Nibelungen*, not least that a ring of power is paramount. Mark Brownrigg notes that Shore's music marks a homology between the *Nibelungen* and the Orcs (2003: 12). So in a way it is apt that Shore chose a similar system of leitmotiv use for the trilogy of films. Shore provides a full range of heroic, bold orchestral themes with a full-blooded orchestral sound and massed choirs, which is something of a rarity in the overwhelming majority of his film scores.

Shore conceived of *The Lord of the Rings* music a single organic piece rather than a fragmentary selection of cues, as is the case in the vast majority of contemporary mainstream films. He worked on the three films as a single entity and the musical score as a central aspect of the trilogy, noting that

> *The Two Towers* has three to five stories all going on at the same time. There's that constant shifting back and forth between them and the music has to do this seamlessly, taking it from one place to another ... The concept is opera and it's the reverse of writing an opera and then having it staged. What I'm trying to do is have the same feeling so that when you watch the film, it feels seamless, it's almost like the film was created to music. (Quoted in 2002: 32–3)

Indeed, at times the conflicts on screen are evident in the interplay of musical themes, embodied in the music, most notably during the battle for Helm's Deep in *The Two Towers*, where the Lothlorien theme appears for the Elf archers immediately followed by the Isengard theme for the Uruk-Hai.

The most prominent musical theme in the film trilogy is the heroic 'Fellowship' theme, which underscores the construction of the fellowship of the ring, and marks their togetherness even though it is fragmented in the second and third films. It often appears on horns and is first heard in its full form when Elrond announces the establishment of the fellowship. The secondary theme is the more mysterious 'Ring' theme, which suggests something of the darkness of the ring and its corrupting capacity. It has an Eastern-style sound (often using the Moroccan rhiata, a reed wind instrument that suggests the exotic for Western audiences unfamiliar with such a sound), and is also used to represent Mordor. Another notable theme is the theme for Hobbits and the Shire, which has a bucolic flavour and suggests something of the rustic wholesomeness of the Hobbits, no matter how far they might be from their homeland. It appears first on fiddle, later on whistle and clarinet, and finally as the hymn-like song 'In Dreams'. The film's depiction of Elf culture inspires some exotic sounds. Lothlorien is characterised by an Eastern-style theme which is associated more directly with Galadriel, and also appears towards the end of *The Two Towers* to accompany the arrival of Elven archers at Helm's Deep. The music for Rivendell is less exotic to a degree, and characterised by gentle arpeggios.

The music in *The Lord of the Rings* trilogy has a remarkable array of well-known guest singers, including Enya (a well-known solo artist, once of Clannad), Elizabeth Fraser (of the Cocteau Twins), Emiliana Torrini, Isabel Bayrakdarian, Sheila Chandra (who once had a hit with Monsoon in the 1980s) and Annie Lennox (once of the Tourists and then the Eurythmics). These are not the only singing soloists by far. The films contain songs (diegetically and non-diegetically) and each film of the trilogy has a song on the end titles that was released as a single to publicise the film, following the conventions of many contemporary big-budget Hollywood films.

The Fellowship of the Ring includes the largest number of songs. 'The Prophecy Song', written by Howard Shore with lyrics in Elvish by Philippa Boyens, opens the film (and the soundtrack CD). Gandalf arrives in the Shire singing in a cart and Bilbo's party includes folk-style music with a strong beat to allow dancing. The Black Riders are accompanied by vocal chants. At Rivendell, Enya sings the slow elegiac Aniron in Elvish, which is a love theme for Aragorn and Arwen. This song was written and performed by Enya, rather than being her vocal performance on a piece of music written by Howard Shore, as was the case in the overwhelming majority of musical pieces in the film. Enya is a very individual singer, who is fierce about artistic integrity. She turned down the offer to provide music for James Cameron's *Titanic* (1997), which led to James Horner's score pastiching Enya's musical style at points in that film (Donnelly 2004: 208–9). She has another song on the film's end titles, which was the scout single serving as publicity for the film ('May It Be'). 'Moria' includes the sound of a male-voice choir, the Maori Samoan Choir, singing in Dwarvish. 'The Lament for Gandalf' is heard in 'Lothlorien' and is sung by Scottish singer Elizabeth Fraser in Elvish as the fellowship talk, and has the sort of ethereal and exotic quality that is matched by the visuals in the woodland kingdom. This is aided by copious amounts of reverb, giving more space and distance to Fraser's highly individual voice. Indeed, she has been one of the most individual voices in British popular music over the last twenty years or so. After singing for the ethereal post-punk group the Cocteau Twins throughout the 1980s and early 1990s, she appeared as guest vocalist for Peter Gabriel on his *Music for the Millennium Dome* (1997) and for Craig Armstrong on the hit single 'This Love' (1998). She has also sung for This Mortal Coil and Massive Attack. Her early records included a characteristic warbling, making a rapid vibrato between two sung notes. Later she abandoned this technique in favour of esoteric words and highly otherworldly tones, usually aided by electronic studio reverberation and echo.

There are some notable missing sections. The whole incident with Tom Bombadil is completely absent. The songs sung at the Prancing Pony Inn in Bree are also lost, meaning that the film has to change the moment where Frodo puts the ring on and become invisible. In the book, he falls from the table after singing while in the film he is simply knocked over by accident by a Breelander. Indeed, the Hobbit songs are excised too, notably the bath song and the drinking song: 'Ho! Ho! Ho! To the Bottle I Go' sung by Sam and Pippin under a tree and 'Sing Hey! For the Bath at the Close of Day' by Pippin and other hobbits at Crickhollow.

However, *The Fellowship of the Ring* has used music to evoke most of the key points of musical representation in Tolkien's book. The Hobbits have a rustic theme that reappears for them, while both Rivendell and Lothlorien are evoked through the use of musical exoticism. *The Two Towers* introduces some new cultures of Middle Earth. Rohan, for instance has a sound as well as a theme, characterised by the use of the Norwegian Hardanger, a type of folk violin. It is recorded with some reverb to isolate the sound slightly from the rest of the instruments. The Norse character of the music is a direct counterpart to the visual representation of Rohan, which is rooted in northern Europe, particularly in Viking design and imagery. Some of the choral music in *The Two Towers* associated with Rohan is sung in Anglo-Saxon ('Old English'), cementing the cultures of men in the invasive peoples of dark-ages Europe. (It is interesting to note that at some point earlier, men have arrived in Middle Earth, while now the Elves are leaving for elsewhere.) The music for Isengard retains an oriental or Arabic flavour, and Mordor follows suit, with music featuring the rhiata. Indeed, this seems to be a fairly problematic use of musical representation in that it identifies the evil in the film with the sounds of the Maghreb and the Arabic world. According to Howard Shore:

> The first things I worked on in *The Two Towers* were Rohan and Fangorn ... The major cultures of film two are Fangorn/The Ents/Treebeard, and then Rohan ... I started to create the sound and the world of Rohan, which is essentially the largest new culture that you're entering in film two. (Quoted in Koppl 2002: 31)

Shore's music for the Ents of Fangorn forest is sung in Sindarin (one variety of Elvish), although it does not match the four songs sung in English by Ents in Tolkien's books. However, Shore's score doubles the Ents with wooden sounds, such as log drums and bass marimbas, as well as the deep sounds of bassoons and double-basses.

The Return of the King has a very distinctive, heroic theme for Minas Tirith, the city heart of Gondor. The broad, sweeping melody (including a substantial interval leap of a fifth) is reminiscent of heroic themes from westerns, being played predominantly on brass as a form of fanfare and on occasion with the sort of rhythmic accompaniment that has been used in films to invoke horseriding. This resemblance is all the more strong when the melody is in full cry, with a brass counter-melody and busy strings giving a strong sense of movement in combination with the staccato beat. The use of choirs evident in the first two films is sustained into the third, and extended as accompaniment to the large-scale battle sequences. For instance, the Ringwraiths are accompanied by mixed choir singing in Adunaic (an ancient language of men, according to Tolkien), while the boys choir of the London Oratory School and the London Voices (a mixed choir), join in the awe-inspiring sonic backdrops to the battles with the forces of Mordor. In addition, *The Return of the King* includes two instances of diegetic singing by the film's characters. At Minas Tirith, Pippin sings the song 'The Edge of Night' unaccompanied, although some of Shore's orchestral score creeps in to support as it goes on. This is an addition, absent in the book. At his coronation, Aragorn sings a brief song in Elvish, with lyrics from Tolkien. (Mortensen released an album, *One Man's Meat* (Lightening Creek/Smart Art Press, 2000), which included live studio recordings and guest musicians such as Exene Cervenka (previously with X) and Buckethead). The film's end titles were, as was the case in the previous two films, partially occupied by a scout single which served to publicise the film. In this case it was Annie Lennox's 'Into the West', which she co-wrote with Shore and Walsh.

Overall, Howard Shore's music for the *Lord of the Rings* trilogy mixes the sort of musical cues provided by Tolkien's writings with a use of music that is traditional to music in films. In other words, it mixes highly individual music that invokes the specific cultures and representations in Middle Earth, while also using the orthodox techniques and orchestral sounds of mainstream Hollywood films. This manifests itself most clearly in the thematic structure of leitmotivs for characters, places and ideas on the one hand (as can be found in many film scores), while on the other the music is leavened with a succession of highly individual singers who serve to provide the different flavours of the radically diverging cultures and peoples of Middle Earth.

The use of choirs (sung in different languages) adds a highly particular element to Shore's music, allowing for distinctive differentiation between cultures represented in the film. Also, it allows for big awesome sound, such as the chanting massed choir for the battle of Pelennor Fields, which mixes London Voices with the Oratory School Choir. In the documentary extra about music on the DVD release of *The Fellowship of the Ring*, Shore states that the character of the music is concerned with 'getting some of the [book's] detail back into the film'. This is borne out in the use of Elvish languages, as well as other exotic elements to flesh out the on-screen world (such as choirs singing in Anglo-Saxon or Nordic or North African solo instruments). So the film's music mixes the traditional functional aspects of scores, underscoring action and clarifying narrative and events, with musical aspects derived from songs and other particular aspects in the book, some of which appear as songs and others as part of the orchestral score. Some of Shore's musical pieces on disc carry the same title as book chapters, demonstrating an attempt to stay close to Tolkien's intentions, although the CD release changes the order of events to provide a more coherent listening experience. More of Shore's music appears on the expanded DVD versions, where he rescored additional sections and transitions, and rerecorded some of the music (Adams 2002: 20).

There have been a number of arrangements of Howard Shore's music from Peter Jackson's films. Nic Raine and the City of Prague Philharmonic Orchestra (with the Crouch End Festival Chorus) released *Music from the Lord of the Rings Trilogy* (Silva America, 2004). They have made a habit of cheaply-done but high quality re-recordings of film scores. Three separate suites of Shore's music appeared on *Themes from the Lord of the Rings Trilogy* (Music Club, 2004). Chris Cozens released *Music Inspired by the Film The Lord of the Rings: The Fellowship of the Ring* (EMI International, 2002), which was a version of Shore's incidental music (and the two pieces in the film by Enya) played on synthesisers. As such, I am unsure about why this album bears the 'inspired by' moniker. The Hollywood Studio Orchestra and Singers released *Music from The Lord of the Rings: The Fellowship of the Ring, Music from The Lord of the Rings: The Two Towers* and *Music from the Lord of the Rings: The Return of the King*. These were all brought together in a set as *The Trilogy of The Lord of the Rings* (Wonderful Music, 2004). Added to the healthy sales of Shore's original soundtrack CDs, clearly the music in Peter Jackson's trilogy had a significance of its own and corresponding consumer attraction.

Another musical aspect of the film trilogy that is worth mentioning is the music used on the film's trailers. This creates an extension of the films and their musical world. The trailers for *The Fellowship of the Ring* used James Horner's 'Attack on Murron' (from *Braveheart* (Mel Gibson, 1995)), Graeme Revell's *The Crow: City of Angels* (Tim Pope, 1996), Christopher Field's 'Gothic Power' and some used music by Immediate Music and original trailer music by Daniel Nielsen and Michael Giacchino. *The Two Towers* trailer music memorably used a remix of Clint Mansell's music from *Requiem for a Dream* (Darren Aronofsky, 2000). While *Braveheart* arguably deals with similar representations and themes, *Requiem for a Dream* is a film about the disintegration of a number of people through drug abuse. This demonstrates how far a single piece of music can go to fit radically different concepts and visuals. *The Two Towers* also used some of Shore's music from *The Fellowship of the Ring*, as did the third film in the trilogy. Some of Shore's music (the Gondor theme) was used as by Simone Benyacar and Craig Stuart Garfinkle, who are part of a company called The Ant Farm that mostly provides music for advertisements. It is the regular procedure for current mainstream Hollywood film trailers to use music from other films or elsewhere. The fact that *The Lord of the Rings* was such a large project, allowing Shore a long time to write its music, meant that the musical signature of the trilogy was largely in place on the trailers by the time of the last film instalment.

In the wake of the films

The *Lord of the Rings* books had already inspired plenty of musicians, but the success of Peter Jackson's film trilogy has in turn stimulated the production of a welter of 'inspired by' albums. Rick Wakeman recorded and released *Songs of Middle Earth: A Tribute to the Lord of the Rings* in 2002 (BMG Records). It comprises mostly keyboards, which is no surprise in the light of Wakeman's pop career in the Strawbs and Yes. The album is reminiscent of his most well-known work, the solo albums in the early 1970s where he attempted to picture through sound such historical narratives as *The Six Wives of Henry VIII* and *Journey to the Centre of the Earth*. Some of the pieces retain the sort of progressive rock character that Wakeman had developed during his tenure in Yes, while others are piano solos that show off his virtuoso skills at the keyboard. This album follows his previous work very directly and makes nothing in the way of concessions to the books' representations or to representing the exotic through changing its idiom.

A seemingly large project was David Arkenstone's *Music Inspired by Middle Earth* (Neo Pacific Recordings, 2001), attributed to The Elbereth Orchestra, which included a number of musicians under Arkenstone's leadership. On the cover it says 'a powerful musical portrait of Middle Earth, these cinematic compositions unfold with an evocative sensitivity'. It runs like a soundtrack without a film, following the narrative development of the books, although almost all the tracks are descriptive of episodes in *The Fellowship of the Ring* rather than the rest of the trilogy. It mixes the sound of an orchestra with electronically-derived sound, ethnic instruments and a full choir. It has an impressive sound and is primarily instrumental, mixing some orchestral sounds that owe at least something to the conventions of music for films with more folk-inspired sections, both in terms of musical style and instrumental texture, although some subtle drum beats slightly suggest 'New Age' ambient music. The album fails to represent the incident with Tom Bombadil, and Arkenstone's invocation of Lothlorien is regal and slow, having an emotional effect rather than being musically exotic, although it includes some tin whistle and xylophone-type sounds. Arkenstone has something of a reputation for producing 'New Age music', a form of music that proved particularly suited to representation of *The Lord of the Rings*, with its concerns of an accessible musical language and a style premised upon invocation of images and a regard for folk music, particularly of the Celtic variety.

Russian ensemble Caprice released *Elvenmusic* (Prikosnovénie, 2001), and are made up of musicians from the Russian National Symphony and the Bolshoi Theatre. They had previously released an album based on William Blake's *Songs of Innocence and Experience*. Despite Caprice's second album of *Elvenmusic* being titled *The Evening of Iluvatar's Children* (Prikosnovénie, 2003), it appears to follow *The Lord of the Rings* precisely. Tracks include 'Bath Song', 'Galadriel's Song', 'Sam's Song' and 'The Last Ship'. The album's second track, 'Of Beren and Luthien' is derived from a song about Tinúviel sung by Aragorn (Strider as he is known at this point) before they reach Weathertop ('The leaves were long, the grass was green/ The hemlock umbels tall and fair' (Tolkien 1966: 208–9)). The song starts with a fairly conventional Celtic folk sound but increasingly adds more exotic elements, including short bursts from a variety of instruments, concluding in a slightly baroque-styled waltz. 'Bath Song' includes female vocals with harpsichord, with additional wood and string instruments. It is taken directly from the song sung by Pippin and other hobbits at Frodo's new home at Crickhollow. Caprice have a very eclectic and quite distinctive sound, taking a folk rock influence, although hardly sounding like a traditional folk group. There is some influence from classical music (at times most notable in the female vocal) and some from rock, using many solo instruments such as clarinet and harpsichord, and a use of modal scales that aids the construction of a seemingly antiquated sound.

Mostly Autumn recorded *Music Inspired by The Lord of the Rings* (Classic Rock Legends, 2002) broadly within a rock format; the music ranges in style from epic heavy metal to folk rock. It produces music for most of the key musical points in Tolkien's books. Furthermore, 'Out of the Inn' not only realises the song sung by Frodo at the Prancing Pony at Bree, but also includes Inn noise and calling for a song. Its conclusion leads to a section of tin whistle playing, followed by a synthesiser solo and then a guitar solo over a folk rock-style backing. While the Elf kingdom of Rivendell is invoked through bell-like keyboards and a dulcimer-like sound, making a bright and airy waltz, Lothlorien is more conventionally rock-based. It neglects to manifest the Tom Bombadil episode. The Texan group Brobdingnagian Bards recorded the album *Memories of Middle Earth: A Tribute to J.R.R. Tolkien's The Hobbit and The Lord of the Rings* (Mage, 2003), although their name was derived from Swift's *Gulliver's Travels*. They performed at the New Line Cinema Oscar party for Peter Jackson's first film of *The Lord of the Rings*, and mix Scottish and Irish folk songs with Middle Earth music; their album topped the Celtic music charts. In a similar vein, The Hobbitons produced *Songs from Middle Earth*, which was derived directly from the songs that appear in *The Lord of the Rings* books, although it failed to have any songs concerning Tom Bombadil. Old Forest Sounds produced *The Music of Middle Earth: A Musical Journey from the Shire to Rivendell* (1991) and *The Music of Middle Earth: A Musical Journey from Khazad-dûm to Gondor* (1991), both of which were available as both recordings and sheet music. They also have an *Adventures of Tom Bombadil* (1991) – which is something of a rarity among representations of the world of *The Lord of the Rings*. Broceliande's *The Starlit Jewel: Songs from J.R.R. Tolkien's The Lord of the Rings and The Hobbit* (Flowinglass Music, 1996) is primarily a settings of Tolkien's poems and songs in a Celtic style with singing accompanied by harp, acoustic guitar and recorder. As in many cases, it neglects to deal with Tom Bombadil but includes a number of hobbit songs (such as 'Bath Song') and has an interpretation of 'Galadriel's Lament'. This is one of the only albums that can boast an official authorisation from the Tolkien Estate. Retaining a broad folk idiom, Everstar's *Enchanted Journey: Music Inspired by the Lord of the Rings* (Sequoia Records, 2003) depicts Rivendell and Lothlorien, mixing harp, flute, guitars and strings in a Celtic-style with classical overtones. Another similarly titled album, *Music Inspired by J.R.R. Tolkien's Lord of the Rings*, was by Andy Street and the Westwind Ensemble (Brentwood, 2003), realising many of Tolkien's songs, in fact most of the Hobbit songs and including some quasi-religious Gregorian-style chant.

Conclusion

In general, musical manifestations of *The Lord of the Rings* have followed certain strategies. These include invoking the exotic though music for Elves and to a lesser extent other unfamiliar cultures; this means that certain aspects of the books are more prominent in representations than others. Rivendell and Lothlorien, for example, appear in musical form in almost every manifestation. On the other hand, the episode in *The Fellowship of the Ring* where the party of Hobbits meet Tom Bombadil is erased from many versions. Neither of the film versions chose to retain this incident. Indeed, the film versions of *The Lord of the Rings*, in musical terms at least, are probably the least faithful to Tolkien's original.

Questions of fidelity to Tolkien's original are important for many of these musical versions of *The Lord of the Rings*. However, they clearly prefer fidelity to certain aspects over others. Tom Bombadil is marginalised or erased – indeed, he is the only major character excised from Peter Jackson's *The Fellowship of the Ring* and makes no appearance in Ralph Bakshi's film either. Jackson's trilogy loses this highly musical section of the book, but occasionally adds or changes music in other places, such as having Eowyn singing at Theoden's funeral and having Gollum sing a song about fish beneath Hennen Annun rather than at the Dead Marshes, as it appears in the book.

Howard Shore's scores for Peter Jackson's film trilogy extensively wields musical archetypes. The music translates the broad themes of the films into fairly standard musical codes, delineating good on one side and bad on the other. Additionally, the music in the films has to express the exotic for Elven culture and the negatively exotic for the evil forces of Isengard and Mordor. The film uses sedate, rustic folk-inspired music to represent the Shire and hobbits, while the large-scale battles use regal and military fanfares and awe-inspiring religious choirs. Notably, Shore's music is the only one that uses self-consciously 'oriental', perhaps even pastiche, Arabic musical style to represent the evil forces of Mordor and Isengard. It should not go without mention that this version of Tolkien's story has been reformulated at a historical juncture notable for the United States' antagonistic relationship with large swathes of the Arab world and some Islamic culture more generally.

Since the advent of Peter Jackson's *Lord of the Rings* trilogy on film, there has been a proliferation of albums that have attempted to ride on the popularity of the films and the interest in Tolkien's world they have generated. Not simply the films in general but the music from the films has proved a major inspiration for those producing folk or ambient-styled music the world over. In the case of the heavy metal music, there is less pressure on the groups to produce music that emanates directly from the books, more that they feel they should be consonant with the spirit of the world of Middle Earth. In many cases, the precise references that the books make to music are ejected in favour of an attempt to evoke an impression of Middle Earth, sometimes a highly-selective impression. The most clear case of this is in the exorcism of the episode with Tom Bombadil from a number of versions. Most obviously in Ralph Bakshi's *The Lord of the Rings* and Peter Jackson's *The Lord of the Rings: The Fellowship of the Ring*. This incident and its music is not easily altered or redirected. It is also the most obvious incidence of traditional British folk music in the books. It is tempting to speculate that the current aesthetic status of British folk music might have contributed to the seeming desire to erase this incident.

Undoubtedly, almost all musical releases since Jackson's film trilogy have ridden the tide of the films' publicity. In some cases musical releases have masqueraded as being connected to the project while in the vast majority of cases they merely become part of the general welter of interest in *The Lord of the Rings* that has been inspired by the films' scale, success and cultural prominence.

Works cited

Adams, D. (2002) 'Towering Achievements: Howard Shore Returns to Middle Earth for *The Two Towers*', *Film Score Monthly*, 7, 10, 20–4.

Brownrigg, M. (2003) 'The Music of Middle Earth: Hearing *The Lord of the Rings*', *Media Education Journal*, 33, 11–14.

Donnelly, K. J. (2004) 'Riverdancing as the Ship Goes Down', in S. Street and T. Bergfelder (eds) *The Titanic in Myth and Memory: Representations in Visual and Literary Culture*. London: I. B. Tauris, 205–14.

Hargrove, G. (2005) 'Music in Middle Earth'. Online. Available at www.phil.unt.edu/~hargrove/music.html (accessed 17 January 2005).

Koppl, R. (2002) 'Climbing into Darkness: Scoring *The Two Towers*', *Soundtrack*, 21, 84, 31–7.

Tolkien, J. R. R. (1966) *The Lord of the Rings: The Fellowship of the Ring*, second edition. London: HarperCollins.

Tolkien Dirty

I. Q. Hunter

It is not at all clear that academics view porn in a way that is compatible with the way nonacademics watch porn. (Burt 1998: 122)

One of the more unlikely spin-offs from *The Fellowship of the Ring* was a clutch of erotic spoofs and trash film parodies.[1] *Whore of the Rings* (Jim Powers, 2001) and *Whore of the Rings II* (Jim Powers, 2003) are hardcore pornographic movies; *Lord of the Cockrings* (Nick Zedd, 2002) is a short underground film based on a stage-play; and *Quest for the Egg Salad: Fellowship of the Egg Salad* (Chris Seaver, 2002) is a fan-accented gross-out comedy. The most engaging of these spoofs is *The Lord of the G-Strings: The Femaleship of the String*, directed by Terry M. West (2002), a sexploitation film from Seduction Cinema, a New Jersey-based outfit that special-ises in erotic take-offs of mainstream movies.

Seduction's distinctive brand of softcore straight-to-DVD parody has pumped new blood into the sexploitation market, and achieved a remarkably high profile with consistent package design, budget prices (in the UK, at any rate), and the promotion as cult figures of in-house starlets such as Misty Mundae, the pasty-faced, small-breasted lead in *Play-Mate of the Apes* (John Bacchus, 2002), *Roxanna* (Ted Crestview, 2002) and *Lord of the G-Strings*. Seduction's highest profile films, such as *The Sexy Sixth Sense* (Terry M. West, 2001), *Spider-Babe* (Terry M. West, 2003) and *The Erotic Witch Project* (John Bacchus, 1999) rework their sources as ultra-low-budget lesbian erotica, intended, like almost all lesbian-themed porn, for consumption by male audiences.

Softcore and hardcore versions

Exploitation parodies are nothing new. Blaxploitation films ripped off mainstream successes – *Hit Man* (George Armitage, 1972), for example, relocated *Get Carter* (Mike Hodges, 1971) to the ghetto – and adult versions of fairy tales, classic litera-ture and well-known films became popular in the 1970s – *Trader Hornee* (Jonathan

Figure 9: Reflexivity and exploitation: *Lord of the G-Strings* (courtesy Seduction Cinema)

Lucas, 1970) sexed up *Trader Horn* (W. S. Van Dyke, 1931), while *The Opening of Misty Beethoven* (Radley Metzger, 1976) transformed *My Fair Lady* (George Cukor, 1964) into a classic of 'Golden Age' hardcore. Since the 1980s 'hardcore versions' of mainstream films have flourished on video, including such indicative titles as *A*

Midsummer Night's Cream, *Harry Potter Made the Philosopher Moan*, *Lawrence of a Labia*, *The Ozporns*, *The Sperminator* and *Yank My Doodle It's a Dandy*.²

These hardcore versions rarely go much further than punning on the titles and lifting the basic situations of the original films. *The Fast Times at Deep Crack High* series (Stoney Curtis, 2001, ongoing), for instance, alludes in its title to *Fast Times at Ridgemont High* (Amy Heckerling, 1982) merely to indicate that it is set around a school and features cheerleaders. Parody films, like most contemporary hardcore, largely jettison narrative in favour of uninterrupted 'gonzo' depictions of sex, and adhere tenaciously to what Linda Williams called hardcore's 'principle of maximum visibility' (1990: 48). Some films do attempt a measure of fidelity to their sources, and shochorn the obligatory bouts of sex into recognisable imitations of the originals' plots and themes. *A Clockwork Orgy* (Nic Cramer, 1995), for example, replicates not only the storyline of Stanley Kubrick's 1971 film but also its futuristic setting and hard-edged tone. In general terms hardcore versions are raunchy reproaches to Hollywood's squeamishness about sex. As Constance Penley notes:

> The knockoffs cannot be intended simply to ride the coattails of popular Hollywood films because most consumers know that the porn version seldom has much to do with the themes, characters and events found in the original film. What is more likely, as Cindy Patton says … is that they are meant as 'an erotic and humorous critique of the mass media's role in invoking but never delivering sex'. (2004: 328)

Although Seduction's erotic spoofs are softcore, they have a close affinity to hardcore versions. But whereas hardcore quickly abandons narrative for lengthy depictions of sex, *Lord of the G-Strings* pads out its length with story, dialogue and other erotically redundant business. Indeed, an effort is made to reimagine *The Fellowship of the Ring* rather than simply riff on its title. The plot centres on Dildo Saggins (Misty Mundae), a Throbbit of Diddle Earth, who goes on a quest with fellow Throbbits Spam (A. J. Khan) and Horny (Darian Caine) to throw the legendary G-string, once worn by evil Horspank (Paige Richards), back into the Party-Pooper Volcano. Along the way they encounter Smirnof (Michael R. Thomas), a drunken parody of Gandalf the wizard; exiled Queen Araporn of Muffonia (Barbara Joyce); and a Gollum-like creature called Ballem. In pursuit are Sourass (John P. Fedele, in the Saruman role) and his Dork army. Since it is essentially a picaresque road movie, it yields easily to the requirements of pornographic narrative, which demands only that sexual encounters occur with the regularity of set-piece numbers in a musical.

Although its production values recall those of *The Blair Witch Project* (Daniel Myrick and Eduardo Sánchez 1999) – in other words, interminable footage of amateurs tramping through the woods – *Lord of the G-Strings* was actually something of a prestige project. Lavishly budgeted at $100,000, it was shot on 16mm film rather than Seduction's more usual videotape. Online reviews, taken aback by such unprecedented extravagance, generally rated the film Seduction's most successful to date; but were uncertain whether to judge it as a spoof with incidental sex scenes or as a porn film with occasional parodic flourishes.[3] The emphasis on parody and intertextual jokes is intended, perhaps, to extend the film's appeal beyond porn's core audience, and align it with one of the dominant modes of contemporary Hollywood production – the compulsively referential comic parody (*Spaceballs* (Mel Brooks, 1987), *Silence of the Hams* (Ezio Greggio, 1994), *Scary Movie* (Ivory Wayans, 2000)). Intertextual allusions in *Lord of the G-Strings*, however, tend to be scattershot and opportunistic, and it is difficult to attach any consistent satirical purpose to them (as, for example, when Smirnof, semi-quoting *American Pie* (Paul Weitz, 1999), says, apropos nothing in particular, 'Once when I was at band camp I told this obnoxious little girl what she could do with her flute'). But it is worth noting that *Lord of the G-Strings*, in spite of its lowly position in the cultural hierarchy, is wholly representative of contemporary film practice in its reliance on pastiche, allusion and intertextuality.

Exploitation and trash films

Lord of the G-Strings is of interest, too, in representing a novel and distinctive mode of contemporary exploitation cinema. Roughly speaking, an exploitation movie is a low-budget feature film which caters to a specific demographic, often to the pointed exclusion of other audiences, and which advertises material unavailable in mainstream cinema. The 'classical' exploitation film emerged in the USA in the 1930s with independently made films dealing with topics prohibited by the Production Code. Films like *Maniac* (Dwaine Esper, 1934) and *Reefer Madness* (Louis Gasnier, 1936) offered simultaneously prurient and self-righteous exposés of taboo subject matter, which, in order to appease censors and legitimate the public's curiosity, adopted a moralistic and educational manner. With the waning of classical exploitation in the 1950s, 'exploitation film' acquired a more wide-ranging and largely descriptive application. No longer referring to a discrete mode of film production, 'exploitation' became an all-purpose label for cheap sensational movies that were produced in cycles, intensively promoted and distributed to a sectionalised market.

By the 1970s exploitation cinema in the USA was threatened on two opposing fronts. On the one hand, the New Hollywood encroached on its territory with an unprecedented wave of violent and sexually explicit films; while, on the other, the legalisation of hardcore made available the kind of pornography for which sexploitation had always been a poor substitute. Exploitation filmmakers had to find innovative ways to distinguish their films from both the Hollywood of *The Exorcist* (William Friedkin, 1973) and the hardcore chic of *Deep Throat* (Gerard Damiano, 1972). New sub-genres sprang up establishing fresh directions for exploitation, such as the slasher film (*Halloween* (John Carpenter, 1978)), the ultra-gore movie (*Maniac* (William Lustig, 1980)), and the self-abasing, intentionally bad trash film, contemporary versions of which include the output of Lloyd Kaufman's Troma Films, such as *The Toxic Avenger* (1985) and *Class of Nuke 'Em High* (1986) series.

Trash films, adopting the camp style pioneered by George Kuchar and John Waters (but not, in the main, their gay sensibility), revel in poor taste, gross-out content and reflexive pastiche of the clichés of low-budget filmmaking. The pleasure of watching them, as Carole Laseur (1990) remarks, 'may well be precisely situated in the recognition of its satirical parody of a pompous high cultural (bourgeois) set of aesthetic proclamations'. Their core constituency is young male connoisseurs of disreputable alternatives to the mainstream, the kind of films Jeffrey Sconce labelled 'paracinema':

> seemingly disparate subgenres such as 'bad film', splatterpunk, 'mondo' films, sword and sandal epics, Elvis flicks, governmental hygiene films, Japanese monster movies, beach party musicals and just about every other historical manifestation of exploitation cinema from juvenile delinquency documentaries to softcore pornography. (1995: 372)

Exploitation outfits that specialise in deliberate trash make a virtue of their films' sleaziness, gratuitous nudity and violence, and contempt for politically correctness. By alienating the mass audience they enhance their appeal to trash aesthetes, self-selecting ironists who are proficient in cult appreciation. As Mark Jancovich has pointed out, a taste for paracinema is therefore curiously elitist in its preening, cliquey contempt for the mainstream and those it satisfies. Paracinema, he writes,

> is a species of bourgeois aesthetics not a challenge to it ... at least as concerned to assert its superiority over those whom it conceives of as the degraded victims of mainstream commercial culture as it is concerned to provide a challenge to the academy and the art cinema. (2002: 311–2)

Seduction's films fall squarely into this category of intentional commercial trash, setting them apart from both underground films and straightforward pornography. The calculated ineptitude of *Lord of the G-Strings* is designed to inveigle the viewer into mistaking what some might regard as incompetent rubbish for subversive self-reflexive fun. Trash films like this embrace their viewers as savvy and discriminating insiders, honoured participants in an exclusive postmodern cult. Seduction's brand of high-camp trash is therefore an astute commercial solution to the dilemma of contemporary sexploitation. Recognising the (paradoxical) mass cult appeal of trash films, Seduction offers DVDs like *Lord of the G-Strings* for sale as instant collectibles rather than as anonymous soft porn – prefabricated cult movies for discerning aficionados of 'Alternative Cinema' (the revealing tie-in name of the company's website). To this end, and to position its films as *hommages* to the great tradition of exploitation cinema, the website advertises not only its own DVDs but vintage grindhouse fare. In short, Seduction peddles a curious kind of 'heritage cinema'; its films are paracinematic ready-mades, which mock the conventions of exploitation cinema even as they keep the ailing form alive.

'Description' and masturbation

Craig Fischer has described how in porn films, and porn-inflected exploitation like *Beyond the Valley of the Dolls* (Russ Meyer, 1970), narrative frequently collapses into what he calls 'description' – extended nude and sex scenes with no obvious purpose beyond the non-diegetic arousal of the audience. These descriptive passages, which are generically essential to porn, are the kind of discursive but extraneous matter that classical Hollywood narrative omits in its pursuit of economical storytelling: 'The moments which define pornography as a genre are *descriptive* moments, independent of plot but concerned with rendering ... the properties of the human body, for voyeuristic purposes' (1992: 20). Exploitation films generally fluctuate between storytelling and description, classical narrative and pornography. They may start out as narrative but 'the pre-eminence of sex and violence [in exploitation] breaks down narrative and replaces it with description of sexual acts' (ibid.).

This is certainly true of *Lord of the G-Strings*, which, hovering awkwardly between parody and porn, struggles to develop a coherent narrative while also serving up the necessary quota of descriptive moments of sex. The story is frequently held up by narratively redundant sex scenes, which get longer and more self-contained as the film goes on, and more severely disconnected from the on-screen diegesis. For example, immediately after the opening prologue, a longish sequence of Dildo masturbating brings the narrative to a grinding halt before it has even had a chance to get started. The result is very bad *classical* storytelling (because the scene is gratuitous vis-à-vis narrative development) but very good *porn description* (because Dildo gets nekkid, as Joe Bob Briggs would say, barely five minutes into the movie). The imperatives of narrative cinema on the one hand and porn's cinema of attractions on the other are in continuous warring opposition.

Subsequent sex scenes in *Lord of the G-Strings* progress from solo masturbation to one-on-one heterosexual fucking to a climactic lesbian orgy. None of the scenes moves the narrative along; mostly they are parachuted in when a bit more sex is required and some are barely integrated into the plot at all. One lesbian scene, for example, takes place against a black background in isolation from storyline, diegesis and temporal location. The major sex scenes, incidentally, are spared the parodic handling of the dialogue sequences, which are steeped in camp irony, 'bad' style, and the low-culture equivalent of Brechtian alienation effects. The result is a weird inconsistency of tone: passages of comic narrative alternate mechanically with solemn bouts of sexual description, which seem designed – though it is hard to be sure – to enhance masturbation.

Pornography and reflexivity

Lord of the G-String's ideology, insofar as it has one, is consistent with the libertinism of pornography. The Throbbits are 'trisexuals' – 'they'll try anything, the horny little bastards', according to Dildo – and Diddle Earth is a pornocopian land of single-minded sexual indulgence without reference to marriage, monogamy or exclusive relationships (except for one poor soul jealous at being dropped by a Wood Dryad). Multiple partners and orgiastic promiscuity are taken for granted, and women are generally presented as strong and sexually active. (This modest feminism chimes with the latest wave of teen films, such as *American Pie*, which are more women-centred than predecessors like *Porky's* (Bob Clark, 1982) and *National Lampoon's Animal House* (John Landis, 1978) as well as more forthcoming about male inadequacy and sexual embarrassment.) Far removed from the moralism of classical exploitation, *Lord of the G-Strings* is evangelical about the virtues of masturbation, voyeurism, troilism, male defloration, lesbianism and lesbian sex.

Needless to say, the film's take on lesbianism owes little to the documented lifestyle of that social group, but rather corresponds to how lesbians *ought* to behave in the perfect porn universe. (Porn habitually presents women as its protagonists and narrators, a device intended to legitimate the male fantasies they are required to respond to and act out.) Pornography is an account of what men want sex to be like (in the case of lesbian sex, a sort of contact spectator sport with opportunities for audience participation). A chronicle of male yearning, porn registers disappointment in, rather than hatred of, the subtlety and difference of female sexuality, along with relief that women are rarely so demanding in real life. The central fantasy of porn is that women are *up for it*; that, in defiance of their evolved sexual nature, they are no less indiscriminate and sexually driven as men.

Lord of the G-Strings is not only an exploitation film; it is also about how viewers ought to watch and respond to an exploitation film. First, in the accepted style of a postmodern trash film, it draws attention to its stupidity, gratuitousness and budgetary limitations. Second, and more interesting, it tries to second guess and mirror back to the viewer his reactions to what he is seeing on screen – for example, in reflexive scenes of characters watching and commenting on the action as if anticipating the audience's response at home. This works both to naturalise the viewer's voyeurism (everyone in Diddle Earth does it, so why shouldn't you?) and also to indicate the kind of viewing situations most appropriate to consuming the film. The first lesbian scene, for example, is interrupted by male warriors led by General Uptight; the girls insist on carrying on making love but permit the men to watch. (One of the men is gay and agrees to watch only if he can imagine that one of the girls is a man.) The resulting set-up, in which men ogle women who are performing sexually for them, is significant in two ways. First, it confirms that the sex scenes, even within the story, are public performances staged only in order to be observed and appreciated. Second, it constructs one preferred scenario for the viewing and correct appreciation of *Lord of the G-Strings* – as a sociable viewing activity with your mates, probably with a six-pack and a take-away. Unlike hardcore porn, which smacks of furtive solitary entertainment, *Lord of the G-Strings* presents itself as ideal for collective laddish enjoyment. Its softcore naughtiness and referential humour identify it as titillating eye-candy for the guys rather than as straightforward pornography.

The implied audience for *Lord of the G-Strings* therefore, is men young enough to get the references to contemporary cult and teen films. There are interesting moments, however, when the film's address to the audience switches and it seems to target women. For example, at one point the trio of female Throbbits ogle a sex session and the film adopts a nominally female point of view. Perhaps the film is suitable after all for viewing on a girls' night in. There is also a very peculiar moment during a dialogue scene when Sourass turns to the camera and says 'Hello girls', thus seeming directly to address women in the audience (or, possibly, since it is implied that he is gay, impertinently feminising male viewers). He then becomes very self-conscious and, with one of his sidekicks, starts playing up to the camera. How do we read this? Camp improvisation? Pretence that the film, against all generic logic, might count women among its viewers? Or simply a random moment of reflexivity, of a piece with the film's scrappily developed trash aesthetic? Reflexivity of this sort, acknowledging the viewer in order to unsettle his or her response to the film, is standard in parody films (*Airplane!* (Jim Abrahams, David Zucker and Jerry Zucker, 1980)) and not unusual in pornography, which often draws the viewer's attention to its staged quality the more powerfully to emphasise the reality of the sex. Richard Dyer has noted that gay porn lures the audience into the film by emphasising its artificiality and hailing the viewer:

> Paradoxically there is a kind of realism in pornographic performance that declares its own performativity. What a porn film really is is a record of people actually having sex; it is only ever the narrative circumstances of porn, the apparent pretext for the sex, that is fictional ... This realism in turn has the effect of validating the video and the genre to which it belongs. By stressing that what we are enjoying is not a fantasy, but porn, it validates porn itself. (2004: 109)

The reflexivity of *Lord of the G-Strings* can seem confusing if it is interrogated closely or taken too seriously. As I have suggested, the film's address to its audience as well as its generic self-definition are strategically inconsistent and opportunistic. This is partly because the film (like all exploitation films, perhaps) is interstitial between different kinds of low-budget movie – porn, trash film, sex comedy and so on – and their different but overlapping audiences. With its comic displays of tits-and-arse, *Lord of the G-Strings* is viable as a post-pub DVD for larky collective male viewing; or it might work as a couples' movie, a saucy bargain basement version of the mainstream parody film; it is also, primarily I would argue, a trash film for the cult market and a must-buy for paracinemaniacs. At the same time it is constructed in many scenes as straightforward pornography, whose extended sequences of sexual description invite the sticky-fingered attentions of masturbators.

In other words, it is hard to know exactly *how* the film is watched or indeed meant to be watched. The likeliest explanation is that Seduction is engaged in postmodern multiple coding. Just as every Hollywood film tries to reach out to multiple demographics, so *Lord of the G-Strings* is making a play for the widest possible range of trash, erotic and parody movie fans.

Sexing-up Tolkien

Finally we come to *Lord of the G-Strings*'s intertextual relationship with *The Fellowship of the Ring*, which I shall argue is not necessarily very important. It is certainly difficult to argue that there is a consistent purpose to its parody of Peter Jackson's film, except insofar as it emphasises that sex is not prioritised in Middle Earth. Although *Lord of the G-Strings* is parasitic on *Fellowship of the Ring*, this is not the key determinant of its narrative structure, ideological content and address to the audience. Far more important, as I have suggested already, are the contexts of exploitation cinema, trash movies, pornography and mainstream parody films.

Nevertheless there are a few hints of subversive intent in *Lord of the G-Strings*. Although never cohering into a full-blown critique of *Lord of the Rings*, it does haphazardly unlock – or rather allow an enthusiastic critic to unlock – some of its repressions and erotic possibilities. The most outrageous aspect of *Lord of the G-Strings* is its overt sexualisation of an imaginative world ostensibly purged of significant erotic reference. Indeed the sheer absence of sex in Tolkien's fantasy might be read by psychoanalytically-minded critics as a sign of massive repression and sublimation. Middle Earth cries out to be pornified, not in order to defile its innocence but rather to encourage a healthy return of the repressed. From this perspective, *Lord of the G-Strings* is neither lurid filth nor disfiguring graffiti, but a kind of wild over-correction, substituting the single motivation of sex for Tolkien's complexly interwoven religious, philological and mythic concerns.

The Lord of the Rings (the novel) is arguably brimful with sexual tensions and aspects of inchoate erotic fantasy and repression. In particular it is nervous about women (divided, in stereotypically Catholic style, into Madonnas (Galadriel) and whores (Shelob)) and deeply attracted to an exclusive and clubbishly homosocial world of men. It must be said that Peter Jackson, in all three films, is alert to the alleged misogyny and erotic subtexts of the novel, as well as to its marginalisation of romance, vivid sexual symbolism, and bubbling undercurrents of homoeroticism. (Given Jackson's background in trash exploitation, it is not surprising that he should relish lurid subtexts in respectable material; his *Meet the Feebles* (1989), a truly grotesque trash spoof of the Muppets, makes *Lord of the G-Strings* seem positively cherubic.) On the one hand, Jackson rescues the Aragorn/Arwen story from the appendices of *The Return of the King*, which, along with boosting the role of Eowyn, enhances the role of women in the story. This acknowledges, too, that, post-*Titanic* (James Cameron, 1997), action films are well advised to build in plenty of love interest. On the other hand, Jackson points up the book's unconscious sexual imagery – the recurrence of swords as symbols of power and masculinity; the womb-like cosiness of hobbits' burrows; the terrifying anality of the One Ring; and the resemblance of Sauron's disembodied cat's eye to the vertical slit of a vagina. As Graham Fuller notes,

> this malicious gynecentrism, intended or not, is reiterated in the images of hapless males imperiling themselves by entering clefts, crevices, caves and narrow doorways time and time again: the portals to Moria, the Paths of the Dead, Shelob's lair … the scalding Cracks of Doom. (2004: 26)

Paradoxically, having intended to present *Lord of the G-Strings* as a parody of *The Fellowship of the Ring* and a sarcastic commentary on its sexual subtexts and repressions, I am forced to acknowledge that Jackson may well have got there first.

Lord of the G-Strings is, in fact, more usefully understood in cultural and generic terms as a trashy American retort to, on the one hand, the English prissiness of the original novel and, on the other, the middle-brow pretensions of the fantasy genre. Laura Kipnis (1999) and Constance Penley (2004) both describe porn as class antagonistic grossness, and *Lord of the G-Strings* is indeed a low-cultural fart in the general direction of (in no particular order) bourgeois propriety, sexual purity, good taste, bodily restraint and social hierarchy (though, admittedly, Gimli serves some of these functions in Jackson's films). Given its multi-racial casting, *Lord of the G-Strings* also vigorously rebuts Middle Earth's unrelieved whiteness, which is transferred wholesale into *The Fellowship of the Ring* with its persistent negative association of blackness with Orcs, Maori-ish Uruk-Hai, and other subhumans from the East. In short, *Lord of the G-Strings* is, in very general terms, *The Fellowship of the Ring*'s generic Other – scatological, disrespectful, pervy, democratic (mostly) in its sexual tastes, racially relaxed, cheap, American, unpretentious and overrun with sexually-confident female trailer trash.

Although widely read as an allegory of the Cold War, *The Lord of the Rings* can also be interpreted as a homoerotic sexual myth, which, in flight from female sexuality, constructs a fantasy world of sublimated homoerotic desire. Consider, for example, Roger Kaufman's ingenious theory that Gollum is Frodo's homosexual other. Kaufman remarks that Tolkien 'created an incredibly rich and detailed fantasy world from which heterosexual romance is almost entirely absent, and none of the primary characters is married' (2003: 32), and then offers a brisk reading of the novel from a revisionist Jungian perspective. According to Kaufman, Sam is Frodo's 'double' who accompanies Frodo on an archetypal 'hero's journey' of individuation towards his true actualised self. Because Sam is both Frodo's soulmate and erotically-charged helper,

> the relationship between Frodo and Sam is not only an ode to same-sex love but also an archetypal dynamic within each gay man, where self-reflection may reveal the existence of an inner lover or a 'soul figure' and guide who loves us just as Sam loves Frodo, and who, like Sam, can spur us to reach our greatest potential. (ibid.)

But to achieve individuation the hero, Frodo, must confront his 'shadow', the most shameful part of himself, represented here by Gollum, Frodo's dark, unconscious twin. Kaufman argues – oddly, in my view – that the films downplay the homoeroticism between Frodo and Sam in favour of an eroticised relationship between Frodo and Gollum (for example, when they struggle inside Mount Doom Gollum wraps himself around Frodo from behind as if endeavouring to bugger him). Gollum, Kaufman concludes, represents the gay man's feelings of inadequacy and inferiority, but he is also energetic and vital and 'in many ways the least repressed creature in Middle Earth' (2003: 33). Frodo's growing empathy with Gollum (himself a divided creature) suggests how the shadow can be wrestled with, confronted and integrated into the self.

Jackson seems to acknowledge the homoerotic passion between Frodo and Sam. In *The Return of the King* Frodo comes across not only as gay (he exchanges lingering glances at Sam; nearly kisses him on the lips at the harbour; and goes off at the end with Gandalf, whose sexuality, inflected extra-textually by Ian McKellen's, is fascinatingly indeterminate) but as a gay Christ, who says 'It is done' when the ring is destroyed and who must die to save the Shire ('it is saved, but not for me'). The crucial difference with *Lord of the G-Strings* is that, even if it registered these layers of homoerotic implication, it could not deal with them, at least not openly. Although the film transforms the central characters from implicitly gay men into porn-lesbians, male homosexuality is strictly off-limits as a sexual permutation. It is true – and a valuable inversion of Tolkien – that *Lord of the G-Strings* converts Middle Earth from a hierarchical, male-centred world into an erotic paradise. It is also true that, in turning the male characters into lesbians, the film asserts a sexual identity unthinkable in the original novel (and perhaps in the films, too) and cancels out its fear of women's sexuality. The price, however, is the elimination of male homoeroticism.

The preponderance of lesbian scenes in Seduction's films, as in porn generally, might be seen, in fact, as an attempt to neutralise the homoerotic aspect of viewing straight porn – that it involves men getting aroused by watching other men have sex. (Watching straight porn has unexpectedly queer possibilities. If men watch porn together, the event becomes discomfortingly homosocial; if one watches it alone and masturbates – well, masturbation, from a weird, fatuous but interesting point of view, is a species of homosexual act, in which a man has sex – incestuously? – with a man.) Since *Lord of the G-Strings* draws the line at male homosexuality (except as a joke), this unexpectedly renders it more homophobic than the *Lord of the Rings* films, if one is persuaded that they intentionally allude to homoerotic subtexts in the novel. For example, whereas the lesbians in *Lord of the G-Strings* are liberated, polymorphous and sympathetically portrayed, Sourass, the film's villain, seems to be a hostile depiction of gayness. Crabbily repressed and appalled by sex, he is a compilation of disgusted allusions to male homosexuality, which range from obscurely-coded references to *The Wizard of Oz* (Victor Fleming, 1939) (he calls the Dorks 'my pretties', like the Wicked Witch of the West) to insistent anus and fart gags.

It is worth very briefly contrasting *Lord of the G-Strings* with 'slash fiction', which also appropriates *Lord of the Rings* for sexual fantasy.[4] Slash fiction is a genre of fan stories about homoerotic affairs between male characters in popular films and television series, such as, classically, *Star Trek*. Slash writers are almost exclusively women, who, as Milly Chen remarks in a magazine piece on Sam/Frodo slash, find that slash 'lets them write about relationships without having to deal with traditional sexual power struggle [and] take control of men's bodies for their own fun, just as men have been taking control of women's bodies for centuries' (2004: 16). There is an extensive archive of *Lord of the Rings* slash at The Library of Moria (http://www.libraryofmoria.com), including stories like 'When the Wizard's Away…' by 'Sam Littlefoot', which imagines Sam and Frodo making love under the friendly gaze of Aragorn:

> Sam stroked his fingers, in and out, touching Frodo deeply – massaging the opening to a body he knew almost as well as his own. Frodo's body arched with a cry as Sam touched that one special spot, the one that filled his lover with indescribable pleasure. Again and again he stroked the dark-haired Hobbit, watching him writhe each time the fingers found their mark. (2005)

Not all slash is quite so 'NC-17'-rated. In fact, according to Catherine Salmon and Donald Symons, who analyse slash from the perspective of evolutionary psychology, slash fiction seems to be as much about friendship and intimacy as sex; its core theme is 'building a romantic/sexual relationship on the solid foundation of an established relationship' (2001: 95). Slash is a variation on the romance novel, whose goal is never sex for its own sake but rather the establishment (or in slash, the fulfilment) of a lasting pair bond: 'In mainstream romances love originates in sexual passion, whereas in slash it originates in friendship; slash protagonists were comrades long before the scales fell from their eyes and they realised the existence of mutual love' (2001: 92). Now, the comparison between *Lord of the G-Strings* and slash is not entirely apt; the former is a commercial film rather than a fan production, and therefore constrained by generic obligations that a slash writer may ignore. But the differences between the two – one essentially porn for men, the other fanfic by women – are nevertheless revealing. For, according to Salmon and Symons, porn and slash are wholly incompatible genres that reflect abiding differences between male and female psychologies and mating strategies. Whereas slash – as in the passage cited above – highlights emotional as well as physical intimacy, porn such as *The Lord of the G-Strings* is exclusively interested in maximising opportunities for impersonal sexual encounters. Considered as porn, *Lord of the G-Strings*, for all its supposed 'lesbian' content, is a clear-cut product of the evolved characteristics of male psychology, and its vision of sex is anathema to the romantic, female world of slash. One interesting result is that slash, unlike straight porn and exploitation, can frankly cope with the *Lord of the Rings*'s homoerotic subtexts (though lesbianism does not get a look in); indeed it finds little else to write about.

In the end, one might conclude that porn versions cannot work as adaptations because the adaptation element is always displaced by the pornography. Whereas adaptation, parody and satire all require specificity of reference for their effect, porn usually tends towards the anonymous, conventionalised and ahistorical. Although *Lord of the G-Strings* starts off as a parody of *Fellowship of the Ring*, its sex scenes are interchangeable with the ritualised, nude caresses of countless other softcore movies. Richard Burt, discussing porn and trash versions of Shakespeare, argues that such versions do in fact add up to an ideological project: they 'rewrite Shakespeare so as to undo the romantic couple and the institution of marriage. They give reign to a sexual pornotopia, including gay and lesbian sex and even incest, rather than uphold heteronormative sexuality' (1998: 82). But this is what happens when *any* text is reworked as porn and it tells us very little about the subtexts or repressed content of the original. Burt also notes of Shakespearean porn that the porn elements cannot really function within the parodic frame. Since we do not know, for example, what 'Shakespearean sex' would be like, what we get instead is the standard repertoire of sexual acts. Similarly, with *Lord of the G-*

Strings, there is nothing intrinsically 'Tolkien-esque' – if one can imagine such a thing – about the sex scenes. (*Whore of the Rings II*, by contrast, makes a couple of its sex scenes vaguely relevant to *The Two Towers*; an Ent, for example, is fellated until it ejaculates out of a branch.) As soon as the sex scenes begin, the parody stops and all narrative coherence is lost.

Sex work

In luridly re-imagining *The Lord of the Rings* as a sexual fantasy, one is struck by three thoughts: first, that it is quite easily done, if one is not too fastidious, and has a relatively dirty mind; second, that sexing-up the classics has become an obligatory exercise given the post-Freudian belief that sex is the measure of all things, the *real* real signified; and, third, that *Lord of the G-Strings* is, essentially, doing what is now standard practice among highbrow critics – recklessly queering the text and imposing its own grid of predictable obsessions. My conclusion is that a merely textual account of the movie, whether as exploitation or pornography or both, misses out what is crucial about it as a 'sex work', the British Board of Film Classification's term for a film intended solely for erotic arousal.

It is perfectly reasonable to interpret *Lord of the G-Strings* in narrowly generic, ideological and historical terms, which is more or less what I have tried to do here. But pornography needs to be thought about in relation to its *use* (Attwood 2002: 102–3) and this is where my treatment of *Lord of the G-Strings* is seriously – if inevitably – flawed. Although I have described the kind of audiences the film caters to – from trash film devotees to solitary masturbators – I have no idea how they actually use it in the sense of integrating it into their lives. This is an acute problem with erotic films because to understand the experience of watching them requires more than delicately unpicking their subtexts from a safe academic distance. As Jennifer Wicke remarks

> It needs to be accepted that pornography is not 'just' consumed, but is used, worked on, elaborated, remembered, fantasised about by its subjects. To stop the analysis at the artefact ... imagining that the representation is the pornography in quite simple terms, is to truncate the consumption process radically, and thereby to leave unconsidered the human making involved in completing the act of pornographic consumption. Because of the overwhelming focus on the artefacts or representations of pornography, such 'making' has been obscured in favour of simply asserting that these artefacts have a specific or even an indelible meaning, the one read off the representation by the critic. That act of interpretation is a far remove from what happens in pornographic consumption itself, where the premium is on incorporating or acquiring material for a range of phantasmic transformations. When the pornographic image or text is acquired, the work of pornographic consumption has just begun. (2004: 181)

So, for example, if an account of watching porn in a dedicated porn cinema assumed that viewers attended to the films no differently from in a multiplex, it would be leaving out everything that mattered about the weird, edgy and homoerotic world of the grindhouse – the comings and goings of the clientele, the shadowy assignations, the irrelevance of the film itself sometimes to the performances in the stalls. Similarly to make sense of domestically-consumed porn and exploitation DVDs and videos, we need some sense of the context of their use and private significance – a phenomenology of masturbation, if you like. We should consider the circumstances in which porn is enjoyed by viewers primarily engaged *not* in comprehending the narrative of a film but rather in the co-ordinated physical and cognitive task of *masturbating to it*. As Laurence O'Toole remarks:

> it has never occurred to anyone to ask porn users what's going on … folks think they already know all there is to know about porn users: they look at dirty images, they become aroused, they're sad. (1999: 284)

Crucial to understanding a film like *Lord of the G-Strings* are such quirky and impertinent questions as the following. Do people watch porn DVDs all the way through, or just in satisfying bursts? (One of the unusual characteristics of porn DVDs is that they are not necessarily intended to be watched all the way through in one sitting.) Do men always masturbate to porn, or are there more subtle, curious or sinister reasons to view it? Do men typically delay orgasm till the cum-shot happens onscreen? How often do men watch porn films communally? Do viewers *ever* interpret a porn film or care about its meaning?

Getting stuck into these questions is no less rewarding than textual analysis and theoretical speculation; it is just harder to do. I would be fascinated to know how *Lord of the G-Strings* is actually viewed, consumed and used by people in the home, whether as amusing trash film, male bonding exercise, wannabe cult object or incitement to erotic play. My guess is that its parodic relation to *The Lord of the Rings* would quickly fall away as a topic of interest. More compelling by far would be an intimate exploration of its role in the life of an individual viewer, modelling one's approach, perhaps, on a closely-focused study by Martin Barker (1997) of one fan's political engagement with *Judge Dredd* (Danny Cannon, 1995) (for an example of this approach, in the form of autoethnography, see Hunter 2000). Admittedly, this sounds like a complete non-starter: it is hard to imagine *Lord of the G-Strings* securing in anybody's life – even in mine – a place of special cult affection or erotic significance. More valuable would be locating the film within the vast eroticised multiverse spun out from *The Lord of the Rings* in the form of fanfic, cos-play, slash fiction, film parodies and even fan-boy essays like this one; and discovering how all this creativity appropriates, sabotages and, to borrow a phrase from the Surrealists, 'irrationally enlarges' Tolkien's world of fantasy.

Notes

1 Published, non-erotic, spoofs include *Harvard Lampoon's Bored of the Rings*, written in 1969 during the hippie Tolkien cult, and, more recently, *The Soddit* and *The Sellamillion*.

2 On hardcore versions, see the documentary, *Shaving Ryan's Privates* (tx Five, 3 November 2003).

3 See, for example, the largely positive reviews at culturedose.net (http://culturedose.net/review.php?rid=10004676) and Modamag.com (http://modamag.com/Lord%20of%20the%20G-Strings_DVD.htm).

4 On Tolkien slash fiction, see Smol 2004.

Works cited

Attwood, F. (2002) 'Reading Porn: The Paradigm Shift in Pornography Research', *Sexualities*, 5, 1, 91–105.

Barker, M. (1997) 'Taking the Extreme Case: Understanding a Fascist Fan of Judge Dredd', in D. Cartmell, I. Q. Hunter, H. Kaye and I. Whelehan (eds) *Trash Aesthetics: Popular Culture and Its Audience*. London: Pluto Press, 14 – 30.

Burt, R. (1998) *Unspeakable ShaXXXspeares: Queer Theory and American Kiddie Culture*. New York: St Martin's Press.

Chen, M. (2004) 'When Frodo Met Sam', *Sunday Times Style*, 18 July, 16.

Dyer, R. (2004) 'Idol Thoughts: Orgasm and Self-Reflexivity in Gay Pornography', in P. Church Gibson (ed.) *More Dirty Looks: Gender, Pornography and Power*. London: British Film Institute, 102–9.

Fischer, C. (1992) '*Beyond the Valley of the Dolls* and the Exploitation Genre', *The Velvet Light Trap*, 30, 18–33.

Fuller, G. (2004) 'Kingdom Come', *Film Comment*, 40, 1, 24–9.

Harvard Lampoon (1969). *Bored of the Rings: A Parody of J. R. R. Tolkien's 'The Lord of the Rings'*. New York: Signet.

Hunter, I. Q. (2000) 'Beaver Las Vegas!: A Fan-Boy's Defence of *Showgirls*', in X. Mendik and G. Harper (eds) *Unruly Pleasures: The Cult Film and Its Critics*. Guildford: FAB Press, 187–201.

Jancovich, M. (2002) 'Cult Fictions: Cult Movies, Subcultural Capital and the Production of Cultural Distinctions', *Cultural Studies*, 16, 2, 306–22.

Kaufman, R. (2003) '*Lord of the Rings* taps a gay archetype', *The Gay and Lesbian Review Worldwide*, July–August, 31–3.

Kipnis, L. (1999) *Bound and Gagged: Pornography and the Politics of Fantasy in America*. Durham: Duke University Press.

Laseur, C. (1990) 'Australian Exploitation Film: The Politics of Bad Taste', *Continuum: The Australian Journal of Media & Culture*, 5, 2). Online. Available at http://wwwmcc.

murdoch.edu.au/ReadingRoom/5.2/Laseur.html (accessed 30 July 2004).

Littlefoot, S. (2005) 'When the Wizard's Away…', *The Library of Moria: Lord of the Rings Slash and RPS Fanfiction Archive*. Online. Available at http://www.libraryofmoria.com/aragornfrodo/whenthewizardsaway.txt (accessed 3 March 2005).

O'Toole, Laurence (1999) 'The Experience of Pornography', in J. Elias, G. Brewer, V. L. Bullough, J. Douglas, V. Diehl Elias and W. Jarvis (eds) *Porn 101: Eroticism, Pornography, and the First Amendment*. Amherst, NY: Prometheus Books, 284–93.

Penley, C. (2004) 'Crackers and Whackers: The White Trashing of Porn', in L. Williams (ed.) *Porn Studies*. Durham and London: Duke University Press, 309–31.

Roberts, A. R. R. R. (2004) *The Sellamillion*. London: Gollancz.

_____ (2003) *The Soddit, or, Let's Cash in Again*. London: Gollancz.

Salmon C. and D. Symons (2001) *Warrior Lovers: Erotic Fiction, Evolution and Female Sexuality*. London: Weidenfeld & Nicholson.

Sconce, J. (1995) 'Trashing the Academy: Taste, Excess and an Emerging Politics of Cinematic Style', *Screen*, 36, 4, 371–93.

Smol, A. (2004) '"Oh … Oh … Frodo!: Readings of Male Intimacy in *The Lord of the Rings*', *Modern Fiction Studies*, 50, 4, 949–79.

Wicke, J. (2004) 'Through a Gaze Darkly: Pornography's Academic Market', in P. Church Gibson (ed.) *More Dirty Looks: Gender, Pornography and Power*. London: British Film Institute, 176–87.

Williams, L. (1990) *Hard Core: Power, Pleasure, and the 'Frenzy of the Visible'*. London: Pandora.

Index